Permanency Planning
for Children

Permanency Planning for Children

CONCEPTS AND METHODS

Anthony N. Maluccio
Edith Fein
and Kathleen A. Olmstead

Tavistock Publications
NEW YORK · LONDON

First published in 1986 by
Tavistock Publications
in association with Methuen, Inc.
29 West 35th Street, New York NY 10001

Published in the UK in 1986 by
Tavistock Publications
11 New Fetter Lane, London EC4P 4EE

Typeset in Great Britain by
Scarborough Typesetting Services
and printed in the United States of America

Library of Congress Cataloging in Publication Data

Maluccio, Anthony N.
Permanency planning for children.
Bibliography: p.
Includes indexes.
1. Social work with children—United States.
2. Child welfare—United States.   3. Custody of
children—United States.   I. Fein, Edith.   II. Olmstead,
Kathleen A.   III. Title.
HV741.M344 1985   362.7′95   85–17333

ISBN 0–422–78840–6
ISBN 0–422–78850–3 (pbk.)

British Library Cataloguing in Publication Data

Maluccio, Anthony
Permanency planning for children: concepts
and methods.
1. Child welfare—Great Britain
I. Title.   II. Fein, Edith.   III. Olmstead,
Kathleen A.
362.7′0941   HV751.A6

ISBN 0–422–78840–6
ISBN 0–422–78850–3 Pbk

To children who wait – and their families

Contents

Preface

Permanency planning – the movement to promote plans ensuring permanency or stability in the lives of children and youth – has in recent years been shaping the philosophy, goals, and services of child welfare agencies in the USA as well as other countries. Permanency planning may be defined as the systematic process of taking prompt, decisive, goal-directed action to maintain children in their own homes or to place them permanently with other families.

Building on the above definition, this book presents a permanency planning framework for child welfare practice. It discusses the philosophy and theory underlying permanency planning; develops a systematic practice approach; and delineates and illustrates practice guidelines. Since decision-making by social workers, other child welfare personnel, judges, attorneys, parents, and others is at the heart of permanency planning, much of the contents deal with the responsibility of the social worker in the decision-making process. Emphasized are those concepts and principles, program components, methods, and techniques that promote assertive decision-making and case management, facilitate timely action on decisions, and encourage alternative strategies when a given decision cannot be implemented.

As the permanency planning movement has spread in the USA, educational programs in schools of social work and staff development programs in public and private child welfare agencies have been increasingly focusing on preparation of social workers, child care staff, and others in the philosophy, theory, and practice of permanency planning. Numerous courses, workshops, and seminars have emerged to fill the need for education and training of a large number of practitioners engaged in delivering services to children and families in such settings as public and voluntary child welfare agencies, residential centers, group homes, family agencies, juvenile delinquency programs, and child guidance clinics.

As these educational programs have expanded, there has been a need for relevant educational materials. Although a variety of such materials has been published in the past few years, there has been no text that focuses on permanency planning in a cohesive and comprehensive fashion. The present volume is intended to fill this gap. It is a practice-oriented text with a strong theoretical and research base.

Part I presents the theoretical and practice framework for permanency planning. Chapter 1 defines permanency planning, places it within a theoretical and philosophical context, and delineates its key components. Chapter 2 discusses the emergence of permanency planning as a movement and a practice method and reviews related research. Chapters 3 and 4 consider, respectively, guidelines for determining which children should be considered for permanency planning and criteria for deciding which permanent plan should be chosen for a particular child. Chapter 5 examines the variety of roles that social workers are called upon to play in permanency planning. Chapter 6 explains that the ecological perspective is especially suited as a guide for permanency planning, in light of its emphasis on the dynamic interaction between human beings and their environments.

Part II focuses on social work practice with parents and children involved in permanency planning cases. Chapters 7 and 8 discuss guidelines for assessing parents and children and engaging them in a helping relationship. Chapter 9 delineates the use of service agreements in practice, while Chapters 10 and 11 discuss principles and methods of ongoing work with parents and children, respectively. Chapter 12 considers the provision of support services for children and parents. Chapter 13 stresses guidelines for maintaining the permanent plan that is selected.

Part III covers collaborative and administrative aspects, especially issues affecting the large number of agency personnel and community resources typically involved in permanency planning in each case. Following examination of the crucial importance of collaboration in Chapter 14, there is discussion of working with the legal system (Chapter 15), methods of record keeping (Chapter 16), and guidelines for creating an agency context that is conducive to permanency planning (Chapter 17). Chapter 18 is an epilogue that critically examines the 'state of the art' in the practice of permanency planning and looks toward the future.

The book is designed to be useful as a text for students in formal educational programs and in-service training programs as well as a reference guide for practitioners. It is addressed to students in courses on family and children's services in graduate and undergraduate schools of social work, particularly courses in permanency planning; educators and staff development persons in schools of social work and child welfare agencies; and administrators, planners, social workers, child care staff, and other child welfare personnel in public and voluntary child welfare agencies. It should also be of interest to practitioners in other practice settings dealing with children and youth, such as family service agencies, youth centers, child guidance clinics, public schools, and juvenile delinquency programs.

Although permanency planning as a formal program originated in the USA, its concepts and methods have universal applicability. Indeed, the issues with which it is designed to deal, such as the drift of children in out-of-home care, are problems encountered the world over. While the authors draw primarily from their experiences in the USA, it is hoped that the contents will also be of value in other countries, by helping to recognize, and prevent or correct, the adverse effects of impermanence.

Acknowledgements

This book has come into existence not only through the efforts of its authors, but with the support, advice, and encouragement of a host of others. It is gratifying to realize that advances in child welfare practice are built on the contributions of many. We are grateful to those we mention, without whose collaboration this would have been a poorer work indeed, although there are probably others who should be acknowledged, but whose names are inadvertently omitted.

Of central importance were the contributions made by a number of colleagues. Ramona Beckius, Joan Benham, Jack Casey, Brian Charbonneau, Joyce Hamilton-Collins, George Howe, Michaele Kelly, Hugh MacGillis, and Katharine Miller, presently or formerly of Child and Family Services, participated in the formulation of many of the ideas presented here or provided useful case materials. Arlene Jackson, formerly of Child and Family Services, Attorney Eliot Nerenberg, and Barbara Pine and Mary Frances Libassi, of the University of Connecticut School of Social Work, reviewed early drafts of various chapters and made significant contributions. Catherine Olmstead was a valuable editorial assistant and greatly improved the accuracy of the references.

Deep appreciation must also be extended to a number of organizations. First, the Connecticut Department of Children and Youth Services, a forward-looking agency, has participated in a number of projects mentioned in the text and continually demonstrates its commitment to the children in its care by its support of research and related planning activities. Thanks are due to Mark Marcus, Commissioner; Charles Launi, Deputy Commissioner; Ray Farrington, Director of Children's and Protective Services; and Walter Pawelkiewicz, Director of Research and Evaluation, for their cooperation.

Second, the Administration for Children, Youth, and Families, of the US Department of Health and Human Services, provided invaluable encouragement by funding grant 90-C-1794 to study the outcomes of permanency planning; similarly, a graduate training grant in social work education, 5T01MH15971, by the National Institute of Mental Health, supported the development of many of the ideas elaborated on in the book. The role of the US government is vital in promoting knowledge-building in child welfare; its contributions cannot be overestimated. Particularly helpful, among many others, were Charles Gershenson, Cecelia Sudia, and Nielson Smith.

Third, the University of Connecticut School of Social Work, through its Child Welfare Training Center, provided excellent opportunities to test and refine many of the ideas presented in the book. The support of its Dean, Robert Green, is gratefully acknowledged.

Finally, Child and Family Services of Hartford, CT, provided general support and tangible services in the writing of this book. Child and Family Services, a large voluntary, child welfare and mental health agency, is unusual in its support of an active Research Department, its encouragement of training and new programming, and its assumption of responsibility to contribute to the profession. The previous Executive Directors, Robert Beers and Warren Braucher, the current Executive Director, William Baker, and the Associate Executive Director, Chester Brodnicki, are especially to be commended.

We have been blessed with expert and cheerful secretarial services and would like to extend thanks to Margaret Partridge, Lois Pye, and particularly Valerie Morris, secretary of the Research Department of Child and Family Services. Her dedication and commitment make her a valuable colleague and team member, her initiative and speedy typing make her indispensable, and her competence greatly facilitates our work. She is a true professional. Our editor, Gill Davies, gave gentle support and intelligent encouragement to make a difficult task manageable, and we are grateful for her patience and understanding.

Our most profound thanks, however, are to the children and families whose lives are touched by the child welfare system. We have learned much from them over the years, and our admiration for their strengths and perseverance cannot be acknowledged deeply enough. We hope this book will help make their lives better.

Throughout this book we have reprinted excerpts or adapted materials from our earlier writings, listed below, and gratefully acknowledge the publisher's or editor's permission to do so:

Fein, E. (1984) Dangerous Clients. *Social Casework* 65 (9): 531. Copyright 1984 – Family Service America.

Fein, E., Miller, K., Olmstead, K., and Howe, G. (1984) The Roles of the Social Worker in Permanency Planning. *Child Welfare* 63 (4): 351–60. Copyright 1984 – Child Welfare League of America.

Maluccio, A. N. (1981) An Ecological Perspective on Practice with Parents of Children in Foster Care. In A. N. Maluccio and P. A. Sinanoglu (eds) *The Challenge of Partnership: Working with Parents of Children in Foster Care.* New York: Child Welfare League of America. Copyright 1981 – Child Welfare League of America.

Maluccio, A. N. (in press) Biological Families and Foster Care. In M. Cox and R. Cox (eds) *Foster Care: Current Issues, Policies and Practices.* Norwood, NJ: Ablex Press.

Maluccio, A. N. and Fein, E. (1983) Permanency Planning: A Redefinition. *Child Welfare* 62 (3): 195–201. Copyright 1983 – Child Welfare League of America.

Maluccio, A. N. and Fein, E. (in press) Permanency Planning Revisited. In M. Cox and R. Cox (eds) *Foster Care: Current Issues, Policies, and Practices*. Norwood, NJ: Ablex Press.

Maluccio, A. N., Fein, E., Hamilton, V. J., Klier, J., and Ward, D. (1980) Beyond Permanency Planning. *Child Welfare* 59 (9): 515–30. Copyright 1980 – Child Welfare League of America.

Miller, K., Fein, E., Bishop, G., Stilwell, N., and Murray, C. (1984) Overcoming Barriers to Permanency Planning. *Child Welfare* 63 (1): 45–55. Copyright 1984 – Child Welfare League of America.

Olmstead, K. A. (1983) The Influence of Minority Social Work Students on an Agency's Service Methods. *Social Work* 28 (4): 308–12. Copyright 1983 – National Association of Social Workers.

Olmstead, K. A., Hamilton, J., and Fein, E. (1985) Permanency Planning for Children in Outpatient Psychiatric Services. In C. B. Germain (ed.) *Advances in Clinical Social Work*. Copyright 1985 – National Association of Social Workers.

Ward, D. E., Maluccio, A. N., Hamilton, J., and Fein, E. (1982) Planning for Permanency Planning in Foster Care. *Children and Youth Services Review* 4 (3): 223–37. Copyright 1982 – Pergamon Press.

Permanency Planning
for Children

PART I
THEORETICAL AND PRACTICE FRAMEWORK

1 What is permanency planning?

In order to grow up satisfactorily, children need to know that life has predictability and continuity; they need the reliability of knowing *where* they will be growing up. Yet too many children throughout the world find themselves in uncertain or impermanent living arrangements – in settings such as foster homes, group homes, and institutions, or in precarious family situations. The plight of these children has led in recent years to the emergence of permanency planning as a popular movement in the delivery of services to children and youth in placement or at risk of being placed out of their homes.

What is permanency planning? What are its underlying values and theories? What are its central programmatic features and methodological components? This chapter addresses these questions and presents a framework for permanency planning as child welfare practice. The framework, together with emphasis on decision-making and assertive case management, is further elaborated and illustrated in the rest of the book.

DEFINITION

The concept of permanency planning has been undergoing a process of revision and redefinition since it emerged a decade ago in the publications of the so-called Oregon Project, a federally funded demonstration project to place foster children in permanent homes, to be discussed in the next chapter (Emlen 1981; Emlen *et al.* 1977; Pike 1976). The term has been applied to many aspects of child welfare practice, including a philosophical perspective on the primacy of the family as the preferred environment for child rearing; a problem-solving process; adoption; a program to reduce the numbers of children in foster care; a case management method; and 'good' or active casework (Maluccio and Fein, in press; Maluccio *et al.* 1980).

Cutler and Bateman (1980: 46) point out that it 'can mean anything from "planning" to "facilitating" to "achieving" permanency placements for children'. Stein (1981: 99) describes it as 'a systematic process of gathering and using information, making informed decisions, formulating case plans, providing problem-solving services'. Maluccio *et al.* (1980: 519) indicate that it 'refers to the idea of moving the child as soon as possible out of temporary substitute care and returning him or her to the family as the preferred alternative or to an adoption home as the second priority, or, if necessary, to another permanent alternative such as a family with legal guardianship.'

Carbino (1982: 10) notes that it consists of 'a commitment through action by foster care system representatives to ensure a child's sense of continuity and stability of family relationships by prompt decision-making and intervention'.

Reflecting the original emphasis in the Oregon Project on children already placed in foster care, Pike *et al.* (1977: 1) initially defined permanency planning as follows: 'Permanency planning means clarifying the intent of the placement, and, during temporary care, keeping alive a plan for permanency. When a temporary placement is prolonged, foster care may have the appearance of permanency, but it lacks the element of intent that is crucial to permanence.'

Emlen *et al.* (1977: 10–11) further explain that the quality of permanence includes the following features:

1. *Intent* – the home is 'intended to last indefinitely', although it is not guaranteed to last forever.
2. *Commitment* and *continuity* – the family is committed to the child, involves the assumption of a common future, and provides continuity in the child's relationships with caretakers and other family members.
3. *Legal status* – the family offers the child a 'definitive legal status' that protects his or her rights and interests and promotes a sense of belonging.
4. *Social status* – the family provides the child with 'a respected social status', in contrast to the second-class status typical of prolonged foster care.

For many, permanency planning continues to mean a focus on children already placed out of their families. For example, a supervisor in a child welfare agency stated in a recent article:

'Permanency planning, as used here, refers to the timely return of the child to his/her biological or extended family, or where this is not feasible, to an adoptive home. It is recognized that for some children placed in foster care, neither of these objectives is a viable option and permanent foster homes may be considered as the only plan offering any semblance of permanence.'

(Villone, 1982: 81)

We see permanency planning more broadly, encompassing attention not only to children and youth in foster care but also, and perhaps more importantly, to those who are at risk of such placement. We see it as the process of planning for permanence, that is, 'the process of taking prompt, decisive action to maintain children in their own homes or place them permanently with other families' (Maluccio and Fein 1983: 195). The foremost question to be asked and answered in each case is: Will the child have a family when he or she grows up?

In other words, permanency planning encompasses both prevention and rehabilitation and serves as a guiding metaphor for all child welfare services,[1] perhaps for all child mental health services. Such an expanded perspective is consonant with the definition of child welfare contained in Public Law 96–272, also known as the Adoption Assistance and Child Welfare Act of 1980, which was enacted by the federal government in the USA. This Act, which will be discussed in Chapters 2 and 15, defines child welfare services as follows:

'*Child welfare services* means social services that are directed toward accomplishing the following purposes:

A. Protecting and promoting the welfare of all children, including handicapped, homeless, dependent, or neglected children.
B. Preventing or remedying, or assisting in the solution of problems which may result in the neglect, abuse, exploitation, or delinquency of children.
C. Preventing the unnecessary separation of children from their families by identifying family problems, assisting families in resolving their problems, and preventing breakup of the family where the prevention of child removal is desirable and possible.
D. Restoring to their families children who have been removed by the provision of services to the child and the families.
E. Placing children in suitable adoptive homes, in cases where restoration to the biological family is not possible or appropriate.
F. Assuring adequate care of children away from their homes, in cases where the child cannot be returned home or cannot be placed for adoption.'[2]

Drawing from the above definition and the varied perspectives to be discussed later in this chapter, we define permanency planning as follows: '*Permanency planning is the systematic process of carrying out, within a brief time-limited period, a set of goal-directed activities designed to help children live in families that offer continuity of relationships with nurturing parents or caretakers and the opportunity to establish life-time relationships*' (Maluccio and Fein 1983: 197).

This definition reflects the emphasis in the permanency planning movement on such aspects as the primacy of the family in a child's growth and development; systematic planning; time limits; goal-directed activities; and the continuing need of each human being to belong to a family. It leads to a framework for permanency planning – and child welfare practice in general – that, as shown in *Figure 1*, embodies the following key interrelated and complementary components: (1) values and theory; (2) program; (3) methods; and (4) collaboration.

VALUES AND THEORIES

The permanency planning movement is based on various premises, particularly the value of rearing children in a family setting, the primacy of parent–child attachment, and the significance of the biological family in human connectedness. These premises are supported by theoretical perspectives and bodies of

Figure 1   Framework for permanency planning

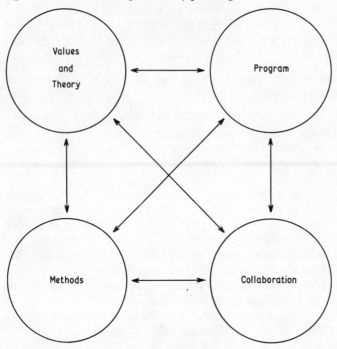

knowledge from diverse sources, particularly child development. Numerous studies of child growth and development emphasize the importance of stability in living arrangements and of continuity and security in parent–child relationships (Neubauer 1976).

Parent–child attachment

Hess (1982) is among those who elaborate on the primacy of parent–child attachment, holding that it provides the rationale behind permanency planning. She stresses that 'all children need a stable and continuous relationship with a nurturant person or persons, in order to develop physically, socially, emotionally, intellectually, and morally' (Hess 1982: 46). Hess (1982: 47–8) summarizes some of the conditions that affect the process and quality of parent–child attachment and thus the child's growth:

* ⋆ *Continuity:* the parent's consistent, constant, and predictable availability in the child's life.
* ⋆ *Stability:* a nutritive environment that supports the parent–child relationship and 'the capacities of both parent and child to engage in the bonding process'.
* ⋆ *Mutuality:* parent–child interactions that are mutually rewarding and that reinforce the importance of one to the other.

In line with these perspectives, numerous writers have underscored the importance of permanence in living arrangements and continuity of parental relationships for every child. For instance, stressing the concept of 'psychological parenting', Goldstein, Freud, and Solnit (1973) have advocated legislation to provide each child with a permanent relationship to those adults who have functioned psychologically as his or her parents. Schaefer (1977), also highlighting the child's need for consistent care, has recommended the use of permanent 'professional' parents whenever necessary.

Significance of biological family[3]

On the other hand, arguing that 'the psychological parent' is an oversimplification of a very complex human situation, Laird (1979) underscores the importance of the biological tie, with its concomitant sense of human connectedness. She therefore maintains that the guiding conviction in child welfare practice should be the fundamental importance of the biological family in the child's life:

'Every effort is thus made to support the family, to enhance its functioning, and to avoid separation and placement. When separation is necessary, the importance of the family continues to be recognized through active efforts to maintain family ties, to support shared parenting by biological and foster parents, and to work, wherever possible, toward reuniting the family.'

(Laird, 1979: 205)

Impact of separation and placement

Reflecting conviction about the significance of the biological family in human development, others have written extensively about the negative impact of separation and placement on parents as well as children. It has been stressed that children who are placed away from their parents experience loss related to the separation. The 'tie that binds' (Jenkins 1981), that is, the tie between parent and child, is like an invisible cord providing a child with a biological, emotional, and symbolic sense of connectedness to his or her environment and affecting his or her basic identity. The severing of the parent–child tie has a differential impact, depending on the child and the circumstances (Sinanoglu and Maluccio 1981: 237). In general:

'The child who must be placed in substitute care at any age, and regardless of the reason, is torn from the biological and symbolic context of his identity. No matter how nurturing the substitute care, the child's ongoing task will always be to reweave the jagged tear in the fabric of his identity, to make himself whole again.'

(Germain 1979: 175–76)

Littner (1956), a well-known child psychiatrist, has written from a psychoanalytic perspective about the traumatic effects of separation and placement, especially for younger children. In particular, he underscores that unless the child is allowed to come to terms with the internalized image of the parents, his or her identity is impaired. He, therefore, argues that contact with the parent is crucial to help the child deal with feelings generated by the separation experience.

Echoing Littner's themes, Colon (1978), a psychologist and former foster child, highlights the role of the child's experience of continuity with the biological family in establishing his or her sense of self and personal significance. As discussed in Chapter 6, the importance of parent–child contact is also strongly supported by research showing that visiting is the 'key to discharge from foster care': foster children who are visited by their parents are more likely to be returned to the biological families rather than to grow up in foster care (Fanshel 1975, 1982).

Separation from their child through placement can also be traumatic for the parents. For example, in a study of parents whose children were in foster care, Jenkins and Norman (1972) found considerable evidence of 'filial deprivation', that is, the feelings of loss, sadness, emptiness, and depression experienced by the parents. These feelings are poignantly described by McAdams (1972), whose own six children were placed in foster care. While appreciating the help provided through placement at a time of family crisis, McAdams captures the pain, turmoil, and sense of failure that she experienced, especially whenever she went to visit her children in their foster homes.

Ecological perspective

Additional theoretical support for permanency planning comes from the so-called ecological perspective, an approach to social work practice which draws on the study of the interactions between living organisms and their environment.

This perspective will be discussed in depth in Chapter 6, since we think that it is especially suited to child welfare practice in general, and permanency planning in particular. We should at this point highlight its chief contributions: it helps heighten the practitioner's awareness of the many factors that contribute to problems encountered by children and parents. It stresses the importance of basic services and supports in the family's environment. It highlights the need for continuity and for interdisciplinary collaboration in the delivery of services; and it provides avenues to preventive as well as rehabilitative services.

PROGRAM

The values and theoretical perspectives discussed thus far lead to a distinctive service delivery program focusing on systematic, goal-directed planning within specified time frames for children at risk of placement or already placed in foster care. Planning becomes a central, deliberate, and ongoing component in all aspects of service delivery – from the helping process in a particular case situation to an agency's broader programming. The emphasis is on making and implementing case-specific as well as agency-wide service plans, priorities, and decisions about resource allocation that contribute to the goals of continuity of care, stability, and permanency in the lives of children coming to the agency's attention.

Major program features

Major programmatic emphases include:

* Comprehensive and intensive efforts to keep children in their own homes.
* Where this is not possible or appropriate, early intervention and early consideration of long-term plans for the child, beginning even before he or she is actually placed in substitute care.
* Identification of different options for moving the child out of temporary foster care, with establishment of priorities among the available options.
* Delineation of a time-limited service plan to achieve an appropriate permanent placement. The plan should spell out goals and the roles, tasks, and responsibilities of all parties involved. It should incorporate, in particular, active encouragement of parent–child visiting.
* Determined use of legal and judicial processes, including organization of legal evidence for a plan, if necessary (e.g. termination of parental rights).
* Use of periodic case reviews (internal, external, or a combination) to assure that cases are moving according to plan.
* Provision of comprehensive services to the child's biological family, especially his or her parents. Such a panoply of services should be planned within an ecological perspective, to optimize the interaction of people with their environments and promote the parents' strivings to care for their children.

Various agencies have restructured their services to incorporate key programmatic features of permanency planning, such as those outlined above. In particular, in response to the mandates of the previously mentioned Public Law 96–272, in the USA public agencies are redesigning their services along the lines of permanency planning.

Systemic issues

The programmatic features that have been noted thus far, and the restructured agency services that have resulted, refer primarily to programs or approaches designed to provide direct help to children and families who come to the attention of the agency. In addition to direct services, agency programs increasingly need to focus on improving or reforming child welfare service delivery at other levels, including legislation, policy, law, institutional systems, and agency management. Much more needs to be accomplished to make agency and community programs more broadly responsive to the values, goals, and principles of permanency planning. Indeed, currently numerous problems or issues exist not only in the foster care system but also in the legal, adoptive, and social service spheres.

In the legal system, for instance, increased emphasis on plans for adoption multiplies the need for legal assistance and court hearings (Ward *et al.* 1982). Lawyers and judges are asked more often to make permanency decisions in which they may lack expertise (Emlen *et al.* 1977). As more social workers attempt to obtain termination of parental rights or establish adoption status, the court backlog stretches further. Studies have shown that 'there were often delays in getting the hearing date set, summonses issued, and witnesses prepared, and further delays were caused by continuances, postponements, and long waits between the time of hearing and announcement of the judge's decision' (Emlen *et al.* 1977: 61). The procurement of a permanent placement for a child is strongly dependent upon the legal system, its statutes, and its ability to process and enforce decisions. More effective relationships between social agencies and judges and attorneys are therefore essential.

Another systemic issue concerns the availability of funding. Prior to the enactment of Public Law 96–272 in the USA, financial support for foster care was more readily available than for preventive services, supportive programs for biological parents, or after-care services (Knitzer and Allen 1978). This barrier may have encouraged agencies to place a child in foster care as the most expedient solution to the family's problem. In fact, it has been argued that public policy and service delivery in child welfare reflect a deep anti-family bias by providing incentives to agencies to keep children in foster care rather than returning them to their biological families (Hubbell 1981; Knitzer and Allen 1978; Pare and Torczyner 1977).

The funding problem may be alleviated as a result of the Adoption Assistance and Child Welfare Act of 1980, if sufficient funds are appropriated by the government. It is likely, however, that ways will still need to be found to influence funding bodies by demonstrating, for instance, the potential cost benefit of supportive services for parents.

A related issue involves the growing emphasis on keeping children with their parent(s) or returning them to the biological family as soon as possible if placement cannot be averted. Since over half of all foster children typically have been in temporary care for two or more years (Knitzer and Allen 1978), families will have difficult adjustments to make. Even if there were parental or sibling contacts with the child while in foster care, the situation is drastically altered when the biological family again becomes the permanent home for the child. The biological parent(s), siblings and foster child(ren) may need special services and a variety of social supports to cope and alleviate stressful problems. Furthermore, 'much of this intensive work with families is for naught if adequate housing, income, day care and homemaker services cannot be obtained when needed' (Jones, Neuman, and Shyne 1976: 10).

As this discussion suggests, to fulfill the promise of permanency planning, we must improve the substance of services so that they become more responsive to the needs and qualities of children and parents. Among other aspects, this means systematic changes in service delivery (e.g. appropriate allocation of staff time and caseload responsibility) to enable workers to implement permanency planning; a more explicit focus on the family as the unit of service; provision of adequate resources and supports to parents and other caretakers; and greater emphasis on after-care services needed to sustain a permanent plan (Maluccio *et al.* 1980: 527–28).

Through staff, administrative, and community supports, agencies can plan effective programs to reduce the numbers of children in foster care (Ward *et al.* 1982). As envisioned in this book, however, permanency planning for children in care is not enough. Planning is one of the initial and essential steps toward alleviating the problems of drift and impermanence; but it remains only a first step if it is not followed by careful implementation and adequate supports and resources. Ultimately, a truly effective network of home-based services is the best means of going beyond permanency planning by preventing removal of children from their own homes in the first place (Bryce and Lloyd 1981; Maybanks and Bryce 1979). Permanency planning *after the fact* cannot substitute for preventive services and for increased investment in our children (Maluccio *et al.* 1980: 528).

METHODS

Inherent in permanency planning programs are techniques or case management methods emphasizing specific practice strategies such as contracts or service agreements with parents; time deadlines for goal-directed activities by parents and social workers; and record-keeping to structure and reinforce decision-making procedures. In using these methods and strategies, workers carry out a variety of roles that will be discussed in depth in Chapter 6, particularly those of case planning, case management, therapy, client advocacy, and court witness.

These methods and strategies can be employed to monitor and test the responsiveness of agency programs to the needs of parents and children. In addition, they can be used to help clarify the parents' responsibilities, test their motivation, and mobilize their capacities. Through active involvement in the helping process, parents can better understand what is needed in order for the child to be able to return home and stay there, or to work toward another plan, if necessary.

Above all, incisive decision-making, frequent case reviews, and assertive case management are important elements in all permanency planning methods. They underlie the techniques and strategies used and form the basis for sound judgment and flexibility in providing services. Decision-making is perhaps the most crucial component of permanency planning methodology. It consists of the process of actively and deliberately making choices among alternative options by following specific steps and procedures, so as to lead to a permanent plan for a child. The plan is decided upon and implemented within a reasonable length of time.

As delineated by Gambrill and Stein (1981: 109–34), a decision-making framework for child welfare practice involves, first of all, making a choice as to which permanency planning option is best for a particular child and family, that is, keeping the child at home; returning the child home from foster care; adoption; and so on. Once the best option is selected, the implementation of that decision proceeds in a timely fashion, from identification of problems and needs

to be worked on – to designing, implementing, and evaluating intervention .
plans.

These steps will be discussed and illustrated in subsequent chapters. The
central theme to be highlighted at this point is that agencies, social workers,
courts and others need to adopt a decision-making mind-set reflecting these
features:

* Making explicit choices among different goals and options.
* Pursuing choices that are made in an assertive, deliberate manner.
* Actively involving parents, children, and collaborators in the decision-
  making process.
* Specifying in writing goals and plans that must be achieved to implement
  the decision.
* Keeping accurate records to facilitate evaluation and monitor the progress
  and outcome of intervention activities on an ongoing basis.
* Changing decisions when evaluation makes it necessary.
* Adhering to time frames that assure children of protection from lengthy
  time in drift or limbo.

In short, deliberate, purposeful, and aggressive decision-making, even in the
midst of uncertain or incomplete knowledge, should replace the passive decision-
making through inertia or inaction that, as discussed in the next chapter, in the
past too often led to impermanence and the neglect of children in out-of-home
care or at risk of such placement.

COLLABORATION

The final feature of the framework for permanency planning is collaboration
among various individuals, disciplines, and organizations. In most case situations
coming to the attention of child welfare agencies, formulation and implementation of an effective permanent plan for a child require mutual respect and a
spirit of active collaboration among child welfare personnel, lawyers, judges, and
others working with children and their parents.

Collaboration is important to assure that the professionals involved are not
working at cross-purposes and that all of them participate in *one* focused plan. It
is also essential to provide a continuum of services, including after-care services
that help sustain the permanent plan.

In preparation for reunification of the child with the biological family, for
instance, it is crucial to involve resources such as self-help groups, school personnel, or child guidance clinic staff – in short, anyone who might provide
ongoing help to the child and parents. The progress that a child and his or her
parents have made during the course of temporary foster care frequently needs to
be buttressed by services and supports in such areas as counseling, health,
education, and respite care. As discussed particularly in Chapter 12, there should
be no reluctance to try innovative services, such as parent aides, homemakers,
home management specialists, or older persons who model effective parental

behaviors to help meet the needs of parents, enrich the family's environment, and prevent placement or re-placement.

Moving from the individual case level to the agency or community levels, successful permanency planning also involves extensive and ongoing collaboration among many persons and systems, including policy-makers, administrators, practitioners, biological parents' groups, organizations of adoptive and foster parents, service systems, and society in general. Such collaboration is necessary to plan for and implement laws, programs, and activities that allow more children to grow up in homes providing continuity and stability. Permanency planning is not a simple, ready-made approach applicable to any situation; also, it 'is not easily achieved' (Krymow 1979: 103), but is within reach if we have time, commitment, and resources to plan and implement effectively.

CASE ILLUSTRATION

We have been discussing permanency planning from a variety of theoretical perspectives, outlining its major components. The importance of permanency planning as a framework for child welfare, however, may be illustrated by a case example. We have deliberately chosen the following case of an older child who for a long time had been left to drift in foster care, so as to highlight the changes in practice and philosophy that are required to promote permanency planning.

Chris, age twelve, was the youngest of three children. At one year of age he had been removed from his home on an emergency basis because of abuse and neglect. The personal problems of his parents had interfered with their ability to provide adequately for him, though they loved and wished to provide for him. Both parents had histories of psychiatric hospitalization and diagnoses of mental disorders, including such symptoms as fluctuations in moods, variations in ability to function, periods of withdrawal, and times when reality became distorted. Consistent parental behavior was not in Chris's environment during his first year of life.

What ensued was not unusual. Chris was placed in a foster home under the auspices of a public welfare agency. Placement was to be temporary 'until his parents could resume care'; 'temporary', however, turned into years. Four years later, as permanency planning concepts were introduced, the agency was mandated to assure Chris a permanent home within a limited period of time (two years at most). His parents, who had been absent from the picture or from treatment efforts, were contacted by the agency. Visiting between Chris and his parents commenced in an effort to assess the possibility of their reuniting.

For the next four years, uncertainty existed for Chris, his biological parents, and his foster parents. Chris, whose adjustment with the foster family had been satisfactory, developed behavior problems, divided loyalties, and confusion about identity. He started school and was soon labelled as a troubled child, with both behavior and learning problems. During this time, it became clear that his biological parents did not have the capacity to care for Chris on a continuous basis.

Chris's parents voluntarily relinquished their parental rights, requesting that he be adopted by the foster family who would be willing to have an 'open adoption', a phrase meaning that they would know where he lived and could still have contact on a basis that would be comfortable for child and adopting parents. The adoption process could not proceed at once because Chris's behavior had deteriorated to the point that his ability to remain at home and in a public school was questioned. His behavior had become violent and there was concern that he might hurt himself or others. He was depressed and was not learning in school. While he was attached to his foster-mother, his admiration for his biological father seemed to preclude acceptance of the foster-father. Chris was then hospitalized for a complete 'workup' (physical, social, psychological, psychiatric) and as a result a recommendation for residential treatment was made. A pre-placement visit at a residential facility was interrupted because Chris ran away and returned home to his foster parents. The foster parents concluded that a placement away from them could only be detrimental for Chris and they decided to keep him at home while receiving outpatient services.

Thus, at age nine, Chris and his foster parents were referred to a child guidance clinic. For two years Chris was seen for weekly individual sessions, as were his foster parents. Initially the foster parents were helped with their commitment to Chris so they could make a decision about adoption. This resulted in their adopting him when he was ten. Subsequently, the primary goal became for Chris to remain at home. Sessions with parents focused on day-to-day management of Chris and provided a place for them to discuss their own frustrations and feelings of discouragement. School conferences were attended by the therapist; individual tutoring was arranged; community experiences such as scouts and martial arts were planned; and individual therapy was planned on a weekly basis.

Chris's use of individual therapy was typical of that of children who have limited capacity to trust. For a long time, he presented himself as a sweet, well-behaved child who quietly played benign games. Eventually, he gained the courage to display more of the troubled feelings that his regular behavior at home and school attested to. He became demanding (often for food); his play became more aggressive and limits had to be set; his language became a stream of un-acceptable words; when he was not a winner, a game would land on the floor. Later, there were times when discussions substituted for the behavior. Chris was then able to talk about his anger at his learning disabilities; to acknowledge the confusion of two sets of parents; and to recognize that a relationship existed between him and his worker. He gained some trust, feeling that the therapist still cared for him, even though she had seen his 'bad' behavior and heard his 'bad' language.

Chris is now twelve. Although his reading has improved considerably, it is still well below grade level. He is more comfortable with it, accepting that he is intelligent despite the reading problem. He is comfortable in having others read to him, confident in his ability to understand content. He joins a regular class for certain subjects and knows that his understanding of science is on a par with classmates. Chris's aggressive behavior at home continues, but with less intensity.

Previously it was impossible to predict his behavior because there were not identifiable precipitants to his outbursts. Currently, his outbursts are not as constant and there usually is an incident that can be cited as causal. Occasionally, Chris now rewards his adoptive father with a 'crumb' of affection, but this is not routine. His ambivalence about loyalty to his biological father remains, though he can verbalize that it is all right to care about both.

No one can safely predict the future for Chris, or accurately speculate on how things might be different for him now if the past had been handled more skillfully. Twelve years ago, when he first came to the attention of the child welfare system, permanency planning was not a prime consideration. Although it was recognized that it was not good for children to move from one foster home to another and there was always a hope that parents would rehabilitate and resume care of their children, there was no emphasis on intensive work with parents or on the need to make permanent decisions within reasonable lengths of time. There was no consideration of adoption for children unless parental rights had already been terminated, nor was there significant attention paid to visiting arrangements for children and biological parents.

In retrospect, one can see how much better it would have been if his parents' inability to care for him had been determined during Chris's second year of life. This would have resulted in an earlier resolution for both Chris and his parents. Parental rights could have been terminated and Chris might have been adopted at age two. One can only speculate that this would have been more comfortable for Chris's parents and also that it would have allowed Chris to take on an adoptive family with less ambivalence, guilt, and fear of being like his disabled parents.

In the current emphasis on permanency planning for children, it is recognized that time is of prime importance; that decisions about where a child shall grow up need to be made quickly, preferably in no more time than a year; and that such decision-making allows for optimum growth of a sense of identity, self-assurance, self-respect and worth, and intellectual development. With long-term support and therapy, Chris may grow to be a responsible and happy adult. His chances for this might have been more optimistic if permanency planning thinking and techniques had been used when he was one year of age.

SUMMARY

We have introduced the concept of permanency planning, defining it as the systematic process of taking prompt, decisive action to maintain children in their own homes or place them permanently with other families. We have argued, in addition, that permanency planning can serve as a framework for child welfare practice and a guiding metaphor for all child welfare and child mental health services.

The permanency planning framework embodies the following features, which we have delineated in this chapter:

* a *philosophy* highlighting the importance of the biological family and the value of rearing children in a family setting;

* a *theoretical* perspective stressing that stability and continuity of relation-ships promote a child's growth and functioning;
* a *program* focusing on systematic planning within specified time frames for children who are in care or at risk of placement out of their homes;
* a *case management method* emphasizing practice strategies such as case reviews, contracting, and decision-making, along with active participation of parents in the helping process; and
* active *collaboration* among various community agencies, child care person-nel, lawyers, judges and others working with children and their parents.

The significance of these features and the impact of permanency planning on practice were illustrated through a case example. The next chapter focuses on the emergence of permanency planning, as a prelude to discussion of its implemen-tation in the rest of the book.

NOTES

1. Suggested by Thomas D. Morton in personal communication to one of the authors, dated May 25, 1983.
2. From Public Law 96–272 – June 17, 1980 – Adoption Assistance and Child Welfare Act of 1980, Section 425 (a) (1).
3. One of the questions we faced in writing this book was how to refer to parents of children in out-of-home placement, when necessary to differentiate them from substitute caretakers. Various possibilities emerged, including biological parents, natural parents, bio-parents, birth parents, and genetic parents. We chose *biological parents* as a neutral term that is objective and descriptive. Others may prefer a different designation.

SUGGESTIONS FOR FURTHER READING

Emlen, A., Lahti, J., Downs, G., McKay, A., and Downs, S. (1977) *Overcoming Barriers to Planning for Children in Foster Care*. Portland, OR: Regional Research Institute for Human Services, Portland State University.

Maluccio, A. N. and Fein, E. (1983) Permanency Planning: A Redefinition. *Child Welfare* 62 (3): 195–201.

Maluccio, A. N., Fein, E., Hamilton, V. J. Klier, J., and Ward, D. (1980) Beyond Permanency Planning. *Child Welfare* 59 (9): 515–30.

Pike, V., Downs, S., Emlen, A., Downs, G., and Case, D. (1977) *Permanent Planning for Children in Foster Care: A Handbook for Social Workers*. Washington, DC: US Department of Health, Education, and Welfare. Publication (OHDS) 78–30124.

2 How did permanency planning emerge?

Reggie, age thirteen, is a 'difficult' boy who has been living in a series of foster homes and group care placements during the past five years.

Laura, whose teenage mother is trying to work out a way to take care of her, is six months old and has been placed in a foster home since birth.

Bobby, age eight, was removed from his family due to physical abuse from his father, who visits him occasionally in the foster home.

Frank, age ten, and his family have been referred to the child protection unit of a local welfare department, following a teacher's complaint that the boy was neglected at home.

As with Reggie, Laura, Bobby, and Frank, too many children and youth through-out the world live in a state of limbo. Limbo is not healthy. Consequently social workers and other practitioners in the human services regularly struggle with crucial questions: What is the best way to help these children and their families? Should children be removed from their own homes? If they are removed, should they be returned to their parents? How can the children be provided with sufficient stability in their living arrangements? What role should the worker play in this human drama?

As noted in the preceding chapter, permanency planning has emerged as a response to these questions and the plight of countless children such as the ones mentioned above. Permanency planning implies the right of every child to a stable home, quickly, and with as few moves or temporary situations as possible. It demands increasing efforts to keep children out of substitute care or, once there, to move them back early into their own homes, into adoptive homes, or into some other permanent living arrangements.

What has led to the emergence of permanency planning as a movement? What has contributed to its further development? What is its impact on service delivery? This chapter addresses these questions, by examining permanency planning within an historical and research context.

DOES FOSTER CARE WORK?

Substitute or foster care emerged out of concern for rescuing potentially 'good' children from their 'bad' or 'inadequate' parents, and rearing them to become productive citizens. The more modern concept of foster care as child-rearing by a substitute family, on a temporary basis, evolved gradually and unevenly over time. According to this concept, the thrust of foster care is to serve as a temporary service whose goal is to reunite the child with his or her own family as soon as possible or to provide a substitute but stable home in which the child may grow up and experience security and continuity of relationships with surrogate parents.

A recurring question, however, is whether the system of foster care is effective in reuniting children with their own families or providing secure substitute families. By foster care, we mean not only foster family homes, but also group child care programs, such as group homes, halfway houses, residential treatment programs, and institutions for children and youth.

Much of the evidence is negative. For instance, over two decades ago, in an extensive nationwide survey, Maas and Engler (1959) reached some startling conclusions: Many of the children in foster care had at least one parent living, but the parents rarely visited them and generally had no plans to assume responsibility for their care; nearly two-thirds of the children were unlikely to return to their own homes; for most of the children in foster care, future plans were indefinite and there was little sense of stability in their living arrangements. Similar findings were gathered in a later British study of children in care (Rowe and Lambert 1973).

These early findings have been supported by subsequent investigations demonstrating that many children who enter the system are likely to grow up in out-of-home placement (Fanshel 1971; Fanshel and Shinn 1978; Gruber 1978; Wiltse and Gambrill 1974). As Gruber observed in his analysis of the foster care program in Massachusetts, research shows that, 'despite the temporary purpose of foster care, it is more often than not a permanent status for the child' (Gruber 1978: 176). Gruber's findings exemplify the status of most foster care programs throughout the country: 'About 68% of the children have been in foster home care between four and eight years. The average length of time spent in foster care is more than five years, yet 83% of the children have never been returned to their parents, not even for trial periods' (Gruber 1978: 176).

Similarly, following a comprehensive review of a large public foster care program in California, Wiltse and Gambrill (1974: 14) stated: 'The fact remains that public foster care programs tend more to be long-term child caring programs than short-term or crisis-oriented treatment programs'. Furthermore, until recently, little effort was made to prevent placement or keep the family together. In one study it was found that almost one-third of the biological parents did not have any contact with the social worker from the child-placing agency, while more than half had not seen a social worker for at least six months (Gruber 1978). Other investigators have reported that there is minimal casework contact with parents (Jameson and Sugg 1979).

Careful planning to prevent or shorten placement out of the home has long been urgently needed, especially since until the late 1970s the number of children in foster care had been steadily increasing. Whereas in 1961 there were 177,000 children in out-of-home placement in the USA, in 1978 there were 503,000 children (Shyne and Schroeder 1978: 33). Moreover, there is extensive evidence that many of these children come from families with limited social supports, insufficient income, and multiple needs and problems in such areas as health, education, housing, employment, and family relationships (Fanshel and Shinn 1978; Fein *et al.* 1983; Jenkins and Sauber 1966; Jenkins, Schroeder, and Burgdorf 1981; Shyne and Schroeder 1978). For instance, in a study of the family situations of children during the year prior to entry into placement, the authors concluded that 'the overall picture of the retrospective year shows marginal families, without sufficient resources to sustain themselves in the community when additional pressures or problems are added to their pre-existing burdens' (Jenkins and Sauber 1966: 61).

As found in a national survey of services to children conducted in the USA in 1977, children from poor families and/or minority groups are disproportionately represented in the group of 1.8 million children who come to the attention of the child welfare system. In 38 per cent of the families of these children, the main source of income was 'Aid to Families with Dependent Children' (AFDC), a public assistance program; 37 per cent of all children in care were Black, Hispanic, Asian, or American Indian; and one out of twenty Black children under eighteen years of age was involved with the child welfare system, in contrast to one out of fifty Caucasian children (Shyne and Schroeder 1978: 23–43). As noted by Meyer (1984: 499), 'foster care remains a social service for poor and minority children'.

The above statistics refer to all children and youth who come to the attention of the child welfare system. A later national survey provides data on the rates of those actually placed in out-of-home care, by ethnic/racial category: 'Compared with the national placement rate of 4 per 1,000, Black children are placed away from home at a rate of 9.5 per 1,000, followed by American Indian children with a rate of 8.8 per 1,000. Other groups – Asian, Hispanic, and White – ranged between two or three per 1,000' (Mech 1983: 661). Sensitivity to racial and ethnic variations is therefore crucial in the planning and delivery of services to these children and their families.

EMERGENCE OF PERMANENCY PLANNING

The increasing number of children entering substitute care, the growing concern about the impermanence of such care, and other developments such as awareness of – and interest in – children's rights and writings on the 'best interest of the child' (Goldstein, Freud, and Solnit 1973, 1979) have led to dissatisfaction with the impact of the foster care system on children and families.

As a result of these mounting concerns, the value of permanency planning for each child began to be asserted with renewed conviction, as two leading investigators did upon conclusion of a longitudinal foster care study in New York: 'We emerge from our research with the view that all children should be afforded permanency in their living arrangements if at all possible' (Fanshel and Shinn 1978: 479).

Such conviction of course is not new in human history. Children without homes have always been with us. Romulus and Remus found nurturance with a she-wolf, and Moses was plucked from the bulrushes to be cared for by an Egyptian princess, the Pharaoh's daughter. Decision-making about these placement options is always hard; Solomon's solution of dividing the child in half has become a metaphor for all difficult decisions.

Within social work itself, permanency planning as such appears to have been first mentioned formally in the literature by Epstein and Heymann (1967) in an article on adoption planning for older children. These authors described a voluntary agency's efforts to prevent long-term foster home placement by confronting the parents early with the need to make a permanent plan either through adoption or return to the child's own home. Even earlier, noted child welfare writers such as Henrietta Gordon (1941) referred to the importance of promoting permanent ties for children in foster care, developing plans providing security, and avoiding prolonged temporary placements.

During the 1970s the permanency planning movement grew in both the UK (Fitzgerald, Murcer, and Murcer 1982; Morris 1982) and the USA (Emlen 1981). It was promoted in the latter country by a landmark, federally funded special project carried out by the Regional Research Institute for Human Services at Portland State University in Oregon. The 'Oregon Project', as it came to be known, began in 1973 with a three-year demonstration program called 'Freeing Children for Permanent Placement'. The project soon demonstrated that children who had been adrift in long-term foster care could be returned to their biological families or placed in adoption through intensive agency services emphasizing aggressive planning and casework techniques (Pike 1976).

Building on these experiences, the Oregon Project developed a variety of training materials and provided extensive training and technical assistance to public and private child welfare agencies interested in incorporating permanency planning into their programs (Downs et al. 1981; Emlen et al. 1977; Pike et al. 1977; Regional Research Institute for Human Services 1976).

Thanks in large measure to the Oregon Project's dissemination efforts and the impact of subsequent demonstration projects, the goal of permanency planning for every child or youth has begun to shape the philosophy and practice of many American child welfare agencies. Arthur C. Emlen, a long-time leader in the Oregon Project, reflects this trend in the following statement:

'The notion that all children should be living with their natural or adoptive families and that foster care should not be a permanent status has taken on such force in recent years that we face the prospect of a radical shift in the expectations placed on service providers in child welfare'

(Emlen 1981: 1.11)

As a matter of fact, as Fanshel and Shinn (1978: 478) point out, the adequacy of an agency's performance is increasingly being assessed on the basis of its success in assuring permanence in living arrangements and continuity of relationships for children in its care.

Permanency planning originally emerged as a movement to deal with the problem of *drift* in out-of-home care – the situation of many children living away from their own families, with little sense of stability or continuity in their living arrangements. Because of ongoing concern about the needs of children in sub-stitute care, many agencies continue to regard permanency planning as a remedial program. As noted in the preceding chapter, the concept has evolved to encompass prevention of placement of children out of their own homes; indeed, prevention is being regarded more and more as the primary goal of permanency planning. Consequently, it is argued that permanency planning principles and values should guide the professional activities of social workers and others not only in traditional child welfare agencies but also in child guidance clinics, family service agencies, hospital pediatric wards, and other settings which serve families and children at risk; timely, early intervention with these families can avert out-of-home placement (Olmstead 1983; Olmstead, Hamilton, and Fein 1985).

ADOPTION ASSISTANCE AND CHILD WELFARE ACT OF 1980

The permanency planning movement was given further impetus with the enact-ment of Public Law 96–272, the Adoption Assistance and Child Welfare Act of 1980, by the Congress of the United States (Sinanoglu 1984). This federal law, which has been widely hailed as a major piece of legislation, is explicitly designed to reform child welfare services by promoting permanency planning for children and youth coming to the attention of the public child welfare system, through a comprehensive set of fiscal incentives to state agencies as well as through procedural reforms. The law has had a widespread impact, since nearly all children in out-of-home care are directly or indirectly served by public agencies. Each state has enacted legislation to implement its mandates and provisions.

Because it has such great significance for permanency planning, the major provisions and approaches reflected in Public Law 96–272 are summarized below. In addition, the law will be referred to throughout the book and will be considered in further detail in Chapter 15, in conjunction with discussion of working with the legal system.

Public Law 96–272 amends the Title IV-B Child Welfare Services Program and the AFDC-Foster Care Program, creating a new Foster Care and Adoption Assist-ance Program under Title IV-E of the Social Security Act, effective October 1, 1982. Its major features involve: (1) prevention of unnecessary or inappropriate placement of children out of their own homes; (2) improvement in the quality of care and services provided for children and their families, especially home-based services; and (3) achievement of permanence for each child who must be separ-ated from his or her own family, through reunification with parents, adoption, or other appropriate means. The law seeks to promote permanency planning through a variety of approaches, including:

* provision of pre-placement prevention services and post-placement supportive services to keep children in their own homes or reunite them with their families as soon as possible;
* requirement of case plans, periodic reviews, information systems, and other protections intended 'to ensure that children enter care only when necessary, are placed appropriately, and are moved on to permanent families in a timely fashion' (Allen and Knitzer 1983: 121);
* redirecting federal funds away from inappropriate out-of-home placement and toward permanent alternatives such as adoption;
* establishment of adoption assistance programs, including federally funded subsidies for adoption of children with special needs, such as older, handicapped, and minority children.

The approaches incorporated in this law reflect and exemplify the following hierarchy of priorities in service delivery that has characterized the permanency planning movement since its inception:

(1) providing supports to families in order to prevent separation of children from their homes;
(2) where separation is necessary, developing permanent plans and providing support services to enable children to be reunited with their families;
(3) where these options are inappropriate, providing highly active services that enable children to be adopted or, where it is the plan of choice, to be placed in a permanent foster home.

In short, Public Law 96–272 establishes 'the federal legislative framework for meaningful reforms on behalf of the over one-half million children and their families affected by the child welfare system' (Allen and Knitzer 1983: 124). It does have some limitations, including insufficient attention to groups such as adjudicated delinquent youth and developmentally disabled or emotionally disturbed youth. At the time of writing, there is also doubt as to whether adequate funding will be made available by the federal or state governments to implement the legislative intent. On the whole, however, the law represents a national commitment to the goals and philosophy of permanency planning. Consequently, as Allen and Knitzer (1983: 123) suggest, it 'is likely to play a significant role in the development of child welfare policy that goes well beyond its specific mandates for services and protections'. This impact is already being seen in the beginning reforms initiated by many states to prevent out-of-home placement or reduce its duration, as seen in a progress report recently submitted to Congress by the US Department of Health and Human Services:

'There has been a significant decrease in the number of children in foster care, from more than 500,000 in 1977 to 243,000 in 1982. The duration of placement of children in foster care decreased from an average of 47 months in 1977 to an average of 35 months in December 1982.

The number of children who are free for adoption has declined dramatically in the last five years from 102,000 to 50,000. However, the proportion of these children who are in adoptive placement, but not yet adopted, has also declined from 49% in 1977 to 34% in 1982.'

(US Department of Health and Human Services 1984: 14)

RESEARCH

As permanency planning emerged as a significant component of child welfare philosophy and practice, researchers have increasingly been engaged in studies seeking to shed light on its processes and outcomes.

Effectiveness of intensive services

A number of studies have explored the effectiveness of intensive services to children in out-of-home placement or at risk of such placement. The focus has been on demonstration projects designed to minimize the drift of children in unplanned long-term placements. The results are varied.

Jones, Neuman, and Shyne (1976) examined a sample of 549 families with at least one child at risk of placement in substitute care. The purpose of the study, which involved a range of public and private child welfare agencies, was 'to test the effectiveness of intensive family casework services to prevent the occurrence or reoccurrence of foster care placements' (Jones, Neuman, and Shyne 1976: 118). Effectiveness was measured by means of outcome criteria such as number of children placed in foster care; duration of placement; whether the child returned to the biological home; and the child's problems and functioning. These researchers concluded that the demonstration project was successful in preventing or shortening placement and in helping children and parents: 'The effectiveness of the intensive service provided in the demonstration units as compared with the regular program was strongly supported by the consistently more favorable outcomes for experimental than control cases' (Jones, Neuman, and Shyne 1976: 22). Variables that were positively related to successful outcome in the above study included an intensive worker–client relationship and provision of needed services (such as housing and health) to the family.

These findings were corroborated in another study of a special project serving families at risk of dissolution; over a two-year period, only 4 per cent of the children in the 'special services' experimental group entered foster care, as compared with 17 per cent of those in the 'regular services' control group (Halper and Jones 1981).

On the other hand, these results were not congruent with another study of 413 children placed through a public child welfare agency, in which the authors examined the relative effectiveness of the following alternative service approaches: (1) regular services; (2) administrative case monitoring; and (3) administrative case monitoring plus special workers to provide intensive services to parents. The conclusion was that 'it could not be demonstrated to a statistically significant degree that the special intervention strategies worked better than regular practice' (Sherman, Neuman, and Shyne 1973: 98). However, the authors recognized that the design of their research was not truly experimental, since it was not possible to assign cases randomly to experimental and control groups and thus control the effect of extraneous variables.

Demonstration projects of new strategies often produce exciting effects; studies conducted in public agencies in California and Iowa have demonstrated the effectiveness of using service contracts and case planning to move children out of temporary care more rapidly (Iowa Department of Social Services 1977; Stein, Gambrill, and Wiltse 1978). Similarly, the Oregon Project found that a higher percentage of project children were in permanent homes than in the comparison groups characterized by customary casework activity (Lahti 1982; Lahti and Dvorak 1981; Lahti *et al.* 1978). The project's casework techniques emphasized decision-making guidelines for devising appropriate plans and court procedures for terminating parental rights (Lahti 1982; Lahti *et al.* 1978).

Barriers to permanency planning

Other investigations have pointed to the existence of numerous barriers to permanency planning (Fein *et al.* 1983; Miller *et al.* 1984a; Regional Research Institute for Human Services 1976).

This is an issue that has been explored in depth by the staff of the Oregon Project, which identified a complex set of obstacles to permanency planning in these areas:

* systemic barriers, e.g. legal constraints or lack of supports to parents;
* worker-related barriers, e.g. negative attitude toward biological parents;
* parent-related barriers, e.g. serious illness; and
* child-related barriers, e.g. severe physical impairment (Regional Research Institute for Human Services 1976).

In another study of a special permanency planning project that emphasized inter-agency cooperation, Miller *et al.* (1984a: 49–50) documented a total of 157 barriers in forty-eight of the fifty-five cases in their sample. These included system-related barriers such as non-completion of termination of parental rights; problems in inter-agency coordination; lack of homes; and legal delays. Case-related barriers included problems with foster parents or biological parents; the child's behavior problems or school issues; the child's need for continued therapy or evaluation; and financial/subsidy issues. Miller *et al.* (1984a) found that workers were able to overcome these barriers as a result of the extensive resources and services available through this special project.

As mentioned in the previous chapter, a particular barrier to permanency planning that is just beginning to be examined is the role that the courts play in dealing with children in care or at risk of placement. Delays in court proceedings, unclear expectations for parents by judges, and non-uniform review times and procedures have been documented. To counter these difficulties, a variety of case review procedures have been proposed. The evaluation of one such program, which uses volunteers to record the judge's expectations, monitor compliance, and write a summary report for the court hearing, found that neglect cases were expedited in their course through the court system (Wert, Fein, and Haller in press). Children were being freed for adoption in less time. A child entering the court system had a 50 per cent chance of having his or her case reach disposition within three months; before the review program the wait had been approximately twice as long.

As a result of these findings, many writers have argued for elimination of barriers to permanency planning through improved and intensified training of child welfare personnel as well as changes in legislation, court processes, and service delivery (Emlen et al. 1977; Jones 1978; Krymow 1979; Miller et al. 1984a).

Follow-up studies

What happens to children *after* a permanent plan is selected and implemented? Various investigations have shown that the majority of children who are placed in permanent homes are reunited with their biological families (Fanshel and Shinn 1978; Fein et al. 1983). At the same time, these studies have indicated that these are families with considerable need for social supports and concrete services in such areas as health, education, employment, recreation, and income. Beyond these findings, the few studies reporting on the outcome of permanent placements in foster care do not provide clear-cut answers regarding the issue of the outcome of permanent plans.

There are questions about the stability of the children's placements: Are they truly 'permanent?' The Oregon Project's follow-up study of 259 children revealed that 90 per cent of the children remained in the same placement eighteen months later, with the adoptive homes being the most stable and returns-to-parent the least, although this difference was not statistically significant (Lahti 1982; Lahti et al. 1978). On the other hand, another study found that only 66 per cent (nineteen out of twenty-nine) children discharged from a time-limited foster care program remained in their permanent placement at the point of follow-up (nineteen to twenty-four months); however, this program served primarily emotionally disturbed children, which may account for the discrepancy (Fein, Davies, and Knight 1979). These researchers found no difference in stability of placement between discharges to adoptive and biological parents.

The results of a broader investigation at the New Jersey State Division of Youth and Family Services suggested evidence that findings from the Fein, Davies, and Knight (1979) study of emotionally disturbed youngsters may also be true of other populations (Claburn, Magura, and Chizeck 1977). In the New Jersey study, a follow-up of a sample of 612 children who had spent at least one week in out-of-home placement showed that 19 per cent of the discharged cases had at least one distinct re-opening during a four and one-half year period. This figure, moreover, does not include additional children or youth who may have entered the juvenile justice or mental health systems or re-entered the foster care system in other ways, for example out-of-state placements and private agencies.

In a comprehensive study conducted in New York City, it was found that, by the end of five years, 16 per cent of the 381 children in the sample had been returned into foster care at least once (Fanshel and Shinn 1978: 159). Again, these figures do not account for additional children who may have experienced other types of changes in their living arrangements following their discharge from foster care.

In a longitudinal investigation of a statewide sample of 187 children placed in permanent plans following temporary placement through a public child welfare agency in Connecticut, it was found that 22 per cent of the children were known to have left their permanent homes within twelve to sixteen months (Fein et al. 1983: 535).

In another study at a New York private child welfare agency, it was reported that there was a recidivism rate of 16.1 per cent among 527 children under age eighteen who had been discharged from foster care in 1978 and 1979 (Block and Libowitz 1983: 17). Moreover, in the same study children who were discharged to parents, relatives, friends, or who were adopted experienced a recidivism rate of 27.3 per cent (Block and Libowitz 1983: 68). Recidivism was defined as return into substitute care or entry into the health or criminal justice systems.

As Block and Libowitz (1983: 15–22) indicate in their extensive consideration of this issue, major problems are encountered in efforts to define and measure recidivism or disruption. These problems make it impossible to arrive at valid comparisons or sound generalizations on the basis of the findings of various studies, since they differ in such aspects as sample selection, definition of disruption, and time period examined.

It is apparent, however, that a substantial proportion of children placed in 'permanent plans' enter another system such as mental health or re-enter the child welfare system and are likely to remain in care indefinitely. Many of these are older children or youth who return to their biological families from temporary care. Extra efforts need to be made to identify and support these especially vulnerable children and their families.

Looking beyond permanence *per se*, several studies have also examined whether there are differences in adjustment between children placed in permanent homes and those remaining in temporary foster care. No significant differences in child's adjustment have been found between these types of placement in two comprehensive studies (Iowa Department of Social Services 1977; Jones, Neuman, and Shyne 1976). Similarly, in the follow-up study of the Oregon project it was found that there was no difference in adjustment between children placed in temporary foster care and those in permanent placements (Lahti et al. 1978). The latter investigators noted, moreover, that the parents' or caretakers' perception of the child's sense of permanence, rather than the legal status of the placement, seemed to be most closely related to the child's well-being: 'Whether the child was in a legally permanent placement, adoption or returned home, or was in legally temporary foster care made very little difference in his level of adjustment and health at the time of the interview. Perception of permanence was the key' (Lahti *et al.* 1978: 9.3).

The results of these studies are consistent with the longitudinal evaluation of the effects of foster care carried out by Fanshel and Shinn (1978), who noted the complexities involved in this type of evaluative research and the inconclusive nature of the findings:

> 'We are not completely sure that continued tenure in foster care over extended periods of time is not in itself harmful to children. On the level at which we are able to measure the adjustment of the children we could find no such negative effect. However, we feel that our measures of adjustment are not without problems, and we are not sure that our procedures have captured the potential feelings of pain and impaired self-image that can be created by impermanent status in foster care.'
>
> (Fanshel and Shinn 1978: 479)

More recently, an extensive study of over 500 children in long-term foster care was conducted in Great Britain by Rowe *et al.* (1984); their findings suggested that foster care does not provide sufficient security and stability for the children, although many of them seem to flourish while in care.

While the research evidence is not clear-cut, other writers have pointed to the damage resulting from the tenuous status in which many foster children find themselves – a status that supposedly makes it difficult for the child to develop his or her identity, to achieve a sense of belonging, to establish meaningful relationships with people, and to deal successfully with developmental tasks (Bryce and Ehlert 1971; Frank 1980; MacIntyre 1970).

Follow-up studies of adults who have been placed in substitute care do not support the conclusion that such care is damaging. In the most recent study, Festinger (1983) comprehensively examined the views, experiences, and functioning of nearly 300 young adults who had 'graduated' from foster care in New York City. She concluded that, in general, they 'were not so different from others their age in what they were doing, in the feelings they expressed, and in their hopes about the future' (Festinger 1983: 294):

> 'The assumptions and expectations that abound concerning the dire fate of foster care children seem to have little validity. The products of foster care – the young adults whom we followed in this study – did not measure down to such dire predictions. They were not what might be described as problem ridden when they were discharged nor did they become so in subsequent years; there was no support for the generational repetition of foster care; there was no evidence of undue economic dependence on public support; and their records of arrest were not excessive.'
>
> (Festinger 1983: 293–94)

Triseliotis (1980) reached similar conclusions in a British follow-up study of forty young adults who were born in the mid-1950s and who had spent from seven to fifteen years in a single foster home prior to age sixteen:

'people who grow up in long-term foster homes, within which they are wanted and integrated as part of the family, generally do well. Those who were perceived and judged as doing well were placed in the foster homes at different ages. Most children were able to overcome the serious social handicaps of their natural families and the traumatic situations to which they were exposed before and after coming into care.'

(Triseliotis 1980: 156)

In most of the cases in this study, both foster mothers and former foster children reported that the foster care experience had been a mutually satisfying one; and the children appeared to have been able to form psychological bonds with their foster parents (Triseliotis 1980).

Follow-up research on post-placement functioning continues to be a neglected area in the field of child welfare. The few studies that addressed this issue prior to Festinger and Triseliotis (Gil 1964; Meier 1965; Murphy 1974) relied on small samples and looked at their subjects in adult life, rather than concentrating on the events immediately subsequent to the foster care experience. More importantly, the results of these earlier studies are now outmoded and have few implications for today's practice, since they reported on a different type of service; for example, it was not uncommon for over half of the respondents to have spent more than seven years in foster care (Maas and Engler 1959).

Similarly, Festinger (1983: 295) noted that her study was 'based on a highly selected group of young adults, most of whom were in placement for a very long time, much of which was spent in a stable placement'. Moreover, most of the respondents in her study, and all of the ones in the Triseliotis (1980) research, had grown up as part of another family, which is not typical of children currently in foster care, who tend to have a history of multiple placements. In view of the many new emphases in the field, current follow-up data and evaluation are sorely needed.

IMPACT ON SERVICE DELIVERY

As the preceding summary indicates, research conducted thus far in the area of permanency planning provides few definitive answers. There is a need to explore further the processes, methods, and outcomes of permanency planning. But there is no question that the philosophy of permanency planning has been influencing service delivery in various ways, beginning by raising consciousness about the needs of children in substitute care, leading to changes in the programs of many agencies (Fanshel and Shinn 1978; Jones 1980; Sisto 1980), and resulting in reduction in the numbers of children entering care, as noted earlier in this chapter.

In particular, there has been growing awareness of the special needs of the disproportionate numbers of minority group children who are placed in substitute care, often on a long-term basis. Various studies have indicated that these children and their families are inadequately served by the child welfare system (Mech 1983; Olsen 1982; Shyne and Schroeder 1978).

Following an in-depth analysis of data from the Shyne and Schroeder (1978) national study, Olsen (1982: 583) concluded that minority group children 'are urgently in need of permanency planning, for they truly have been lost in the system'. For example, 'Black children and their families showed several indications of neglect by the child welfare system', including having fewer service plans, fewer contacts with their parents, and longer placements (Olsen 1982: 583).

As a result of this increasing sensitivity, permanency planning as a goal is being increasingly adopted in the field. Some agencies have successfully restructured their services to counter the drift of children in their care and to promote permanency (Levitt 1981; Sisto 1980). Others have found that 'a modest investment of time, staff and money' can be productive in increasing workers' skills and making stable placement plans for children (Jones 1980).

One especially interesting project, a combined public agency–voluntary agency effort, succeeded in finding permanent homes for over fifty 'hard-to-place' children over a two-year period (Miller et al. 1984a). This project, which was subsequently incorporated into the structure of the public agency, involved a number of special features, including in particular: strong inter-agency collaboration; intensive training of all staff on permanency planning skills; frequent opportunities for staff to share specific case problems and discuss possible solutions; and persistent efforts to overcome barriers to permanency planning (Miller et al. 1984a: 48).

One of the most concrete changes in service delivery resulting in part from the emphasis on permanency planning has been the creation in many agencies of case review procedures, even before these became required by Public Law 96–272. These structural devices are designed to control the phenomenon of foster care drift. Although their value has been questioned (McDonnell and Aldgate 1984) and their impact is yet to be documented (Claburn, Magura, and Resnick 1976; Magura and Claburn 1978), it is widely believed that mandatory periodic review of cases of children in foster care is a promising method of preventing children from languishing in 'limbo' (Krymow 1979). There is some evidence that case review systems result in moving children out of temporary care (Poertner and Rapp 1980). One study has found that volunteers monitoring all abuse and neglect cases in a juvenile court resulted in faster movement of cases through the judicial system (Wert, Fein, and Haller in press). Definitive data for other programs do not yet exist and their relative effectiveness remains to be seen through experience.

In short, there are indications that the thrust toward permanency planning is leading toward significant changes in child welfare programs and methods, including:

* more emphasis on carefully evaluating a child's needs in the context of the family situation;

* prevention of out-of-home placement as much as possible;
* careful planning of a child's placement, if it is appropriate, to achieve continuity of care and help assure stability in his or her life;
* more explicit attention and intensive help to the parents; and
* greater awareness of the importance of aftercare services.

SUMMARY

We have explained that permanency planning originally emerged as a movement to deal with the problem of drift of children and youth in out-of-home care, with little sense of stability or continuity in their living arrangements. The movement gained strength following recognition of the increasing number of children entering substitute care, growing concern about the impermanence of such care, and other developments such as advocacy for children's rights. As the concept has evolved, permanency planning has also come to encompass prevention of placement of children out of their homes.

The permanency planning movement was given further impetus in the USA with enactment of Public Law 96–272, the Adoption Assistance and Child Welfare Act of 1980. This federal law was designed to reform child welfare services by promoting permanency planning for children and youth coming to the attention of the public child welfare system, through a comprehensive set of fiscal incentives to state agencies as well as procedural reforms. Its major features involve: (1) prevention of unnecessary or inappropriate out-of-home placement; (2) improvement in the quality of care and services provided for children and their families; and (3) achievement of permanence for each child who must be separated from the family, through reunification with parents, adoption, or other appropriate means.

The philosophy and methodology of permanency planning have already had a significant impact on service delivery, as seen in such areas as provision of preventive and supportive services to children and families; program changes emphasizing more careful planning and timely decision-making on behalf of children coming to the attention of child welfare agencies; reduction in the number of children entering out-of-home care; and widespread acceptance of the goals of permanency for each child. Research, however, reveals continuing issues and gaps in knowledge in areas such as barriers to permanency planning; the effectiveness of intensive services or demonstration projects; and the long-range impact of foster care placement on the functioning and development of children and youth.

SUGGESTIONS FOR FURTHER READING

Allen, M. L. and Knitzer, J. (1983) Child Welfare: Examining the Policy Framework. In B. McGowan and W. Meezan (eds) *Child Welfare: Current Dilemmas—Future Directions*. Itasca, IL: F. E. Peacock, pp. 93–141.

Emlen, A. C. (1981) Development of the Permanency Planning Concept. In S. W. Downs, L. Bayless, L. Dreyer, A. C. Emlen, M. Hardin, L. Heim, J. Lahti, K. Liedtke, K. Schimke, and M. Troychak *Foster Care Reform in the 70's – Final Report of the Permanency Planning Dissemination Project*. Portland, OR: Regional Research Institute for Human Services, Portland State University, pp. 1.1–1.15.

Maluccio, A. N. and Fein, E. (in press) Permanency Planning Revisited. In M. Cox and R. Cox (eds) *Foster Care: Current Issues, Policies, and Practices*. Norwood, NJ: Ablex Press.

Olsen, L. (1982) Services for Minority Children in Out-of-Home Care. *Social Service Review* 56 (4): 572–85.

Pike, V. (1976) Permanent Planning for Foster Children: The Oregon Project. *Children Today* 5 (6): 22–25.

3 Who needs permanency planning?

Should permanency planning take place in certain agencies only? How do we decide whether a child or family coming to our attention would best be served through a permanency planning approach? What are the indicators for setting in motion the process of permanency planning? Following a brief discussion of children and families at risk, this chapter considers these questions and formulates and illustrates criteria useful in determining whether children should be considered for permanency planning.

CHILDREN AND FAMILIES AT RISK

Judy is a three-month-old girl who is brought to the hospital emergency room by her eighteen-year-old single mother. The child has a number of injuries, including a skull fracture and a broken arm. After initially explaining that Judy fell out of her crib, her mother admits that she has been under so much strain lately that she frequently beats her child.

Bobby, age twelve, has been in a small children's institution ever since his widowed father was hospitalized over a year ago for a psychiatric disturbance.

Eric, age six, has just returned to his parents, following a year-long stay in a foster home, where he was placed by the child welfare authorities because of physical abuse by his father. The parents have been responding to psychiatric treatment and the court determined that they were ready to resume their child's care.

Mr and Mrs Jones have been receiving counseling at a family service agency in regard to their persistent fighting and dissatisfaction with each other. They are at the point of considering separation and possibly divorce, and are concerned about how they can go on caring for their four school-age children.

These vignettes have at least one thing in common: the child or children involved in each can be regarded as actual or potential candidates for permanency planning, since they come from vulnerable families – that is, families with children who are at risk of out-of-home placement or who are already placed out of their homes. There are countless children like these and they come to the attention of professionals in diverse settings, from public child welfare agencies to hospitals to family counseling programs.

In the USA alone, a 1977 survey based on a stratified sample of nearly 10,000 children under age eighteen found that 1.8 million children were receiving services through the public child welfare system (Shyne 1980; Shyne and Schroeder, 1978). These were children who had come to the attention of the agencies for a variety of social services, including:

Placement services	adoption
	foster family care
	group home care
	residential treatment or institutional care
	emergency shelter care
At-home-services	day treatment
	day care
	homemaker service
	protective service
	counseling

Selected findings from the above study convey some understanding of the families and children coming to the attention of these agencies (Shyne and Schroeder 1978: 23–52).

* The median age of children was 9.2 years, with 39 per cent between 11.0 years or over.
* Most children (68 per cent) were living with at least one parent (usually the mother) or with relatives. Only 15 per cent lived with both parents. Almost one-third of the children were living in some type of out-of-home placement (22 per cent in foster families, 2 per cent in group homes, 4 per cent in institutions, and 2 per cent in other facilities).
* The most common reason for receiving services were: neglect or abuse; emotional problems of parents or child; financial need; conflict in parent–child relations; and behavioral problems of the child.
* Minority group children were over-represented in the population: 62 per cent of the children were White, 28 per cent Black, 7 per cent Hispanic, 1 per cent Asian-Pacific, 1 per cent Indian-Alaskan, and 2 per cent other. The ratios of children served to the general population were: White, 20:1,000; Black, 51:1,000; and Hispanic, 25:1,000.
* Most children were from families where public assistance or another cash transfer program was the primary source of income (e.g. 38 per cent were from families receiving 'Aid to Families with Dependent Children'). Forty per cent came from families for whom the major source of livelihood consisted of wages or other means of self-support. A court had been involved with 39 per cent of the cases; the most common type of involvement was in relation to custody issues, protective services, or judicial review.

Because of reasons such as poverty, racial or ethnic discrimination, and behavioral or family problems, many of these children live in stressful situations and are at risk of drifting in one type of placement or another. The Shyne and Schroeder (1978) study summarized above deals with children and families formally coming to the attention of the public child welfare system. An indeterminate number of similarly vulnerable children come to the attention of voluntary agencies (e.g. child guidance clinics, family counseling services, private hospitals) or other public services (e.g. mental health agencies, correctional or juvenile delinquency programs, public hospitals). In addition, some children at risk may not be known to any formal agency (e.g. children in informal adoption, informal day care, or informal foster care placements). The pool of potentially vulnerable children and families is vast.

IDENTIFYING CHILDREN FOR PERMANENCY PLANNING

Since children who are potential candidates for permanency planning are found in diverse settings – not only agencies traditionally associated with child welfare needs but also many others – how do we determine whether permanency planning should be put in motion in a particular case? Should the permanency planning process be initiated for every child who comes to our attention?

Regardless of the particular agency setting, social workers should be alert to the possible need for permanency planning whenever they come in contact with the type of family or child whom we have described as vulnerable or at risk. Moreover, as we shall discuss in Chapter 16, agencies can institute mechanisms such as case reviews or record-keeping procedures to help identify children in need of permanency planning.

General indicators of vulnerability

Various criteria or guidelines are available to help social workers assess whether children coming to their attention in foster care or other settings should be considered for permanency planning services. Prior to considering these, however, we should note a variety of general indicators that can serve to alert workers to the possibility that a child or family is at risk. These include:

* poverty
* minority status
* multiple family problems in basic life areas
* adolescent parents
* single-parent family with no other adult in the home
* child abuse or neglect
* child sexual abuse
* chronic substance abuse

In cases that contain one or more of these indicators, workers should quickly ascertain whether the family is vulnerable – that is, whether there is a child at actual or potential risk of out-of-home placement. If so, workers should immediately adopt a permanency planning stance; in addition to providing services that respond to the family's presenting problem or request, workers should consider intensive services designed to maintain the child at home, make efforts to place the child with relatives or family friends if removal from the home is indicated, or develop another permanent plan if appropriate.

Various authors offer guidelines for determining whether out-of-home placement is necessary (Janchill 1981; Meddin 1984; Snyder and Ramo 1983; Stein and Rzepnicki 1983). Snyder and Ramo (1983) have written a comprehensive manual that can be used by child welfare staff as a reference book, a self-study guide, or a tool in staff development programs; the manual spells out specific indicators to guide the decision regarding placement. A particularly useful set of criteria is also provided by Stein and Rzepnicki (1983: 60–1), who explain that out-of-home placement may be necessary in cases of child abuse or neglect involving one or more of the following conditions:

'1. There is no adult willing to care for a child, or the child refuses to stay in the home.
2. There is medical evidence that physical abuse or nutritional neglect is so severe as to be life-threatening.
3. There was intent to kill the child, even if injury is not severe. Medical evidence should support a hypothesis of deliberate poisoning, or marks on the child's body should indicate assault with a deadly weapon or repeated beating with a heavy object.
4. There is medical or psychological evidence of abuse or neglect that, without intervention, may threaten the child's life, *and* the parent refuses help.
5. Medical evidence of repeated abuse exists. This reference is to previous untreated injuries, generally identified through X-rays, where the location or type of injury suggests prior maltreatment.
6. Severe abuse or neglect recurs after services were offered.
7. Severe emotional abuse or neglect is evidenced by behavioral disturbance or withdrawal by the child, *and* the parent rejects the child.
8. Medical or psychological evidence suggests that the parent is incompetent to provide minimum child care and there are no resources (e.g. family, friends, or community services) to help in the home while assessment is under way.
9. A child has been raped by a related adult or a non-related adult known to the parent, *and* the parent did not attempt to protect the child.'

(Stein and Rzepnicki 1983: 60–1)[1]

A recent study of placement decisions in a large public agency in the USA found that workers were essentially guided by very similar criteria: Risk to the child of further abuse or neglect was the 'primary variable used to decide whether to place the child' (Meddin 1984: 372). In addition, 'severity of the current incident, functioning and cooperation of the primary caretaker, and age of the child' were the other most critical variables (Meddin 1984: 372).

Children most susceptible to drift and impermanence

Children who are about to enter foster care or who are already placed in it are among those most susceptible to the dangers of drifting and impermanence; they should therefore be prominently regarded as children in need of permanency planning. As noted previously, by foster care we mean not only foster family care but also group child care or residential treatment. Children and youth in residential care are especially at risk because they are more difficult (or have been so labelled) and it may be tempting to have the group or institutional setting become the 'permanent' plan.

Children who have entered – or are entering – the foster care system should be designated as in *urgent* need of permanency planning, receive concentrated efforts, and quickly have the permanency planning machinery set in motion, especially if they are vulnerable in one or more of the following areas (Shireman 1983):

*   length of time in foster care;
*   number of placements;
*   minority status; and
*   special needs.

Each of these areas is briefly described below, and a case vignette is included to illustrate the type of case that would require the 'urgent' label.

LENGTH OF TIME IN FOSTER CARE

It is difficult to assess what is an appropriate period of time in foster care, since children's needs vary in accordance with factors such as their age, developmental status, and reason for placement. However, it is known from various research studies that the longer the child remains in care, the less likely he or she is to return to the biological family or to go into an adoptive home; moreover, it has been found that the likelihood of the child's returning home or going into some permanent plan is drastically reduced once he or she has been in foster care beyond one and one-half years (Fanshel and Shinn 1978; Maas and Engler 1959).

Case Vignette: Ellen, age nine, has been in foster family care since age six, when she was removed from an abusive home. Parental rights were terminated when she was seven. Ellen has been placed in adoptive homes twice, first at age seven and then at age eight. Both placements failed within three months and each time she was returned to the foster family. Reasons for the failures included excessive demands for attention and inappropriate seductive behavior with the adoptive father and male children in the adoptive home.

AGE OF CHILD

Since older children are more difficult to plan for, it is crucial to make permanent plans as soon as possible, particularly if adoptive placement needs to be contemplated as a possible option. Early permanency planning is also urgent in the case of younger children, particularly infants: 'a few months of unplanned time in foster care soon moves an infant into a "hard to place" category' (Shireman 1983: 382).

Case Vignette: Alice, age twenty-three months, has been in foster placements for ten months. She was placed at the request of maternal grandparents who had cared for her for two months. They had taken custody of her when their drug-dependent daughter was clearly unable to provide care. While this was a first placement for Alice, the care of two older children had been assumed by the maternal grandparents on three other occasions when the mother's drug use made it impossible to provide adequate care.

NUMBER OF PLACEMENTS

Many children are placed more than once in some type of substitute care arrangement, and some children indeed are placed repeatedly. 'Repeated placement within the foster care system may also automatically be taken as an indicator that a child is experiencing difficulty and should receive special attention' (Shireman 1983: 382).

Case Vignette: Timothy, currently placed in a foster home, has the following background: placements with mother, biological father, and paternal grandmother for varying periods of time prior to age six; residential placement for two years, age six and seven; specialized foster placement for three months; and now five months in present placement, which is designated as temporary. History is one of suspected physical abuse in each placement with parents or grandparents and during home visits. Mother, while proclaiming her inability to manage him, will not release him and wishes to wait for him to 'get better'. Mother shows no capacity to have age appropriate expectations of Timothy.

MINORITY STATUS

The child's minority status is another variable pointing to the need for systematic permanency planning. It has been shown that children from minority backgrounds tend to remain in foster care longer than other children, have multiple placements, and are placed less often into adoption (Chestang 1978; Olsen 1982; Stehno 1982). A recent analysis of census data (Jenkins and Diamond 1985) demonstrates that time in foster care is related not only to the child's problems and the child protection agency's procedures, but to external social, economic, and political realities. Jenkins and Diamond (1985) found that length of stay in foster care is influenced by the percentage of families with children in poverty and the percentage of Blacks in the population. Further, there is a greater probability of Black children being placed when Blacks are a smaller proportion of the population than when they are a larger proportion. Special precautions consequently need to be taken to formulate and accomplish permanent plans for minority children in a timely and deliberate fashion.

Case Vignette: Janice, age thirteen, a Black/Hispanic child, was placed as an infant with a White adoptive family. Her struggles with identity and her failure to bond with the adopting mother, combined with friction between the parents over appropriate responses to Janice's behavior problems, resulted in their giving her up. Janice was placed in a Black 'therapeutic' foster home where she has been for nine months.

SPECIAL NEEDS

Children with special emotional, physical, or developmental needs also should be recognized early to receive intensive permanency planning services. It should be stressed that, 'without permanency planning efforts, these children are probably the most likely to "drift" in the foster care system and to suffer replacement within it' (Shireman 1983: 383).

Case Vignette: Amy, a two-year old mentally retarded daughter of two retarded parents, was not being appropriately cared for by her parents and was in foster family care for nine months. Her foster parents then discovered that Amy had been sexually abused when on home visits. Since the foster family was not interested in providing long-term care or in adopting Amy, she was moved to a 'therapeutic' foster home where she has been for three months and is making some developmental strides.

Vulnerable children in outpatient settings

The permanency planning perspective has been increasingly incorporated into services for children and families coming to the attention of typical child welfare agencies, such as child placing agencies, children's protective service agencies, and group child care services. The cases exemplified by the vignettes in the preceding section would therefore be recognized in these settings as needing permanency planning attention.

The very same cases might appear in outpatient settings. Indeed, as indicated earlier, many vulnerable children come to the attention of social workers in practice contexts other than typical child welfare agencies. These include schools, family counseling agencies, hospital emergency rooms or pediatric wards, mental health services, community centers, and others. In these settings, workers need to be especially alert to the potential need for permanency planning services, since the indicators of the child's or family's vulnerability may not be as apparent as those described in the preceding section (Olmstead, Hamilton, and Fein 1985).

Typical agency procedures can be adapted to help staff members identify cases requiring permanency planning services. Through such identification, agencies requring permanency planning services. Through such identification, agencies would be better able to provide services that support and rehabilitate families and also prevent the unnecessary placement of children out of their homes. For example, most child guidance clinics have formal or informal systems for labeling cases at the point of referral. Common categories include school refusal, suicidal potential, delinquency, and learning disability. The case of a child exhibiting school refusal, for instance, brings a quick response: waiting list priority; immediate efforts to return the child to school; school conferences; and examination of the parent–child relationship. Furthermore, labeling cases at referral permits a clinic to assign particular categories of clients to workers who have demonstrated special interest or skill in those areas (Olmstead, Hamilton, and Fein 1985).

For these reasons, child guidance clinics and other mental health or social service agencies could add the label of 'permanency planning' to the more familiar categories. The label would designate, among others:

* children referred for outpatient therapy who are already placed out of their home;
* pregnant women in conflict about keeping or giving up their unborn child;
* children currently at home but with a history of one or more previous placements;
* children referred for a trial of outpatient care prior to consideration of residential care;
* parents referred for help as a prerequisite for resuming care of children in placement;
* children referred for intra-family sexual abuse;
* foster children referred for school or behavior problems; and
* parents who are seriously questioning their ability to keep a child at home (Olmstead, Hamilton, and Fein 1985).

On the basis of any of these or other early warning signals, a case could be clearly identified and assigned to staff members with expertise in permanency planning, or referred to a permanency planning expert for consultation. As emphasized throughout this book, a timely and explicit decision is essential at this point in the helping process, as well as later on.

The permanency planning label would trigger responses assuring that appropriate service is offered to maintain the child with his or her family or consider alternative plans, if necessary. Workers' responses would include some or all of the permanency planning methods and emphases delineated in this book, such as support to parents or other caretakers; services delivered within an ecological perspective; use of time frames and service agreements; collaboration with other agencies; and aftercare services.

CASE ILLUSTRATIONS

The following examples illustrate the kinds of cases that require permanency planning, whatever the setting. It will also be shown how labelling a case as 'permanency planning' and explicitly adopting a permanency planning perspective can help practitioners to be more responsive to the needs of vulnerable children and families. In particular, they can focus more clearly on timely decision-making and enhance parental functioning, even when alternate permanent plans become necessary.

Case of John Sawyer

Mr and Mrs Sawyer, a Black couple in their early twenties, were referred for outpatient services at a child guidance clinic by the public agency charged with protecting children, because their three-year-old son, John, had been severely burned. John, who had been in his mother's custody, was then temporarily placed with his maternal grandmother, after a brief time in a foster home. Both parents, who were separated, had visited John for one and a half hours per week while he had been placed. The parents were in conflict and presented discrepant information regarding how, and with whom, the burn occurred. The public agency worker referred the case to the outpatient clinic with the request that a recommendation be made as to the mother's ability to resume care of the child. A court date was scheduled for three months later regarding this issue.

Without knowledge of permanency planning on the part of the clinic staff, intervention in this case would have been primarily with the mother, probably including the other family members only in the assessment phase. The focus would have been on gathering information about the mother's parenting skills, assessing conflicts between the parents, and attempting to determine if the mother were capable of parenting. The mother in all probability would have succumbed to the stress of her life situation and to the interrogation and would have dropped out of treatment. Most likely, there would have been a recommendation to terminate her parental rights.

Instead, the following occurred, as the clinic staff followed a permanency planning perspective. An initial interview was scheduled with the public agency worker and Mrs Sawyer to clarify the reason for the referral and what was expected of the mother as well as the agency. Individual roles and responsibilities were clarified, emphasizing the appropriateness of parent aide services for the mother and the need for the public agency worker to remain involved. During this session, Mrs Sawyer expressed a wish to resume custody of her child.

Weekly parent aide visits and weekly counseling sessions with Mrs Sawyer followed, to develop parenting and child management skills, alternate ways of handling stress, the ability to ask for help and utilize appropriate community resources, confidence in being able to understand the needs of the child, and better communication among family members. Monthly family sessions were held with both parents, maternal and paternal grandmothers, the child, the public agency worker, and the parent aide; the purpose of these sessions was to discuss issues and facilitate communication among family members. The maternal grandparents were found to be especially concerned and supportive. Parent–child visiting progressed from one and a half hours a week to two overnight visits with the mother and monthly weekend visits with the father. A service agreement was used, which clearly listed what the mother had to do to resume care of her child, and what the worker's responsibility was in keeping records of scheduled appointments and notes indicating progress. There was weekly contact with the maternal grandmother regarding the child and the visitation schedule, and the mother was helped to obtain needed furniture for her apartment.

In addition to her therapeutic functions, the worker's role involved advocating on behalf of child and mother; collaborating with a court monitor, the public agency worker, and a parent aide assigned to the case; and utilizing community resources to assist the mother in developing the skills and confidence she needed to resume care of her child.

Within eight months, Mrs Sawyer resumed care of her child. The outcome was dependent on several factors: an awareness of permanency planning, effective consultation, appropriate use of collateral resources, timely intervention, and sensitivity to the needs of the mother.

Case of Mrs Monte

Ruth Monte, a White 35-year-old mother, agreed to see regularly her worker in the public agency charged with protecting children, to assess her ability to learn and apply parenting skills before the agency would consider a return of her two children, Mark, nine, and Jim, eight, from foster care. She had voluntarily placed them after a suicide attempt; the children had been in placement for eight months, and the case was scheduled to appear in court in seven months.

Mrs Monte had been reared in residential child care settings because of abusive and neglectful parents. She had limited ability to parent her children, being unable to separate their needs from her own. Due to financial difficulties and the distance between her home and the foster home, Mrs Monte was not able to maintain the pre-arranged visits with her children.

With a permanency planning focus in mind, the worker became involved from the beginning in a comprehensive assessment and treatment program. In her initial interview with Mrs Monte, the worker clarified the objectives of the planned sessions, as well as the expectations and responsibilities of the agency worker and the child's foster parents. There was an immediate assignment of a parent aide to work with Mrs Monte twice a week, assisting her with housing, financial aid, budgeting, appropriate use of medication, nutrition, parenting, and child management. The parent aide accompanied Mrs Monte bi-weekly to visit with her children and the children's worker. This assured continuity of visits, and permitted the aide to observe the quality of interaction between mother and children and to address problem areas through role modeling.

A service agreement was used to outline what was required of Mrs Monte and the children's worker regarding a permanent plan for her children. Adoption was mentioned as an alternative to returning the children home. It was agreed that weekly sessions with Mrs Monte would focus on helping her care for herself, develop child management skills, learn to deal with crises and stress in a less self-destructive way, and function more competently on her own. The children's worker's responsibilities included keeping a record of attendance at appointments, assessing and monitoring progress, and providing support to the mother.

Following three months of weekly sessions, it became clear that Mrs Monte was not ready to resume responsibility for the care of her children. She understandably found it difficult to be confronted with her limitations and required extensive support to consider adoption. An agency adoption worker was brought in as an outside collaborator to explain the adoption process more fully to Mrs Monte;

the children's worker postponed filing for termination of parental rights to give Mrs Monte more time to make a decision. The permanency planning perspective – using a parent aide, becoming involved with the visitation, collaborating with foster parents, and using a time-limited service agreement – provided sufficient demonstration, to Mrs Monte and to others, of her inability to parent.

Termination of parental rights seemed the most viable course. Although Mrs Monte could not bring herself to surrender the children voluntarily, she was able to understand their need for permanence. The worker continued to offer support and helped Mrs Monte accept the evidence of the previous few months. All of this helped her live with the court decision to terminate parental rights and allowed her to release the children emotionally so they could attach to a new family.

Case of Ms Harris

Sonia Harris and her two children, Joseph, age nine, and Keisha, age seven, were referred for counseling at a child guidance clinic by their public assistance (AFDC) worker. Ms Harris, a 26-year-old White mother, was concerned because both of her children were doing poorly in school; they were reported as falling asleep frequently in class and not 'getting along' with their peers. The clinic worker, after two initial sessions, labelled the case as a permanency planning case because Ms Harris was having great difficulty managing day-to-day care of the children. She was depressed to the point that she often stayed in bed, cited financial difficulties, and indicated that food was not always available.

Ms Harris's own background reflected lack of continuity. She was the youngest of five children and her parents separated when she was six. Her mother suffered from periods of hospitalization for depression, and Ms Harris was placed with different relatives when her mother was in the hospital. At age ten she was placed with an aunt who agreed to keep her; however, she ran away, to return to her mother, when she was thirteen. At age sixteen, Joseph was born, and two years later Keisha was born.

Ms Harris did not marry the children's father but did live with him off and on. Since Joseph's birth she had lived with Joseph's paternal grandparents, on her own, with the maternal grandmother, and with a new boyfriend. For almost a year she had left the children with her mother while she and her new boyfriend moved to a different state seeking employment. She returned to live with her mother and the children. At the time of referral, Ms Harris had just secured her own apartment in a town adjacent to that of her mother. It was clear that she felt lost without the support of her mother and isolated in her new apartment and new town where she knew no one.

Although the children were at home with Ms Harris, the case was labelled as permanency planning because they had lived in so many settings, had been placed with the maternal grandmother for about a year, and were clearly at risk of being placed again. A preventive approach was taken, using permanency planning techniques.

A service agreement was drawn up. Ms Harris agreed to keep weekly individual appointments for herself and weekly individual appointments for her children. A twelve-week contract was agreed upon. A parent aide was also assigned to the family for twelve weeks. Ms Harris agreed to use her individual sessions to discuss her need for support, to talk about her depression, and to become more aware of the needs of the children. Mother and parent aide agreed to discuss the mother's feelings of isolation and find new ways of socializing; to discuss budgeting and shopping; and to look for housing in her home town where she would be closer to the maternal grandmother, a source of support. Mother agreed that it was import-ant for Joseph and Keisha to know where they would grow up and that she needed to assess her ability to care for them on a continuing basis.

In addition, as work progressed, it was possible to include the maternal grand-mother in a session with the parent aide and to discuss how she could be support-ive to Ms Harris. The latter was also helped to use inter-city buses, to attend school conferences for the children, and to explore job training opportunities for herself.

At the time of closing, Ms Harris was still in the new apartment but was feeling less isolated. She had met some neighbors and was able to use public transpor-tation to visit her mother, usually on weekends, finding that this helped her depressed feelings. She had learned a great deal about budgeting and was pleased with her ability to have food in the house consistently. She felt committed to raising her children.

The value of labelling the case as a permanent planning case was that there was an immediate and serious focus on the need for these children to know where they would grow up. Ms Harris could understand this need because she could relate it to the lack of consistency in her own growing up and the effects this had on her. In addition, clinic staff were better able to focus on those case aspects which had particular bearing on this mother's ability to care for her children: reducing depression, handling budgeting, and obtaining necessary support from the maternal grandmother and other resources.

SUMMARY

Permanency planning is a goal for all children. This chapter highlighted the importance of identifying those children for whom permanency planning should be specifically considered, because they are at risk of out-of-home placement. They come to the attention of social workers and other professionals in a variety of agency contexts – from traditional child welfare programs such as foster care or residential treatment to child guidance clinics or hospitals. Many of them are from single-parent families that are poor or come from minority backgrounds and have multiple problems in basic life areas.

The chapter also delineated criteria useful to social workers in determining whether a particular child or family should be approached from a permanency planning perspective. For children who are already in foster care, the major criteria to be considered include: length of time in foster care; age of child; number of placements; minority status; and special needs. For children in settings other than foster care, a variety of early warning signals were proposed, alerting staff members to the need to label a case as 'permanency planning' and triggering responses assuring that appropriate service is offered to maintain the child with his or her own family or to consider alternate plans if necessary.

NOTE

1. Reprinted by special permission of the Child Welfare League of America, Inc. from Stein and Rzepnicki (1983: 60–1). Copyright © 1983. All rights reserved.

SUGGESTIONS FOR FURTHER READING

Chestang, L. W. (1978) The Delivery of Child Welfare Services to Minority Group Children and Their Families. In *Child Welfare Strategy in the Coming Years*. Washington, DC: US Department of Health, Education and Welfare. DHEW Publication No. OHDS 78–30158, pp. 169–94.

Olmstead, K., Hamilton, J., and Fein, E. (1985) Permanency Planning for Children in Outpatient Psychiatric Services. In C. B. Germain (ed.) *Advances in Clinical Social Work*. Silver Spring, MD: National Association of Social Workers.

Shireman, J. F. (1983) Achieving Permanence after Placement. In B. G. McGowan and W. Meezan (eds) *Child Welfare: Current Dilemmas – Future Directions* Itasca, IL: F. E. Peacock Publishers, pp. 377–423.

Shyne, A. W. (1980) Who Are the Children? A National Overview of Services. *Social Work Research and Abstracts* 16 (1): 26–33.

Shyne, A. W. and Schroeder, A. G. (1978) *National Study of Social Services to Children and Their Families*. Washington, DC: US Department of Health, Education, and Welfare. DHEW Publication No. OHDS 78–30150.

Snyder, E. and Ramo, K. (1983) *Deciding to Place or Not to Place*. Revised edition. Cheney, WA: School of Social Work and Human Services, Eastern Washington University.

Stehno, S. M. (1982) Differential Treatment of Minority Children in Service Systems. *Social Work* 27 (1): 39–46.

4 Which permanent plan?

Social workers are accused of playing God when they make decisions that affect a child's future. The wish to be omnipotent and omniscient when given the responsibility of recommending where a child should grow up is a natural reaction to the importance attached to such a decision. In many instances, however, decisions are not made, since social workers feel poorly equipped to take on such responsibility. Children can then grow up in unsuitable plans because ambiguous case situations do not support definitive action. Sound permanency planning work, therefore, requires a firm and timely commitment to make decisions and recommendations about where a child will grow up.

How does one make a responsible decision? What options are available? What children do best in what kinds of placements? What are the obstacles that must be considered? This chapter will address these questions and present guidelines to help social workers in recommending permanent plans for children. Foolproof formulas or precise prescriptions are not possible. Every decision must be based on the uniqueness of the child and the circumstances of that child and his or her family; often the best recommendation cannot be acted upon; and many times plans that are meant to be permanent can backfire. Despite these challenges, social workers must strive to make responsible decisions, and avoid the ambivalence that can result in no decisions and in the drifting of the child and family.

RESPONSIBLE DECISION-MAKING

Decision-making in child welfare is extremely complex, not only because it often involves crucial issues affecting the lives of children and parents, but also because available information and knowledge are not always clear-cut and options are not easily set forth. In addition, social workers may be inclined or pressured to relegate certain decisions to the 'expert', such as a psychiatrist or a legal authority. For instance, recognition of the courts' final decision-making authority may allow the social worker simply to provide data and leave conclusions to attorneys and judges. Further, because courts often do not recognize them as expert witnesses, social workers tend to define themselves as impotent in effecting important decisions. In this regard administrative structures of social agencies do not always provide clear guidelines about decision-making, and social workers are reluctant to take the responsibility.

Although these and other limitations are real, social workers do have an expertise that should be exercised in making timely decisions involving permanent plans for children. In spite of the many complexities and uncertainties in each case situation, social workers must respond in an assertive fashion to help create and implement plans for a child's future. Various guidelines are available to assist in these efforts.

The ingredients for responsible decision-making are not unique to social work, and the process is not new. We can look to the *Spiritual Exercises* written by St Ignatius in the sixteenth century, which offer guidelines for decision-making:

'To place before my mind's eye the thing on which I wish to make a choice. . . . At the same time I must remain indifferent and free from any inordinate attachments so that I am not more inclined or disposed to take the thing proposed than to reject it, nor to relinquish it rather than to accept it . . . I will likewise consider and weigh the disadvantages and dangers . . . I will proceed in like manner with the other alternative, that is, examine and consider the advantages and benefits as well as the disadvantages and dangers . . . After having thus weighed the matter and carefully examined it from every side, I will consider which alternative appears more reasonable. Acting upon the stronger judgment of reason and not on any inclination of the senses, I must come to a decision in the matter that I am considering.'

(*St Ignatius* 1964: 85–6)

St Ignatius was not far from our modern methods of 'gathering all the facts', 'considering the consequences', 'thinking about the complications', 'not doing anything rash or impulsive', 'knowing what is possible'. As we reflect on how people learn to make decisions, from simple childhood decisions about colors to more adult decisions about careers and life styles, it becomes clear that patterns are established through the influence of parents, cultural mores, and principles of logic learned in mathematics, philosophy, and science. Adults come to be proud (or despairing) of their impulsive, clear, or deliberative decision-making characteristics. The reader is invited to reflect on personal decision-making styles.

Recently there has been increasing attention to training in the area of decision-making in child welfare. For example, guidelines have been set forth for decision-making at intake, for supervision, and for general assertiveness in professional life (Gambrill and Stein 1983; Sundel and Sundel 1983; Stein and Rzepnicki 1983). Gambrill and Stein (1983), for instance, recommend that services be provided as soon as possible following the placement of a child, that there be frequent contact between social workers and parents, that parents be encouraged to visit children, that there be clearly defined case objectives, and that service be confined to objectives directly related to reaching a decision concerning the child in care.

Equally important is the support that an agency gives to decision-making (Wiltse 1981). This is manifest in a variety of ways, including time for teams, contracting for necessary consultation, planning for training, and so on (Ward *et al.* 1982). Certainly parents should be involved, and their active participation facilitated, in all aspects of the process. Decision-making can be further promoted by involving children, perhaps in finding their own placements and thereby increasing the number who are placed with people from their own community (Bush and Gordon 1982). Children in care want to be listened to, and have much to say about their living arrangements and life plans (Kufeldt 1984). In a follow-up study of the views of young adults who had grown up in foster family or group care, Festinger (1983: 281–83) found that a 'recurrent theme in their comments was the importance of consulting with children and allowing them to share in, and contribute to, decisions that need to be made'.

In permanency planning, decision-making is a serious responsibility which is carried out by careful scrutiny of options and facts, by objective evaluations of children and families, by sound knowledge of theory and techniques, and with a firm commitment to the right of every child to self-identity that comes from an enduring sense of belonging to a family.

WHAT OPTIONS ARE AVAILABLE?

Hierarchy of permanency planning options

There is a hierarchy of options for a child's living arrangement, which, as discussed in Chapter 1, reflect cultural and personal values regarding children and families. This hierarchy is supported in the USA by federal law, Public Law 96–272, which was outlined in Chapter 2. Beginning with those considered the most desirable, the options are:

1. A child should remain with his or her biological family, while receiving the supports necessary to maintain home placement.
2. When a child must be removed from the biological family temporarily, he or she should be placed with relatives or in a foster home as geographically close to the family as possible, to encourage parental visiting. The child should return to the parents at the earliest possible date, following intensive work with the family and child. The family should continue to receive the necessary supports so that another removal of the child does not occur.
3. When a child must be removed from biological parents and a return home is not possible, a permanent plan with responsible and caring relatives should be sought. To assure that the intent for such a placement is permanency, adoption should be given serious consideration. When adoption is not possible, the relatives should be given legal guardianship.
4. For a child for whom the first three options are not possible, a legal adoption by non-related persons, preferably of similar ethnic or cultural backgrounds, who have been approved through sanctioned home studies, should be sought.
5. For a child who cannot remain with the biological family or with relatives and who cannot be adopted, specialized long-term foster care is considered

the next best option. If foster parents can be given legal guardianship, this again symbolizes the intent that the plan is permanent.

6. The final option for a child is planned long-term residential care in non-family settings. Choice of such settings could range from least restrictive to most structured. An open, family-style group home would be a least restrictive choice, with, at the other end of the continuum, a closed hospital setting. Opportunities for ongoing contact with a family should be built into this plan.

As noted in Chapter 1, the rationale for this hierarchy of options is based on various philosophical and theoretical perspectives, especially the tasks inherent in child development. Children who suffer separation from biological parents, or the loss of their parents, can be hampered in their ability to form significant attachments to other people; suffer developmental lags and subsequent feelings of inadequacy; grow up without internalizing the values that account for a person's respect for other human beings; and fail to develop self-identities that include pride, belonging, and self-respect. A child who experiences a minimally traumatic disruption has a better capacity to mend wounds and continue to make developmental strides.

The majority of children who need permanency planning can be cared for through one of the first four options, but there will always be children for whom the least restrictive options will not work. One group is those who have been in the child welfare system for some time. When permanency planning procedures first began to be applied diligently in some agencies in the 1970s, caseloads consisted of parents and children in a system that had not actively supported early decision-making about a permanent plan.

Many of the children on those caseloads had already been in placement for many years and had already had multiple placements. Their biological parents, in many instances, had not been actively involved in treatment programs and may have cared for their children only sporadically. The least restrictive permanency planning options were thus more difficult to implement for these youngsters who had been in the system for some time.

Others for whom the least restrictive options may not be appropriate are older, severely troubled children who have maintained contact with chronically disturbed families; it is for these children and parents that options five and six may be particularly necessary. Some agencies have demonstrated, however, that intensive residential treatment can be used to achieve permanent plans such as adoption for youngsters who are emotionally disturbed or have special needs (Weitzel 1984).

It can be hypothesized that if every child entering the system now were treated in accord with permanency planning philosophy and techniques, within a decade there would be few children suffering the consequences of drift. Further, most children would be accommodated by options one through four while the last options, long-term foster family care or non-family residential care, would be reserved for those children whose physical, intellectual, or psychiatric problems require the constant attention of trained caretakers in other than traditional family settings, or for older children whose relationships with their disturbed biological families do not allow for a more permanent legal connection with another family.

When the latter options are used, strenuous efforts should be made to maintain the child or youth in a stable placement. As suggested by the follow-up studies of foster care graduates reviewed in Chapter 2, growing up in a single foster family placement does not necessarily lead to damaging effects due to separation from one's biological family; it may result in satisfactory development and functioning (Festinger 1983; Triseliotis 1980).

Controversy about options

The literature includes extensive descriptions of various options, especially maintaining or reuniting the child with the biological family (cf. Bryce and Lloyd 1981; Maluccio and Sinanoglu 1981; Maybanks and Bryce 1979); adoption (cf. Churchill, Carlson, and Nybell 1979; Jewett 1978; Sachdev 1984; Triseliotis 1980); and foster family care (cf. Horejsi 1979; Kadushin 1980; Triseliotis 1980). These and other writings reflect disagreement as to which option should be chosen for a particular child.

For instance, there are those who believe that a child's ability to sustain abuse, neglect, or inappropriate care is greater than a child's ability to sustain permanent or temporary separations from parents. These 'kinship defenders' assert that only in unusual and extreme situations should the family unit be disrupted (Fox 1982). They argue that defining abuse in any given situation is not simple, and that emotional abuse is particularly difficult to measure and its consequences are unclear. Moreover, the medium- and long-term sequelae of abuse are not known, treatment for abuse is inadequate, and incidence and identification of risk for abuse are statistically unreliable (Newberger, Newberger, and Hampton 1983). The 'kinship defenders' are also concerned that economic or cultural bias often labels parental behaviors as emotionally or physically abusive, and that such labelling victimizes the culpable parents and threatens family integrity. They feel that data supporting the relationship between poverty and child removal are clear (Mech 1983). All of these considerations underlie the strong feeling that damaged emotional development occurs with removal of the child from the biological family.

On the other hand, those who believe that society can intervene beneficially to protect children, the 'society-as-parent protagonists', dismiss the supremacy of the blood tie and denounce the price a child must pay waiting for inadequate or immature parents to grow up (Fox 1982). They cite data on successful adoptions and foster parenting, and proclaim the rights of children above those of parents.

The nature of this controversy is complicated by the lack of consensus about the criteria that dictate removal of the child. Attempts have been made to standardize and define criteria (Janchill 1981), but children are still removed without conformity to guidelines. In addition, as discussed in Chapter 12, adequate in-home services and community supports can make it appropriate or feasible for an at-risk child to remain at home. It is the social worker's difficult task to assess all aspects of the situation and make a recommendation that guarantees the child's right to protection while respecting the family unit's integrity. Perhaps there will be less controversy when appropriate support services are acknowledged to be as essential as foster care services, and become readily available to families in distress.

HOW TO CHOOSE A PERMANENT PLAN

Although there is a certain hierarchy of permanency planning options, it does not mean that one or another option is best or preferable for all children. Adoption, permanent foster family care, placement with relatives, or reunification of children with their families are not inherently good or bad for everyone. It is essential to weigh which is best for a particular child and family. This is especially true when considering if two placement decisions may need to be made. Often one placement decision is the one designed as the permanent plan, and the other is the temporary placement that may be necessary during the permanency planning process. The ideal plan is for a child identified as needing permanency planning to continue at home during the planning process and then to remain at home as a permanent plan, with the family being provided the necessary support services for the entire period. Since this is not always possible, other options must be considered.

For children whose parents are deceased or whose parental rights have already been terminated, it is sometimes possible for a first placement also to be a permanent placement. Certainly there is less disruption for these children if they can move directly to the home of the relatives or adopting parents with the knowledge that the intent is permanency. When time constraints do not allow this option, or concerns about a child's special needs prevent it, interim placements are necessary.

As indicated in the preceding chapter, guidelines are available for determining whether a child should be placed out of the home for a temporary period (Janchill 1981; Snyder and Ramo 1983; Stein and Rzepnicki 1983). There are situations in which a time-limited placement may be useful as a tool in efforts to rehabilitate the family and accomplish a permanent plan. Decisions concerning the type of placement that is best in these situations should be governed by the child's needs, in conjunction with a number of considerations consistent with the purposes and values of permanency planning. These considerations are concisely described by Stein and Rzepnicki (1983: 62):[1]

'In sum, children should be placed:

1. As geographically close to the home of their parents as possible. If the child has special needs that cannot be met in his or her community, arrangement should be made for parent–child visits.
2. In the home of a relative when the child is familiar with the home and when there is evidence to suggest that the youngster will benefit from ongoing contact with family members.

3. In the least restrictive setting that most closely approximates a family environment.
4. With a family of the same race, whenever possible, and in a home that will reinforce the child's religious, ethnic, and/or cultural heritage.
5. In accordance with criteria set forth in rule 307 of the Indian Child Welfare Act, if a child is of American Indian heritage.'[2]

Various writers advocate the use of the 'decision tree' as a guide to the worker in the decision-making process about such issues as removal of a child from the home or choice of a permanent plan (Emlen *et al.* 1977; Stein and Rzepnicki 1983). The decision tree is a set of questions in a flow chart format setting forth all the issues that must be addressed to come to a conclusion about a course of action (see *Figure 2*). Some workers find a decision tree useful. Others are uncomfortable with a diagram to guide their action; moreover, they feel the decision tree can oversimplify a complex process in which the worker or service team needs to take into account a changing array of factors pertaining to the child, the parent, legal aspects, and available resources, among others.

Whatever the technique used in choosing *one* appropriate plan, a number of factors should be assessed:

* child's legal status;
* previous placement experiences;
* child's behavior;
* ability to differentiate reality from fantasy;
* educational needs;
* age and developmental needs; and
* parental resources.

Legal status

A child's status can change legally from one in which parents retain full rights to the child, to one in which parents are denied all rights to the point that the child can be legally adopted by others. Between these extremes are situations where parents temporarily have been denied certain rights by court action that makes children temporary wards of the state or other public authority. In that case, parents usually retain legal guardianship of the children, but decisions about where a child will live and when parents can visit are made by the public agency that holds temporary custody.

When a child is legally free to be adopted, an adoption should be achieved with the least amount of delay possible. Whenever possible, a child's relatives should be given priority; after relatives, unrelated families, preferably from similar cultural or ethnic backgrounds, should be sought for purposes of adoption.

When a child is a ward of the state or other public authority, and it has already been determined that a petition for termination of parental rights will follow, efforts can also be made to prevent an interim placement by identifying foster parents as potential adoptive parents. Similarly, for children for whom a freed

Figure 2   The case planning process

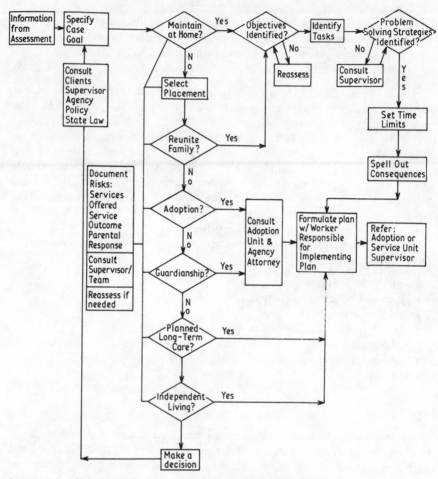

legal status is pending, placement in a foster family with interest in adoption has the potential of avoiding an interim placement. In past years there were strict guidelines for foster parents defining them as temporary caretakers, emphasizing that the foster children were not theirs, and denying they would be in a position to adopt if the children became legally freed. This position, however, has changed and it is now considered acceptable, even desirable, in some cases for foster parents to become adoptive parents (Fanshel 1982: 303; Meezan 1983: 445–48). It may be necessary for the social worker to seek out adoption subsidies or other financial incentives to make this occur. In exploring the option of adoption by foster parents, workers should assess the family's willingness to adopt the child, consider what this will mean to other foster children in the family, anticipate the future with the foster family, and be certain that the foster parents are not acting out of a sense of guilt or obligation that may later be resented.

In the past, it was not considered sound practice to place a child in an adoptive home unless the child was clearly freed for adoption. Again, the thinking has changed. It is now possible for an adoptive family to take a child on a pre-adoptive or foster care status. There is the risk that the child ultimately will not be freed for adoption, but more and more families are willing to accept such a risk. When adoptive families are willing to accept a child with this uncertainty, it again offers him or her the chance for permanency without the potential risks involved in an interim placement.

For children whose parents have every intention of resuming full care, and who have the legal option to do so, an interim plan based on the needs of the child should be made. In these cases, contact with biological parents is one of the greatest needs, and the placement decision should recognize this. As noted earlier in this chapter, considerations such as geographical proximity and accessibility to the biological parents are of prime importance. The caretakers, whether foster parents, child care workers, or others, must be receptive to parents and be able to treat them with acceptance and respect. Ideally, caretakers will be trained to work with biological parents through modeling and instruction.

Previous placement experiences

In choosing a permanent plan it is essential to assess a child's previous placement experiences, which can range from no out-of-home placements to a series of varied placements. Clues to the reasons for failed placements can be obtained from examining the previous experiences, and can serve as guidelines for selecting a permanent placement. For example, if a child's placements in foster homes have repeatedly disrupted, a less emotionally intense setting may be appropriate. For a child whose departures from foster homes seem associated with an inability to relate to foster parents, the attachment to the biological parents may be so strong that there is extreme guarding against new attachments, and a group home or a residential setting, where there are fewer demands for attachment, may be more desirable.

When a child's problems seem related to inadequate structure in previous settings, a more structured environment should be sought. When rivalry with other children in a family has caused disruption, a setting as an only child should be considered. When a child has demonstrated skills in creating conflict between parents, placement with a single parent might be planned. When quiet or withdrawn behavior has allowed the child to get 'lost in the cracks' in a placement that includes many children, a setting which affords more individual attention would be appropriate.

It should be clear that examining previous placements is essential. Mistakes do not need to be repeated. From now on we hope that there will be fewer and fewer children who have been subjected to multiple placements; but it is necessary to take into account a child's past experiences and plan for the future in a way that is intended to provide a permanent home.

Behavior

A child's behavior is an obvious consideration in deciding on a placement in the permanency planning process. A child deserves to be in a place where inappropriate behavior can be adequately handled. Children need to trust that adults can control their unacceptable behavior. When such control is lacking, children may develop fears that their unacceptable or destructive impulses will escalate without restraint, or they may acquire feelings of omnipotence and become less able to form important attachments to caring adults. Thus, a child with a history of suicide gestures or fire setting would not be a candidate for a large foster family with a casual life style.

As a general rule, children who are suicidal or who set fires need to be in a hospital setting; children whose behavior is assaultive, destructive, and overly aggressive need to be in residential treatment centers that specialize in modifying such behavior; children who are oppositional, stubborn, impulsive, and hyperactive can be placed in specialized foster homes or retained in their own homes; and children who are shy, inhibited, fearful, and clinging can be placed in foster homes or remain with biological families. There is also the option for children in these last two categories to remain living at home while participating in day treatment programs designed for such children.

Ability to differentiate reality from fantasy

A child's ability to differentiate fantasy from reality is also pertinent in deciding on a placement. A child who appears to live in fantasy needs a thorough psychiatric evaluation to sort out treatment options. For example, a fantasy life adopted by a child as a means of surviving in a chaotic environment may quickly dissipate once a child is afforded stability; a child who has psychotic episodes may respond to medication in a way that allows a greater grasp on reality; an autistic or blatantly psychotic child clearly needs a highly specialized program.

Children with little grounding in reality will usually require hospital or residential treatment, while children with healthier grasps of reality can be cared for in specialized foster homes, day treatment centers, and their own homes. Despite these general statements, it cannot be denied that there are unique biological, foster, and adoptive parents who have the capacity to care for children with severe difficulties. For this reason, placement with a family should never be ruled out solely on the basis of a child's behavior or grounding in reality.

Educational needs

While public schools are obligated legally to provide for every child's special needs, in reality they are not always equipped to do so. A placement must be made with assurance that a child's educational needs will be met. When these needs can be met only by close collaboration between school and home, the placement must facilitate this working together. For example, when a child needs a consistent and planned approach, a residential placement with an on grounds school may be the best choice, if the facility and its school both employ a behavioral approach to child management. A child with diagnosed learning disabilities may not require a close collaborative arrangement between school and home but rather a school with special programs to deal with the learning needs.

Similarly, if a child's educational needs could be met best by a regular placement with resource room help during part of the day, the school in that community should allow this. In sum, a recommended educational program for a child should be an integral element in deciding on a suitable placement.

Age and development needs

The physical and developmental needs of some children may be so taxing that they are difficult to meet in the context of a family environment. These are children who have a constant need for medical care because of serious illness, or children who have an ongoing need for physical therapy because of severe physical handicaps. Spina bifida, heart and kidney diseases, and severe cerebral palsy are examples of such conditions. Some children are severely retarded and will not develop the capacity to care for themselves even minimally. For these children, biological parents may have made a responsible decision in placing them in residential care. An ongoing relationship with parents, while growing up in a setting that can meet the child's special needs, may be the most appropriate plan. While there are some unusual foster parents who have the stamina to provide continuous care for such children, institutional care designed to meet their needs is more often the plan of choice. Planned long-term institutional care, with continuing support of and contact with biological parents, is particularly suitable when life-long care will be essential because of the physical limitations of the children.

Age is also an important consideration. While diligent efforts can produce families willing to adopt teenagers, this offers no promise that the teenagers will succeed in adoptive placements. Long-term care in a foster family or group setting may well be a better option for some, since it offers the possibility of maintaining whatever identification continues to be felt with the biological parents. Long-term care is suitable for three groups: teenagers with marked parental conflicts; severely mentally or physically handicapped children; and children who have drifted into long-term care, are too old for adoption, and have no biological parents to whom to return.

Adolescents need special consideration when plans for permanency are made. It is vitally important to involve them in the planning, and to trust they can make a valuable contribution to decision-making. Some children may not feel that adoption is the best plan:

'Data suggest that the official, professional view of what is good for children can sometimes be too tidy and too impatient of tangled relationships to be in the best interests of children. Surrogate parents, social workers, and researchers are not always sympathetic to natural parents, who, though they may seem inadequate by some standards, are involved in a mutually rewarding relationship with their children. Some children clearly can benefit from concurrent relationships with surrogate and natural parents. Pushing these children into adoption might destroy an important source of support.'

(Bush and Gordon 1982: 310–11)

Some youngsters may assist in identifying resources in their home communities suitable for them. Others may have ties to relatives or particular foster homes that can be strengthened by the support of an active permanency planner. In any event, each child must be considered individually when decisions are made, and social workers must be open to all options. As with other guidelines, those suggested for teenagers should be carefully tested by the social worker in a particular case.

Parental resources

In choosing a permanent placement for a child, the parents' current resources and their potential for acquiring other resources must also be assessed. Resources refer not only to physical and financial attributes, but also to coping and functioning abilities.

Although some parents wish to relinquish parental rights, in which case efforts should be made to avoid an interim placement and search for an adoptive placement with relatives or non-related persons, most often parents state a strong wish to continue caring for their children or to resume care following a period of placement. All parents have the right to rehabilitate themselves to the point of being able to care for their youngsters, and the permanency planning worker has the responsibility of encouraging them and giving them every opportunity to do so. Principles and methods of working with parents are discussed in greater detail in Chapter 10. While it is vital to maintain the hope that the parent can resume care of the child, it is also necessary to assess realistically the possible outcome.

The assessment of parent's capacity to provide long-term consistent care to a child requires the permanency planning worker to:

* obtain a personal history of the parent;
* examine current social patterns and networks;
* determine how crises are handled;
* observe the relationship between parent and child;
* understand past therapeutic experiences; and
* evaluate the parent's personality.

These will be discussed in the following sections. In addition, assessment of parents will be considered more extensively in Chapter 7.

HISTORY OF PARENT

In addition to routine history taking, which will not be reviewed here, particular areas of information will aid in the assessment of resources. These include:

* Parents' experiences in growing up, particularly in relation to placements outside the family that they may have had. Parents who had multiple placements as children are likely to have an impaired ability to relate, as well as a lack of appreciation for consistency in child-rearing.
* Parents' memories of how they were disciplined as children. Those who were subjected to physical or sexual abuse as children may be more apt to abuse their own children, and often suffer from problems with self-esteem. It is important to explore their feelings about these experiences and how they affect the parent's ability to care for and nurture a child responsibly.
* Parents' stability in adult life. Have there been multiple moves? Has there been an ability to sustain a relationship with an important person, or is there a pattern of superficial or brief relationships? If the parent has been employed, what is the job history? Is there an ability to keep a job or are there frequent changes? How has financial stress been managed? Have there been chronic problems with evictions, loss of utilities, lack of food? It has been determined that experiencing such stressful life events increases susceptibility to illness, decreases coping ability, and is associated with diminished self-esteem (Dohrenwend and Dohrenwend 1977). Use of a 'Stressful Life Events' assessment instrument may be valuable at this point (Holmes and Rahe 1967). If there are patterns of instability of a long-term nature, a prognosis for improvement is less optimistic than if the problems are situational and the history taking reflects periods of better functioning and supportive social networks.

Current social patterns and networks

Assessing a parent's current social patterns and social networks leads to such questions as:

* What kinds of relationships exist in both the nuclear and extended families? Is there closeness between family members? Do they live near each other? Is there trust of family members? Are family members seen as supportive? Are family members available at times of crisis? Can family members be mobilized as resources for the child and parents?
* What associations are there outside of the family? Does a parent have a best friend, someone in whom to confide and call upon in an emergency? Very often the parents of children who need permanency planning do not have close ties with family or close friends. If isolation has not been chronic for a parent, or if it can be reduced through various supports, a more optimistic prognosis can be made. What is a parent's relationship with community supports such as churches, schools, and community centers? It is not unusual for parents to lack trust in such supports, or to feel they are not

important. Isolated parents may find it difficult to respond to the support offered through the permanency planning process, or they may need intensive efforts to build social ties. As discussed in Chapter 12, can additional supports be identified, mobilized, or created?

STYLE OF HANDLING CRISES

Parents whose children need permanency planning often describe a pattern of living as that of a 'series of crises'. The crises may be the separation of the parents, sudden need to move, mental stress that requires hospitalization, dire lack of daily needs, or extreme frustration with the behavior of a child.

It is crucial to assess if such a pattern exists, if solutions to crises result in improved or impoverished functioning, and if parents are able to anticipate and avoid some crises. When crises are unavoidable, it is important to evaluate coping skills and resources. A pattern of repeated crises with little capacity to deal with them constructively affords a guarded prognosis.

RELATIONSHIP BETWEEN PARENT AND CHILD

In assessing the relationship between the parent and the child, answers to the following questions are vital:

* Are the child's physical needs (food, clothing, housing, hygiene, health) adequately met?
* Is there a difference in the physical care of this child, as compared with that of siblings?
* Is the parent able to set reasonable limits with the child?
* Is the parent able to enjoy the child?
* Can the parent describe the child developmentally and emotionally?
* Is there a clear definition of roles between parent and child, or are roles confused or poorly defined?
* Has the child been assigned any unrealistic tasks, such as caring for the parent or carrying responsibility for a sibling beyond what is reasonable according to age?
* Can the parent set aside personal needs at times when the needs of the child require priority?
* Is the parent able to promote development of self-identity and autonomy for the child?

Answers to these questions help to define the ability of parents to promote healthy growth and development in a child, and point to the support needed to enhance parental skills. Some parents will have some skills and not others. Some will be able to respond to the needs of children at certain times but not with consistency. Some will show little capacity to understand or carry out sound child care practices. The more able a parent is to understand the needs of a child and to respond in a consistent fashion, the more optimistic one can be about a permanent plan with the biological parent.

PAST THERAPEUTIC EXPERIENCES

The kinds of experiences parents have had in the past with social workers, psychiatrists, psychologists, and other helping professionals can be useful in assessing their ability to make use of such services. Some relevant questions are:

* Did the parents seek some form of counseling or was it imposed by some authority?
* For how long did the parent continue with a particular helper?
* How does the parent describe the experience:
    * Was it helpful?
    * Did it result in positive change?
    * What were the reasons for ending?
    * How might it have been more helpful?

The parent's feelings about the helping person are also of diagnostic value. For example, if a parent has had previous counseling with a number of people and describes an inability to trust any of them, trust might be appropriately identified as a major concern. There may be a theme of dependence on the worker, with inevitable disappointment because of frequent changes in workers, a phenomenon common in child welfare. Or there may be resentment for having to engage in mandated treatment in order to have the child remain at home.

A parent may have a positive view of past therapeutic experiences and may be eager to have such services again. If the services previously offered focused on child management skills, an assessment should be made of the parent's capacity to internalize the learning and to generalize the application of new techniques. Some parents need continuous reminders, while others are better able to integrate learning and proceed independently.

In addition to assessing participation in counseling, it is important to evaluate a parent's experiences with other kinds of interventions. Has there been involvement with any support groups, such as Parents Anonymous or Alcoholics Anonymous? Has the parent been helped to use public welfare resources, such as food stamps, medical benefits, income maintenance programs, or health clinics? Have opportunities for job training been explored and made available? Have the services of a parent aide been utilized? Have there been home visits for parents who seem unable to keep office appointments? Have community resources available through neighborhood centers, churches, and schools been explored?

It is necessary to understand the kind of help that has been offered, the quality of the services, and their success in helping the parents to achieve the goal of caring for the child adequately. A parent should be asked to participate actively in planning future work together. When a parent can state needs and goals and how they might best be met and accomplished, he or she is demonstrating an ability to become actively involved in the permanency planning process.

PERSONALITY ASSESSMENT

For purposes of permanency planning work, traditional diagnostic labels are not as useful as precise behavioral descriptive terms. Moreover, personality assessment should reflect the ecological perspective presented in Chapter 6. Thus, while pathology must be recognized, emphasis should be on a parent's environmental resources. Using that orientation, a clear, realistic statement of goals should be made. This can afford a sense of hope for both the parent and the social worker that is based on a positive view of assets. When a parent is labelled psychotic, narcissistic, borderline, or neurotic, and supports for the parents are not explored, it is easy to ignore strengths that a more descriptive, ecologically oriented approach can highlight.

In a sense, the personality assessment is a summing up of parental resources. By rating each area – history, social patterns, ability to handle crises, observed relationships with children, and previous therapy experiences – the social worker can get a sense of the goals that need to be accomplished and what the prognosis is.

For parents whose resources suggest the capacity to resume care of their children, or continue care at home with supportive help, the child's interim placement, if necessary, should be designed to achieve permanency for the child with his or her biological parents within a specified time. Intensive work with parents and child must be provided. The setting must be accessible to the parents both physically and emotionally. They must be accorded respect and given every opportunity to achieve the goals necessary for the child to return home.

If the placement is with a relative, it is important to assess the ability of the relatives to support the parents as well as the plan for the child to return home. It would be to everyone's disadvantage to place a child with a relative whose mission was to rescue the child from a 'bad' parent. If the child is to be placed in a foster home, the worker should assess the ability of the foster parent to support the plan of a return home. A foster parent needs to be able to provide nurturance and care in a manner that is neither competitive nor possessive. A foster parent who can form a bond with the biological parent based on the mutual desire for the child to succeed at home is ideal.

With the growth of permanency planning there has been further development of specialized, foster family programs providing time-limited specialized care in therapeutic homes (Bryant 1980; Shaw and Hipgrave 1983). Foster parents in these programs regard themselves as temporary caretakers and as part of the permanency planning team. They share in the belief that, when possible, the biological family is the best permanent plan for a child. They are committed to working toward that plan and accept the participation of biological parents in the process. They welcome parents when they come to visit their children, involve parents in decision-making whenever possible, and willingly discuss child management issues with parents.

For children whose parental resources are limited and for whom a more realistic goal is a permanent placement separate from the biological parents, a home with the potential for being permanent should be sought. Options include placement with a foster family with an interest in adoption, or with an adoptive parent while the child retains the status of foster child. It takes special people to offer this kind of care to children, since they must live with the uncertainty of the outcome, open to the possibility that biological parents can rehabilitate to the point of being able to care for their children.

When a strong bond, either healthy or destructive, exists between a parent and child, a more neutral interim or long-term setting may be preferable. A parent may not be able to tolerate having a child become attached to other parental figures, and a child's loyalty and guilt may make such an attachment impossible. A group home or residential setting, where there is less demand for close attachment, may be a better placement for repair of an unhealthy bond. Placement in such a setting can also help a parent who cannot resume care for a child to give that child permission to relate to other parent figures.

WHAT ARE THE OBSTACLES TO BE CONSIDERED?

When selecting a permanent option for a child, the worker must be aware of the obstacles to achieving what is considered the best plan. As suggested in Chapter 2, barriers to creating permanency plans for children can be divided into case-related and system-related obstacles (Miller *et al.* 1984a).

Case-related barriers

Case-related barriers that are obstacles to permanency planning are as various as the individual cases. In many instances a parent refuses to allow placement. When a parent retains full custody of the child and is not receptive to a particular placement, the placement cannot occur. The social worker must then assess the risks to a child who remains in an environment that is not promoting healthy growth and development. Unless there is clear evidence of neglect or abuse that can serve as grounds for removal, the placement will not proceed. It will be necessary to work with the child and family while the child remains at home, even if it appears that gains could be more readily achieved and have more lasting value if there were a period of placement outside of the home. Where there is clear evidence of abuse or neglect, however, the worker must be willing to take the required steps with the legal authorities to remove the child.

Other case-related barriers may be the physical condition and needs of the child, particular financial needs of a potential adoptive family, or emotional and behavioral characteristics of the child.

System-related barriers

Difficult to work through as some case-specific barriers may be, the most complex obstacles encountered are those related to various systems: public agencies, voluntary agencies, the courts, the legal system, schools, police, and so on. Some typical barriers are:

NON-COMPLETION OF TERMINATION OF PARENTAL RIGHTS

Unwillingness to terminate parental rights is a widely documented barrier to adoption. This unwillingness reflects an acknowledgement of the importance of the biological family to any child and the desire to return the child to the biological home if at all possible. This value exists among both workers and judges. For

unwilling to terminate parental rights - shows importance of biological family -

example, in one case, workers planned to terminate parental rights and place three siblings for adoption. While the legal process was under way, a long-absent father came forward and expressed an interest in parenting the children. All involved parties were pleased to be able to return the children to the father and did so. Within six months, two of the children had to be removed and returned to long-term foster care; the third child was also removed shortly after.

In another case involving siblings, the workers agreed that the best plan was to terminate parental rights and place the children for adoption. When the case was heard, the judge disagreed and ordered the children returned to the mother. The workers felt that such an order was given without enough opportunity to assess the parenting abilities of the mother.

Courts will rarely terminate parental rights without worker support for the move, but in numerous cases workers have expressed frustration with the court's unwillingness to terminate parental rights even with the worker support. The judicial system is often an obstacle to the best efforts of permanency planners.

FINANCIAL DIFFICULTIES

Any placement outside of the home is costly, and usually beyond the means of families in need of such care. Many placement facilities will not consider a child for placement until a preliminary determination of financing has been made, and voluntary agencies usually have purchase-of-service agreements with public child welfare agencies. Families that can afford placement outside of the home are less likely to come to the attention of social agencies, and more apt to choose private school placements for children for whom they cannot care. For those who cannot afford such private arrangements, placement of a child usually means that a family enters the public system, with the attendant stigma of dependence on the 'state' and fear of its arbitrary control.

When parental rights have already been terminated, or when a child is already a ward of the state, financing a placement is achieved most readily. Working out intricate financial arrangements, however, can be a sticky problem and can prevent the implementation of the optimum plan. To assist families financially some states insist that their own agencies be used as placement resources, although the facilities may be perceived as undesirable by parents and child, because the expense to the state is less than using private facilities of voluntary agencies.

The inadequacy of financial subsidy for adoptive families is also often mentioned in the literature as a major barrier to adoption (Derdeyn 1977; Fein et al. 1983; Shaffer 1981; Ward et al. 1982), but its prevalence as a barrier is not clear (Miller et al. 1984a). Still, adequate worker support can make a subsidy available to a family and thus facilitate adoption.

CHILD'S LEGAL STATUS

Social workers should become familiar with the child caring system and pertinent legal aspects in the area where they work. In most cases when children become wards of the state or other governmental unit because of abuse or neglect, it is clear that the public agency, within legal guidelines, has control of the child. In some states, however, a child can be placed on a non-committed status, allowing parents to retain custody rights while the public agency cares for the child. Such arrangements are often temporary and not offered for more than two years. When parents retain full rights under non-committed status, the social worker must be aware that the parent is legally free to remove the child from placement at any time. This often subverts the intent and implementation of the permanent plan.

In many instances, it is necessary for children to become wards of the state or other authority in order to receive financial assistance. Since children usually become wards of the state because they are alleged to be neglected or uncared for, it can be difficult for a parent to agree voluntarily to a child's commitment and seemingly seek out the stigma of being neglectful. Some parents are unable to do this and thus a child cannot be placed because there is no clear evidence of lack of care. Where the evidence is clear, a social worker can petition the court and ask that a child be committed to the custody of the state. Placement can then proceed, as parents are temporarily denied the right to decide where the child shall live.

LACK OF AVAILABLE HOMES

Because placement services are expensive to maintain, places in foster homes are not always readily available. A first choice is often not obtainable, and a temporary placement needs to be made. Social workers, however, should always strive for the first placement to be the *only* interim placement during the permanency planning process.

Placement agencies vary in the prerequisites for admission. The social worker should become familiar with available resources and their limitations. Some serve certain age groups, some only one sex, and most specify the kinds of children considered appropriate. Some require active involvement of parents, some serve only children who are wards of the state, and some specify behaviors in children which are not acceptable. The caretaker's understanding of a child's need for permanency planning should be an important consideration. There are still child caring facilities that view a placement as a plan that does not require a time frame and a goal for permanency. Unless permanency planning can be instituted, such placements should be avoided.

Social workers should acquaint themselves thoroughly with available placement facilities; procedures for admission; means of financing; therapeutic philosophies; and populations served. This equips the worker with the information necessary to make a responsible decision based on a sound knowledge of resources.

LEGAL DELAYS

Another system barrier, legal delays, is usually mentioned in conjunction with termination of parental rights. Delays are also associated with revocation of commitment, that is allowing a child to return home, sometimes inappropriately. Continuing pressure for legal resolution is always essential, since permanency planning stresses the importance of time in children's lives, and social workers need to become comfortable with applying that pressure on behalf of children.

PROBLEMS IN COORDINATING BETWEEN THE PUBLIC AGENCY AND VOLUNTARY AGENCIES

In those cases where the public agency has purchased services from a voluntary agency to provide placement, therapeutic, or home finding services, the risk exists for a variety of difficulties. Communication between workers, clear definitions of the roles and boundaries of each, territoriality issues, and susceptibility to manipulation by other collaborators or clients are some areas where problems may arise. A service agreement that includes the expectations for the social workers involved, as described in Chapter 9, can minimize this particular obstacle to permanency planning.

SUMMARY

This chapter has stressed the importance of making responsible decisions regarding where children will grow up. To avoid or postpone such decisions is contrary to the best interests of children and their families. Permanency planning work sometimes requires two decisions about placement, one a time-limited and goal-oriented placement during the permanency planning process, and the other the actual permanent placement. Whenever possible a child should be afforded permanency with the biological family, and temporary placement should be avoided. When a child cannot remain with the biological family and cannot return home, a permanent plan without an interim placement is preferable.

Options for placement have been described and ranked according to their ability to offer a child a sense of belonging and the promise of permanency. In order of desirability, the options include: remaining with biological parents; returning to biological parents following a time-limited placement out of the home; adoption by responsible and caring relatives; adoption by non-related families; specified long-term foster care; and residential care in the least restrictive setting.

As guides for workers making decisions about which of these options should be selected for a particular child, the various factors that need consideration were discussed, including a child's legal status, previous placement experiences, described behavior, educational needs, age and developmental needs, and parental resources. Finally, obstacles that can interfere with implementation of the preferred plan were considered.

The discussion of the choice of permanent plan for a child raises many issues that were not addressed in this chapter. These are concerns about the criteria used by the judiciary in determining a child's legal status, the therapeutic process with children and parents, and the use of supportive services, all crucial to arriving at a child's permanent plan. These issues will be considered in depth in subsequent chapters.

NOTES

1. Reprinted by special permission of the Child Welfare League of America, Inc. from Stein and Rzepnicki (1983: 62). Copyright © 1983. All rights reserved.
2. The Indian Child Welfare Act, enacted by the US Congress in 1978 (Public Law 95-608), mandates that American Indian children be placed, if necessary, in the following order of priority: (1) members of the child's extended family; (2) other members of the child's tribe; and (3) other Indian families, including single parents.

SUGGESTIONS FOR FURTHER READING

Janchill, M. P. (1981) *Guidelines to Decision Making in Child Welfare*. New York: Human Services Workshops.

Miller, K., Fein, E., Bishop, G., Stilwell, N., and Murray, C. (1984a) Overcoming Barriers to Permanency Planning. *Child Welfare* 63 (1): 45-55.

Pike, V., Downs, S., Emlen, A., Downs, G., Case, D. (1977) *Permanent Planning for Children in Foster Care: A Handbook for Social Workers*. Washington, DC: US Department of Health, Education, and Welfare. Publication (OHDS) 78-30124, especially Chapter 3.

Stein, T. and Rzepnicki, J. (1983) *Decision Making at Child Welfare Intake*. New York: Child Welfare League of America, especially Chapter 2.

Stein, T. J., Gambrill, E. D., and Wiltse, K. T. (1978) *Children in Foster Homes – Achieving Continuity of Care*. New York: Praeger Publishers.

5 What are the social worker's roles?

There once was a centipede named Bloom
Who took an octopus up to his room
It was almost a crime
To spend all that time
Deciding who did what, when, and to whom
                              (Anonymous)

Doggerel verse can reflect confusion, whether over multiple arms and legs or the myriad tasks facing social workers engaged in permanency planning:

There once was a worker named Bloom
Who felt confused and mired in gloom
He tried with elan
To write a permanent plan
But couldn't say who did what, when, and with whom

The goals of permanency planning are relatively easy to subscribe to. But how can a social worker make order out of the many tasks that need to be undertaken to accomplish permanency planning? Do these tasks fall into discernible categories? What structure will be useful to assist the worker in understanding the involvement required? This chapter will specify and illustrate through a case example the roles and tasks that are important in implementing a permanent plan.

ORGANIZATION OF PERMANENCY PLANNING ROLES

As discussed in preceding chapters, the concept of permanency planning, in its various definitions, has been influencing service delivery in recent years. Although some agencies or workers have been 'doing' permanency planning without labeling it as such, a number of agencies have begun to restructure their services formally to make permanency a more conscious goal (Levitt 1981; Sisto 1980). Review procedures have been instituted to control drift in foster care (Wert, Fein, and Haller, in press), and service agreements and case planning have been used to move children out of foster care more rapidly (Stein, Gambrill, and Wiltse 1978; Iowa Department of Social Services 1977).

As various programs show, moving from the philosophy to the implementation of permanency planning is a complex process. In particular, social workers practicing permanency planning are faced with a range of responsibilities and functions that are essential to achieve the goal of permanency planning in each case. These responsibilities and functions can be considered as elements of five basic roles (Fein *et al.* 1984):

1. Case planning
2. Case management
3. Therapy
4. Client advocacy
5. Court witness

These roles represent the ingredients that must be combined by the worker in providing a coherent service to the client. They interweave and overlap, each taking priority over other aspects at different times, depending on the evolution and developments in the case. In all of the roles, decision-making and assertive action based on the decisions are key elements.

The structure and organization of permanency planning roles vary from agency to agency, based on factors such as agency size, auspices, and orientation. In some large settings, for example, workers specialize in provision of services; one worker may be the therapist, while another is the case manager. In other agencies, especially smaller ones, the roles are combined and carried out by one staff member. There are advantages and disadvantages in either approach.

When workers specialize and a number of them are involved in the varying roles there are risks that are assumed: insufficient communication between workers, different interpretations by each worker of the goals to be achieved, lack of clarity in assignment of responsibility for tasks, and fractured continuity for the family being served. With specialization the case manager has greater responsibility to clarify roles and monitor completion of tasks. Particular attention must be paid to who is responsible for essential decision-making.

The greatest advantage of specialization is the opportunity to increase workers' expertise. Proficiency in particular areas can develop more easily as experience builds with the division of roles. For example, a worker with limited skills in client advocacy may be outstanding in clinical intervention; someone who cannot negotiate community networks may be strong in case management. Furthermore, specialization may be a deterrent to burnout. Permanency planning cases can be exhausting, and not having to assume all of the different tasks in each case can be a relief. In addition, a feeling of support from workers sharing the case can be helpful.

On the other hand, combining roles in the person of one worker decreases the time needed for communication, minimizes misunderstandings that may result, and may lead to greater efficiency in implementing the elements of the permanent plan. Some may feel that burnout is minimized when roles are combined and workers have the opportunity to perform a variety of functions. Additionally, the client may be more comfortable relating to one worker rather than many, and a supportive therapeutic environment may be easier to establish.

The inherent conflicts between some of the roles and the complexities in carrying them out may support either specialization or combination of roles. There is insufficient research evidence or practice experience to decide which approach is better. What is clear is that in the process of intervening in a case most of these roles must be played, often simultaneously, to achieve optimum results.

While many workers carry out multiple and diverse permanency planning tasks, few have had the time and support to examine critically the roles they perform. These roles are complex and demanding. The range of tasks required of the worker in successfully negotiating each of the roles should not be discouraging to those learning permanency planning. The classification of roles provided in this chapter is a sound basis for the development of training programs and for the acquisition by students and practitioners of the skills necessary for permanency planning. A description of the roles, followed by an example of their implementation, will be presented in the following sections.

CASE PLANNING ROLE

The case planning role involves the development and maintenance of long-range plans (e.g. for the next four to six months). In this role, workers develop the overall plan for a particular case, creating a broad framework for approaching the case over time. The case planning role includes tasks such as:

* Carrying out an *early psychosocial assessment* of the family and the family's environment. Areas to be assessed include potential environmental resources, the family's needs, threats to a return home, the needs of child as a result of family disruption, and the family's capacity to eliminate those things which make abuse or neglect a likely recurrence.
* *Assessing the potential treatment and resource environment*. This includes contacting other providers working on a case; determining what services and resources are practically available; and ascertaining that cultural and ethnic concerns are respected.
* Developing a *preferred plan for permanent placement*, considering alternative options in case the preferred plan does not work out.
* Negotiating a *service agreement* with parents, other family members, or other providers, in line with the preferred plan, and in light of the realities of the legal system.
* Setting that service agreement within a *well-defined time frame*, including specific dates for review, and an estimated deadline for goals to be achieved.
* Developing *goal-oriented treatment plans* congruent with the service agreement, and reviewing these periodically.
* *Maintaining careful case records;* a record-keeping system, such as the one described in Chapter 16, is an essential tool in permanency planning. It

forces workers to make placement decisions, document the decisions, formulate case goals and plans, assign time limits for achieving goals, and review and monitor case progress in plan implementation. The use of time limits for the completion of goals is the most difficult task in planning, and any record system that facilitates this task is especially useful.

CASE MANAGEMENT ROLE

As noted in Chapter 1, most permanency planning cases involve collaboration among numerous intra-agency and inter-agency resources and personnel, in addition to the work to be done by the clients and workers specifically assigned to the case. As discussed in detail in Chapter 14, the case management role, which is receiving increasing attention in child welfare, involves systematic efforts to facilitate coordination among multiple service providers, promote collaboration, bring clients into meaningful contact with various community resources, and monitor progress. As a result, it may be argued that case management should be the chief role of the social worker, especially in public child welfare. Specific tasks include:

* *Evaluating the family's attainment of the goals agreed to*, in an atmosphere of support and assistance; sharing with the families their perceptions about goal attainment; and being available as a support when goals have not been achieved.
* *Negotiating respective roles* with the various providers and court personnel involved in a case.
* *Referring clients* to appropriate community resources in areas such as health care, transportation, housing, or education.
* *Planning and managing parent–child visitation* in those cases in which children have been removed from the home.
* *Helping clients develop social resources*, while respecting and enhancing cultural and ethnic connections. This includes helping parents to re-establish ties with family and friends and become involved with community groups.
* *Monitoring* home-based service providers, such as parent aides, to establish the specific goals on which the aide is working and promote the development of a cooperative team approach.
* *Promoting collaboration among service providers* and checking progress toward achievement of goals. This includes calling people together for case conferences, monitoring service agreements, etc.

In the past, the breadth of this role was often a function of the interest of the practitioner; for example, those with a strong feeling for advocacy or for development of the client's informal social resources have been more active in these areas. The scope of case management, however, should not be limited by particular interests of the social worker, but should be defined by the needs of the family.

As stressed in Chapter 16, the use of goal-oriented records to monitor case management becomes an important planning tool, because careful record-keeping will identify treatment biases as well as document activities in the case. Documentation of efforts is essential for planning, therapy, advocacy and court work, and identifying particular treatment biases. For example, a strong individual therapy orientation, or an ecological perspective, can skew or enhance service delivery. These biases need to be evaluated in the context of each case.

THERAPEUTIC ROLE

In this role, the worker provides necessary clinical services to increase the chances of a successful placement in line with a preferred plan. Tasks include:

* first and foremost, helping families *develop productive and positive child rearing environments*, including the replacement of abusive and neglectful patterns with positive parent–child interaction and improved parental skills;
* helping to *empower the parents* so that they can make positive moves to change conditions in their environment;
* helping families *alter the family dynamics* that support the negative child-rearing environment;
* helping *children overcome or narrow developmental lags* in emotional and behavioral patterns that impede their parenting;
* helping *children overcome or narrow developmental lags* in emotional and social functioning caused by earlier family disruption;
* providing *support and encouragement* to parents in their efforts to change, and being willing to continue with them even if they are not able to care for their children.

This role is central in clinical work; it consists of individual or group therapy sessions with children, adults, couples, or families. For workers who are not experienced with the demands for assertive action of the other roles, this is the role most comfortably assumed and supervised. It is the role most susceptible to extension beyond time limits because of unclear goal-setting and lax monitoring by the social worker. It is also the role dealing with many intangibles, expecting the most from the parents, and therefore the most difficult one in which to engage the family's participation.

CLIENT ADVOCACY ROLE

Initiative and creativity are often required on the part of the social worker to obtain for the child and family the services and supports essential to permanency planning. Social workers may need to advocate within the legal system and the service system to help ensure that the rights of parents and children are maintained and necessary services are provided. Tasks include:

* pressing community resources to *provide or create necessary services* for the child and family, especially those culturally and ethnically comfortable;

* *pressing the agency responsible for the child* to carry its mandate in a case where the planner feels children are not being adequately protected;
* pressing the legal system and/or appropriate agencies to consider *termination of parental rights* when the worker determines that this is essential to a successful permanent plan;
* pressing the legal system and/or appropriate agencies to consider *parent's rights and the importance of biological parents* to the success of a case;
* pressing the court or appropriate agencies to *develop overt and realistic contingencies* for a parent to strive toward in a service agreement.

The initiative required to press for change for clients is not easily instilled. This is a role that requires special commitment, special skills, and an unusual drive to have impact on systems that are not readily responsive. It is an area easily susceptible to frustration and burnout.

ROLE OF COURT WITNESS

Workers are often called upon to provide testimony in court when termination of parental rights is at issue. Testimony is also required in many cases involving custody issues and in many instances when the placement of the child is questioned. Social workers must often testify about the functioning of the family and the child, and they have a grave responsibility to provide pertinent information to the court. We shall discuss testimony and other legal issues in depth in Chapter Fifteen. Here we should note that tasks in the role of court witness include:

* *documenting all important events* during treatment and service provision, even in cases which might not come to court, just to be prepared;
* *working with lawyers, court officers, relevant expert witnesses, court case reviewers, and volunteer monitors* in appropriate ways when a case is actively involved in legal action;
* *presenting information as a witness in court*, and coordinating such testimony with expert witnesses.

Goal-oriented records, with their specific treatment plans and time limits, encourage the kind of record-keeping that is necessary for a social worker to appear as a credible witness. As discussed in Chapter 15, testifying in court is an anxiety provoking situation; clarity and specificity are the best preparation for that difficult task.

CASE ILLUSTRATION

The following case summary shows how the various permanency planning roles and tasks are enacted. Although there is no typical permanency planning case, this one illustrates the multiple roles that a worker must perform. It is a case that contains a reality workers often face: the difference in perspectives between different agencies involved and the conflicts that may arise between workers' perceptions of goals and plans for a child.

John, the client, not quite three years old, was in the care of his unofficial guardian, his aunt. His mother had left him in the aunt's care and disappeared with her boyfriend. The aunt had voluntarily placed the child in specialized foster care six months earlier. John was epileptic and had deficiencies in motor and language development. His aunt was anxious about his welfare; this concern, combined with his frequent falls due to poor coordination, had resulted in numerous hospital admissions. Most of these admissions had been unnecessary and child abuse had not been suspected, but the public agency had been called in on the case. The public agency worker had persuaded the aunt that placement in specialized foster care would enable John to catch up developmentally.

After six months in specialized foster care the case was in a state of administrative disarray. It had been moved from one district office to another in the state, and in the process the worker changed. The specialized foster care worker was leaving and a new worker was asked to replace her. The new worker was determined to implement permanency planning principles in this case. Recent testing had shown that John had caught up developmentally and the aunt was pushing for immediate return of the child. The public agency worker had agreed with the aunt, but the specialized foster care worker felt strongly that the child, aunt, and foster parents needed an opportunity to adjust to the change in the placement. This was important in assessing that expectations for the child's functioning were realistic, that the aunt's anxiety could be defused, and that chances for replacement in foster care were minimized.

This situation forced the specialized foster care worker to act in the role of case advocate in order to protect the interests of the child. Against stiff resistance, the worker convinced the aunt to wait two months before removing the child from placement. It was within this tightly constrained time frame that the worker had to accomplish as much as he could to ease the child's transition from the foster home to the aunt's home. He developed goal-oriented treatment plans within this time frame.

The worker concentrated his efforts in three areas. First, he was instrumental in referring the child to a rehabilitation center for motor and language development assessment. Second, he worked with the aunt to minimize her overly protective parental patterns. He sought to have her accept reasonable expectations for her nephew and to decrease her agitation and anxiety about his safety. Besides short-term therapy, one aspect of this treatment was exploring diverse concrete services appropriate for the child and informing her of their availability. Finally, the worker held meetings with the foster parents to help them deal with termination issues brought up by the sudden removal of the child. This work continued for a month after John was returned to his aunt's home.

This case was unusual because of the brevity enforced by the aunt, but within that time framework it provided a breadth of experience in permanency planning. The worker served in all of the permanency planning roles described. In his capacity as case planner he developed a goal-oriented plan in collaboration with the aunt, the foster parents, and the public agency worker (see *Figure 3*); this involved setting goals with a reasonable chance of success within the short treatment period, writing a service agreement (see *Figure 4*), and reviewing goal achievement during treatment. All plans, goals, and degrees of goal achievement were carefully documented as part of the worker's role as court witness. This case did not go to court during this period; if it had, however, the worker's testimony and case documentation would have been crucial in determining whether the aunt should have been awarded legal guardianship and custody of the child.

The worker also was active as a client advocate, pressing the public agency's worker to assess and monitor carefully the child's return home. His therapeutic skills were demanded in his work with the aunt, the foster parents, and, to a limited degree, the child. In addition, a key role in this case was that of case manager. The aunt had to have access to an adequate community service network in order to parent John. The worker explored numerous services and referred the aunt to the appropriate ones in an effort to insure that she had this access.

The worker's diverse tasks and plans and their relation to the permanency planning roles are presented in *Figure 5*. It can be seen that the case planner role, under which the goal-oriented record (*Figure 3*) and the service agreement (*Figure 4*) were developed, was augmented by tasks assumed as case manager, therapist, client advocate, and possible court witness. An examination and comparison of *Figures 3, 4,* and *5* demonstrate that the creation of the service agreement and goal-oriented records to plan and monitor the progress of the case is only a small part of the work needed to achieve permanency. The tasks are numerous, but more manageable when conceived of as examples of a limited number of roles in the context of goal-oriented service.

SUMMARY

This chapter set forth the tasks and responsibilities that make up permanency planning work; they fall into five categories of roles:

1. Case planning
2. Case management
3. Therapy
4. Client advocacy
5. Court witness

Though each may take priority at different times, depending on requirements in a particular case, all roles are essential. Also, they overlap and mesh with each other, and all require decisive and assertive social work. A case example, accompanied by its service agreement and goal-oriented records, illustrated the diverse tasks and plans and their relation to the various roles.

Figure 3   Goal-oriented record

(John is a three-year-old boy in a voluntary agency's specialized foster home whose aunt, his guardian, has requested his return to her home.)

PROBLEM 1
John needs special services which aunt cannot provide and aunt does not know how to find and use these services in the community.

Resources and client strengths
Aunt is motivated and excited at prospect of resuming parenting role.

Goal
Aunt will have access to a supportive community network to which she can refer for guidance and direction.

Plans
1. Meet weekly with aunt to determine her service needs.
2. Inform aunt of available community services.
3. Support aunt in arranging speech/language evaluation for John.
4. Monitor educational enrichment plans made for John.
5. Support aunt in arranging for psychiatric evaluation for John.
6. Collaborate with public agency worker in introducing aunt to parenting classes.
7. Inform parenting classes of aunt's possible enrollment.

PROBLEM 2
Public agency worker appears supportive of early discharge from specialized foster care program although all goals have not been met; this leaves the aunt confused.

Resources and Client Strengths
Aunt is open about her confusion regarding mixed directives and planning problems.

Goal
Aunt's confusion will be minimized by receiving consistent, agreed-upon message from all workers.

Plans
1. Work with public agency worker to plan and monitor John's return home.
2. Develop visitation plan for public agency worker to monitor John's behavior at aunt's and foster home during transition.
3. Plan September meeting with public agency workers to discuss case.

PROBLEM 3
John and foster parents have developed an attachment which will require some strategic separation work for healthy readjustment to occur.

Resources and Client Strengths
1. John is comfortable with aunt and shows affection toward her.
2. Foster parents understand importance of John's returning home.

Goal
John will have gradual separation from foster parents and reintroduction into aunt's home; foster parents feel supported throughout process.

Plans
1. Develop visitation plan with aunt and foster parents to provide reasonable transition.
2. Maintain open communication link among all parties during transition.
3. Work with foster parents on separation issues.
4. Assess child's readjustment reactions.

Figure 4 Service agreement

(Child and Family Services and Mrs Jones agree that her nephew, John, has a right to a home on a permanent basis and agree to work together on goals to make that possible. If the goals are not met, a plan for John's permanent placement with another family will be made.)

TIME FRAMES
Decision date: October 3, 1985

GOALS

A. Aunt will have access to a supportive community network to which   by Oct. 3
she can refer for guidance and direction.

B. Aunt's confusion will be minimized by receiving consistent, agreed-   by Oct. 3
upon message from all workers.

C. John will have gradual separation from foster parents and   by Oct. 3
reintroduction into aunt's home; foster parents feel supported
throughout process.

TASKS

Aunt
1. Meet weekly with Child and Family Services worker.
2. Get speech/language evaluation for John.
3. Get psychiatric evaluation for John.
4. Attend parenting classes.
5. Visit foster home every day to ease transition for John.
6. Communicate with public agency worker, foster parents, others during transition.

Child and Family Services worker
1. Meet weekly with aunt to determine her service needs
2. Inform aunt of available community services.
3. Support aunt in arranging speech/language evaluation for John.
4. Monitor educational enrichment plans made for John.
5. Support aunt in arranging for psychiatric evaluation for John.
6. Collaborate with public agency worker in introducing aunt to parenting classes.
7. Work with public agency worker to plan and monitor John's return home.
8. Develop visitation plan for public agency worker to monitor John's behavior at aunt's
and foster home during transition.
9. Plan September meeting with public agency worker to discuss case.

Public agency worker
1. Collaborate with Child and Family Services worker to introduce parenting classes to
aunt.
2. Monitor John's behavior at foster home and at aunt's during transition.
3. Meet in September with other public agency workers to discuss case.

Signatures: _____
Aunt

_____
Child and Family Services worker

_____
Public agency worker

Date: August 3, 1985

Figure 5 Permanency planning roles and tasks in John's case

Permanency Planning Roles	Case tasks
Case planning	★ Formulate goal-oriented records ★ Assess appropriateness of John's return home ★ Develop reasonable plans given limited time period, write service agreement ★ Assess child's readjustment reactions
Case management	★ Inform aunt of available community services ★ Collaborate with public agency worker in introducing aunt to parenting classes ★ Inform parenting classes of aunt's possible enrollment ★ Develop visitation plan with aunt and foster parents to provide reasonable transition ★ Support aunt in arranging speech/language evaluation for John ★ Maintain open communication link among all parties during transition ★ Support aunt in arranging for psychiatric evaluation of John
Therapy	★ Meet weekly with aunt to determine her service needs ★ Work with foster parents on separation issues ★ Develop visitation plan with aunt and foster parents to provide reasonable transition ★ Support aunt in arranging speech/language evaluation for John ★ Maintain open communication link among all parties during transition ★ Support aunt in arranging for psychiatric evaluation of John ★ Assess child's readjustment reactions
Client advocate	★ Monitor educational enrichment plans made for John ★ Work with public agency worker to plan and monitor John's return home ★ Develop visitation plan for public agency worker to monitor John's behavior at aunt's and foster home during transition ★ Plan September meeting with public agency's workers to discuss case
Court Witness	★ Review of goal success and implementation of plans

6 What is the ecological perspective?

Social work practice is influenced by our particular conceptual frameworks regarding human behavior and human development – the theories and bodies of knowledge that guide us in our efforts to understand human beings, explain problems, and decide on goals and strategies of intervention. The ecological perspective, which we introduced briefly in Chapter 1, is especially suited to permanency planning practice, in light of its emphasis on the dynamic interaction between people and their environments. In our view, it should be adopted as a framework for working with parents and children.

What is meant by the ecological perspective? What is its contribution? What are its key principles? What are its implications for service delivery with parents and children in the context of permanency planning? This chapter considers these questions and also presents a case example illustrating the shift in thinking about social work practice that is stimulated by adoption of an ecological perspective.

ECOLOGICAL PERSPECTIVE

The ecological perspective refers to an approach to social work practice that draws on the study of the interactions between living organisms and their environments. As noted by Carel Germain, who has contributed substantially to the development of this approach:

> 'Ecology rests on an evolutionary, adaptive view of human beings (and all organisms) in continuous transactions with the environment. As a metaphor for practice, the ecological perspective provides insight into the nature and consequence of such transactions both for human beings and for the physical and social environments in which they function.'
>
> (Germain 1979: 7)

The essence of the ecological approach is that social work intervention is addressed to the interface between people and their impinging environments: 'practice is directed toward improving the transactions between people and environments in order to enhance adaptive capacities and improve environments for all who function within them' (Germain 1979: 8). Social workers seek to influence change in both the person and the environment.

Such a conceptual framework offers a basis for comprehensive analysis of problem situations and relies on a broad array of knowledge and theory from General Systems Theory, biological sciences, cultural anthropology, ego psychology, social psychology, and ecology. It also includes concepts from demography, public health, and organizational and communication theories. It rests on a view of human beings as spontaneously active, seeking, and creative in their ongoing efforts to cope with life challenges and to move toward self-realization. The key ecological principles may be summarized as follows:

* *Interactionism*, which assumes that human behavior is not solely a function of personality or of environmental influences, but rather of the complex interaction between person and environment.
* *Transactionism*, which regards human beings as active participants in transactions with their environment.
* *Adaptation*, which views human behavior in terms of whether it helps people adapt functionally as they interact with their environment.
* A *health/growth orientation*, which focuses on people's strengths and adaptive striving, rather than solely on weaknesses or deficits (Maluccio 1981b).

As suggested by these principles, the ecological perspective is useful for child welfare practice, especially within a permanency planning framework, for a number of reasons:

* It represents a move away from an illness orientation to a health/growth orientation. Utilizing this perspective, practitioners engage the progressive forces in individuals, families, and groups, while simultaneously seeking to render environments more responsive to the adaptive and coping needs of human organisms (Maluccio 1981b: 24).
* It enables practitioners to understand more clearly the relationships between families and their environments and identify the significant sources of support as well as stress and conflict (Garbarino 1982). Workers can assess more objectively the complex personal and environmental factors affecting parents and children, and arrive at more appropriate treatment plans and recommendations for permanency planning (Howe 1983; Olmstead 1983).
* It helps in recognizing and involving parents as full partners in the helping process (Whittaker 1979). The family is regarded as the central unit or focus of attention and service, and practitioners appreciate the importance of preserving family ties (Laird 1979; Maluccio 1981a).
* Above all, it helps to conceptualize child welfare as a comprehensive service with a strong preventive component (Sundel and Homan 1979). As a result, the ecological perspective stimulates a marked shift from a narrow orientation to a broad view of child welfare that emphasizes a multifaceted

practice approach to children and their families in the context of their life situation and environment.

Scholars from diverse disciplines have applied the ecological perspective to policy and practice in child welfare. Brown *et al.* (1982), Garbarino (1982), Maas (1971), and Minuchin (1970) have called attention to the impact of the environment on the child's development. Garbarino (1982), in particular, has underlined the influence of 'socio-cultural risk', that is, the impoverishment of the child's world: 'Children who grow up wanting for food, for affection, for caring teachers, for good medical care, and for values consistent with intellectual progress and social competence grow up less well than those children who do not lack these things. Their absence places a child "at risk" for impaired development' (Garbarino, 1982: 32).

To counteract the adverse impact of sociocultural risks, these and other authors call for active professional intervention in the social environment. Maas (1971) underscores the role of prevention programs in ameliorating the effects of poverty and other stressful environmental factors. Garbarino (1982: 57) advocates 'weaving a strong social fabric around child and parent'; he further observes that 'this wonderous human child can and will become a competent human being, if we only give it the chance' (Garbarino 1982: 57). Whittaker (1979) urges the involvement of parents as 'full and equal partners in the helping process'; he also advocates forming a 'service net' by establishing linkages among child welfare agency, family, school, peer group, juvenile justice system, and other community services. Brown *et al.* (1982) propose a master plan for family-centered child welfare services at the neighborhood level. Bronfenbrenner (1979), an eloquent exponent of the ecological foundations of practice in child and youth services, points out that service delivery should take into account the wide array of rapid societal changes affecting the family; also, it should include the provision of societal supports and resources that are required to promote the development of emotionally and socially healthy persons.

In conjunction with the ecological perspective, permanency planning can be a powerful tool in our efforts to meet the needs of children and parents. In particular, the ecological model leads to a number of implications for practice and service delivery with parents and children.

IMPLICATIONS FOR SERVICE DELIVERY

Preserving family ties

The ecological emphasis on the dynamic transaction between people and their environments highlights the crucial importance of the biological family in the growth and functioning of children in placement.

As many writers have pointed out, the natural bonds between children in care and their parents continue to be prominent for parents as well as children long after they are physically separated, reflecting the significance of the biological family in human connectedness and identity formation (Laird 1979). Workers should therefore view the goal of preserving family ties as a major imperative in child care and use ecologically oriented intervention to facilitate and support continued family interactions:

> 'Every effort is thus made to support the family, to enhance its functioning, and to avoid separation and placement. When separation is necessary, the importance of the family continues to be recognized through active efforts to maintain family ties, to support shared parenting by biological and foster parents, and to work, wherever possible, toward reuniting the family.'
>
> (Laird 1979: 205)

A key means of accomplishing the goal of maintaining family ties is through consistent parental visiting of children in care. The findings of recent studies have highlighted the crucial role played by parent–child contact or parent visitation in the outcome of the placement as well as the child's functioning (Aldgate 1980; Fanshel 1975; Fanshel 1982; Fanshel and Shinn 1978; Rowe *et al.* 1984).

Research has demonstrated that parental visiting of children in foster care is the best single predictor of the outcome of placement and, therefore, is the 'key to discharge' (Fanshel 1975). For instance, in their longitudinal study of foster care in New York City, Fanshel and Shinn (1978: 96) concluded that children who were visited frequently by their parents during the first year of placement 'were almost twice as likely to be discharged eventually as those not visited at all or only minimally'. Similarly, in a study conducted in Scotland, Aldgate (1980: 29) reported that, in cases in which children had been returned to their families, 'there had been some contact between at least one parent and child in 90% of the cases, and contact monthly or more frequently in just under half the cases'. Studies have also found that high frequency of caseworker–parent contact is linked to a higher level of parental visitation (Fanshel and Shinn 1978: 108) and to continued parental involvement with the child (Jenkins and Norman 1975).

There is, in addition, some evidence that visitation is correlated with the child's well-being and improved functioning while in care (Weinstein 1960). In one study it was found that children who had been returned to their biological families from foster care did better in their ultimate permanent plans than those who had not had such a chance for parental connection (Fein *et al.* 1983).

As a result of these findings, researchers have stressed the importance of encouraging and monitoring visiting: 'agencies should be held accountable for efforts made to involve the parents in more responsible visitation' (Fanshel and Shinn 1978: 111). The findings have also led to formulation of practice guidelines for using parent–child visiting as a means of achieving permanency planning (White 1981). It has been stressed that 'the visiting experience can be effectively used as a natural opportunity to provide services that meet the developmental needs of children and promote the competence of parents (Sinanoglu and Maluccio 1981: 444).

As noted by Aldgate (1980: 29–30), parent–child contact can have various beneficial effects, such as reassuring the child that he or she has not been rejected;

helping the child to understand why he or she cannot live at home; preventing the child's idealization of the parent; and helping parents maintain their relationship with their child. In addition, others have called attention to an often neglected dimension – the significance of sibling relationships and the importance of maintaining sibling ties while children are in placement (Harari 1980; Ward 1984). All of these activities can influence the transactional sphere of the family and contribute to the goal of permanency planning.

Viewing the family as the unit of service

Another implication flowing from the ecological perspective is the need to view the family as the central unit of service, as the focus of attention – in short, as the client.

People can best be understood and helped within their significant environment, and the family is the most intimate environment of all. It is here that the child grows up, develops, and forms a sense of identity and competence. The family has the potential for providing resources throughout the life process, especially as its members are sustained and supported through ecologically oriented practice (Hartman and Laird 1983). The family's own natural space/environment can be used as an arena in which the worker and others intervene to help strengthen communication, parenting skills, and parent–child relationships.

The concept of the family as the central unit of service has been difficult to implement, although professionals have long concurred with it. The tendency has been to fragment helping efforts by concentrating variously on the children, the parents, or the foster parents, rather than working with the children and parents as interacting components of one family system. Obstacles such as heavy caseloads, emergency situations, and complex family problems have prevented us from fully incorporating into child welfare practice new knowledge about families and new approaches to intervention with family systems. Other factors, such as rescue fantasies and bias against parents, have complicated efforts to provide adequate services to families (Maluccio, in press, a).

At this time, however, practice is beginning to reflect a trend toward regarding the family as the primary client; there is considerable evidence of innovative efforts by agencies and practitioners to work purposefully and systematically with parents. Some of the impetus for these efforts has come from the previously mentioned Adoption Assistance and Child Welfare Act of 1980 (Public Law 96-272), whose enactment represented the culmination of efforts on the part of many groups to strengthen the role of federal and state governments in promoting permanency planning for children coming to the attention of the child welfare system. Among the Act's most significant features are those mandating state agencies to provide services designed to prevent placement of children out of their homes or to reunite placed children with their families. Included is a range of programs, such as counseling, day care and homemaker services, respite care, and parent education. Also stressed are caseworker involvement with the family and maintenance as well as strengthening of parent–child relationships through frequent and regular visits.

Numerous innovative programs focusing on the family as the unit of service are described in the literature (Bentovim and Tranter 1984; Bryce and Lloyd 1981; Horejsi, Bertsche, and Clark 1981; Maluccio and Sinanoglu 1981; Maybanks and Bryce 1979; Sinanoglu and Maluccio 1981; and Stein, Gambrill, and Wiltse 1978). These efforts have shown that parents can be supported in their adaptive strivings as they are helped to plan responsibly for their children; ecologically oriented practitioners have provided comprehensive help addressed to both person and environment, such as counseling, support services, and systematic case management based on principles of decision-making, goal-setting, and contracting with parents. Even in situations in which children could not be returned home, parents have been helped to participate in the planning process in a way that reflects their caring, helps maintain their dignity, and frees the child to move into another family (Jackson and Dunne 1981).

In particular, the growth of the family therapy movement has led to the application of various family treatment approaches as alternatives to placement of children out of their homes or as methods of speeding up the reunification of placed children with their families. Many of these approaches reflect an ecological orientation, through their explicit or implicit use of the principles enumerated earlier in this chapter.

Some agencies employ intensive family therapy with multi-problem families with children at risk of placement in substitute care. These programs stress the importance of viewing the family from an ecological perspective: assessment and intervention address family's transaction with its kinship system, school, community institutions, and other social networks. Intervention strategies focus not only on engaging the family in treatment but also on changing the social systems that influence it (Tomlinson and Peters 1981).

Other agencies have gone even further in their work with families, experimenting with 'parent–child foster placements', in which single mothers and their abused or neglected children are placed for time-limited periods in specialized foster homes. Along with affording immediate protection for the child, the placement facilitates assessment of the mother's functioning and the provision of intensive services to strengthen her parenting skills (Nayman and Witkin 1978).

The concept of parent–child placement has been extended to residential treatment. Wood (1981), for example, describes a residential program in which parents diagnosed as abusive or neglectful live with their preschool children in a residential setting. The basic assumption of this program is 'that parental behavior is most effectively changed if parents and children live together in a supervised, supportive environment, with service delivery by a multi-disciplinary team' (Wood 1981: 105). Within two years, this program involved fourteen families for an average stay of fourteen weeks. The author concludes that it was effective in helping parents to care for their children in their own homes (Wood 1981).

Renewed emphasis on working with families is also seen in group settings such as children's institutions, many of which are moving toward family-centered services. Keith-Lucas and Sanford (1977), for example, present the concept of group child care as a family service. Increasingly, residential treatment centers stress not only the active participation of parents in the program but also the use of the center as a resource for parents and families (Finkelstein 1980; Whittaker 1979). The staff recognizes the parents' own needs as well as the importance of parents to the child, and mobilizes agency and community resources on behalf of parents and the family as a whole. Implicit in these approaches is the conviction that parents should be meaningfully involved in decision-making in critical areas of their child's life.

The literature offers many examples of practice innovations reflecting a focus on the total family as the client. For instance, a child care agency has demonstrated the effective use of 'family residential centers', that is, group homes where parents of placed children are given almost unlimited visiting privileges and encouraged to participate fully in their children's placements (Simmons, Gumpert, and Rothman 1973). This program has been found to be beneficial not only for the children but also the parents; with agency support of continual interaction between parents and children in placement, parents with severe problems are helped to improve their coping patterns and parenting skills.

In response to the need of many parents for ongoing support, some residential centers as well as community-based child welfare agencies have moved toward becoming an 'extended family'. In these agencies, service programs provide opportunities for parents to meet informally with staff members, to have social contacts that help combat their sense of isolation, and to obtain support as needed (Shyne and Neuman 1974).

Restructuring the environment

From an ecological orientation, a major function of the service delivery system in child welfare is to help families of children in care or at risk of placement to restructure their environment, to modify or enrich it so that it is more suited to their needs and qualities and more conducive to their positive functioning.

As suggested in the discussion of support services in Chapter 12, restructuring of the environment can be accomplished in a variety of ways. In many cases, it involves helping parents to identify actual or potential resources in their social networks – e.g. neighbors, friends, members of the kinship system, or various informal helpers. The extended family may provide resources to help a parent care for a child so as to avert placement in an unfamiliar institution or foster home, or reduce the duration of placement.

In other cases, restructuring the environment may mean involving parents in a self-help group or introducing a new person such as a homemaker or parent aide. Various studies have shown the value of complementing professional help with the services of paraprofessionals such as home management specialists, homemakers, and older persons who model effective parental behavior and coping skills. These aides help to meet the basic needs of parents, enrich the family's environment, and prevent placement or replacement (Spinelli and Barton 1980). They provide parents with better opportunities to learn skills, fulfill needs, and develop competence. The introduction of a new, supportive person such as a grandparent figure or homemaker aide helps meet the needs of parents themselves and enhances their capacity to give to their children.

In response to the multiple needs of families in basic life areas, many programs stress the provision of intensive services and environmental supports to the child's family before placement, during placement, and in the aftercare period. These comprehensive programs seek to avoid placement or reduce its duration and reunite children with their own families by strengthening the parents' coping and adaptive capacities and providing them with necessary services as well as counseling. Some examples are described in Jones, Neuman, and Shyne (1976); Sherman, Neuman, and Shyne (1973); and Weissman (1978). A major feature is collaboration among various community resources. Especially noteworthy is the approach of the Lower East Side Family Union in New York City to avert or limit foster care; it involves coordination and monitoring of services provided to families at risk by a variety of agencies (Weissman 1978). Such an approach takes into account the complex personal and environmental factors that affect family functioning and structure, as underlined by the ecological orientation.

In addition to direct work with families, agencies and workers must become involved in advocacy and social action, to help resolve the systemic or societal problems that lead to out-of-home care in the first place. There is ample evidence of a high correlation between entry into out-of-home care and social problems such as poverty, deprivation, and racism.

The ecological perspective directs our attention to these larger social and economic forces and the environmental context in which families function. It suggests that, ultimately, 'permanency planning cannot substitute for preventive services and for increased investment in our children' and their families long before symptoms emerge (Maluccio et al. 1980: 528).

Redefining the roles of social workers and child care staff

Another implication is the need to redefine the roles of social workers engaged in permanency planning. Workers are often understandably overwhelmed by the complex and intense demands placed on them as they attempt to work with parents. A major problem is that they are, in a sense, asked to be all things to all people: therapists for child and parents; consultants or supervisors with foster parents; case managers; advocates; etc. Moreover, these multiple roles have to be carried out in the context of insufficient training, heavy caseloads, and limited resources.

The ecological perspective suggests that the role of the primary social worker in any case situation should be redefined as that of a *catalyst* or enabling agent – someone who helps the family to identify or create and use necessary resources. The worker uses flexible approaches and calls on a variety of resources to help provide the conditions necessary for parents to achieve their purposes, meet life challenges, and engage in their developmental processes. Above all, rather than relying primarily on traditional psychotherapeutic techniques such as insight-oriented procedures, workers should become experts in methods of environmental modification, use of existing community resources and natural helping networks, creation of new resources that may be needed by their clients, and mobilization of family members' own resources.

Along with redefinition of the roles of social workers, in some programs the relationships between parents and foster parents or other substitute caretakers such as child care staff have been redefined; in contrast to the traditional pattern of keeping them apart or in competition with each other, these programs show the value of having parents, foster parents, and other child welfare personnel regard themselves as partners in a shared undertaking, with common goals and mutually supportive and complementary roles.

This perspective leads to new helping systems that are ultimately more effective and rewarding for everyone concerned. For example, several recent articles describe the involvement of foster parents as resources for parents through such means as role modeling or serving as parent aides (Davies and Bland 1978; Ryan, McFadden, and Warren 1981). These articles suggest that foster parents can become allies of biological parents and be more actively involved in permanency planning, as long as their roles are clarified and they are provided with adequate supports and rewards. In short, we should encourage a foster family to become an *extension* of the biological family, rather than its *substitute* (Watson 1982), as is now the case. In this way the foster family becomes a part of the supportive environment that helps promote the adaptive functioning of the biological family.

Empowering parents and children

Social workers in permanency planning should also stress approaches that serve to empower parents or children – that is, to help them to enhance their competence in dealing with environmental challenges (Maluccio 1981b). Knowledge from ego psychology, biology, ecology, and other fields can guide practitioners in engaging the progressive forces within clients and helping them to develop their competence.

There should be de-emphasis of pathology, especially psychopathology, and greater emphasis on clients as active, striving human beings. For instance, there is a tendency to view the problems leading to foster care as reflecting primarily the psychopathology of the parents. There is inadequate attention to societal conditions that limit the power of parents and interfere with their coping efforts. Minuchin (1970) has urged that social agencies shift their approach from a pathological model to an ecological approach, in order to be more effective in their work with the poor. He points out that practice deriving from the pathological model has tended to fragment families; in contrast, regarding the family as part of an ecosystem can elicit and utilize the supportive resources in the environment and help hold it together. Minuchin (1970: 130) concludes that the adoption of an ecological approach could lead to more 'truly change-producing and helpful' intervention in support of families and their children, poor or otherwise. It could also result in greater awareness of – and increased sensitivity to – the qualities and needs of families from diverse racial and ethnic groups.

In particular, there should be emphasis on the resources and supports needed by parents. At the same time, 'human problems, needs, and conflicts need to be translated into adaptive tasks providing the client with opportunities for growth, mastery, and competence development' (Maluccio 1979a: 290). For example, a parent who is labeled abusing or neglectful can be helped to learn or relearn skills in child care. To accomplish this, the problem has to be redefined as a situation involving lack of knowledge or inadequate parenting skills. In short, as discussed further in Chapter 12, the focus is on providing support services and identifying and removing obstacles that interfere with the parents' coping capacities.

Empowering parents also means regarding them as resources in their own behalf, as partners in the helping process – rather than simply as carriers of pathology, as is often the case. As we shift from a pathological view of parents to a competence or non-deficit perspective, we are better able to identify strengths in parents themselves and involve them in growth-producing activities. Once they are given adequate opportunities, parents as well as children can mobilize their own potentialities and natural adaptive strivings. As demonstrated in recent years by the success of various self-help groups such as Parents Anonymous, parents can be recognized as resources who can help each other. Social workers should aim toward empowering clients to accomplish their purposes and meet their needs through individual and collective efforts.

The concept of empowerment is receiving increasing attention, especially in work with minority clients. For instance, Solomon (1976) explains that empowerment in Black communities involves a process where the worker engages in practice activities that aim to reduce the powerlessness often caused by the negative evaluation associated with membership in a stigmatized group. For clients such as parents of children in foster care, working together to obtain needed resources for a better life for themselves and their children would be one way to counteract feelings of powerlessness and to promote competence and self-esteem.

CASE ILLUSTRATION

As presented in this chapter, the ecological perspective requires the development of a particular mind set – one that helps social workers focus on changing the client's environment and on client assets and potentialities rather than client weaknesses and deficits. Application of this orientation to permanency planning calls for significant shifts in the practitioner's attitudes and approaches. The following case example illustrates how adoption of the ecological perspective by workers helps ensure permanency planning for children and youth.

Summary of Sanchez case

Sandra Sanchez and her two sons, Jamie, age six, and Eddie, age five, were referred to a child guidance clinic by the public welfare agency because the boys were having frequent nightmares. Ms Sanchez, age twenty, had several siblings and was the child of a Black mother and a Puerto Rican father who separated when she was three. At age ten she was placed with an aunt in a neighboring town because her mother was hospitalized with a nervous breakdown; two years later she ran away and returned to live with her mother. At age thirteen she became pregnant. A year after Jamie's birth, Eddie was born. Sandra and the children's father married and had a variety of living arrangements, including living with the paternal grandparents, with the maternal grandmother, and, briefly, on their own.

After this marriage ended, Ms Sanchez entered a new relationship and re-married. She and her new husband, also a Puerto Rican, went to Puerto Rico for an extended visit, leaving the children in New York with the maternal grand-mother. They returned, got their own apartment, and assumed care of the children. When her husband began to abuse her physically, Ms Sanchez separated from him and returned to live with her mother. At the time of referral, Ms Sanchez and her two children had just moved to their own apartment in a housing project a few miles from the maternal grandmother's apartment. The family's problems included, besides the nightmares, the children's refusal to accept their mother's rules and discipline and their reluctance to go out and play because they feared older youths from the neighborhood.

When Ms Sanchez and Eddie went to the clinic for the second interview, Eddie looked depressed and seemed to be lacking in energy. It was subsequently learned that he had not eaten for two days because there was no money for food. In addition, the mother clearly felt isolated; she left her apartment only twice a month, when her welfare checks came and she joined her mother to go grocery shopping. She slept most of the day and watched television at night. Jamie often missed school because his mother was not awake to get him ready.

Traditional clinical approach in the Sanchez case

In following a traditional clinical approach, the clinic staff would most likely formulate a diagnostic and treatment plan such as the following:

> Sandra Sanchez, an immature young mother whose need for nurturance causes her to depend on relatives, is depressed and unable to function as a responsible parent. It appears that her relationships with men have been motivated by emotional needs rooted in unhappy childhood experiences. And just as her own childhood was fraught with insecurity and lack of nurturance, so Jamie and Eddie have not had the kind of consistent nurturance important to their sense of security. Their night fears may symbolize anxiety about losing what little security they feel. Although Eddie responds in a more openly frightened, unsure, and untrusting manner, Jamie responds with bravado. He sees himself

as the strong and powerful head of the house and is afraid to allow himself to be what he is, a six-year-old boy.

The treatment plan will include weekly individual sessions for Sandra and Jamie, and psychiatric evaluation will determine Ms Sanchez's need for anti-depressants. She will be encouraged to join the boys when they go out to play, and will be instructed in child management techniques. Assistance in budget planning will be provided to her. Jamie will be offered supportive therapy wherein he can be allowed to assume the role of a little boy. If progress is not noted, a referral to a child protection agency might be necessary to assure that the children are not neglected.

Ecological approach in the Sanchez case

On the other hand, by approaching and analyzing this case according to an ecological model, the staff would arrive at a rather different diagnostic and treatment plan:

Sandra Sanchez is a young mother who is striving to cope with the challenges of single parenthood and who has the potential to nurture and enjoy her children. She functions best with the support of her extended close-knit family, particularly her mother. Her housing, in a project several miles from her mother's home, has meant the loss of significant support. While Ms Sanchez's mother and her mother's neighborhood are familiar and safe to the children, they find their own neighborhood frightening, particularly because they fear the older youths residing there. Ms Sanchez's isolation, which has resulted from her separation from her husband and the move away from her mother, leaves her feeling depressed. This contributes to her inability to care for the children appropriately. Jamie, seeming to recognize the absence of support for his mother, has attempted to take on the role of head of family.

The service plan will include assignment of a parent aide to work with the family in their apartment twice a week. The parent aide will offer support to Ms Sanchez, help her learn new child-management skills, and assist her with budget problems. Also, mother needs to learn new ways of maintaining contact with relatives through more skillful use of public transportation and to gain support from people other than extended family members, so that she will not feel so isolated and depressed when the latter are not available. The parent aide will assist Ms Sanchez in going to a health clinic for checkups and to the housing unit to apply for an apartment in the housing project where her mother lives.

Jamie will be seen individually and will be helped to understand that efforts are being made to have people help his mother so that he can be more appropriately involved in school and play. In individual sessions, Ms Sanchez will be helped to think about – and plan for – herself, Eddie and Jamie. She will be encouraged to use the supports available in her extended family while working on ways to become more independent, such as getting job training and learning homemaking skills. She will be helped to understand Jamie's needs so that she will not expect him to be the head of the family. The maternal grandmother will be included in an early session, either at the agency or at her daughter's or her own apartment, so that she can contribute ideas about ways of involving the extended family. A school meeting will be set to explore the possibility of a group experience for Jamie and Eddie, which might help them become more comfortable in their school and in their neighborhood.

Conclusion

As the ecologically oriented treatment plan was carried out in this case, the clinic staff consistently kept in mind the primary goal of permanency planning for each of the children. The parent's pathology and the problems in the family unit were not overlooked; but there was greater emphasis on the strengths and potentialities in the mother and her extended family, as well as sensitivity to their cultural patterns and values.

The problems were defined in ecological terms as outcomes of the transactions between this family and their environment. There was a shift in mind set – from viewing family members primarily in pathological terms (e.g. the mother as depressed) to regarding the family in constructive terms (e.g. as a potentially mutually supportive unit). The thrust of intervention was to help family members, particularly the mother, strengthen their coping skills, modify their environment, and identify and use potential resources.

Following an ecological orientation, the clinic staff engaged in both direct work with the Sanchez family and activities designed to change their environment. Through intensive provision of services from clinic staff and others, the mother was helped to enhance her competence as a parent and the goal of maintaining the children within the family was achieved.

As the above case illustration suggests, the ecological perspective leads to specific practice principles and implications that can guide the worker through the major phases of permanency planning practice: engagement of parents and children in a helping relationship; formulation of the assessment; selection of permanent plan; development of a service agreement and treatment plan; and implementation of intervention. These principles and implications will be discussed in depth in the remaining chapters of Part II, especially in relation to using service agreements; working directly with parents and children; and providing support services.

SUMMARY

The ecological perspective on social work practice has been presented as especially suited to permanency planning, in light of its emphasis on the dynamic interaction between people and their environments. Ecological principles, particularly interactionism and transactionism, reflect various themes useful in child welfare practice: moving away from an illness orientation to a health/growth orientation; enabling practitioners to identify the significant sources of support as well as stress in families; recognizing and involving parents as full partners in the helping process; and conceptualizing child welfare as a comprehensive service with a strong preventive component.

The ecological model leads to a number of general implications for service delivery with parents and children within a permanency planning context, including: the importance of preserving family ties; the value of viewing the family as the unit of services; the need to help families restructure their environment; the need to redefine the roles of workers and child care staff; and emphasis on empowering parents and children by promoting their competence. These implications were discussed, and a case example was presented and analyzed, to illustrate the utility of adopting an ecological perspective in permanency planning practice. Specific practice principles flowing from an ecological orientation will be discussed in the chapters in Part II.

SUGGESTIONS FOR FURTHER READING

Brown, J. H., Finch, W. A., Northen, H., Taylor, S. H., and Weil, M. (1982) *Child, Family, Neighborhood – A Master Plan for Social Service Delivery*. New York: Child Welfare League of America.

Germain, C. B. and Gitterman, A. (1980) *The Life Model of Social Work Practice*. New York: Columbia University Press.

Howe, G. (1983) The Ecological Approach to Permanency Planning: An Interactionist Perspective. *Child Welfare* 62 (4): 291–301.

Maluccio, A. N. (1981a) An Ecological Perspective on Practice with Parents of Children in Foster Care. In A. N. Maluccio and P. A. Sinanoglu (eds) *The Challenge of Partnership: Working with Parents of Children in Foster Care*. New York: Child Welfare League of America, pp. 22–35.

—— (1981b) Competence-oriented Social Work Practice: An Ecological Approach. In A. N. Maluccio (ed.) *Promoting Competence in Clients: A New/Old Approach to Social Work Practice*. New York: Free Press, pp. 1–24.

Olmstead, K. A. (1983) The Influence of Minority Social Work Students on an Agency's Service Methods. *Social Work* 28 (4): 308–12.

PART II
PRACTICE WITH
PARENTS AND CHILDREN

7 Assessing parents and children

As they engage parents and children in a helping relationship, social workers seek to formulate an assessment to guide treatment planning and intervention. What guidelines can social workers follow in their efforts to understand parents and children for permanency planning purposes? How do they formulate an assessment of their clients' functioning, qualities, and overall situation? What are the special aspects relating to permanency planning that need to be considered? This chapter addresses these questions, focusing first on understanding the parents and then the children.

ASSESSING PARENTS

An accurate assessment of parents and their situations is essential to responsible planning and intervention. In particular, the worker needs to comprehend and evaluate the parents' inner strengths; environmental resources; style of relating to others; grounding in reality; ability to adapt to and handle stress; and, most of all, capacity to promote the healthy growth and development of the child. Together with assessment of the child to be discussed later in this chapter, assessment of the parents and the family situation provides the basis for the service agreement (Chapter 9) and for ongoing work with the parents and child.

In formulating an assessment of parents and families within a permanency planning context, workers are guided by principles and techniques that are basic to social work practice (cf. Germain and Gitterman 1980; Holman 1983; Hollis and Wood 1981; Hartman and Laird 1983; Northen 1982). Special considerations pertinent to permanency planning emerge in the following areas:

* family history;
* functioning of family and parents;
* psychological, psychiatric, and medical evaluations of parents;
* parental response to children in different developmental stages;
* recognition of parental strengths; and
* appreciation of the family's environment.

In addition, the characteristics of abusive and neglectful parents should be considered, since a majority of children coming to the attention of permanency planning workers have experienced parental abuse or neglect.

Family history

There should be a review of the history of the 'presenting problem', which is likely to be one of the following:

* A child has been abused and parents need help with child management.
* A child needs to be placed.
* A child is in placement and the parents want the child returned.
* A family has been mandated to participate in counseling before a child can return home.

The review of the presenting problems should search for patterns: Have there been previous placements? Have placements occurred at particular times of the year? Have previous placements been for particular time periods? Are the reasons for this placement and the previous ones similar? For example, if placements have occurred around the anniversary of a grandparent's death when a parent is experiencing depression, the worker and family can search for ways of handling such reactions differently. If placements coincided with periods of extreme marital conflict, the parents can be helped to see that resolution of marital difficulties would be important in preventing further placements. In short, the history of a presenting problem can be a significant diagnostic tool.

Beyond the presenting problem, information about a parent's own experiences in growing up is especially pertinent. Did the parent experience disruptions in permanency during childhood? If parents were placed out of their homes as children, their understanding and feelings about the reasons for the placements should be explored. A parent's sense of belonging should be discussed. It is not unusual to find that parents of children needing permanency planning were themselves victims of drift or impermanence.

The parents' relationships with their own parents should be reviewed. Many parents of children in placement or at risk of placement have experienced abuse, neglect, lack of consistency, and feelings of being misunderstood. The possibility of child sexual abuse should be openly explored. A discussion of how parents were disciplined as children may offer clues to current difficulties in child management. Parents may remember having been assigned unrealistic tasks in their families, such as responsibility for younger siblings or even responsibility for the care of parents. They may remember frequent family moves, hunger, marital strife, and general chaos. Some parents may remember only stable times with nurturing parents. This information can offer the worker clues about the chronicity of a problem, or the situational nature of the current crisis.

Information about the supports that have been available to families should also be obtained. Some parents disclose a history of relying on public welfare services for years. Others hold a staunch philosophy of depending on no one. Some have strong family ties that offer support, or they find support from churches, community centers, and neighbors. Others live in isolation and have nowhere to turn at times of crisis. Patterns in reaching out for support also need to be examined, in order to understand current difficulties or potentialities.

Functioning of family and parents

Various tools for assessing the functioning of parents and families are available. Among the most useful ones are: the *ecomap*, which can help workers and clients to understand the family and its relationship with other people and systems in the environment; the *genogram*, which can aid in learning about a family's history and relationships over time; and *family sculpture*, which can vividly portray the current relationships within the family (Hartman and Laird 1983; Holman 1983).

A family always should be viewed within the context of its kinship system and broader social networks. A single parent with an adolescent child living in an isolated part of the city would present different issues from a single parent with young children living next door to a grandmother in an area where there are many relatives. Early in the helping process information about existing or potential resources available to a family should be part of the history taking.

Observation of the current functioning of the family is an integral part of the assessment process. A home visit to a family provides an opportunity to evaluate basic living conditions such as space, housekeeping style, neighborhood assets, number of household occupants, and adequacy of furnishings. A family may feel less guarded on its own turf, and the worker will be able to observe family interaction and functioning more accurately than in the office setting.

The personal functioning of the parents – fatigue and depression, attention to personal appearance, and the physical care of the child – can, at least in part, be observed. Observations should be formulated as objectively as possible, with recognition that there are many degrees of acceptable standards for home and personal care, based on different socio-cultural, ethnic, and racial styles and patterns.

Interactions between the parent and child should be observed both at home and in the office. Various authors offer detailed guidelines useful to practitioners in learning how to observe parent–child interaction (cf. Gambrill 1977; Greenspan 1981; Sigel, Flaugher, and Johnson 1977).

Careful observation can help to answer crucial questions such as: Do parents pay attention to their children? Do the children look to their parents for responses? Some parents are overprotective or indulgent, while others are highly critical of their children. Parents may be dependent on their youngsters, asking them to make decisions or expecting them to remember appointments. Some are unaware of how to play with them, finding it awkward to engage in fantasy, while others enter into play easily. Some convey a sense of helplessness to their children, while others appear stern and controlling. Parents can express support and warmth, or appear distant and uninterested. Some can be aware of a child's interests and abilities, and others have little understanding of a child's individuality. Observation in each of these areas can offer clues about the depth and quality of the relationship between parent and child, particularly the bonding and attachment between them.

Many aspects of bonding and attachment are still in the process of clarification; for instance, some authors use these concepts interchangeably, whereas others see them as distinct phenomena (Rutter 1972). Also, the assessment or measurement of bonding behavior is not simple or absolute. Nevertheless, bonding and attachment are especially relevant to consider in making decisions regarding permanency.[1]

Attachment or bonding involves a continuously changing process, varying with the development of the child and the situation of the parents, among many pertinent variables. Positive indicators of bonding include: a comfortable parental response to the child's demands, without a sense of cost or reward; the child's feelings of security and comfort in relating to the parent; parent's and child's recognition of each other as individuals; and parental satisfaction in the child's growth (Bolton 1983: 61).

Indicators of poor or incomplete bonding include: early childbirth; poor frustration tolerance on the part of the parent; ignorance of child development; inability to perceive the child's behavior as rewarding; denying the opportunity for relationships between the child and other persons; rigid expectations of the child; and other historical, environmental, and behavioral factors (Bolton 1983: 183–209).

Where bonding seems absent, a permanent plan that separates children from biological parents may not be highly traumatic. Such a lack of bonding, however, raises questions about a child's ability to attach to new parents and indicates that special pains need to be taken in the selection of substitute parents or other caretakers. Where there is evidence of a strong bond between parent and child, it may be inappropriate to think of permanency planning options outside the biological family. In that case, if it is mandatory that permanency be provided by another resource, careful work with parent and child must be done to free the child to attach to new parents.

Observing a parent's interaction with all the members of the family may enable workers to identify clues as to why a relationship with a particular child seems different or problematic. The child may have been assigned a scapegoat role in the family; his or her behavior may remind parents of attributes they have rejected in themselves; or the child may physically resemble a spouse with whom the parent is angry. Such explanations for the relationship are probably not evident to the parent or child, and should be shared only at therapeutically appropriate points.

In addition to observation of interaction between family members and a particular child, workers can note general family communication patterns. Interactions can appear warm, caring, and supportive and suggest that the family has the capacity to nurture and support itself, or they can appear critical and destructive. The atmosphere can be one of sharing, or of blaming; of giving or of withholding; of encouragement or of despair. Clues can be gained about how best to enable families to develop their own capacities to support their members. Families can be helped to become more accepting of individual strengths and weaknesses and learn to complement each other in more constructive ways.

Observation should also include the interaction between workers and parents. Is there initial anxiety? Does it subside as the worker makes efforts to engage the parents? Is the parent able to share thoughts and concerns? Is the parent able to state what must change in order for the child to remain at home, or return home? Does the parent seem to understand a child's need for permanency? Can the parent look at the worker, smile on occasion, display some sense of humor, share disappointments and disagreements? How does the worker feel about the parent? Is there initial fear, positive connection, or anxiety? These details can help in planning appropriate intervention. For example, a parent who is extremely uncomfortable with a worker may benefit more from the services of a parent aide or from group experiences; or the worker's initial feelings may provide hints to explore hidden areas of history such as alcoholism or sexual abuse.

Psychological, psychiatric, and medical evaluations of parents

There are times when formal psychological, psychiatric, or medical evaluations of parents are necessary for accurate assessment. Such evaluations can help clarify areas of concern that workers identify as a result of interviewing and observing parents. Clarification of the parent's capacities and potential can help in setting appropriate and realistic goals.

Since such evaluations are not always readily available, and since they can add to the anxiety already experienced by parents, workers should use them in a discriminating and sensitive fashion. In communicating with the psychological or other consultant, they should specify the unanswered questions which the evaluation could address. For instance, if there is a question about the parent's intellectual ability to care for a child responsibly, a differential diagnosis may be needed to distinguish between intellectual deficiency and depression. Other concerns may be the parent's awareness of reality; the appropriateness of hospitalization for self-destructive behavior; or the possibility of enhanced functioning with the use of medication. Complete medical evaluations can explore complaints of fatigue, depression, or recurring physical symptoms.

Past evaluative material from other community agencies, physicians, private practitioners, and others can also be helpful in arriving at an assessment. Such documents should be obtained only with the knowledge and written consent of the parent and must be considered background materials, not verification of any present condition. The information may be useful, however, to demonstrate gains parents have been able to make over a period of time.

Because decision-making in permanency planning is so difficult and so essential, workers should avail themselves of resources that can facilitate the process. To have the sole responsibility for a decision when a clear-cut course is not evident can inhibit decision-making and perpetuate drift. Agencies should therefore have expert consultation available, and workers should feel free to seek it.

Parental response to children in different developmental stages

In order to assess fully a parent's capacity to care for a child, an evaluation must be made of the parent's ability to respond to the child in varying developmental stages. This is a clinical task not readily amenable to precise measurement and scoring. Black (1982) suggests that different parental qualities are necessary in interacting with young children, from birth to age four, and older children, from ages four to twelve. The most important factors in the earlier years include the amount of time spent with the infant; the responsiveness to the physical needs of the youngster; the ability to respond to the child's needs in preference to one's own needs; the capacity to invoke a sense of trust in the world around the child; and the flexibility to grow with the child in knowing when immediate care is necessary and when needs can be frustrated. The parent must be able to set firm limits and to 'synchronize' with a child's need to separate.

The later stage, after age four, is a time of ego consolidation for the child. The youngster imitates, identifies, acquires traits, and learns values and beliefs. Interpersonal relationships, attitudes toward achievement, morals and conscience formation, and sexual identity are important developmental tasks. Parents who best facilitate growth in this phase are those who are secure in their own sexual identity, have internal senses of right and wrong, are able to be nurturant and involved, can promote autonomy, and have the quality of empathy. Their reality testing must be strong enough to distinguish between thoughts and feelings, fears and actuality in order to make appropriate decisions (Black 1982).

The key therapeutic questions that present themselves are:

* When parents lack these capacities, can they develop them?
* What kinds of interventions can facilitate this development?
* When such qualities cannot be developed, are there other ways of providing them for a child while he or she remains at home?

Recognition of parental strengths

Although the discussion thus far has centered on parental problems and weaknesses, a vital part of assessment is recognition of actual or potential strengths. Evaluating strengths is as necessary in assessment as in engagement of parents and children in a helping relationship, as noted in the next chapter.

In assessing children, we tend to view them with a greater sense of optimism than when assessing parents. For example, we feel encouraged when a child with developmental delays shows growth, although the child may still be below what is expected for age appropriate development; if a child who wets the bed can be dry for even one night; a learning disabled child masters some basic words; or a child with poor impulse control internalizes an appropriate behavior.

While it may be unrealistic to view adults whose personalities are already formed with the same optimism with which children are assessed, it is essential to

concentrate on *assets*, not *liabilities*; on *strengths*, not *weaknesses*. It is therapeutically sound to work with clients by recognizing and supporting their ego
strengths and their healthiest defenses. For example:

> Mrs F. appears depressed. She is out of work and has severe financial diffi-
> culties. She is exasperated with Tim's behavior, saying she simply cannot
> tolerate his demands.

One assessment of this mother's functioning might be:

> Mrs F.'s inability to support herself and her children results in her being
> depressed and unable to respond to them appropriately.

A more useful evaluative response would be:

> While Mrs F. is depressed because of her layoff from work, she is optimistic
> about getting another job soon because of her good work record. She shows a
> great deal of insight in recognizing that Tim's demands exasperate her because
> she feels guilty about being unable to give him the extras she could when she
> was working.

The latter response reflects the worker's sense of optimism and conveys to parents
a renewed sense of hope. This is a valuable therapeutic tool that should underlie
all work with families.

Appreciation of the family's environment

As presented in Chapter 6, the ecological perspective on social work practice
requires that a person's functioning or characteristics not be viewed in isolation
from the environment, taken in its broadest sense (Germain and Gitterman
1980). Perceiving transactions between person and environment that are adaptive
as well as those that are detrimental is the essence of the ecological approach. A
key question in assessment is: What is the 'goodness of fit' between the person
and the impinging environment? To answer this question, the worker considers
such aspects as: 'How nutritive is the environment; that is, does it contain the
ingredients necessary to support, nourish, and challenge the person? What is
interfering with an individual's efforts to use available supports and resources?
What needs to be added, removed, or otherwise changed so as to achieve a better
fit and promote the person's strivings toward growth and fulfillment?' (Maluccio
and Libassi 1984: 53). The answers to these and similar questions will enable the
worker to see better how and where to intervene in order to enhance
person–environment transactions in each case situation.

Pertinent environmental factors include an individual's social network,
neighborhood, community organizations, physical facilities, societal pressures.
Important personal factors include innate adaptive capacities such as sensory and
motor skills, intellectual ability, and motivation for competence, as well as other
qualities such as resilience, identity, autonomy, and coping skills.

Coping skills include the use of problem-solving skills, the ability to control disabling feelings like rage and anxiety, the responsible use of information, and the self-confidence and freedom to try new responses. Coping skills, however, do not reside solely in the person; they are also dependent on the environment and its supports, opportunities, and demands. Assessment in these areas helps to clarify various issues for treatment, such as:

* Can this parent be helped to cope better through the use of resources in his or her social networks?
* Is there a relative who might offer some support?
* Can this family function better if community resources are made available?
* Are there church members who might reach out to the family?
* Are there ways of widening a family's experiences, to enable family members to feel less depressed and isolated?

The ecological perspective compels assessment of competence in persons as well as opportunities in environments, viewing person and environment as they interact dynamically (Maluccio 1981b). Someone who appears to be functioning poorly may actually be coping well, considering the circumstances of poverty and deprivation in which he or she lives. By the same token, a person with excellent environmental supports may appear functional but then show a surprising lack of competence when the supports disappear.

For example, a young mother had three children who were all doing fine while the family lived with the maternal grandmother. When they moved to their own apartment in another part of the city, the children quickly came to the attention of the community because they were late for school, not bathed, and without lunch or lunch money. It became clear that the mother was depressed and unable to function when she was away from her family. When she had their support she felt better and was able to provide adequate care for her children. Labeling her as depressed and unable to care for her children would not be productive or accurate; nor would it be useful to conclude that the problem was that she lived in a poor environment. It would be more accurate to observe that the mother coped best when she had the support of the maternal grandmother, and that without such support her coping capacity diminished because of depression.

A useful assessment is one that leads to a clear plan for intervention. For instance, in the case example above, an assessment of depression might have resulted in medication or even hospitalization. An assessment of depressed functioning because of lack of environmental supports would result in the provision of in-home parent aide services to give needed support, or a search for housing closer to the home of the grandmother to alleviate feelings of isolation.

The ecological explanation of problems contrasts with other perspectives based on a linear rather than transactional view of human functioning. For instance, in their analysis of barriers to returning foster children to their own homes, the Oregon Project staff (Pike *et al.* 1977: 16) categorized the central obstacles in terms of the following parental problems:

'*Parental Absence* refers to lack of consistent contact between parent and child over a period of time.

Parental Condition refers to qualities within the parent which prevent adequate nurturing.

Parental Conduct refers to observable behavior of the parent which indicates inadequacies in parenting ability.'

(Pike *et al.* 1977: 16)

Such a typology broadly classifies parents and their deficits or inadequacies; but it is limiting, since it places the major burden on the parents and their negative qualities, without fully taking into account environmental pressures, demands, or opportunities. In keeping with the ecological perspective presented in Chapter 6, we prefer a more dynamic explanation of barriers to the child's remaining or returning home – an explanation that takes into consideration the complex inter-play between the parents' qualities or problems and the properties of their environment. To arrive at such an explanation, we need to understand as fully as possible not only how the parents are functioning, but also what is going on in their environment that influences their functioning.

Understanding the characteristics of abusive or neglectful parents[2]

As noted in Chapter 3, many children are referred for permanency planning services because of abuse or neglect. To arrive at a sound assessment in each case, workers therefore need to be familiar with the characteristics of abusive or neglectful parents, especially as these relate to their capacity to care for a child (Ebeling and Hill 1983; Faller 1981; Garbarino and Gilliam 1980; Helfer and Kempe 1974).

Abusive parents are actively involved with the child, have strong feelings invested in the youngster, and assign the child the task of gratifying the parent. Many abusive parents were abused as children physically or sexually; have high expectations of their children; are apt to live in isolation without other significant people in their lives; lack self-esteem; and are crisis-prone but poorly equipped to handle crises. Those families where sexual abuse is present may come from any socio-economic class and may apparently be law-abiding and functioning; actually the family structure shows flaws in ability to communicate, substance misuse, sexual problems, and misalignment of power.

Neglecting parents usually lack interest in the child. Basic needs are not attended to. Such parents often live in poverty, have trouble holding jobs, tend to move a lot, and are apt to seek solace in drug and alcohol use. Like abusive parents, they tend to be isolated and not have friends. Many have grown up in families where parents were neglectful. They may tend to deny problems, a defense that has been essential to their own survival.

The characteristic ego functioning of a neglectful or abusive parent includes such defenses as denial, projection, regression, and repression. These defenses are ego-syntonic, in the sense that the parent manages to get by on a day-to-day basis. They are ego-alien in that their use may impair the ability of the parent to care for the child. A parent is ill-equipped to care adequately for a child when repression takes up so much energy that he or she is depressed, regression reaches the point of extreme fantasy, denial impairs the ability to perceive reality adequately, or projection results in exaggerated suspiciousness.

Neglecting or abusive parents have a problem with trust, and parents who lack trust cannot bring up a child to feel trust. Such people have difficulty with traditional treatment modalities. The treatment issues that emerge are:

* Can these parents develop some sense of trust?
* What kind of intervention is best for parents who lack trust?
* Can they raise children to have trust in others?

Neglecting and abusive parents are often preoccupied with fulfilling their own needs. This is not surprising, since meeting their needs has required their complete energy. Nonetheless, it means that such parents are not only blind to the needs of their children but also view the children as potential nurturers and caretakers. This inability to see a child's needs because one's needs are so great raises treatment issues that workers must consider:

* Can such parents learn to look elsewhere to satisfy their own needs?
* Can a worker provide interventions that will facilitate this process?
* If a parent can be helped to seek other satisfactions, can he or she come to understand and respond to a child's needs?

A characteristic of neglecting and abusing parents is poor impulse control which may be consistent with their day-to-day existence. When there is nothing to look forward to and nothing to plan for, the motivation to control impulses is lacking. Poor impulse control can result in children being punished unduly, youngsters being left alone because the parent has momentary opportunity to get gratification, lack of essentials because of unrealistic purchases to satisfy urges rather than necessities, or unpredictable use of and addiction to drugs. People who are least equipped to satisfy impulsive urges are also least apt to be able to control them. Along with poor impulse control comes poor judgment. The poor impulse control prevents responsible action even when the parent knows what is appropriate. Again, various treatment issues emerge:

* Is it possible for these parents to think in terms of the future or can they only exist for today?
* Can they be helped to recognize that certain impulsive behaviors are making it necessary for someone else to care for their children?
* Can they help their children to postpone gratification and learn that there is value in thinking and planning beyond the moment?
* Can these parents be helped to understand that they must exercise reasonable judgment if they are to care for their children?

UNDERSTANDING CHILDREN

Along with understanding the parents, permanency planning work requires careful understanding of the children. To achieve such understanding, workers are guided by generic principles in assessment of children (Cooper and Wanerman 1977· Greenspan 1981; Lieberman 1979; Mishne 1983). Additionally, they need to pay special attention to:

* history of child's growth and development;
* observation of the child in diverse settings;
* child's current functioning; and
* psychiatric and psychological evaluations.

History of child's growth and development

As in any situation where a child is experiencing difficulty, it is important to obtain pertinent history. Parents of children in care or at risk of placement are often considered unavailable, especially when children are committed to state agencies or other authorities. The whereabouts of parents may be unknown or parents may be perceived as uncooperative or uninterested. Social workers must resist the temptation to accept such statements from referral sources and be willing to pursue parents to obtain significant background material.

An assessment of a child includes the kind of information about parents described earlier in this chapter. As noted there, a thorough understanding of the competence of parents, their strengths and limitations, and the family's overall situation is essential to planning appropriate intervention with and on behalf of the child. In addition, significant history regarding the child should be gathered, particularly in the areas of:

* developmental history;
* school;
* health; and
* out-of-home placements.

DEVELOPMENTAL HISTORY

As with any child, the physical, intellectual, and emotional milestones should be noted, since they are essential to a full understanding of functioning and potential. Early developmental milestones are especially important in determining whether a child's development falls within normal ranges. This can be crucial for children who may need special care because of lags. In the event that separation from the biological parents is required, it is necessary to be aware of current or potential developmental problems, in order to choose an appropriate permanent plan.

Developmental problems need to be viewed in the context of the stimulation offered or denied by the parents and the environment. There are times when lags can be attributed to lack of opportunity to develop because of neglect. Some parents can cope well with children whose development is normal but not so well with children having problems such as slow learning, speech deficits, visual or aural impairments, or other handicaps. This requires careful assessment, to clarify whether the child can catch up when the deficit is remedied.

Also noteworthy are the parent's perception and description of a child's developmental milestones, as they offer insight into the parent–child relationship. Parents may remember developmental milestones in great detail or not at all. They may describe them with interest and animation or with flat affect. When asked to describe an infant, parents may use terms like cuddly, quiet, active, fussy, responsive, alert, or placid. Some parents may be unable to offer such descriptions at all. It should be remembered that the description reflects both the child's characteristics and the parent's feelings about him or her. For instance, children who are difficult nevertheless can be well cared for and nurtured. Thus, the affect that accompanies the parent's description is as important as the account itself.

Parents' feelings about a child may vary with the different phases of the child's development. This too can produce insight about the parent as well as the child. For example, a parent may express satisfaction about a child's infancy but discomfort with the child's movement into the explorative stage that comes with mobility. There may be even more discomfort when the child enters the age of self-assertion. The opposite may be true for other parents; some may welcome the stage of development that symbolizes children's growing ability to care for themselves. Such an assessment helps delineate situations of possible deprivation for the child as well as areas of child care where the skills of parents need further development.

The ability of parents to provide information about the child's development offers clues about their relationship with the child. For example, remembering significant developmental milestones for one child but not another may be striking. It is especially useful to discuss what was happening in the parents' lives during the child's first three years. As parents describe the child's infancy, some parents will show affection in describing a baby as cuddly, or in talking about breast feeding, or watching a baby take first steps; others may not remember such incidents or may describe them with flat affect or unpleasant memories. They may relate their expectation that the infant would be different, or may recall that the child seemed more difficult than siblings. Infants in their appeal and attractiveness differ and can elicit a variety of responses from parents. Workers should be alert for clues that a child's personality created barriers for the parents in forming a bond with the child, or for indications that a parent's personality made it difficult to care for a child in a nurturing fashion.

SCHOOL

A comprehensive examination of a child's school history offers the opportunity to evaluate functioning in a setting outside the home. In particular, workers should determine if school has been a positive or negative experience for a child. Special educational needs may not have been met if there have been frequent changes of school due to family moves or placement changes. Frequent changes may also have led to difficulty in making social adjustments. Academic standing, to determine if a child is at grade level, should be reviewed, as should the teachers' reports about a child's desire to please, ability to concentrate, social relationships, general state of mind, and acceptance by his or her peers.

Any special education opportunities that have been provided should be noted, and a prediction obtained of the child's future special education needs. Descriptions of a child's school functioning that suggest the possibility of an attention deficit disorder, a learning disability, or limited intellectual ability should also be noted. This can be relevant information when decisions about permanency are made.

School attendance records are also noteworthy. A child whose attendance at a number of schools has been sporadic in all probability has not had positive learning experiences. Reasons for poor attendance should be explored. Frequent illness, not getting up in time for school, and absence for frivolous reasons characterize some children's school experiences. If a child has a history of school phobia or school refusal, it is possible the parent is giving the child the message to stay at home.

The parent's view of the child's educational needs should be determined. Some parents value education highly, while others are indifferent. The regularity of a child's attendance and the amount of parental encouragement to learn can be significant factors in assessing a child's performance in school. When adjustment is good despite stressful situations, the child's inner resources may be especially strong.

HEALTH

A complete health history is vital in any assessment of children. Records of innoculations, allergies, or any health problems are particularly important when a child is to be placed. An account of eating and sleeping habits is also important. Occasionally, poor nutrition or different routines can explain a child's listlessness or disinterest in the environment. Any child may have trouble adjusting to a placement where food and sleep routines are different. Advance information can help an adoptive, foster, or group home facility accommodate a youngster's individual patterns.

Particular illnesses or disabilities should be noted. For example, children with diabetes may be difficult for some parents; those in wheelchairs require more care and support than children who can walk and run. A disability, if serious enough, can make it impossible for the biological parents to care for the child. Feelings about – and adjustment to – the disability should be assessed to determine if intervention is needed to bolster the child's ability to cope.

The family's health history is as important as the child's health history, especially when a permanent plan outside of the biological home may be necessary. For instance, adopting parents should be aware of any familial health problems that are potential risks for the child, such as heart disease, cancer, high blood pressure, or diabetes. Sometimes such histories offer guides to preventive measures that can be employed when a child is young. As an example, when the family history suggests that a number of members suffered from affective disorders, special attention might be given to preparing a child to deal with stress and depression in adaptive ways.

OUT-OF-HOME PLACEMENTS

A history of previous placements should be obtained, including dates and reasons for each one. Placements might have resulted from escalation of family problems or difficult behavior displayed by the child. Knowledge of any special patterns can be useful in planning intervention. For instance, if a child's placement always followed a parent's loss of a job, anticipatory intervention could prevent this from happening if the father should become unemployed in the future.

The child's adjustment to various placements should also be explored. Poor adaptation in a foster home but a good adjustment in a group setting can provide clues to the child's needs; he or she may do best with structure, or the demands for intimacy in a foster home may be too threatening and conflictual. Reasons for discharge from placement, especially if the child went to a place other than the biological home, should be reviewed. This can enlarge the worker's understanding of the child's adjustment to particular settings and responses to different environmental stimuli.

For children in placement, the views of their caretakers are significant. A child's ability to tolerate closeness, comfort with authority, sense of identity, and manageability can best be conveyed by those who care for the child on a regular basis. An objective caretaker can often pinpoint the characteristics that make a particular child difficult to manage or easy to enjoy.

Observation of the child in diverse settings

To understand a child, the worker must engage in careful observation as part of the assessment process. Ideally, a child should be observed in different settings, such as home, school, or office, and with the family as well as individually. This provides the opportunity to see how the child relates in various situations and with different people. With children who have experienced emotional trauma because of neglect, abuse, or upheaval, there is always a question about their ability to recoup and heal when provided with a secure and permanent home. Past evidence of a child's ability to do well when provided with necessary supports offers an optimistic prediction for a capacity to make strides in an appropriate permanent placement.

As workers observe children in diverse settings, especially noteworthy aspects include:

* Appropriateness of the child's affect in a given situation.
* Interactions with peers and authority figures.
* Nature of the relationship with other family members.
* Nature of the child's behavior.
* The child's verbal skills.
* General level of maturity.

Anything extraordinary may suggest a need for additional information. A child's general appearance should also be observed. The appropriateness of a child's dress for the occasion, general impression of neatness or disarray, attention paid to cleanliness and hair combing, body posture, general coordination, and level of activity all contribute to a worker's evaluation of the child.

Child's current functioning

Observation of the child in diverse contexts contributes to the worker's analysis of his or her current functioning – a fundamental part of the assessment. The components of such an analysis are those typical of all child evaluations: the child's appearance and manner; developmental strides; nature of conversation with the child; the child's ideas about problems; the child's ego strengths and reality testing; and impressions gleaned from techniques designed to reveal a child's fantasies.

As delineated by various authors (cf. Greenspan 1981; Mishne 1983), techniques that can be used to elicit fantasy material include family and person drawings, sentence completions, story telling, and questions about dreams, among others. A child's developmental level can be assessed by such instruments as Beery's Developmental Test of Visual-Motor Integration, Goodenough's Draw a Person Test, and Jastak's Wide Range Achievement Test. These, and others, are discussed in mental measurements compendia (e.g. Buros 1972). In addition, various techniques and guidelines for the clinical assessment of pre-school children are described by Plenk and Hinchey (1985). Social workers should obtain the assistance of psychologists in administering and interpreting any testing instruments.

Recently, Kinetic Family Drawings (Burns 1982) have been employed to understand children's perception of family relationships and to monitor changes in their sense of permanence. To use this technique, workers ask children to draw a picture of their families doing something, and then interpret the results by considering the relative size of the figures, the age-appropriateness of the drawings, the physical closeness of family members, the enclosure of figures within boxes, and other projective measures.

Of particular significance is the nature of the relationship between the child and the parents. Where a strong bond exists, the nature of that bond must be assessed to determine if it will hamper the ability to allow the child to separate and develop an individual identity. When there does not appear to be a strong connection between parents and child, a question must be raised about the child's, as well as the parents', capacity to relate.

In addition, it is crucial to explore children's feelings about permanency planning, especially if they have been removed from the biological family. As Kufeldt (1984: 257) has pointed out, 'when given the opportunity to be heard, children in [out-of-home care] can provide observations that are both relevant and important.' The idea of a placement away from home is generally threatening for children. Some will convey their apprehension with accompanying anger toward the person or agency they hold responsible, while others will hold themselves responsible and promise to be good if only they can stay at home. Others may plead that their parents need them to help, seeming to recognize their parents' shortcomings but not as a sufficient reason for placement. An occasional child may welcome the option of a placement, blaming parents for a horrible experience at home and anticipating greener pastures.

When children are asked what they think it would be like to move to a new place, the meaning of the present environment to the child will emerge. Some children will talk about not wanting to change schools, friends they will miss, or a favorite teacher. Others will not mention losses but will focus on the unknown, either with apprehension or with eager anticipation.

The child's current functioning is a crucial issue when planning for a placement. There may be obstacles because of tension between siblings, the possessiveness of the child, or differences between the child's style of relating to males and females. For example, a child with intensive sibling rivalry problems might do better in a family where there are no other children. A child who fears father figures would do better in a family where the foster father is gentle and soft-spoken.

Psychiatric and psychological evaluations

Some questions about a child's functioning or development need close scrutiny. For example, a child's intellectual functioning may appear low, learning problems may exist, or the child's reality testing may seem distorted. In such cases, it is appropriate to seek formal psychiatric or psychological evaluations. Evaluations should be requested in particular whenever there are unanswered diagnostic questions in areas such as intellectual ability, appropriate school placement, or learning problems that need to be defined for corrective measures to be taken.

Principles and procedures for the use of psychiatric and psychological evaluations are described in basic texts on treatment of children (cf. Cooper and Wanerman 1977; Greenspan 1981; Mishne 1983). Several central points will be noted here.

A clinical psychologist is trained to administer intelligence and projective tests, tools of great value in clarifying diagnostic issues. When referring children for such evaluations, workers should specify the questions of greatest concern, to enable the psychologist to select the most appropriate battery of tests. Psychologists should be given the significant background material, in order to take into account environmental deprivation or socio-cultural differences, since efforts to free tests from cultural bias have not been completely successful.

Psychiatric evaluations are particularly helpful in clarifying the severity of disturbance in a child. For instance, when there is question of psychosis, a psychiatric interview can provide the neurological and other data necessary to formulate a diagnosis. The psychiatrist can also assist with treatment planning, especially when medication is indicated.

Since workers must always be aware of the need to make a decision about permanency, they should take advantage of formal evaluations to clarify diagnostic concerns they may have. The evaluations are also useful when questions of parental rights are raised, since they offer information that courts will value as pertinent to the decision-making process.

Dynamic formulation

After the worker has gathered historical material, made observations, sought appropriate formal evaluations, and analyzed the child's development and functioning, the information must be combined to present a coherent dynamic formulation that characterizes the child, highlights his or her need for permanency, and conveys recommendations for intervention.

The child's sense of identity, ability to trust, comfort in relating to others, self-esteem, relationship to family members, and general level of intellectual and emotional functioning should be described. The treatment plan should consider such aspects as the placement choice, special education programs, individual and family therapy, group therapy, opportunities for socialization in the community, and comments about the kind of service that would enable parents to provide continuous care of the child.

Most critical is a statement about the child's need for permanency. This need should be set forth strongly, and the time frame clearly delineated. For example, it might be stated that the child, within six months time, needs to know what the permanent plan will be, and that the plan should be implemented within a year. Recommendation of a plan that appears open-ended would be a disservice to the child as well as the family.

In short, in conjunction with assessment of the parents, the family, and the overall environmental situation, the dynamic formulation characterizing the child contributes to the creation of the service agreement discussed in Chapter 9 and guides the worker's intervention with and on behalf of the child and the family.

SUMMARY

This chapter has focused on understanding parents and children through a careful assessment of their histories, functioning, qualities, and overall situation. As they engage in formulation of this assessment, social workers are guided by generic principles. They also pay special attention to various aspects relating to permanency planning.

In regard to parents, these include: family history; functioning of family and parents; psychological, psychiatric, and medical evaluations of parents; parental response to children in different developmental stages; recognition of parental strengths; and appreciation of the family's environment. As for children, the areas requiring special consideration include: history of child's growth and development; observation of the child in diverse settings; child's current functioning; and psychiatric and psychological evaluations.

The understanding derived from such a comprehensive assessment of parents and children and their overall situation forms the basis for the service agreement to be discussed in the next chapter and guides the ongoing work with the parents and the child.

NOTES

1. See Sluckin, Herbert, and Sluckin (1983) for an incisive critique of the concept of bonding.
2. Social work practice with parents and children involved in child abuse or neglect, including sexual abuse, is a specialized area beyond the scope of this book. For excellent treatment of this topic, see, among others, Ebeling and Hill (1983), Faller (1981), Helfer and Kempe (1974), and Sgroi (1982).

SUGGESTIONS FOR FURTHER READING

Cooper, S. and Wanerman, L. (1977) *Children in Treatment*. New York: Brunner/Mazel.

Greenspan, S. I. (1981) *The Clinical Interview of the Child*. New York: McGraw-Hill.

Hartman, A. and Laird, J. (1983) *Family-Centered Social Work Practice*. New York: Free Press.

Holman, A. M. (1983) *Family Assessment – Tools for Understanding and Intervention*. Beverly Hills, CA: Sage Publications.

Maluccio, A. N. and Libassi, M. F. (1984) Competence Clarification in Social Work Practice. *Social Thought* 10 (2): 51–8.

Mishne, J. M. (1983) *Clinical Work with Children*. New York: Free Press.

8 Engaging parents and children

The social work literature abounds with references to 'involuntary' clients, that is, persons who do not seek help of their own free will and who are described as unmotivated, untreatable, hard-to-reach, resistant, and so on (Cowan *et al.* 1969; Moore-Kirkland 1981; Oxley 1981). Parents and children coming to the attention of permanency planners in general fall in this category, and they test the worker's skill in engaging them in a helping relationship as in no other field of practice.

As they first meet and begin to work with parents and children, how do social workers engage them in forming a helping relationship? How can they make it clear to both parents and children that their work together must focus on making a decision regarding the child's permanent plan? How do they deal with the parents' and children's feelings as well as their own? This chapter concentrates on these issues and presents guidelines for the initial phase of the helping process with parents and children.

ENGAGING PARENTS

Numerous authors discuss the process of engaging clients in a helping relationship, recognizing that a person must feel comfortable and trust the worker for any change to occur (cf. Germain and Gitterman 1980; Hollis and Woods 1981; Maluccio 1979b; Shulman 1984). Especially noteworthy are those principles and techniques that can enhance the worker's skills in interpersonal helping in areas such as attentive listening, self-expression, empathy, warmth, and genuineness. The reader is referred to excellent, in-depth discussions of such principles and techniques by Fischer (1978) and Gambrill (1983), among others.

Guidelines that pertain especially to practice with biological parents of children who require permanency planning will be discussed here, as follows:

* examining the worker's own feelings and biases;
* relating to parents as persons in their own right;
* building trust;
* forming an alliance based on a child's right to permanency;
* recognizing strengths in parents;

* offering concrete help;
* delineating simple parent tasks; and
* allowing initial dependence.

Examining one's own feelings and biases

Parents of children involved in permanency planning tend to stimulate strong feelings, such as outrage, anger, and rejection, in social workers, foster parents, child care workers, and others in child welfare. Many workers typically identify with the child and experience a rescue fantasy – the wish to save children from their 'bad' parents. Furthermore, there are various cultural and professional biases against parents who have not 'done well' by their children and who in general come from low-income families and/or minority groups (Maluccio, in press).

Many of these feelings and biases are easily aroused in workers as a result of dealing with so many painful situations involving loss, separation, and abandonment. In addition, their own childhoods may be the basis for their current reactions. They may identify with the abused or abandoned child, or recall a similar experience from their own younger years. The possibility of becoming abusing parents themselves may be a vague but lurking threat needing to be defended against. Workers also may have biases about minimal standards for parenting. For example:

* there may be concerns about returning a child from a rural foster home to a crowded city ghetto apartment;
* it may seem wrong to move a child from a suburban school to an inner city school with limited funds for special services; and
* it can be wrenching to move a child from foster parents, who stimulate curiosity and desire to learn, to biological parents who are less interested or competent in promoting the child's development.

Feelings about cleanliness, personal hygiene, dress, and nutrition are also areas where personal standards and values come into play. To make work with the families succeed, it is urgent that social workers examine their own feelings, prejudgments, and biases in each case and learn how to handle their reactions in a constructive way.

Relating to parents as persons

The social worker must be able to relate to parents as persons in their own right. This means avoiding the tendency to focus immediately on the child's needs. For example, 'You are having a hard time' or 'You are feeling overwhelmed' is a better opener than 'We are terribly concerned about your child.' Such an approach offers parents the assurance that the worker is interested in the wellbeing of all family members, including *them*. Above all, the parents must know that their value as human beings does not rest solely on their capacity as parents.

This recognition of the parents' feelings must come early in the process. In particular, parents may need permission to be angry with workers and agencies. Parents of children in placement or at risk of placement are typically irate about what has happened and about what they anticipate will happen. Unless this is recognized as natural, progress in forming a relationship will be impeded. 'Two people working hard together won't always agree' is a way of acknowledging the reality. 'It will be important to know when we don't agree so that we can work things out' is a way of inviting parents to share disagreements. 'At times you may feel I'm being unfair' is another means of stating what is almost certain to occur.

Parents who are concerned about the potential loss of a child often feel they must be on their best behavior. Their idea of 'best behavior' may be not to disagree with what authorities say to them. They must be assured that their expression of anger or disagreement is acceptable, in order to acknowledge it in the present and help them deal with it with their children in the future. The feelings of helplessness and anger can be generalized. 'All parents at some point get angry with their children' is an example of the kind of statement that enables parents to feel they are understood.

Building trust and being honest about the worker's role

Many parents who are involved in permanency planning have no reason to feel a sense of basic trust in anything or anyone. Their life experiences have taught them to be guarded and suspicious. Especially in the early stages, workers can help by acknowledging the parents' fears and mistrust. For instance, 'I know it's hard to discuss things with strangers, particularly personal problems' is a way of eliciting the concerns parents have. 'I know it isn't easy to trust social workers and social agencies and that you may even have heard stories of how they take children from you' again identifies the anxiety that parents may be feeling. Identifying and labelling fears lead to a better chance for building trust in the client–worker relationship.

The process of building trust also involves clarity and honesty about the worker's role. Most often parents do not know what to expect from a worker or may have inaccurate perceptions of the worker's role in the family's life. It must be made clear that the major function is the worker's early decision-making about permanency for the child. Parents must understand that the child needs to be assured of permanency even if it means termination of parental rights and adoption. A specific statement should be made that the worker's job includes making an assessment, keeping records, and using courts when necessary. Such a forthright explanation eliminates confusion and helps build a foundation for trust in the worker's honesty, the essential ingredient for a working relationship.

Forming an alliance

Engagement includes the forming of an alliance based on mutual concern for the child and the child's right to permanency. 'It must be hard for you to see your child's life disrupted' is a way of recognizing that most parents do care about their children and want what is best for them. It can be a means of assuring parents that their affection or concern for their child is not in question.

Since most clients involved in permanency planning do not openly verbalize their need or readiness for help, their motivation may be disguised and expressed as anger or in indirect pleas for help. If, for example, there is excessive concern for the child, workers must be ready to help mobilize that concern and be particularly sensitive to any other indications of latent motivation on the part of the parents.

If appropriate, the concept that giving a child up can be the most responsible decision a parent can make should also be introduced. This is especially effective if workers offer themselves as an ongoing source of help regardless of what happens to the child.

In order to engage the parent, the worker can emphasize that both of them must work together in a joint effort to provide permanency for the child. If the child is to be placed out of the home, parents need to know that their participation in making plans, giving the child permission to be placed, and approving the placement are vital steps in the process. The partnership of parent and worker becomes real when parents understand their involvement influences the outcome. In particular, in discussing the placement of the child, the crucial importance of visits between parent and child must be emphasized. This informs the parent, from the beginning, that parental participation is valued and necessary for the child's well-being. As parents become aware of their roles in the permanency planning process, they can begin to feel less threatened, more in control of what happens, and more respected as part of the permanency planning team.

As discussed in Chapter 9, the use of a written service agreement is another means of underscoring that parent and worker can join together to achieve permanency for a child. The agreement provides opportunity for further clarification of roles, goals, and tasks and assures parents that they are a vital part of the process. This joining of worker and parent for the purpose of assuring permanency for a child cannot be emphasized enough as a basic element of the engagement process.

Recognizing strengths in parents

Because families whose children need permanency planning are characteristically those with more than their fair share of problems, it is easy to overlook their positive aspects. Recognizing and commenting on strengths in parents is essential to the engagement process.

This acknowledgment of strengths is easily overlooked. If a group of workers is asked to consider parents whose child is in placement and list adjectives that best describe the parents, the result is likely to be a list describing weaknesses rather than strengths. In this regard, it has been argued that social work training encourages workers to concentrate on the pathology or deficits of clients rather than their assets (Maluccio 1979b: 197–98).

While a parent's limitations should not be overlooked or minimized, actual or potential strengths should be deliberately identified and labelled. Comments such as the following can help to build trust and facilitate the engagement process as well as the ongoing work together:

* 'I can see that you really care about your child.'
* 'You certainly are handling your job well.'
* 'You feel good about your other children.'
* 'You are wanting to make things better.'

Offering concrete help

The engagement process will also be promoted if the worker can offer something concrete to the parent, whenever possible and appropriate. Tangible supports often have more meaning than words. For example, something as simple as an appointment card for clarity about the next appointment is useful. Written directions to a foster home where the child is placed provide tangible evidence that the worker endorses parental visits to the foster home. The promise of transportation to the next appointment, reading materials, phone numbers, and appointments regarding financial aid are examples of concrete ways of letting parents know how important they are to the permanency planning process – and to their child.

Delineating simple parent tasks

Specifying a task that a parent can complete can be a beginning step toward a renewed sense of competence. It helps parents to feel more in control of what is happening to them and their child and also facilitates their ongoing participation in the permanency planning process.

Initial tasks should be simple in nature and within the parent's ability to accomplish them. Parents, for example, may be asked to contact a school for the name of a social worker, call a doctor to learn about immunization shots a child has had, talk to an employer about release time for keeping counseling appointments, or inquire about a group for parenting skills. Role playing between social worker and parents may help the latter to overcome their anxiety sufficiently to attempt these or other tasks in real life.

Allowing initial dependence

Finally, since biological parents need to feel that they have an ally, permitting them some dependence on the worker can be an important part of developing the working alliance. For instance, it can help relieve immediate pressures and leave a parent feeling less overwhelmed.

Care should be taken to avoid the pitfall of the eternally dependent client. This can be done, in particular, through the use of time frames. An example would be to provide transportation for a parent to visit a child, but to do it for a limited time only. 'I know how difficult it is for you right now, so I've arranged for a driver to take you to visit your child for this first month. After that I think you'll feel more comfortable taking the bus, because you won't be so nervous about the visits and you will know the way.' This is an example of allowing, but not perpetuating, dependence.

ENGAGING CHILDREN

Various texts cover the principles and techniques for engaging children and youth in helping relationships (Cooper and Wanerman 1977; Crompton 1980; Lieberman 1979; Mishne 1983). To extend these principles and techniques to permanency planning practice, social workers must appreciate the feelings, fears, and reactions of children who are threatened with out-of-home placement or who are already in foster care.

The experience of actual or potential removal from the biological family for indefinite periods is a problem for the child that can be expressed in a number of symptoms, including learning difficulties in school; problems with eating or sleeping; poor socialization skills; shyness; fearfulness; phobias; undue aggression; stealing; running away; suicide gestures or threats; failures to cooperate; lack of concern for others; and general unhappiness.

As research has shown, these children typically suffer from poor self-esteem, lack of ego ideals, identity confusion, and inability to develop trusting relationships with others (Bryce and Ehlert 1971; Frank 1980). To engage them in a helping relationship, social workers need to remember that children have the right to understand what is happening to them and what to expect of the future. It is tempting to protect children from painful information; to feel that they are too young to understand and do not need to know everything; to think that they ignore adult conversation and do not hear what is being said; or otherwise to treat them as unable to participate fully in what is happening in their lives.

Children may not be as verbal as parents, and they may be equally, or more, adept at avoiding certain topics of conversation, but this should not lead the social worker to view their participation as unnecessary. Efforts to engage children are as important as those to engage parents, and reflect similar principles, including:

* relating to children as persons in their own right;
* building trust;
* forming an alliance based on a child's right to permanency;
* dealing with feelings;
* recognizing the strengths in the child and family.

Principles and techniques pertaining to each of these areas are discussed in the following sections. These should be applied in accordance with the child's age, developmental status, and other unique qualities and needs.

Relating to children as persons

Social workers need to address children's immediate concerns and convince them that the worker is interested in their well-being. While it may be necessary to talk with children about topics such as school, play activities, and games as an initial icebreaker, it is vital to bring up the issues the child is concerned about, if only to acknowledge the worker's awareness. 'I know you're worried about where you'll be living' or 'I know you're concerned about when you'll be able to return home' are appropriate comments, even if the child does not respond actively. Children gain assurance from such worker sensitivity to their lives.

Building trust

Their parents' lack of a sense of trust in the world is reflected in children, either because they have learned parental behavior or because of their own internal response to the world. Workers can comment about how difficult it can be to talk with someone new, and that children may have been told to be careful about what they say to social workers. They should explain that it will be important to get to know one another so it will not feel like talking to a stranger. Young children may be told that it is sometimes easier to get to know someone by playing together. Since play often is a more comfortable way for children to communicate, it can be used to create a relaxed atmosphere for the child that will lead to a relationship based on trust.

Children have little idea of what to expect from a social worker, unless they have had previous workers, in which case there may be misconceptions. Workers, therefore, should explain to children how often they will see the worker, how the time will be used, who else the worker will see, what various collaborators will be doing, and how decisions will be made. Children do better if they are not left guessing about the process. In particular, the worker needs to be honest about the task of reaching a decision within an agreed upon period of time about where the child will grow up. The worker also must be honest about what needs to happen for the child to return home, and about the worker's role in facilitating and evaluating progress.

Forming an alliance

Just as parents may be engaged in treatment by forming an alliance based on the best interests of the child, that is the child's right to permanency, a similar alliance can be formed with the child.

Statements that serve to promote an alliance with children, based on their right to permanency, include:

'I know it's hard for you to be living away from home.'
'What's really important is for you to know where you'll grow up.'
'The big job for all of us – you, your parents, and myself – is to decide the best place for you to grow up.'

'I know that both you and your parents want things to work out so that you can grow up at home.'

Despite a worker's skill in engaging most clients, it is often difficult to form an alliance with children, who can be highly resistant to participating in the permanency planning process. Consider the risks they take in giving up their resistance. They have ambivalent feelings about their parents (e.g. love/hate; trust/fear), which make them guard against any disloyalty. Their strong wish to be 'normal' that is, to grow up in their own family – makes them reluctant to share family experiences honestly, while their guilt about being the cause of difficulties can be too painful to share. Also, because they feel powerless, their fears about what will happen in the future are magnified. For these reasons, workers need to be patient in their efforts to form an alliance with a child, and persistent until the resistance is overcome.

Dealing with feelings

Another area in which workers must persevere is in helping children express and deal with their feelings. Children needing permanency planning are helped by knowing that other children are in the same circumstances and have similar feelings. They should be told that many children who cannot live with their parents feel confused because they care about their parents and are angry with them at the same time. Moreover, workers should let children know they are justified in feeling as they do. Understanding how children in similar circumstances feel makes it easier for them to acknowledge their own feelings. When they can be assured that feelings are neither 'right' nor 'wrong' but important to understand, they may be more willing to share them.

Some children in out-of-home placements, like parents, may feel that the best route back home is to be acquiescent, compliant, and well-mannered in the worker's presence. In that case, children will fail to communicate their real feelings about their lives. Workers must convince children it is acceptable to disagree with decisions that have been made; it is appropriate to protest if something does not seem fair; and it is natural to be angry with the worker, parents, or other people who are deciding where the child will grow up.

Children, in addition, should be told that their parents may feel angry at the worker sometimes, that this is understandable, and that people are not always expected to agree or to think alike. They must be made aware that the best decisions are made when everyone expresses what he or she feels about prospective plans for permanence. Workers may need to remind children of this again and again, especially whenever they suspect that a child is not communicating feelings that must be present but remain hidden.

Recognizing strengths

A worker's acknowledgment of the strengths in the child and his or her family facilitates the formation of a helping relationship. Children who have been removed from their homes because of abuse or neglect are already familiar with the problems their parents experience. It can be helpful to them if workers recognize the assets in parents along with the problems. As an example, when the worker can suggest some hope, based on a realistic assessment, that the child will return home, the therapeutic relationship is strengthened.

SUMMARY

This chapter considered the initial phase of working with parents and children, that is, engaging them in a helping relationship. Principles for engaging parents include: examining the worker's own feelings and biases; relating to parents as persons in their own right; building trust; forming an alliance based on the child's rights to permanency; recognizing strengths in parents; offering concrete help; delineating simple tasks; and allowing initial dependence. Similarly, engaging children involves relating to them as persons, building trust; forming an alliance; dealing with feelings; and recognizing strengths in the child and family.

SUGGESTIONS FOR FURTHER READING

Crompton, M. (1980) *Respecting Children: Social Work with Young People*. London: Edward Arnold.

Jackson, A. D. and Dunne, M. J. (1981) Permanency Planning in Foster Care with the Ambivalent Parent. In A. N. Maluccio and P. A. Sinanoglu (eds) *The Challenge of Partnership: Working with Parents of Children in Foster Care*. New York: Child Welfare League of America, pp. 151–64.

Moore-Kirkland, J. (1981) Mobilizing Motivation: From Theory to Practice. In A. N. Maluccio (ed.) *Promoting Competence in Clients – A New/Old Approach to Social Work Practice*. New York: Free Press, pp. 27–54.

Oxley, G. B. (1981) Promoting Competence in Involuntary Clients. In A. N. Maluccio (ed.) *Promoting Competence in Clients – A New/Old Approach to Social Work Practice*. New York: Free Press, pp. 290–316.

9 Using service agreements

While service agreements did not originate with permanency planning and are not unique to it, they are considered essential to the sound practice of permanency planning, especially since they aid in decision-making and taking timely action to achieve a permanent plan.

What is a service agreement? How is it written? What is its content? How is it used? What are the advantages and disadvantages in using it? This chapter will address these questions and present a sample service agreement, so as to help social workers understand and use this vital tool to achieve permanency for a child.

BACKGROUND

Social workers in most agencies are required to keep detailed records, sometimes even verbatim accounts of interviews with clients. These records may be used as documentation of social work activity for reimbursement; as material for supervision, statistical reporting, and continuity when a case is transferred; and as a teaching vehicle (Wilson 1980). Confidentiality of records is strictly maintained, although with the permission of the client they may be shared with other professionals, and, under subpoena, made available to courts. As a rule, clients neither participate in the writing nor read what is written. Records have not routinely been considered part of the treatment process itself, and social agency files abound with records that have never been read by anyone except the worker who wrote them.

With the advent of the brief treatment therapy movement of the late 1960s and early 1970s, the use of records in the form of treatment contracts came into practice (Mann 1973; Reid and Shyne 1969). Such contracts became increasingly popular because of their potential for clarifying the purposes of treatment, helping in case planning, facilitating worker–client communication, and establishing the mutuality of the treatment situation. The contracting process was also expected to have an impact on premature discontinuance of treatment, which was thought to be related to lack of clarity about goals (Maluccio and Marlow 1974; Stark 1959).

There is some controversy as to whether contracts should be written or not. One study reports on the advantages and disadvantages of written and verbal contracts, recommending that one or the other be used on a differential case basis, matching the contract's characteristics to the client's needs (Klier, Fein, and Genero 1984). Others feel written contracts are tangible reminders of mutual commitment to the therapeutic relationships and that they influence and reward positive interactions within the family (Fatis and Konewko 1983).

In child welfare services, studies in public agencies in California and Iowa have demonstrated the effectiveness of using service contracts in case planning to move children out of care more rapidly (Iowa Department of Social Services 1977; Stein, Gambrill, Wiltse 1978). Some formal communication among the participants in the treatment situation as they embark on their work together, whether it is called a treatment contract, service contract, or service agreement, is now seen as a desirable technique in many modalities and areas of interaction.

WHAT IS A SERVICE AGREEMENT?

A service agreement, as used in permanency planning, is a written statement of concurrence among a biological family, the permanency planning worker, and other collaborating professionals. Its overall purpose is to give a child the promise of permanency in an environment that promotes healthy growth and development. Its primary function, therefore, is to facilitate the process of deciding within a specified time frame where a child will grow up.

The service agreement emphasizes the mutual concern of the parents and the social worker for the child's right to permanency. It identifies a preferred permanent plan and sets forth specific tasks that must be accomplished to attain goals necessary for implementation of the plan. It specifies responsibility of the social worker, parents, and collaterals. It includes both short-term and long-range goals and time frames for each. Times for review are also specified. When children need to achieve particular goals as part of the decision-making process, these goals are also included.

A service agreement is neither a legal document nor a binding contract, and should not be presented as such. If it were, it could promote an adversarial relationship between the family and the permanency planning worker. Rather, it should be viewed as a tool for facilitating development of – and agreement about – a preferred permanent plan and the steps necessary for its achievement; it should be the basis for open and honest communication between worker and family.

In short, the service agreement is an integral part of the therapeutic process in permanency planning and serves a variety of purposes, including in particular:

* facilitating decision-making on the part of parents, social workers, children, and collaterals;
* specifying time frames for decision-making;
* encouraging participation of parents and thereby promoting their sense of competence and control;

* maintaining a focus on the child's need for permanency as the central issue;
* ensuring clarity of tasks, goals, and purpose for clients, workers, and collaterals; and
* providing for periodic review and assessment of progress.

HOW IS THE SERVICE AGREEMENT WRITTEN?

Although some prefer to use oral agreements, we strongly encourage the use of *written* service agreements in permanency planning practice, to promote clarity, emphasize their importance, and provide a vehicle for periodic review.

Who writes it?

In most permanency planning cases, there are many parties involved. There may be the public agency worker, the voluntary child welfare agency worker, the family, the foster family or child care workers, a parent aide, school personnel, lawyers, and others. Each may play a significant role in the permanency planning process and such roles should be considered in a service agreement.

The person designated as the case manager, usually the public agency worker or the social worker in the voluntary agency caring for the child, assumes the responsibility for the service agreement, which is written with the family and is reviewed with all parties involved in the permanency planning process at strategic points.

It is essential that the family, including the child if old enough, be involved in the preparation of the agreement. The kind and degree of participation in the writing will vary itself with the literacy and sophistication of the client, but involvement in determining and agreeing on content is vital. The agreement should be 'owned' by both family and workers, thus facilitating mutual commitment to achieving its terms.

When is it written?

Service agreements should be written in the early phase of the permanency planning process and revised in later phases as appropriate. The concept of a service agreement might be introduced in an initial session with the family. It sets the stage for goal-directed work and mutual involvement of the social worker and family. The worker might say: 'One thing we want to do is write down the goals we agree to be important in making a decision about where your child will grow up.' A reasonable deadline for completing a service agreement would be during the first six sessions with a family. This too should be stated: 'By the end of six weeks, it will help us if we put in writing the goals and plans we can agree on.'

Forming an alliance with the family

As discussed in other chapters, particularly Chapter 10 on working with parents, in permanency planning the importance of forming an alliance with the client cannot be overlooked. In fact, a viable service agreement is difficult to write without such an alliance between worker and family. Many families are not accustomed to regarding social workers as allies; they perceive social workers as child snatchers, unfair critics, meddlers, self-righteous judges, or 'out to get you'. It is important, therefore, to determine how a family views the social worker. This might be done by asking the family to describe earlier experiences with other workers. The worker needs to listen for patterns in these descriptions and must convey to the family the themes that have emerged. Some examples follow:

* 'It seems that you've often felt that workers haven't been honest with you.'
* 'You feel that workers haven't kept promises.'
* 'You've often disagreed with decisions that have been made.'
* 'You felt that people wanted to keep you from visiting your child.'

Positive themes should also be noted, such as:

* 'You felt the foster mother wanted to help you.'
* 'You appreciated the worker coming to your home when you had transportation problems.'

The idea of a service agreement usually can be introduced as a means of avoiding pitfalls that have been described, through statements such as:

* 'By putting in writing the things we agree on, we will avoid the chance of misunderstanding each other. Things will be clearer for both of us.'
* 'By both of us signing an agreement, we will know we are both committed to working toward the same goals.'
* 'If we have a visiting schedule written down, then everyone will be clear about it.'

Workers should encourage a family to be clear about their goals. When a family's goals do not seem realistic, or when goals are not in the best interests of a child, the worker will need to point that out. By listening to the family and honestly discussing their wishes and hopes, the worker may be able to help family members arrive at more realistic goals. In many instances, the worker needs to play an educational role to enable parents to understand the needs of children.

Most often, a family's immediate goals and those of the worker will complement each other. Parents may say: 'My child needs a place to stay until things are better at home,' or, 'My child needs to learn to behave better so I can manage at home.' These statements can be viewed as short-range goals with which a worker usually can concur. The worker's more difficult task is to introduce the long-range goals of permanency and improved family functioning that can be sustained. Workers may convey messages such as these:

* 'Most important is that, when your child comes home, it won't be necessary to consider placement again. You want your child to know that another placement won't be necessary because things are better.'
* 'In addition to wanting your child to behave better, you'd like to learn

what to do when there are tantrums. If you can learn to handle tantrums, when your child comes home you'll feel certain that another placement won't be necessary.'

Through these statements, the worker is introducing the idea of permanency to the family, although the parents or other family members may not see beyond the immediate crisis and may not readily attach importance to the worker's concern about permanency.

The worker must teach parents about the importance of permanency. It should not be assumed that parents understand that disruptions in care by biological parents, or disruptions in other placements, can be damaging to children. Parents may need to become aware that children can lose their ability to attach to other people, withdraw their trust from adults, and suffer from problems with self-esteem when they do not grow up with consistent, nurturing caretakers. They may not know that such damage can be irreparable. It is the responsibility of the worker to inform the family of these risks and to assure them of the worker's commitment to assisting them so that the child is protected from such emotional scars.

Since parents of children needing permanency planning have often experienced out of home placements in their own childhoods, the worker also needs to be sensitive to the emotional scars the adults may have. Parents may be aware of their fears of relationships and inability to trust but may not have related them to their own childhood experiences. Making this connection can heighten their understanding of the importance of permanency for their child.

The social worker's alliance with the family, based on mutual conviction that a child needs permanency, provides the groundwork for proceeding with writing the service agreement. With the goal of permanency as the framework, the worker engages the family in a discussion of what must happen for that goal to be achieved. Short- and long-term goals, with time frames for each, are agreed upon and put in writing. Tasks that must be accomplished as steps toward goal achievement are spelled out and assigned to the various persons involved in the permanency planning process.

CONTENT OF SERVICE AGREEMENT

A service agreement should be concise, written in clear specific language, and focus on those goals that are pertinent to the major objective of permanency. Goals which are too global or not relevant to the permanency planning process should be avoided, even if they have value for other reasons.

The content of a service agreement – that is, the goals, tasks, plans, time frames, and so on – should be based on careful understanding or assessment of the children, the parents, and their social situation, as discussed in Chapter 7. In essence, the written agreement incorporates the service or treatment plan that results from the dynamic interaction between worker and clients in each case situation. The agreement serves as a guide to treatment; some workers equate it with a service or treatment plan.

In their discussion of decision-making in child welfare, Stein and Rzepnicki (1983: 104–13) indicate that written service agreements should cover these areas: case goals; problem-solving objectives; tasks; time limits; and consequences. More specifically, we find that, for permanency planning purposes essential ingredients of a service agreement consist of the following:

I. Identification of *participants* in the agreement.
II. Statement reflecting a *mutual commitment* to a child's rights to permanency.
III. Statement of the *preferred permanent plan*.
IV. *Time frames* for decisions to be made about a permanent plan and implementation of that plan.
V. List of *goals*, with time frames, which are steps toward achieving the permanent plan.
VI. List of *tasks*, toward goal achievement, with time frames, for parents, worker, child (when appropriate), and collaterals;
VII. Periodic *progress review* meetings and dates.
VIII. Appropriate *signatures*.
IX. *Date of agreement*.

Before discussing the elements of the service agreement, we should point out that the stress on dates and time frames is deliberate; as noted in earlier chapters, early and timely decision-making is the goal, although there is always the need for flexibility, since each agreement reflects the unique circumstances of the particular case at any given time.

Participants in the agreement

All persons participating in the service plan – and therefore in the agreement – should be identified. This includes not only the social worker and other collaborators, but also the parent(s), the child when appropriate, and other significant family members. For instance, the initial statement might be:

This agreement is entered into among *(parents)*, *(child)*, *(social worker from child placing agency)*, *(parent aide)*, and *(parent's attorney)*.

Mutual commitment to permanency planning

Every service agreement should begin with a statement that reflects the child's right to permanency and the bond between the family and the social worker based on their mutual commitment to this right. Samples of such statements, which should be simple and brief, follow:

* *(Name of agency)* and *(name of parent)* agree that *(name of child)* has a right to a permanent environment that is stable and nurturing. We agree to work together to establish this and agree that, if the necessary goals cannot be achieved, a suitable permanent plan other than with *(child's name)* own family will be sought for *(child's name)*.

* The major goal of *(name of agency)* is to return a child home on a permanent basis. However, if we are not able to help parents modify their relationship with their child, cope with their child's behavior, or meet their child's physical and emotional needs, a recommendation will be made to *(court or other authority)* to pursue another permanent plan for the child, such as adoption.

Preferred permanent plan

The service agreement should also have a clear statement of the preferred permanent plan. Most often this will be that a child remain with, or return to, biological parents, as set forth in the initial statement of commitment to permanency planning in the example above. When this is a mutual goal of agency and family, it should be so indicated. Again, statements should be simple and brief, as follows:

* *(Name of agency)* and *(name of parent)* agree that the best plan is for *(name of child)* to return home.
* *(Name of agency)* and *(name of parent)* will work together to achieve the goals that are necessary for *(child's name)* to return home on a permanent basis.

These examples are appropriately used when both worker and family share the conviction that return home is a viable option. There are times when such mutuality cannot be achieved. For instance, when a parent wishes the child to return home but the worker's assessment of the situation is that this may not be realistic, the statement should reflect such a disagreement:

* *(Parent)* wants to achieve the goals that are necessary for *(child)* to return home on a permanent basis.
* *(Agency or worker)* agrees to work with *(parent)* to achieve this goal, recognizing that other plans may need to be considered if the goals cannot be met.
* *(Parent)* wants *(child)* to return home on a permanent basis. *(Agency or worker)* understands *(parent's)* wish and will assist in efforts to make this possible.

The purpose of the statements is to be as realistic and honest as possible with parents, while not depriving them of their right to rehabilitate to a point of being able to reassume responsibility for their child. Until court action deprives parents of their rights, they are entitled to receive comprehensive services to enable them to achieve goals. Realistic statements, however, do not have to be negative statements. The parents should feel that the worker and agency are their advocates, not that they want to prove their incompetence. An *inappropriate* statement would be:

(Parent) wants *(child)* to return home but has made no efforts, despite agency support, to make this possible. While *(agency)* will work with *(parent)* to

achieve the goals necessary for *(child)* to return home, *(agency)* feels that a permanent plan separate from *(parents)* is preferable.

This statement is inappropriate because it does not reflect any agreement between worker and client, suggests that the worker's efforts will be directed toward pointing out a parent's lack of capacity, conveys a punitive attitude toward the parent for past behavior, and does not communicate support for the plan. Although a parent might sign such an agreement, perhaps hoping to prove the worker wrong, it is not the basis for a therapeutic bond between them. Parents should not be blamed for past performance in any of the statements contained in the service agreement. Often parents feel that their questionable performance in the past is only a reflection of poor assistance from agencies. The service agreement should offer the promise of a fresh and objective approach to the situation.

In some cases workers should also introduce the idea of a second option for a permanent plan, to allow parents to begin to deal with the possibility that a child cannot return home. Following is an example that reflects a commitment to a permanent plan, a preferred permanent plan, and a second option:

> Mrs Stoner agrees with *(public agency)* that Terry has been in placement too long and that he needs to have a permanent home. While Mrs Stoner would like to take Terry home, she understands that certain goals need to be achieved in order to do this. Mrs Stoner and the agency agree to work together to achieve the necessary goals; furthermore, they agree that these need to be achieved within the next six months. Mrs Stoner agrees that, if she is not able to care for him, Terry will remain with his foster parents, who have expressed interest in adopting him.

Time frames for decision about a permanent plan

Essential to any service agreement are the time frames to be followed. There are five parts of the agreement that should incorporate such time statements:

* making a decision about a permanent plan;
* implementation of the plan;
* goals toward achievement of permanent plan;
* completion of tasks essential to implementation and achievement of goals and the permanent plan as a whole; and
* review of progress.

A child's sense of time, so different from an adult's, requires that permanent plans be achieved as quickly as possible. A year is a reasonable amount of time for achieving a permanent plan for most children. Less than a year should be allotted for infants or other young children. Up to two years may be acceptable in cases with complicated circumstances or when children have therapeutic needs best met by a longer stay in a setting such as a residential treatment center. When decisions can be made in less time, the child is offered the promise of permanency rather than the pitfall of lengthy uncertainty.

Time frames relating to the first two parts above will be discussed in this section, whereas those pertaining to the latter three parts will be considered in the appropriate sections later. In general, service agreements should be written with time frames of three-month intervals. Short-term tasks may be given a three-month time frame, short-term goals six months, the decision about a permanent plan a nine-month time frame, and implementation of the plan twelve months. Three-month review times will facilitate progress review and permit making necessary changes.

The time frame for decision-making can be included in the initial statement, which conveys the commitment to permanency planning and a preferred plan, as in the example of Mrs Stoner and Terry above. Time frames for implementation of the plan can also be included in an initial statement. The plan should be stated concisely, and all the elements of the agreement delineated readily and clearly.

A sample initial statement that includes a commitment to permanency planning, a preferred plan, a second option, a time frame for decision-making, and a time frame for implementation follows:

> Family Service Bureau and Mrs Juarez agree that a decision about a permanent plan for Tommy needs to be made in nine months' time. Mrs Juarez wants to provide a permanent home for Tommy and knows that the Family Services Bureau will work with her toward that goal. Mrs Juarez also knows that the Family Service Bureau must evaluate progress and seek another permanent plan for Tommy if agreed upon goals are not met. If Tommy cannot return home, a permanent plan arrangement with his grandmother as legal guardian will be considered. Mrs Juarez and the Family Services Bureau agree that Tommy needs to be in his permanent home within one year.

Goals toward achievement of permanent plan

Another essential element of service agreements is delineation of the goals that must be attained if the preferred permanent plan is to be achieved. Goals should relate specifically to achievement of the agreed-upon permanent plan. When families have other, unrelated goals, these should not be part of the permanency planning agreement, since their achievement or lack thereof would not affect the decision regarding permanency. This does not mean that other goals are inappropriate. For example, a young mother employed as a waitress may wish to take some business school courses in order to secure employment in the clerical field. Although this is a significant goal for the mother, it would not play a role in a decision about her child's permanent placement. Goals such as this one may be verbally agreed upon or written in a separate contract. They should not detract from the emphasis on a child's right to the promise of permanency.

Goals for permanency planning service agreements, when the preferred plan is for a child to return home, will address areas that must change if a child is to live at home. They may relate to a parent's personal struggles, such as those involving alcoholism, depression, or destructive relationships; a parent's environmental situation, such as poverty, lack of housing, job insecurity, or lack of community support; a parent's lack of skill in money management, child care, homemaking, or use of resources; or a parent's relationship with the child. In articulating each of these goals, the worker must ask if its achievement is necessary for a parent to provide permanent care for the child. If not, the goal may reflect a worker's value judgments rather than essential attributes for permanency planning. The worker's appreciation of his or her biases and values is especially crucial in work with clients from other socio-economic, ethnic, or racial groups.

As previously indicated, all goals should be accompanied by time frames. The statement of specific goals and time frames facilitates the decision-making which is a major purpose of the service agreement. Clear goals and time frames also communicate that the service agreement is a tool that will be used seriously in the treatment process.

Goals should be written in simple and specific language defining the *outcome* that is desired. The key question is: What should happen in the family to assure the child of permanency? Although all goals need to be determined according to individual case needs, the following samples may be useful to the permanency planning worker who is learning to write service agreements:

Sample goals regarding a parent's personal struggles
* In six months Mrs Juarez will manage alcohol and drug use to the point that she can responsibly attend to the needs of her child.
* In nine months Mrs Stoner will manage depression to the point that she is available to her child in the morning, so that her child gets to school regularly and on time.
* In three months Mrs Bates will protect herself from beatings that result in hospitalization or physical disability, so that her child can count on her being available on a consistent basis.

Sample goals regarding a parent's environmental needs
* Within three months Mrs Juarez will be receiving benefits from the Aid to Families with Dependent Children program (AFDC).
* Within six months Mrs Stoner will have housing that includes at least two bedrooms.
* Within three months Mrs Bates will have a regular job which she can reach by public transportation.

Sample goals regarding a parent's skills
* Within three months Mrs Juarez will prepare meals that are nutritionally sound.
* Within nine months Mrs Stoner will manage her child's behavior problems in a consistent fashion.
* Within three months Mrs Bates will know how to use city buses to go to the public welfare agency and the housing authority.

Sample goals regarding a parent's relationship with the child
* Within three months Mrs Juarez will enjoy playing with her child and will have expectations that are realistic for a three-year-old.

* Within nine months Mrs Stoner will understand her child's needs better and will be more accepting when her child's behavior reminds her of parts of herself which she dislikes.
* Within six months Mrs Bates will be able to encourage her child's movement toward independence by allowing the child to make small decisions (such as choice of cereal), and by teaching the child to dress himself.

Goals are always stated in positive terms that reflect an optimistic stance. They should not be punitive or judgmental. The temptation to state that a parent will stop being drunk, beating a child, or blaming a child for marital problems should be avoided. Such statements are not action-oriented, are constant remainders of a parent's failures, and cannot form the basis of a therapeutic bond between worker and parent. Parents do not like to be reminded of the unsuccessful past and resent its being used to deprive them of their children on a permanent basis. The service agreement provides the opportunity to put the past aside and make decisions based on the parent's potential to achieve mutually defined goals.

Tasks toward goal achievement

In addition to a permanent plan for a child, goals for achieving the plan, and time frames, service agreements should specify tasks for assuring goal achievement. Tasks are steps that must be taken for a goal to be attained, and they too require time frames. They also require assignment to specific persons, namely, parents, children, workers, or collaterals. If there are tasks for everyone, the service agreement reflects a mutual effort toward achievement of a permanent plan for the child.

As with other parts of the service agreement, tasks should be written in clear and concise language. They should be regarded as the elements most apt to change at times of progress review. Tasks are apt to have the shortest time frames, and may be seen as stepping stones to additional or more complex tasks once they are achieved. For example, as part of a goal to locate suitable housing, a parent's initial tasks would be reading newspaper advertisements and contacting a housing authority. Subsequent tasks might be examining available apartments and checking locations of neighborhood schools. A later task might involve furnishing an apartment. When task achievement is reviewed, new tasks can be added, as appropriate for goal achievement.

Tasks, like goals, should be action-oriented (Maluccio 1981c). This allows participants to work actively toward goal achievement and offers specific guidelines. 'Tell me what I am supposed to do' or 'Nobody ever told me what I was supposed to do' are statements often made by parents who feel frustrated or 'caught in the system'. Clear tasks assignment helps to answer these complaints. The service agreement provides a guide for all.

Time frames for accomplishment of certain tasks can vary, according to what is realistically possible and what is necessary if the preferred permanent plan is to be implemented. What cannot vary is the *inclusion* of time frames, because they add clarity to the agreement and provide a means of measuring progress. For instance, it is better to state that a parent agrees to attend a six-week parenting course beginning on a certain date than to state merely that a parent will attend a parenting course. This facilitates clarity and also implies that the feasibility of achievement has been investigated.

Tasks may be listed according to assignment. For example:

Parent tasks

* For the next twelve months Mrs Juarez agrees to keep weekly appointments with the social worker.
* For six weeks, beginning in one month, Mrs Stoner agrees to attend the parenting classes offered at the community center.
* Beginning immediately, and continuing as long as necessary, Mrs Bates will attend AA meetings at least twice a week.
* By the end of three months Mrs Rodriguez will discuss her disappointments about her child in sessions with the social worker.
* By the end of three months Mrs Lambert will have met with the consulting psychiatrist and will be following her recommendations regarding medication for depression.
* For the next twelve weeks Mrs Forte will meet with the assigned parent aide twice a week and work with her to gain skill and confidence in meal preparation and homemaking.
* During the next three months Mrs Thomas agrees to pick child up at the foster home at noon on Saturday and return child on Sundays at 6 p.m.

In light of the significance of parent–child visiting that we described in Chapter 6, a common parental task is to visit the child, if placed out of the home. Visiting schedules are therefore important parts of service agreements. Because they may need to be detailed and include specific dates, times, and pick-up arrangements, it is often desirable to have a visiting schedule attached to the service agreement rather than incorporated in its body.

Child tasks

* For the next three months *(Bob)* agrees to meet weekly with the social worker.
* Beginning immediately, *(Judy)* agrees to attend school on a regular basis while living in a foster home.
* Within the next three months *(George)* agrees to meet with parents on three occasions to work with them on a list of rules and chores for weekend visits.

The inclusion of child tasks in no way should imply that the child carries full responsibility for being in placement, or that his or her actions can solely determine the decision regarding a permanent plan. In many instances, as with very young children, it may not be appropriate to include tasks for them. Where adolescents are involved and their actions do have an important bearing on a parent's ability to manage, tasks should be assigned to them and incorporated in the agreement. Refusal to attend school, for example, might well be a factor that could prevent an adolescent from returning to the biological home.

Social worker tasks

* Beginning immediately, *(social worker)* will be available to meet with parent on a weekly basis, and will make a home visit once per month.
* Within six weeks *(social worker)* will assign a parent aide to the family to meet with them in the home twice a week for twelve weeks.
* Within three weeks *(social worker)* will obtain the schedule for parenting classes offered at the community center.
* Beginning immediately, *(social worker)* will meet with the child on a weekly basis.
* In three months time, and every three months thereafter, *(social worker)* will review progress with family and collaterals.
* Beginning immediately, and on an ongoing basis, *(social worker)* will keep records designed to assess progress; i.e., records of kept and missed appointment, the visiting schedule with the child, attendance at meetings, and impressions and incidents that can contribute to evaluation of progress.
* Within one month *(social worker)* agrees to write a home visiting schedule for the child for the next three months and to give copies to the parent, child, and foster parents.

Tasks of collateral workers

Tasks for collateral workers may be grouped together or categorized by worker when a particular worker has many tasks. When a parent aide service is used, a separate agreement should be prepared to spell out the elements of that service.

Beginning at the time of placement, *(foster parents)* agree to have the child ready for home visits according to the schedule worked out with the social worker.

* Beginning in six weeks, and once a month thereafter, *(foster mother)* agrees to meet with the parent for one hour to discuss child management.
* In three months time, and then every three months, *(therapist from child guidance clinic)* agrees to attend progress meetings with the parent, social worker, and other collaterals.
* Beginning in six weeks, and for a period of twelve weeks, *(parent aide)* agrees to visit the parent in her home twice a week to work on goals stated in the parent aide agreement.
* Beginning in one month, and once per month thereafter, *(school counselor)* agrees to send the social worker a report on the child's school attendance and academic progress.
* In three months' time, and every three months after, *(parent's lawyer)* agrees to attend progress meetings to be apprised of how the parent is succeeding in meeting goals necessary for resuming care of the child on a permanent basis.

Depending on the situation, other collaterals might be grandparents or other relatives, child care workers, probation officers, private therapists, group home parents, group leaders, and so on. Any party who is participating in the work toward assuring a child the promise of a permanent home might appropriately be included.

Periodic progress review

As a means of facilitating the use of the service agreement for evaluative purposes as well as renegotiation, periodic review meetings should be set for every three months, unless there is a reason for them to be sooner. Participants in review should be the social worker, the family, and significant collaterals. The progress review meeting should be seen as a prominent component of the decision-making process. It should identify areas of progress, as well as lack of progress, in a clear manner.

Time frames for review of progress are essential because they provide a technique for assuring that the reviews occur and thus give the opportunity to talk realistically about the feasibility of achieving the preferred permanent plan. They also offer the chance to make changes in the agreement, as new circumstances may dictate. The review dates make the service agreement a therapeutic tool, rather than another paper exercise for the case record. The dates serve to make both worker and parents constantly aware of the primary goal of permanency for the child. In general, a review date of every three months is recommended.

In the review, progress on the tasks and goals set forth in the service agreement and within stated time frames should be acknowledged. If some progress is made, but not to the expected level in the given time, this too should be noted. When realistic factors such as illness interfere, limited progress may indicate a need to consider alternate options. If tasks have not been completed, this must be recognized, and reasons for lack of progress, when known, should be stated. If opportunities for task achievement have been available, the need to consider other options for permanency must be discussed.

Progress review meetings should focus on decision-making regarding a permanent plan for a child. Parents may need to be reminded that the goals in the agreement must be achieved if a child is to return home on a permanent basis. It may also be necessary to remind them that a child cannot return home unless there is conviction that he or she will be able to remain at home.

When progress has not been made, a parent may be able to consider alternate options. It is at this time that the social worker can tell a parent again that it may be a responsible decision to allow a child to grow up with adoptive parents. Parents sometimes need permission to give up their parental rights, and require help in realizing that the inability to parent does not mean failure as a person. A parent's readiness to recognize limitations and allow a child to have other nurturing parents can be a demonstration of love for the child. Parents may be ready to hear these messages, following structured efforts at goal achievement where tasks and roles have been clear.

The review meeting can also be a time to ask parents how they can be helped differently. They may feel that a social worker or collaterals are impeding progress, or that an additional service or a change in tasks or goals would be useful. These should be discussed and negotiated. It is the responsibility of the social worker or case manager to be certain that all parties remember that their basic mission is for the child to have a permanent plan within the agreed-upon length of time.

In addition, the review provides an opportunity to assure parents of the interest of all parties in assisting them to achieve the goals necessary for the child to remain with, or return to, the parents on a permanent basis. The social worker's attention to time frames, goals, and tasks can assure parents of the worker's commitment to a permanent plan for the child. The review minimizes the chance of a child getting lost in the system, and keeps the parent from being forgotten while others make plans for the child's life (Krymow 1979; Poertner and Rapp 1980). It ensures mutual direction on the part of collaborators; regular, honest reports to parents on their progress; and an opportunity to promote goal achievements by appropriate shifts in focus.

The three-month review is less formal than the six-month case review mandated by Public Law 96-272. As discussed in Chapter 15, the latter is also crucial; it involves administrative and judicial procedures designed to make certain that a child is not being forgotten by the child welfare system.

Appropriate signatures and date

The final component of a service agreement consists of the signatures of the parents and social worker. It is also important for the service agreement to be dated, emphasizing the significance of the time frames. The signing is an acknowledgment by social worker and parents of the content of the agreement and their concurrence with the goals, tasks, and time frames set forth in it. It symbolizes the partnership of parents and social worker and other collaborators in the mission of creating a permanent plan for the child. The mutuality of this goal creates a bond between the parents and the worker that can facilitate progress.

The parents should know that the agreement is not legally binding, but that it could be submitted to court as evidence in making a decision regarding a permanent plan for the child. They should also know that progress in goal achievement will be noted, and could be submitted to the court as part of the process of reaching a decision about a permanent plan. The parents should be aware that use of such information in court can influence the outcome for the child, in a way that favors the parent's desire to care for the child as well as against it. The social worker must emphasize that the permanency planning decision should be one that favors the best interests of the child, but that both worker and parent need to be prepared for the possibility that the court's decision about what is best for the child may not be the one selected by parents and worker.

The signing and dating of the agreement can be the occasion for reiterating the commitment of parent and worker to achieving the promise of permanency for the child. It is a time for being certain that goals and tasks are clear, and for restating that alternate options may need to be considered if goals cannot be achieved.

ADVANTAGES AND DISADVANTAGES

Along with various advantages to which we have alluded thus far, there are disadvantages or difficulties in the use of service agreements. One potential problem has to do with the relationship between client and social worker. As indicated earlier, alliance between client and worker is essential, if the client is to participate in writing an agreement with honesty based on trust in the worker. Such an alliance may be difficult to achieve in the early phase of intervention, which is when agreements must be written in permanency planning. Many parents of children in care or at risk of placement struggle with the issue of trust and are not able to place confidence in their workers immediately. They may therefore give lip service to the whole process, to avoid jeopardizing the chance of their child's returning home. Their concurrence with the social worker may not be based on a true investment in the issues set forth.

Another potential difficulty with service agreements centers around lack of accord about the content of the agreement, particularly the goals. As in social work practice in general, discrepancies in goals and expectations between clients and workers often lead to mutual frustration, resentment, and lack of effectiveness of the service (Maluccio 1979b; Mayer and Timms 1970). When worker and parents can struggle with disagreements and arrive at workable compromises, the chances of success are greater than when clients verbally agree because of their fear of the consequences of challenging the worker. If parents cannot accede to goals essential for a child to be returned home, the social worker should acknowledge the disagreement but point out that parents may have to work on that goal because the court or other authority has identified it as necessary before the child can return home. The social worker should not attempt to 'sell' the goal without recognizing either the disagreement or the legal incentives for compliance. This gives parents the opportunity to express their feelings and eventually reach a decision with full knowledge of the consequences.

Service agreements are also subject to corruption. This occurs when one of the parties has a hidden agenda, or when the terms of the agreement are not shared with all those involved. If such sharing does not occur, opportunity for mixed messages, contradictory actions, and counter-productive communication increases. The importance of dealing directly with disagreements is underlined by Seabury (1979: 35):

> 'An important principle in contracting is that conflict should not be avoided, differences must be teased out and negotiated, and the sooner differences are revealed the better it is for the service process. Even if a conflict cannot be resolved and no contract is agreed upon in the beginning, at least no time and energy will have been wasted on a corrupt contract.'

Finally there is a danger of formulating the service agreement in such a way as to place the burden on the client. This is especially evident when the client is presented with unrealistic expectations; examples would be expecting parents to visit a foster home located many miles from the city when transportation is not available, or expecting parents to find housing without assistance in negotiating the system.

Despite the problems that can surface when service agreements are used, the advantages far outweigh the obstacles. As Brady (1982) observes, the advantages can be summarized as follows:

Clarity of expectations. Writing down the issues early in the treatment process sets clear guidelines for all. Moreover, when there is a progress or court review, clients can use completed contracts to demonstrate efforts at cooperation and positive changes.

Measurement of success. 'Rather than using the nonspecific sentence "You're doing better," the worker can offer some specific feedback to changes already achieved. Lack of progress is just as plain. Conversely, the client can hold the worker accountable for such commitments as visits, referrals, and appointment times' (Brady 1982: 275).

Treatment focus on key issues. There is always a tendency in treatment to bring in all the problems the family might be having. By specifying in writing expectations for changes in areas germane to permanency planning, the central issues become clarified and work can proceed without extraneous interference.

Minimizing drift into foster care. With review dates and renegotiation times set forth, the significance of decision-making is highlighted. Cases move more easily 'either toward closing or more intensive treatment and court action' (Brady 1982: 275).

SERVICE AGREEMENT OUTLINE AND SAMPLE

An outline for a written service agreement and a sample agreement reflecting the principles presented in this chapter follow in this section.

Outline for written service agreement

    I. Participants in this agreement
   II. Mutual commitment to permanency planning
  III. Preferred permanent plan
  IV. Time frames for decisions about permanent plan
      A. Date for decision to be made:_____
      B. Date for decision to be implemented: _____
   V. Goals and time frames for achievement of permanent plan
      A.
      B.
      C.

VI. Tasks toward goal achievement and time frames
   A. Parent tasks:
      1.
      2.
   B. Child tasks:
      1.
      2.
   C. Social worker tasks:
      1.
      2.
   D. Collateral tasks:
      1.
      2.
VII. Periodic progress review meetings:
   1.
   2.
   3.
VIII. Signatures: Parent: _____
                      Social worker: _____
                      Child (if appropriate)_____
                      Other:_____
IX. Date:_____

Sample service agreement – the Shaw family

James Shaw, age ten, and Mrs Shaw had come to the attention of the child protection agency when a neighbor filed a 'Suspected Child Abuse Report'. Investigation revealed that Mrs Shaw often ignored James's inappropriate behavior; was lax in assuring that he was adequately supervised; and at times of frustration would yell, scream, and hit him in an uncontrolled manner. James was inattentive, very active, and impulsive. Mrs Shaw acknowledged her frustration with James and expressed interest in using assistance that would allow her to maintain James at home. James Shaw will enter the Day Treatment Program of Family Service Agency in September 1984.

  I. *Participants in this agreement*
  Mrs Shaw, parent; James Shaw, child; Mr Milner, Family Service Agency worker; and Ms Coty, Child Protection Agency worker.

 II. *Mutual commitment to permanency planning*
  Family Service Agency, Child Protection Agency, and Mrs Shaw believe that James has a right to remain at home on a permanent basis and agree to work together on goals to make that possible. If the goals are not met, a plan other than living with his own family will be sought for James.

III. *Preferred permanent plan*
  The agreed-upon plan is to return James to his home. If this should not be possible, another permanent plan will be chosen.

IV. *Time frames for decisions about permanent plan*
Date for decision to be made: ___June 5, 1985___
Date for decision to be implemented: ___September 4, 1985___

V. *Goals and time frames for achievement of permanent plan*
A. James will remain in Day Treatment for one year, beginning in September 1984, and will re-enter public school in September 1985.
B. Within six months, Mrs Shaw will demonstrate an ability to care for James.
C. Within six months, Mrs Shaw will learn how to discipline James appropriately.

VI. *Tasks toward goal achievement and time frames*
A. *Parent tasks*
Within six months:
1. Beginning in September 1984, Mrs Shaw agrees to keep bimonthly appointments with the agency social worker.
2. Beginning immediately, Mrs Shaw agrees to use means other than physical punishment to discipline her son. Within three months, she will understand and use new approaches such as time-outs and restrictions.
3. Beginning immediately, Mrs Shaw will provide proper baby-sitting rather than leaving James home alone with smaller children.
4. Beginning in September 1984, Mrs Shaw will have James ready to be picked up on Monday mornings, to go to the Day Treatment Program, and be sure that an adult is home when he returns in the evening.
5. By the end of two months, Mrs Shaw will be able to discuss her son's progress or lack of progress in her sessions with the social worker.

B. *Child tasks*
1. Effective immediately, James agrees to leave the house only with his mother's permission, and to return home when asked to do so.
2. By the end of three months, James will have become attentive to his mother's requests, especially when his younger siblings are involved.

C. *Worker tasks*
1. Mr Milner (Family Service Agency worker) will be available to meet with Mrs Shaw individually every other week, beginning September 1, 1984.
2. Beginning in November of 1984, three month progress reports will be sent by Mr Milner to the public agency that referred the child. In addition, monthly phone calls to Ms Coty (worker from child protection agency) will be initiated, to keep her apprised of progress made by the family.

3. Beginning in October 1984, Mr Milner will meet with mother and son once a month.
4. Within two weeks, Mr Milner will provide mother with a list of community resources (with phone numbers) that provide support services.
5. Beginning immediately, Mr Milner will keep records designed to assess progress, such as appointments kept and missed and disciplinary measures taken.

   D. *Collateral tasks*
1. Beginning immediately, Ms Coty agrees to keep in close touch with family and make monthly home visits to support the mother in her efforts, observe the mother's interaction with the younger children at home, and discuss progress.
2. Ms Coty agrees to be present at all review meetings.

VII. *Periodic progress review meetings*
1. December 2, 1984
2. March 6, 1985
3. June 5, 1985
4. September 4, 1985

VIII. *Signatures*   Parent: _____

                    Child: _____

       Social worker: _____

                     (Family Service Agency)

       Social worker: _____

                    (Child Protection Agency)

IX. *Date:* September 1, 1984

SUMMARY

Written service agreements can be a valuable tool in decision-making toward achieving a permanent plan for a child. This chapter covered the use of the service agreement in permanency planning, the process of writing such agreements, their appropriate content, and their advantages and disadvantages. Also considered were the importance of service agreements in clarifying the responsibilities of agency and family in assuring a child of permanency, and how the service agreement can specify goals and tasks clearly to facilitate a working relationship between workers and family, to reinforce decision-making, and to monitor progress. An outline for a service agreement and a sample agreement reflecting principles presented in the chapter were included.

SUGGESTIONS FOR FURTHER READING

Brady, J. (1982) Advantages and Problems of Using Written Contracts. *Social Work* 27 (3): 275–77.

Klier, J., Fein, E., and Genero, C. (1984) Are Written or Verbal Contracts More Effective in Family Therapy? *Social Work* 29 (3): 298–99.

Seabury, B. A. (1979) Negotiating Sound Contracts with Clients. *Public Welfare* 37 (2): 33–8.

Stein, T. and Rzepnicki, J. (1983) *Decision Making at Child Welfare Intake.* New York: Child Welfare League of America, especially Chapter 3.

10 Working with parents

The importance of involving biological parents actively in the helping process has long been recognized in child welfare; in practice, however, there has been insufficient attention to direct work with parents. As noted earlier, particularly in Chapter 6, this is now changing and we are witnessing a resurgence of interest in work with parents, who are increasingly seen as partners in permanency planning for their children (Maluccio 1981a, 1984).

As suggested in earlier chapters, there is an extensive rationale for involving parents, even in situations in which the child must be permanently removed from the biological home. First, there is a strong philosophical orientation to the value of rearing children in a family setting. Second, the importance of the family is supported by theory in such areas as the role of parent–child bonding in the development of human beings, and the significance of the biological family in human connectedness and identity formation. Third, in research as in practice, there is evidence of the negative impact of separation on parents as well as children. And, finally, there are pragmatic reasons for involving parents; a follow-up study of children discharged from foster care by a public children's services agency found that over two-thirds of the children were returned to their parents (Fein et al. 1983). As Fanshel (1981: ix) has noted, biological 'parents are by far the most likely source of permanency for children'.

In order to work effectively with parents, we need to ask a variety of questions: How can we build on the assessment and engagement phases for the purpose of treatment planning? What are the key principles useful in working with parents? What special aspects should be emphasized for permanency planning purposes? How do we know when we have gone far enough in trying to help parents to rehabilitate themselves? This chapter will address these questions, underscoring the prominent role that parents can and should play in the process of deciding where a child should grow up as well as implementing a chosen plan.[1]

BUILDING ON THE ENGAGEMENT AND ASSESSMENT PHASES

In Chapters 7 and 8 we considered the process of formulating a comprehensive assessment and engaging parents and children in a helping relationship. Assessment of the parents' functioning, qualities, and situation contributes to formulation of the treatment plan, whose essence is embodied in the service agreement discussed in the preceding chapter. In accordance with the assessment and the service agreement, in permanency planning the worker and team members engage in a range of activities, including provision of support services (covered in Chapter 12), direct work with the child (discussed in the next chapter), and direct work with parents – the focus of this chapter.

All therapeutic work begins with the first contact between parents and social worker. In permanency planning, the initial steps provide the framework for a working relationship and for the ongoing focus on decision-making about a permanent plan for a child. Worker and family must not forget that decision-making is the single most important task to be accomplished within a stated period of time. Keeping this task constantly in mind, various elements that contribute to its completion may be addressed with the following questions:

*   What style of intervention by the worker is most productive?
*   How is decision-making emphasized?
*   How is the service agreement used?
*   What focus is placed on issues of separation and loss?
*   How can parents be empowered to make decisions and take action?
*   How are parents helped to deal with their ambivalence toward their child?
*   How is the parent–child relationship enhanced?

PRODUCTIVE WORKER STYLE

Permanency planning work requires practitioners to be persistent, well organized, able to tend to detail well, think logically, and employ a variety of techniques. For example, the worker needs to be assertive in working with collaterals. When telephone calls are not returned or reports not received, the worker must persist in getting responses. This becomes important not only because the communication may be vital, but also because it models for parents that the worker is committed to following through on agreed-upon tasks. It can also demonstrate to the parents that the system is not hopeless and there is a point in trying.

In direct work with the parents, a combination of support, confrontation, and honesty leads to the greatest progress. A passive worker who listens in a supportive manner may not succeed in motivating a client to work on necessary tasks or insights. An aggressive worker who does not offer enough support may leave a client feeling hopeless. A blending of honesty, support and confrontation allows the client to feel understood in his or her struggles, while recognizing that progress needs to be made and that appropriate steps are being taken: 'I know that keeping appointments is hard for you because of transportation problems. It concerns me that we aren't meeting regularly because it means that we don't have opportunity to work on the problems between you and your child. Perhaps we can go over the bus schedule once again to be certain that we both understand that this is a reasonable way for you to get here.' Responses such as these are more productive than a simple supportive statement about how hard it is to take buses, a confrontive statement that appointments must be kept, or a simple statement that progress is not being made.

Another example: 'I understand how depressing it can be to look for housing when you've had so many frustrating experiences in the past. I'm concerned because we know that you must have a place to live if your child is to come home on a permanent basis. When we discussed new ways to approach the problem, such as going to the housing authority with a parent aide, you seemed willing to do that. I think it is important that we discuss what happened and whether or not you can follow through.'

Reflection, interpretation, and recapitulation are tools that are part of the social worker's training and should be applied in permanency planning practice. Because time is of the essence, however, these tools may not be sufficient. Again, confrontation and honesty, coupled with support, are essential to facilitate decision-making within specified time frames.

EMPHASIS ON DECISION-MAKING

Social workers are taught to have a central, significant theme in mind during a client interview, and to focus deliberately on that theme. For permanency planning work, *the major theme is that a decision regarding a permanent plan for a child needs to be made*.

Workers cannot remind themselves or parents too often of this need for a decision, and that there is a time frame to be followed. In brief treatment, for example, where one theme is always separation from the therapist after a limited treatment contract, it is necessary to keep track of the number of appointments remaining in a contract (Sifneos 1972). This is done in order to deal with separation from the beginning, so that worker and client will be prepared at the end. Permanency planning workers can deal with the issue of decision-making in the same fashion. A decision may need to be made in twelve months, then in eleven months, and so on. This is not a 'back burner' item in the intervention process. Workers must not wait until month twelve to state that a decision will be made. Decision-making must be regarded as a process, and progress toward its achievement should be reviewed regularly.

USE OF SERVICE AGREEMENT

The service agreement, which was discussed in detail in Chapter 9, is a basic tool in ongoing intervention with a family. It should be employed frequently as a reference for measuring progress, remaining task-oriented, and meeting time frames. Its use is important for both parents and workers. Time can pass quickly and the service agreement can be a constant reminder that there are deadlines. Periodic review of the service agreement indicates whether tasks have been accomplished.

For example, if the service agreement states that a parent agrees to attend a six-session parenting course scheduled for a particular time, a review clarifies whether the parent has done so. If the parent has, the worker is able to be supportive and a discussion of learning from the group can be initiated. If the parent has not attended, the reasons must be examined. The worker will take the opportunity to state honest concern that the parent was unable to complete the task. Reference to decision-making can be made by reminding the parent that a decision for the child to return home may be contingent upon ability to follow through on tasks agreed upon in the service agreement. Questions may be raised about the problem the parent may have had and an alternative plan, such as starting a new course, may be considered and agreed upon.

Most service agreements will contain times for review of progress every three months. These reviews will often include persons other than the worker and the parent, such as representatives from another social agency, foster parents, child care workers, school personnel, supervisors, and lawyers. These should be considered formal times for review, but the worker and parent can also refer to the agreement on a more frequent as well as informal basis. In this way, review meetings will not be as threatening for parents, since they will be clear on the status of their progress. For some parents, review of the service agreement may produce more rapid progress; for others, it might require breaking initial tasks down into smaller steps in order for a parent to feel able to get started.

Reference to the service agreement also facilitates the addition of tasks as early ones are completed. For example, when the task of attending parenting classes has been carried out, it may be important to assign new tasks that help the parent to practice this new learning. Thus, if techniques such as time outs were discussed in the parenting class, a parent's use of the technique when a child exhibits certain behaviors may be initiated.

When frequent review of the service agreement continues to reflect a parent's inability to make progress, it may become apparent that a parent will not be able to offer a permanent home to a child. This can mean that the worker begins to focus on consideration of alternate options. Since parents need a great deal of help in facing this as a potential reality, the process is facilitated if the worker can assist the parent in the early phase of intervention by acknowledging that other plans sometimes need to be considered.

To emphasize the importance of using the service agreement as part of the ongoing work, workers may want to have the agreement available at all interviews with parents. Workers should also be certain that parents have copies of their own, to which they may refer as time goes on. When the worker demonstrates that the service agreement is significant in the treatment process, the parent is more apt to accord it the same importance.

FOCUS ON SEPARATION AND LOSS

Workers are usually prepared to discuss issues of separation and loss when they relate to children. When children are placed away from home, the implications are apparent and readily discussed with parents. Workers explain the fears a child may have; talk of the potential for the child to feel uncared-for, unwanted, or rejected; point out the child's fear of abandonment; and discuss with parents how they can be helpful to their children to minimize the trauma. This is appropriate, in fact necessary, in sound work with children and their families. In addition, issues of separation and loss may be equally traumatic for parents.

Workers also need to be sensitive to the feelings of the parents, particularly those who were in foster care themselves, and who are likely to know all too well how their children are feeling. Parents may even resent being reminded of separation issues, when their own experiences provide an awareness much keener than that of the worker. Workers need to be extremely supportive and demonstrate that they understand the parent's past and present pain. Parents then are more apt to regard the worker's concern about the child's pain as genuine. Otherwise, parents may feel that the worker is scolding them for inflicting such pain on the child. Only if the worker can feel honestly that parents do not want the child to experience the pain they are too familiar with, will the parents feel understood and connected to the worker.

It can be extremely difficult for a parent to allow the child to go, whether on a temporary or permanent basis. The reactions typically experienced by parents include: the arousal of earlier feelings of abandonment in their own childhood; the fears of loss of the child's love; the loss of the child's emotional support; loss of gratification of dependency needs which a child may have met; and feelings of helplessness, guilt, low esteem, failure, and inadequacy. These reactions and feelings have been vividly portrayed by researchers (Jenkins 1981; Jenkins and Norman 1972, 1975) as well as a parent herself (McAdams 1972).

Workers must be able to empathize with these feelings and support parents in experiencing them. Parents need help with these emotions so they can respond to the needs of their children, and give them permission to leave and adjust to new surroundings. Without this permission, children will find it even more complicated to form new attachments in the new setting. When parents can understand this, they bolster their self-esteem with the importance of their role in facilitating the child's adjustment to a difficult situation.

EMPOWERMENT OF PARENTS

It is characteristic of parents whose children are in placement, or at risk of placement, to feel a sense of helplessness or powerlessness. They perceive themselves as victims of a system that controls them, and feel that they have no power over the decisions others are making about their lives and the lives of their children. These reactions can inhibit progress in a number of ways.

First, parents can respond with a sense of resignation. When they feel that their actions will have no impact, it is easy to give up, and depression about their situation can immobilize them. The more prolonged the difficulties, the more helpless parents may feel, and the less hopeful that things will improve. They may feel their past efforts have gone unnoticed and that the same will be true now. Unless they believe that they have some power in the decision-making process, it is unlikely that they will mobilize themselves to make changes.

Second, parents can hold on to these feelings as a way of exonerating themselves. When one has no power in a situation or a decision, one cannot be held accountable. The attitude that 'the system will do what it wants anyway' allows the parent to feel victimized and, in a sense, innocent. Thus, this lack of power can become the parent's strongest defense because it can alleviate guilt and responsibility. It also provides the parent with a legitimate reason for being angry with the system, creating an external target for anger that might otherwise be internalized. Displacing guilt and projecting anger are defenses that permit the parent to derive some secondary gains from feeling powerless.

Workers have a responsibility to acknowledge the feelings parents have and help them regain some power and control. Parents must become convinced that their participation in the permanency planning process is vital, that the decisions to be made are contingent upon the parents' feelings and actions, and that the best decision for a child can only be made when parents participate actively. Past experiences of being excluded from participation can be reviewed and the groundwork for new procedures or coping patterns begun. Workers should talk about how it will be different: 'You felt left out before because you were not invited to meetings where your child was discussed. This time, we will be certain that you are included. In fact, we will ask that you agree to attend because your participation will be essential.' Using past disappointments as a contrast to the present plans will show a parent that the procedures will be different, and rekindle a sense of hope.

The service agreement is another way of restoring the sense of hope and the feeling of some power over what will happen. An agreement about goals and tasks put in writing, and signed by parent and worker, gives the parent a strong sense of active participation. The parent's agreement that certain things must happen for a child to return home is different from simply being told what must happen.

Even when there is disagreement, honest communication is important. For example, a worker and parent may not agree that a parent's drinking is a serious problem which must be controlled if a child is to live at home. Such a disagreement can be recognized, and the worker can inform the parent that a recommendation for the child to return home will not be made if the drinking continues. This allows the parent to make a decision about what to do, knowing the consequences. The outcome is known in advance, minimizing the feelings of outside control and helplessness.

Workers should check with parents periodically about feelings of being victimized. Parents need to be asked if they are satisfied with the way things are progressing. Are there services they would like changed? Is there a different kind of help they would like? For example, if talking with a foster parent about child management is useful, a parent might like to do it more often. Workers should encourage parents to state their wishes, especially in areas where flexibility is possible.

Most of all, parents need to feel that they have a part in the decision-making about where the child will grow up. It must be understood, however, that the actual decision is made on the basis of the opinions of all the parties involved.

Parent, worker, court, lawyers, parent aides, and others may be asked to offer facts and opinions that will lead to a responsible permanent plan for the child. For a parent to feel some power in this process, he or she must know the basis for the decisions and recommendations of others, which can be conveyed through comments such as the following:

* 'The parent aide will be able to recommend that your child go home after you've been able to learn appropriate ways of disciplining.'
* 'The foster parents will be able to talk about your ability to take care of your child if you show that being on time for visits is important to you.'
* 'When I see that you are coping with your depression better, I'll feel that you can care for your child.'

When a parent knows what is expected, in as specific terms as possible, he or she is more likely to be helped to meet them, and can feel more power and hope. As highlighted in the presentation of the ecological perspective in Chapter 6, workers should stress approaches that enable parents to take action on their own behalf (Solomon 1976) and enhance their competence in dealing with environmental challenges (Maluccio 1981a).

When attention is not paid to the feelings of powerlessness, little progress may take place. Parents will be labelled resistant when they simply feel helpless. If workers do attend to these feelings and parents still fail to make progress, there may be a need to address the reality of parental ambivalence toward the child.

DEALING WITH PARENTAL AMBIVALENCE

Often parents are not certain about wanting to care for their children on a permanent basis. The stigma attached to giving up children prevents them from admitting, even to themselves, that they have questions about their ability or desire to care for a child. Ambivalence is common among parents of children in foster care or at risk of foster care, although it is not usually acknowledged.

Ambivalence stands in the way of therapeutic progress because it signifies that a parent does not want to succeed. Ambivalence may be operating when parents stubbornly persist in their feeling of being victimized when efforts are being made to empower them. They may find it more comfortable to blame society for its denial of their parental rights than to admit the socially unacceptable feeling of wanting to be free of their child.

If there are periods when things go better, followed by parental behavior that undoes the improved functioning, again ambivalence may be the problem. For example, a parent may demonstrate consistent management of a child and routine promptness at visits but then disappear for a week or have unusual complaints about the child's behavior. It is not unusual for workers to defend themselves with a device similar to the parent, that is, ambivalence about the appropriate permanent plan.

When workers identify ambivalence, it should be discussed and used for therapeutic purposes (Jackson and Dunne 1981). Parents need permission to admit these feelings, which can then be generalized: 'Often parents feel that life would be better without children'; 'Often parents feel guilty about feeling bothered by children.' Workers should share the information which alerted them to the ambivalence in the parents: 'Even though we've talked of just what you may do to help, you continue to feel helpless. It makes me think that you aren't certain about taking your child home.' The ambivalent behavior observed in parents should be clearly described for them.

Parents then need permission to make a decision not to care for the child. Many parents are not aware they have a right to terminate voluntarily their parental claims. They do not know that this can be a responsible decision, one that reflects their desire for the child to have a permanent home in the child's best interest. Also, parents may not feel comfortable that workers will respect such a decision and respect them for being able to make it. They may not know that they are entitled to continued services and support in their adjustment to the decision, in dealing with their own issues, and in bolstering their self-esteem.

When parents know that workers will continue to care about and respect them and offer ongoing service even if they choose to relinquish a child, they can come to realize that their value as human beings does not rest solely on their ability to be parents. To help parents further, separation from the social worker should not occur at the same time the child is taken from the home. The parent's feelings of separation and loss should be handled with sensitivity to the potential trauma that he or she may experience.

ENHANCING THE PARENT–CHILD RELATIONSHIP

Children who are in placement, or threatened with possible placement, often feel a strong bond with parents, despite the reality of the neglect or abuse. Because it is difficult to regard their parents as unable to care for them, the children resort to defenses that protect them from this reality. It is typical of them to blame the system, as do their parents. They also blame themselves, labelling themselves as 'bad', and promising they will be 'good' if they can go home.

A goal for therapeutic action is for parents to be honest with their children about what has happened. If parents have blamed the children for misbehavior, the parents need to share their own struggles so the children can understand the problems their parents have. The parents also need to talk to the children about their efforts to solve problems that will make it possible for them to provide care.

Consistency and appropriate discipline are areas in which most parents need to make changes. They must understand that consistency is especially important to children who have experienced disruptions in their lives. For children in placement, regular visiting on the part of parents is often the best example to use in talking with parents of the importance of consistency. Parents must learn that if they are expected at a given hour, their children will be waiting at that time and will experience great anxiety if they are late because of the fear that they will not come. If there is an agreement that parents will call the child at a particular time of the week, the parents need to appreciate that the child will be waiting by the telephone. Parents can be helped to understand that consistency is important in rebuilding a sense of trust in their children. In this way, they are not simply being put to some test to prove themselves as fit parents, but are actively participating in the therapeutic program for their children.

Discipline needs to be administered in a consistent manner and in appropriate ways. Parents will often mete out discipline according to their own impulses rather than the child's infraction. Depending on the mood of the parent, a spilled glass of milk will be overlooked or result in a spanking. Parents should be helped to discipline according to the child's behavior rather than their own levels of frustration, in order to give clear messages to the child.

Parents should also be taught that the techniques of discipline should relate directly to unacceptable behavior, so the children can understand that the behavior is unacceptable rather than that they themselves are bad. Thus, it is better to have a child clean the floor dirtied by muddy feet than to deprive the child of television. It makes more sense to give an earlier bedtime to a child who refuses to get up in the morning than it does to take away the child's allowance. Parents can be helped to learn the skill of allowing the punishment to fit the crime in disciplining children.

Sometimes parents do not know how to play with their children or enjoy time with them. Their own lives may not have included such experiences, nor do their childhood remembrances include pleasant memories of play times. Parents should learn that it is acceptable to enjoy playing with children, using their own childlike qualities to enter a child's fantasy world and play 'pretend' games. It can be fun to be silly and giggle, or get on the floor to play cars or house.

Parents may feel so removed from their children, or their own needs are so compelling that the adults are blind to the interests of their children. They may be so involved in telling the children their own troubles that it does not occur to them that the children may have problems to tell them. Workers can help, perhaps by scheduling a parent's visit with a child specifically with the goal of having the parent learn more about the child's activities and interests. Workers, in observing parents with their children, can point out areas of difficulty and help parents interact with the children differently.

When there are particular problems in the relationship between a parent and child, they need to be examined carefully. Parents need permission to talk of their anger with or dislike of a child, in order to understand the reasons for their feelings. The resolution of such feelings can be vital to the success of a permanent plan. Parents should learn that such difficulties are not unique to them, but that they must be faced if things are to get better. Parents may not be aware of the basis for their negative reactions to a child, or they may need help and support to explore the reasons for their feelings.

In working with parents on their relationships with their children, consistency, appropriate discipline, the ability to enjoy children, and sorting out negative feelings about a particular child are important areas to deal with in the therapeutic milieu. Parents, in short, need help to learn, relearn, or strengthen their parenting skills.

Much can be accomplished toward this purpose in individual sessions between worker and parent, in family sessions that include the child or other family members, or in groups with other families. In addition, as discussed in Chapter 12, further assistance often needs to be provided through a range of support services to parents and children, including:

* modeling child-caring behavior by foster parents;
* parenting classes;
* in-home parent aide services;
* public welfare services;
* Parents Anonymous and other support groups of various kinds; and
* resources available in churches, neighborhood centers, and other community agencies.

As will be noted in Chapter 12, all of these can be adjuncts to the sessions with the worker and can be planned to address specific goals delineated in permanency planning.

ENDING WITH PARENTS

Thus far in this chapter we have presented an optimistic perspective on work with biological parents. This is not accidental; there is no doubt that many parents, when approached with care, sensitivity, and skill, will respond positively to the services provided. Some parents will be sufficiently rehabilitated to be able to sustain or resume care of their child, while others will accept their inability to do so and participate in making an alternate permanent plan. There are, however, parents who are not able to respond or who cannot be helped toward rehabilitation. These are the cases in which workers are compelled to ask:

* How far do we go in trying to help the parents?
* When is it time to give up?
* When should we move decisively to make another plan for the child?
* How do we manage to help the family overcome its difficulties within a time scale that does not damage the child?
* How do we balance the parents' needs and at times slow pace of growth with the child's urgent need for permanency in a timely fashion?

These are appropriate questions with which workers frequently struggle. Although there are no precise prescriptions that can be offered, there are certain factors that should be considered in deciding when workers have gone 'far enough' in a particular case. These include:

* a reasonable length of time;
* previous efforts at rehabilitation;
* chronicity of problems;
* history of abuse or neglect;
* parents' investment;

* history of drug or alcohol addiction;
* legal obstacles;
* age of child; and
* predictable outcomes.

Reasonable length of time

A parent's potential to rehabilitate 'over time' is not a sufficient reason for delay in decision-making. There must be an ability to rehabilitate within a 'reasonable length of time', which must be determined on the basis of the child's best interests. As noted early in this book, there is empirical evidence that the longer the placement, the less likely the child is to return home. Currently, it is widely believed that more than two years of 'temporary' placement is too long and that, in general, one year or less is preferable. An exception would be when a child's particular medical or emotional needs require a long period of hospitalization or residential care for the child's rehabilitation.

Case example: Evelyn, age nine, has been in foster care for almost two years. The agreement had been that, within one year's time, a decision would be made about where she would grow up. The preferred option was for her to return home. If that were not possible, adoption was recommended. Evelyn's mother has made some progress in managing her depression. In fact, her worker felt that she would be able to resume care of her five-year-old, who has also been in placement. Evelyn's attachment to the foster parents is growing stronger. She wants to call them 'Mommy' and 'Daddy' instead of Catherine and Richard, as she has referred to them up to now. Catherine and Richard do not wish to adopt Evelyn and are concerned that she have a permanent family soon.

It becomes clear that an extension of time for Evelyn's mother to rehabilitate presents concerns that things will happen that are not in Evelyn's best interests. There is the possibility of a move to another foster home, since the current family is clear in not wanting long-term placement. Evelyn's 'adoptability' may change as she gets older, as her trust of adults becomes more tentative, or as her attachment to the foster family grows. A *reasonable length of time* must be decided upon with these concerns in mind.

Previous efforts at rehabilitation

Where there is evidence that comprehensive services (service agreement, time frames, support services, parent aide services, parenting groups, and so on) have been provided to a family on previous occasions for a sustained period of time (such as one to two years) with no indication of progress, the only value of additional efforts may be to document the inability of the parent to change, especially if the parent is unable to acknowledge the situation. In such instances, no more than six months should be allowed.

Case example: Kara, age ten, is in her fifth placement, a residential treatment center. With each placement, the public agency worker made clear definite plans with Kara's mother regarding regular appointments, visits with Kara, and specific goals that needed to be achieved if Kara were to return home. Goals included mother having a place for her and Kara to live; being able to support Kara (through public assistance, if necessary); and protecting Kara from mother's male friends who had physically abused her in the past.

Mother was unable to demonstrate any efforts to work toward these goals. She changed her place of residence, leaving no forwarding address; failed to keep appointments; and did not visit Kara. After several months she returned, made promises to Kara, renewed her agreement to work toward Kara's return, but then failed to follow through again.

Chronicity of problems

When the family history shows that no stability and dysfunction has been a 'way of life', there is not much optimism about the potential for positive change. When the history reflects no evidence of rehabilitative services provided to the family, such services must be made available, so that the family's readiness to use them can be tested and assessed. If, however there is considerable evidence of the family's inability to use rehabilitative services that have been provided, less time is necessary to document the family's inability to change.

Case example: Tommy is age three. He was placed in a temporary foster home six months ago when his tantrums and night terrors left mother unable to care for him. His mother has never felt 'settled'. While she only feels secure if she has a man to live with, it has never worked well for her with any man. She has suffered repeated physical abuse and has been used, sexually and financially, by men. She has had individual psychotherapy for the past three years, has gone to a woman's shelter on four occasions, and has been in a self-help support group.

It is evident that extreme anxiety about her dependency needs and failure in meeting them successfully is incapacitating this mother and leaves her unavailable to Tommy emotionally. In view of the chronicity of her problems, it is unlikely that she will be able to provide a permanent home for her son.

History of abuse or neglect

When there have been reports of repeated instances of abuse or neglect, it must be assumed that the parent does not abuse or neglect only at times when the child is particularly irritating or when the parent has 'lost his or her cool', but that abuse and neglect are typical patterns of interacting with the child. The parent who does not or cannot change the patterns, following reports to authorities, may not be able to change. If the parent has a history of having been abused or neglected, there is further doubt about his or her ability to rehabilitate.

Case example: Sara, age four, was brought to the emergency room by her mother with a severe cut over her eye. She had 'fallen down the stairs and hit the banister'. When the doctor noticed other scars on her arm, she examined her and discovered welts on her back and legs. X-rays revealed a healed fracture of the collar bone. Mother initially indicated surprise, then confessed that her husband cannot bear to hear Sara cry and 'beats' her. This has been going on for three years. Mother has threatened to leave her husband, but 'forgives' him when he promises it will not happen again. Sara's father grew up in an abusive home.

Parents' investment

If parents feel no need for therapeutic intervention and are unwilling to partici- pate in rehabilitative efforts, and their refusal is not related to feelings about a particular worker, an extended period of time to test progress is inappropriate. This is particularly true if their problems in parenting are severe, reflecting extreme neglect, physical or sexual abuse, alcoholism, or absolute rejection, and the parents are unwilling to examine their parenting styles and personal problems.

Case example: George, age eight, was placed in a foster home six months ago because of aggressive behavior in school. His parents were angry about his behavior, stating that he was just as bad at home. They asked that he be 'put somewhere to find out what was wrong with him.' While they have taken him home for weekend visits every six weeks, they have refused to keep appoint- ments themselves, maintaining that they are good parents and that they had no problems with their three other children, who are now grown. They maintain that George is the one who needs help, and that they will take him home when he is 'better'. George is eight years younger than the next child in the family, was not planned, and has 'always been a problem'; his parents admit never wanting or liking him.

History of drug or alcohol addiction

When there is a parental history of long-standing, incapacitating drug addiction, and treatment has been refused, a good prognosis is doubtful. If the addiction is denied, there is less hope.

Case example: Carla, age fourteen months, has been in a foster home since birth, when her twenty-eight year-old mother could not care for her. Her mother has been addicted to heroin since age eighteen and was unable to care for her first two children, who have been living with her older brother and his family. While she has participated in detoxification programs on four different occasions, she has never stuck with any one for the full thirty days and has always returned to drug use within six months. She says she wants to care for

Carla and is about to begin a detoxification program. She has never followed through on previous recommendations for therapy.

Legal obstacles

Judges often decide how much time is enough to allow parents to rehabilitate. If workers fear too much time will be allowed, it is crucial to have clear service agreements, specific time frames, and accurate documentation of events. All of this helps to remove possible legal obstacles to permanency planning.

Age of child

In general, the younger the child, the more quickly a decision needs to be made. Children should not have to wait until their age makes them undesirable candidates for other permanent plans, such as adoption.

Predictable outcomes

Outcomes that are reasonably predictable should require minimal time for decision-making about a permanent plan. Examples include: the severely retarded parent who will never understand appropriate child care; chronic psychosis where long-term hospitalization or only marginal self-care is predicted; terminal illness of a parent.

Conclusion

In each situation workers need to consider a variety of factors in resolving the complex issue of when to terminate efforts with parents. Here again, the service agreement can be an effective means of documenting when sufficient efforts have been made or when the parents have gone as far as they can. Through systematic, therapeutic use of the service agreement, workers and parents can recognize when goals have been achieved, when there is reason to renegotiate new or additional goals, and when it is time to stop because the parents have demonstrated that they are unable to effect change or make use of the service. In some of these situations, as discussed in Chapter 15, termination of parental rights needs to be pursued.

SUMMARY

This chapter has focused on working with biological parents, building on the process of engagement and assessment as well as the service agreement considered in preceding chapters.

Special aspects of intervention discussed were: productive worker style; emphasis on decision-making; use of the service agreement; focus on separation and loss; empowerment of parents; dealing with parental ambivalence; and enhancing the relationship between parent and child. In addition, various concerns in relation to ending with parents, particularly if little or no progress is being made, were considered. The emphasis throughout the chapter was on the positive aspects of involving parents in decisions about their children, and giving them every opportunity to participate in the permanency planning necessary for their youngsters' stability.

NOTE

1. For an excellent discussion of parental involvement in foster care agencies, see Blumenthal and Weinberg (1984), which was published following completion of our manuscript.

SUGGESTIONS FOR FURTHER READING

Bryce, M. and Lloyd, J. C. (eds) (1981) *Treating Families in the Home*. Springfield, IL: Charles C. Thomas.

Horejsi, C. R., Bertsche, A. V., and Clark, F. W. (1981) *Social Work Practice with Parents of Children in Foster Care – A Handbook*. Springfield, IL: Charles C. Thomas.

Maluccio, A. N. and Sinanoglu, P. A. (eds) (1981) *The Challenge of Partnership: Working with Parents of Children in Foster Care*. New York: Child Welfare League of America.

Maluccio, A. N. (1984) Permanency Planning: Implications for Practice with Natural Parents. *Adoption and Fostering* 8 (4): 15–20.

Maybanks, S. and Bryce, M. (eds) (1979) *Home-Based Services for Children and Families*. Springfield, IL: Charles C. Thomas.

Sinanoglu, P. A. and Maluccio, A. N. (eds) (1981) *Parents of Children in Placement: Perspectives and Programs*. New York: Child Welfare League of America.

11 Working with children

Permanency planning work with children must emphasize the need for a decision to be made about where a child will grow up. Work with children, as with their parents, must proceed with this focus in mind. This chapter, therefore, will cover direct practice with children as it should proceed when the focus is on making a decision about the child's permanent placement. It will highlight issues that must be addressed to support the decision-making process as well as implementation of a permanent plan.

INTERVENTION WITH A PERMANENCY PLANNING FOCUS

A typical referral to a child guidance clinic is that of a child living in a foster home who is presenting behavior problems in school. In response, the clinic worker is likely to attend a school conference, prescribe individual treatment for the child, and see the foster parents on occasion to discuss appropriate child management techniques. The individual treatment might be supportive in nature and include a behavioral approach. Therapeutic goals might focus on the child's feelings about placement, wishes to be at home, issues of separation and loss, and guilt. The overall purpose would be to enable the child to make a more adequate adjustment to the foster home placement.

Although these responses may be appropriate, practice in such cases often neglects to focus on the child's need for permanency. The question of where the child will grow up may not even be raised. The status of the biological parents may not be discussed beyond considering them unable to care for a child, and their involvement in the helping process may not be contemplated. The symptoms are treated and the child may feel better, but the underlying issue of permanency is not addressed. In all work with children this issue must be kept in mind constantly.

As in practice with children in general, intervention within a permanency planning framework should offer support and create a therapeutic environment that allows the child to develop and use the relationship to work out concerns, worries, fears, angers, and confusion. Building on their work with the child in the engagement and assessment phases as well as the service agreement discussed in preceding chapters, workers need to consider a variety of issues of particular importance for permanency planning purposes:

* honesty with the child;
* confidentiality;
* guilt;
* loss and separation;
* use of Life Story Books;
* visits with parents; and
* acceptance of reality.

These issues will be discussed in the rest of this chapter.

HONESTY WITH THE CHILD

Consider the following excerpt from an interview with a child about to move from a residential placement to a foster home:

Worker: Do you remember what we talked about last week?
Child: Uh, huh.
Worker: Tell me what.
Child: About me going home.
Worker: About you going to a foster home. Remember? Mrs H's house. What did I say?
Child: I forgot.
Worker: OK. I am going to tell you again. Listen to me. It may not be easy to hear because you don't want to hear it, but there is a plan for you which we think is the best plan right now and the plan is that you'll be going to Mrs H's house and you'll be going to public school in September.
Child: I know. I didn't want to ask when I am going to go home with my mother.
Worker: You know, we're not sure when you're going home with your mother. The plan right now is that in two weeks from today you're going to go to Mrs H's house and stay there for a while.
Child: And then I'm going home?
Worker: And then we still are not sure. It all depends on your mother and how she is doing. How do you feel about that?
Child: Sad.
Worker: You feel very sad because you wanted to go home really badly, didn't you?
Child: What year am I going to go home?

This excerpt portrays a worker's attempt to be honest with a child about the plans that are being made. It falls short in that it does not answer the child's basic question about permanency. The child wants to know the date for returning home. One might guess, from the content, that there is no certainty that the child will go home at any point. It is important to be honest with the child about the process and about the possibility of a permanent plan separate from the biological parents.

In the excerpt cited, time frames for decision-making evidently had not been established. The child should have been told that a time for making a decision would be set. In addition, the worker might have stated that it is important for children to have one place to grow up and to know where that place is. If the child had been informed that everyone was going to work hard together for six months, and at the end of that time a decision would be made about a plan to return home or grow up in another home, the youngster might have felt reassured about being included in the process.

It is also essential to be honest with the child about what must happen in order to return home. Workers, in their own words, need to convey to the child messages like the following:

'Your mother needs to have a place to live that is her own, because there are too many fights where she lives with her friends. Your mother has a problem with drinking and when she drinks too much, she isn't able to take care of you well enough. We hope your mother can solve these problems because you want to be home and she says she wants you home.'

'We can't wait a very long time because you need to know where you will grow up. If things aren't better in six months' time, then it will be necessary for you to have a home with a new family. You will know what will happen in six months' time, and in a year's time you will either be home with your mother or you will be with new parents who will adopt you.'

It is most effective if parents themselves also can communicate to their children the ideas just described. Of course it is difficult for parents to do so. Most of them understandably prefer to promise children that things will be better, and often workers must help parents speak honestly with their children about permanency. Sometimes workers need to explain to children that it is hard for parents to talk about their troubles because they wish the problems were not there.

It can be as difficult for workers as for parents to be honest with children; they may prefer to tell them that everything will be fine, or to leave things up in the air. Workers must examine their own comfort with the honesty children deserve and increase their skills in this critical area of the treatment process.

CONFIDENTIALITY

In traditional psychotherapy, the therapist often speaks of confidentiality in the first session. The child is informed that whatever is said stays in the room and is just between the therapist and the child. In permanency planning it is not realistic to offer such a promise of confidentiality to children. The fact that a momentous decision must be made about where a child will grow up means that communication among permanency planning team members is essential.

Children need to know that when the important decisions are made about where they will grow up, all pertinent information must be considered by the appropriate parties. They must be told that things that happen at home are significant; that secrets cannot be kept about their getting hurt or being left alone; that information about the things going well is necessary too; and that all information is used to help make the best decisions about where they will grow up. They should be made aware that the sharing of relevant information can assist their parents in their efforts to care for their children.

Workers should mention that a child may fear punishment as a result of sharing certain incidents. When possible, this can be discussed in the presence of both child and parents, with an agreement made that children will not be disciplined as a result of sharing information. Children can be told that they may want to know how their parents are doing and that they have a right to ask and to be told. For instance, if a goal for a parent is to find appropriate living quarters, the child has a right to know how the parent is progressing. It can help children to know that this kind of confidentiality works both ways. Just as others need to know how things are going for children, so children need to know how things are going for parents.

Children can still be offered assurance of confidentiality in the sense that they will not be quoted. For example, a child may share information that conveys a particular feeling. It may be necessary to let others know that the child feels frightened when left alone with mother's boyfriend, while not sharing the specific content of the child's conversation. The child can know that this will help the worker to work with the mother so that the latter can understand things better.

Most children will accept an honest agreement about confidentiality, which offers them something that is credible and that can be a first step toward building trust in the future.

GUILT

Because of their fragile self-esteem, their experience of being blamed, and their actual misbehavior, children who come to the attention of permanency planners typically feel responsible for and therefore guilty about their potential or actual placement, believing they have caused it. These feelings are reinforced when parents attribute the need for placement to the child's behavior.

When children have some understanding of their parents' inadequacies, they may also feel guilty because they have not assisted their parents enough. They feel that they could have prevented the disruption if they had been more helpful. Some children may assume that it is their job to hide their parents' inadequacies, and feel guilty because they have not protected their parents from exposure. Often children have been instructed by parents to take care of them, have been blamed for causing trouble, and have been described as unmanageable. They feel bound by their love for their parents, yet compelled to cry out for help.

Workers need to recognize these feelings and listen to the children. At the same time, children should not be reassured prematurely about their lack of involvement in the problem. They need to sense that workers understand how responsible they feel, and they need assistance to absolve themselves. Workers can help children think about how they might have handled things differently or realize that good options were not available. They can be assured that, whatever actions they might have taken, something needed to be done so that aid could be made available to the family.

Eventually, workers can point out that the children were expecting themselves to act as mature adults, an unrealistic expectation. As children are able to feel less responsible for what has happened, they may begin to recognize the anger they feel about their parents' inadequacies or rejection. This anger also needs expression, and parents require help in accepting it as a natural way for children to feel when parents are not able to care for them on a consistent basis.

It is a long-term process for children to move from guilt to anger and then to an acceptance of their parents as persons who want to be good parents but lack the ability to do so. We all know adults who are stuck at a point of self-blame or blaming parents. It is perhaps naive to hope that young children can succeed in reaching a point of mature understanding and acceptance. Workers can, however, acknowledge a child's current feelings, and comment on how things will seem different as time goes on, in ways such as the following:

* 'Right now, you feel mad at your mother because she can't take care of you. Sometime later, you may not feel so angry because your mother may be able to explain it to you more.'
* 'You are understandably very angry because your mother can't take care of you. We want to help you so that you are not so angry that you won't allow someone else to love and care for you.'

The suggestion that there will be a time when things will be different can offer the child a sense of hope. Being told that a time will come when they will feel better can help provide children with the motivation to struggle toward growth, despite the pressure to feel depressed, regress, or become fixated. Children should be assured that an important part of helping them to feel better is the making of a decision about where they will grow up: 'Once you know where you will grow up, it will be better for you. You won't have to worry about changes anymore, and that's important for children.' It is urgent for both workers and children to recognize there is a process involved in making things better and that the process can take a long time.

LOSS AND SEPARATION

Loss and separation are key issues for children just as for parents, especially when the permanency plan is for living away from the biological parents (Moss 1966). The impact of separation can be the same regardless of the reason for it. Children are not apt to understand rational explanations for separations. They simply feel the pain that separations bring. The pain can be as great with the parent ill and in the hospital as when the parent has abandoned the child. The fears that accompany the pain can also be enormous, regardless of the reason for the separation.

When children experience separations, particularly those for which there has not been careful planning, they feel the pain of the loss of the person and are frightened about the potential permanency of the separation; they may not understand the time limits of a temporary separation; they feel abandoned, unloved, and all alone; and, most of all, their ability to trust is threatened.

Everyone has experienced a separation at some point in life. People cope with separation, and life goes on. When a parent is absent in a planned way and for a specified time, things often return to normal when the parent returns. Regressed behavior on the part of the child soon disappears, and the child's sense of trust is not seriously damaged. Subsequent, planned separations are less traumatic; children learn that such separations are temporary, that the parent does return, and that substitute care is provided.

On the other hand, experiences with separation may have been different for children who require permanency planning. Separations from their families were probably unplanned. Adequate substitute care may not have been readily available, and the time limits may not have been known. Explanations for the separations may not have been given, and the separations may have been frequent rather than infrequent. The effect of any of these conditions can be traumatic.

With each separation, the child's ability to trust adults may diminish. Children may develop stronger needs to control their environments, so as to avoid feeling totally helpless. It becomes easier to avoid attachment, lest another separation be faced. A child may even adopt a pattern of forcing a separation just to avoid its anticipation. With each new placement, the capacity to relate and to trust is lowered further. Eventually, the child is defined as not a suitable candidate for living in a family setting, because he or she cannot tolerate the demands for intimacy. The system has indeed created a monster! The danger of such a reaction to separation is one of the most prominent reasons for early decision-making about permanent homes for children.

When dealing with issues of separation and loss, perhaps more than with other issues, workers must carefully examine their own comfort with the accompanying feelings. The tendency of workers to avoid talking of loss and separation is common, since such conversations are likely to upset children, and most of us are reluctant to do that. Moreover, such discussions may be painful because they reactivate workers' own experiences around loss and separation. Because children are not likely to initiate such conversations, the process of denial is perpetuated. With this awareness, workers must be willing to grapple with separation and loss and to be forthright with children while they struggle with their own accompanying feelings.

Principles and techniques for helping children cope with separation and loss in situations such as adoption and foster care have been described by Fassler (1978) and Jewett (1982) among others. Above all, workers need to empathize with children as the pain of separation is acknowledged. They can recognize that children who have had to move are not happy about it; that they can feel frightened it will happen again; that they can worry about what will happen next; and that they can feel unsure about getting close to someone again.

Even if children deny these feelings, the worker is giving them permission to feel as they already do. Workers can also talk of how confusing it is when there are a lot of changes of places to live and when they have lived with a number of different people. Children should be told that it helps to know all about where they have lived and who the important people have been in their lives. A helpful tool in facilitating the child's understanding is the Life Story Book, which is increasingly being used in permanency planning.

LIFE STORY BOOKS

A Life Story Book is an informal book that depicts major events in a child's life in writing, pictures, and drawings. The book is usually put together jointly by the worker and the child, along with participation by other significant persons when appropriate. The process of creating a chronicle of the child's life not only connects his or her past and present life experiences but also helps develop a more positive self-image (Aust 1981). Various authors have described the uses of a Life Story Book and explained how to construct one (Aust 1981; Backhaus 1984; Beste and Richardson 1981; Wheeler 1978).

Making a Life Story Book can promote a sense of history for a child, facilitate a developing sense of identity, and provide an arena for reviewing past events. The process of creating the Book can take a long time, perhaps months, and should proceed at a pace that is comfortable for the child. In addition to providing factual information, it offers children the opportunity to remember how they felt when certain events were occurring.

The Book should be accurate in its explanation of events that have transpired, and misconceptions can be corrected in the process. Workers will want to phrase things in as objective a manner as possible, leaving judgments for children to make. For example, the Book could state the child's mother's age when the child was born but not that the mother was too young. It might note that the parents were divorced because they had a lot of fights, but no judgment about blame would be included.

The Book should incorporate information about parents that is neutral and positive. For children who are not returning home, a description of the biological parents can be included, with pictures if possible. The interests, talents, and occupations of parents can be listed and children can be encouraged to take pride in the positive attributes of their parents. Children should be told the Book will be theirs to keep forever, so that they will always be able to hold onto significant memories.

When children have lived in many places, each one can be identified with a date and related pictures of houses, schools, foster parents, significant child care-takers, acquaintances, and important neighborhood places. All of this assists the child in understanding what the past has been, and gives the worker the opportunity to convey appreciation of how difficult it can be to have lived in so many places.

Because children are not apt to have accurate information themselves, the worker needs to collect many details from various sources in order to assist the child with the Book. Parents can be supported to involve themselves by giving information, providing pictures, or describing what some events were like, thus participating in the child's development in a substantial way. Sometimes workers will need to seek information from relatives or foster parents. Sometimes children can benefit from going back and revisiting former places where they have lived; this can help make their memories more real and also facilitate their ability to move on to new settings.

As with most biographies, the Life Story Book will start with the child's name, date of birth, names of parents, and place of birth, and then proceed with the life story up to the child's current age. While the finished Book will record the child's life in sequence, the child may wish to work on it out of sequence. It may be more comfortable to start with the present, or with some period of life that was a less threatening time. Workers need to be sensitive to the child's level of comfort, keeping in mind that the making of the Book is an integral part of the therapeutic process.

A Life Story Book should always reserve a space for the future, which becomes the place for indicating what the child's permanent home will be. When a child is to return home, comments can be made about what has transpired to make the return possible, and the intent to have this plan be permanent.

When the permanent plan is adoption or long-term foster care, the future space can describe the new family. Adopting families can be helpful in supplying information and pictures that can be included as the child and worker talk about the future. The whole process provides the opportunity for the child to review the past, gain a better sense of identity, and acquire some optimism about the future.

Life Story Books can be made of construction paper covers with plain paper for writing, drawing, and pasting pictures. If possible, photo albums with plastic-covered pages are preferable because the Book can be better preserved. When photographs of significant people are not available, children can be invited to draw people as they remember them, or write or dictate a description. Their active participation in making the Book is important. To prepare the Book for children deprives them of the therapeutic benefits of the process and of the potential pride in the finished product.

Children differ in their capacities to participate in the Life Story Book process, and workers need to judge the appropriate level for each child. While the Book can be appropriate for any youngster, the child's interest and ability to participate will vary with age. Children between six and twelve years of age are the easiest to engage because of the appeal of making something. For younger children, particularly those who will have a permanent plan separate from biological parents, the Book is important for them to have as a reference in later years. While their actual participation in putting together the Book may be limited, its value should not be minimized.

The interests of adolescents is unpredictable; some may become thoroughly engaged in a Life Story Book project while others will openly rebel. For some adolescents, an 'in vivo' experience may serve the same purpose. For example, when a fifteen-year-old foster child who had not seen her mother or father for eight years began raising questions about her past, the worker and child set off on a day's excursion (camera in hand) to the area where the child remembered living. The child was able to recreate her past by stopping in familiar places in the small town where she had once lived. She even asked people in a familiar coffee shop if they knew her mother and was able to learn that her mother had lived in a particular apartment but had moved from the area. She learned of siblings living with their paternal grandmother in another part of the country, and a second excursion was planned. On the way home, it was possible to visit with her first foster family. While none of this ended up in a Book, the child did have pictures and did gain some connection with her life story.

Workers sometimes need to be imaginative in creating ways to accomplish the goal of the Life Story Book: facilitating a child's perception of the past so that a sense of continuity is established and the present can be better understood and accepted.

VISITS WITH PARENTS

As indicated in earlier chapters, the value of parental visiting with children in out-of-home placements has been demonstrated through research findings as well as practice experiences (Colon 1978; Fanshel 1975; Fanshel and Shinn 1978; White 1981). Whether a child will be returning home or not, regular visits with the biological parents are essential to the permanency planning process for a number of reasons, even in cases in which it is likely that parental rights will be terminated.

In the past, visiting between parents and children in placement was approached tentatively. There was conviction among workers that the child needed time to adjust to the placement. Visits were seen as interfering with the adjustment, were usually delayed for at least a month, and then were scheduled only gradually. Without the framework of a permanency planning philosophy, the duration of the placement was not an initial concern; work with biological parents was not given priority; long-term foster care was an accepted plan for many children; and time frames were not crucial. In contrast, permanency planning philosophy and goals do not allow time to delay visitation. There is less emphasis on the need for the child and parent to separate in order to adjust, and greater attention to the need for them to work actively toward a permanent reunion.

Regularly scheduled visits are valuable, as a means of helping the child maintain his or her sense of connectedness and identity with the biological family. Even when children cannot live with their biological parents, they continue to belong to them. This is particularly true when children are living in 'limbo', that period in which there is grave uncertainty about where they will grow up, that state of feeling that they belong to nobody. Regardless of the outcome, their sense of roots and heritage should be theirs to keep. This identity is best preserved when regularly scheduled visits are planned and encouraged.

Visits are also useful as a way of keeping parents and children aware of what is happening and the reality of their situation. When there are long periods of no visitation, both children and parents can lose sight of the true state of their affairs. Memories become fuzzy and conflicts can be forgotten. Both can begin to think that things are fine, that there was no need for the separation. These feelings are based on the fantasies that can develop when there is absence of contact. Frequent visits help maintain, for child and parent, a sense of how things really are. Children, in particular, want to think of their parents in positive ways and can refuse to accept what others tell them. Regular contact is essential for them to develop a realistic picture of their parents' strengths and weaknesses.

Additionally, regular contacts provide parents and children with the opportunity to try out new styles of relating. For example, if a parent is learning a more consistent method of child management, it is important that he or she have opportunity to interact with the child to put it into practice. Greater sensitivity and responsiveness to the child's needs can only be demonstrated when there is an opportunity to interact with the child.

With frequent contacts the worker will be better able to assess progress. A parent can describe how a visit went; a child can talk about the time together; foster parents can observe a child's attitudes about anticipating a visit and returning from one, as well as the interaction between child and parent when the child is picked up; and workers can observe the parent–child interaction in the context of family sessions. Since the quality of the relationship between parents and children is crucial to the decision about a permanent plan, an opportunity must be provided for parent and child to work on the problems in that interaction.

The capacity of parents to make and keep commitments to visit their children should also be assessed. Parents who are not able to give priority to such a commitment may be indicating that they cannot delay personal gratification in order to respond to the needs of the child. For some parents, this can be an educational process; they can learn how vital it is that they honor commitments made to their children.

Regular visiting is also instrumental in assuring parents of the agency's commitment to work toward a permanent plan with them. It emphasizes their participation in the decision-making process, and keeps them vividly aware of their responsibilities as parents, as they must plan for their children on a regular basis.

There can be situations when visiting is inappropriate. When a parent's home environment is such that a child is not guaranteed protection, it is unsuitable for the child to visit home. If a parent appears for a visit intoxicated, the child should not be allowed to go with the parent. If a parent comes at other than a scheduled, agreed-upon time, it may be inappropriate to allow a visit to take place. When these or other conditions make it impossible to allow parents to take children home for visits, efforts should be made to have structured and supervised visits in the foster home or office. The goal would be to progress to the point where parents can responsibly take children home for visits.

The terms regarding visitation must be clear for workers, parents, children, foster parents, and other staff members involved, and should be spelled out in the service agreement discussed in Chapter 9. All parties, including the children, need to know that parents cannot visit if they are not sober; that visits must take place at agreed-upon times; that children must be returned at the specified hour; and that they cannot be taken to places considered unsafe, such as the mother's house, when her boyfriend, who is known to be abusive, is present. Children can be helped to understand that parents sometimes have to make hard decisions in order to care for them properly, and that they have a right to be protected. If parents cannot provide the necessary protection, children need help in understanding and accepting this reality.

The purpose and pattern of parent-child visiting are related to the particular plan for that child. For instance if a child in foster care is to return home within a year, the visitation in the last few months of the placement continues as preparation for the return. On the other hand, if the decision is that the child cannot return to the biological parents, another permanent plan must be made. At that point, visits with the biological parents should focus on termination of that relationship, so that the child can be prepared to become engaged with new parents. Visits with new parents should begin by the end of nine months and increase until the time of the permanent placement.

Whenever possible, children should visit parents routinely on weekends, particularly when the goal is for the child to return home. The overnight visit guarantees that parent and child will have a sustained period of time together and provides a long enough opportunity for assessment. The traditional hour in the park followed by ice cream cones gives unrealistic or false impressions of how things are going.

In placing children, workers should bear in mind the accessibility of the foster home to the biological family. A rural foster home away from a bus line can be exceedingly difficult for a parent to visit if the parent has no car. It may be impossible for a parent, especially one who has few friends or resources, to arrange transportation on a regular basis. Unless workers take such practical matters into consideration, the parent – and the plan – can unwittingly be set up to fail. In many cases, workers need to assist parents actively in their efforts to visit. Foster parents may need to bring children to bus stops to greet parents. Children may need to be transported to a central agency location where parents can pick them up.

It does not make sense to set up impossible tasks for parents, particularly for those who are struggling to function at minimally adequate levels. When workers do set up such impossible tasks, they need to examine closely their own feelings. For instance, do they hope or wish that a permanent plan separate from the biological parents will be necessary? Parents have a right to rehabilitation, and workers have a responsibility to offer them aid in their efforts.

Finally, foster parents and other caretakers such as child care workers can play a vital role in enhancing the child's ability to handle visits, separations, and new relationships. Children need their support and encouragement. When foster parents understand their role in the permanency planning process, they are better able to help children with visiting. Well-trained foster parents will share in the belief that, when possible, the biological family is the best permanent plan for a child. They will be committed to working for that plan and accepting parental involvement in the process. They welcome parents when they come to visit their children, involve parents in decision-making whenever possible, and willingly discuss child management with them.

Trained foster parents accept the reality that children belong to the biological parents. They share in the parents' and child's pleasure when things go better, and do not compete with the biological parent for ownership of the child, or for the child's favor. Their commitment is time-limited, and children and parents know this. Thus, they are pleased when children and parents are able to share holidays, and have good feelings when weekend visits at home go well. There are disappointment and empathy when things do not go well. Foster parents can be assisted by agency training and by the worker to cultivate such an orientation to encourage and reinforce comfortable visiting as an integral part of permanency planning.

ACCEPTANCE OF REALITY

One of the functions of workers in permanency planning is to help children accept the reality of their situations. Reality is not always a situation the worker or child likes. A child's parents may not be able to provide ongoing care; or, if parents can provide ongoing care, the environment may be far from ideal. It may be necessary that a child grow up in other than a family setting. Whatever the reality, the intent should be that the plan which is worked out is permanent.

In using the permanency planning process, workers should feel assured that efforts were made to obtain the best plan for a child, even if the plan is not ideal. Children, because they have been a part of the process, will have some understanding of why things turned out as they have. Workers will need to be sensitive to the disappointment children experience, acknowledging the hope that matters might have turned out differently.

When permanent plans are for placement with caretakers other than the biological parents, there usually is a court hearing for the termination of parental rights. This too can be helpful to children in their struggle to accept reality. Workers can tell children it is important to give a judge all of the information, and that it is the judge's responsibility alone to make the decision. In addition, as indicated in Chapter 4, children themselves, especially older children, should be involved in reaching a decision regarding the permanent plan that is best for them.

If we are to engage children successfully and gain their trust, we must assure them they will be listened to (Kufeldt 1984). Children, particularly older ones, have thoughts about the best way for them to grow up (Festinger 1983: 281–82). There are many teenagers, for example, who need to be away from home, temporarily or permanently. Some may become temporary members of a friend's family; some may run away and become part of a communal living arrangement; and others may be allowed to choose boarding school arrangements. The causes and outcomes vary, but many pre-adolescents and adolescents have an understanding of their own needs and capacities to adjust.

Children can make responsible contributions to decisions about:

* the frequency of visitations while in placement;
* the ability to carry a load of responsibility in order to remain in a home where parents tend to be disorganized;
* choices between boarding school and foster home, foster home and group home, adoption and foster care, or open adoption and a complete break with the biological family; and
* choice of a responsible relative with whom to live.

It is possible for a child to come up with an option that others have not considered. Participating in decision-making will give the child a greater investment in making the decision work out well.

The following case example illustrates how persistent children can be in getting adults to listen to their thoughts.

John is thirteen and has lived with his adoptive parents for three years. His 'final' goodbye was said to his biological parents when he was eight and in a foster home while a decision was being made about where he would grow up. He is brought to the outpatient clinic for counseling by his adoptive parents because of 'behavior difficulties'. The underlying problem is that John has never felt attached to his adoptive parents and constantly talks about returning to his biological parents. Clinically, it appears that adolescence has raised questions for John about identity issues, and curiosity about being unable to live with his biological parents.

John had a Life Story Book which he was asked to bring in. The worker also was able to talk with the original adoption worker and learn that parental rights had been terminated voluntarily because of the biological mother's severe rejection of John. In reviewing the Life Story Book, John could not accept the statement that his parents had trouble with three children: 'I know lots of families that have more than three children.' John listened while the worker talked of how it can happen that there are families for whom it can be difficult to have another child. John acted resigned to the 'fact' that he could not see his biological parents or return to them.

It soon became clear, however, that John had been simply placating the adults with his acceptance that he could not be with his biological parents. He now announced that he did not wish to stay with the adopting parents, that he would not even try to behave there, and that he needed a new family. Although the adopting parents tried to 'live through' this phase, John's negative behavior escalated to the point that they agreed John could leave.

The adoptive mother asked if it were possible for John to see his biological parents. She felt it might help him, recognizing that a move to another family would not help because his past was still not resolved for him. The worker agreed, contacted the biological parents, learned that John had been very much on their minds, and heard that they were eager to see him. They felt they had gained some insight into the mother's feelings about him as an infant and as a child, indicated that they gave him up because they did not feel able to give him the love he needed, and felt that they could explain this to John. They raised the question about being able to take John back but agreed with the worker that it was too early to even consider. A visit was set up.

When John saw the worker prior to the visit, he said: 'I don't know why everyone is giving my mother credit for the idea of this visit. I've been saying it all along.' The worker could only comment that the important thing was that his mother listened to him and helped the visit to happen.

At this point, John has agreed to delay his request to leave the adoptive home until he knows how he feels after the renewed contact with his biological parents. While the outcome is not known, there is optimism that it will not be a series of placements with no resolve.

SUMMARY

This chapter considered direct work with children, as it should proceed when the focus is on determining and implementing a permanent plan. It highlighted the special issues that must be addressed in intervention with children, including honesty; confidentiality; guilt; separation and loss; use of Life Story Books; visitation with parents, and acceptance of reality. Work in these areas should be carried out within the framework of a therapeutic alliance with the child that is founded on a supportive relationship with the worker as well as conviction about the child's right to permanency.

SUGGESTIONS FOR FURTHER READING

Aust, P. (1981) Using the Life Story Book in Treatment of Children in Placement. *Child Welfare* 60 (8): 535–36, 553–60.

Beste, H. M. and Richardson, R. G. (1981) Developing a Life Story Book Program for Foster Children. *Child Welfare* 60 (8): 529–34.

Colon, F. (1978) Family Ties and Child Placement. *Family Process* 17 (3): 289–312.

Kufeldt, K. (1984) Listening to Children – Who Cares? *British Journal of Social Work* 14 (3): 257–64.

Mishne, J. M. (1983) *Clinical Work with Children*. New York: Free Press.

Moss, S. Z. (1966) How Children Feel About Being Placed Away From Home. *Children* 13 (4): 153–57.

White, M. S. (1981) Promoting Parent–child Visiting in Foster Care: Continuing Involvement Within a Permanency Planning Framework. In P. A. Sinanoglu and A. N. Maluccio (eds) *Parents of Children in Placement: Perspectives and Programs*. New York: Child Welfare League of America, pp. 461–75.

12 Providing support services

Permanency planning work is complex and time-consuming, and it requires the skillful enactment of many roles. One of the most important ones is that of the case manager, who must often expend extraordinary energies to assure that appropriate support services are made available to families. In line with the ecological perspective presented in Chapter 6, adequate supports must be made available to families, in order to promote or test their capacity to care for the child. Only when families do not respond positively to a full array of remedial and supportive services can the case manager or team confidently recommend that a decision be made for a permanent plan separate from the biological parents.

This chapter will present the rationale for provision of support services for client families; describe the services most significant to permanency planning work; and discuss the importance of collaborative efforts between case manager and support systems.

RATIONALE FOR SUPPORT SERVICES

The rationale for emphasis on providing support services to families comes from the ecological view of human beings and their living situations that we discussed in Chapter 6, as well as research and clinical evidence that children involved in permanency planning come from families with extensive needs in basic life areas, as presented in Chapter 3.

Various studies lead to the conclusion that these are children at socio-cultural risk (Fein, Maluccio, and Goetzel 1983; Shireman 1983; Shyne and Schroeder 1978). Their support systems are 'undermined, impaired, eroded, or destroyed', resulting in social and cultural impoverishment (Garbarino 1982: 56). Consequently, 'the pressing need is to establish an effective partnership between formal and informal support systems so that each child is protected and nurtured by both, directly as in the case of the small school, and indirectly as through the child's parents and primary care givers' (Garbarino 1982: 57). Adequate support services could help to prevent out-of-home placement of children, or to accelerate their reunification with their families (Turner 1984).

As described in Chapter 6, various ecological principles also provide a rationale for provision of support services to families. These include, in particular, the assumption that human behavior is a function of the complex interaction between person and environment; the view of human beings as active participants in transaction with their environment; emphasis on the person's adaptive processes; and a health/growth orientation stressing people's strengths and potentialities rather than their deficits.

In accordance with these principles, an accurate assessment of ability to cope must take into consideration the quality and quantity of the environmental supports available. The ecological model suggests that it is a bias of clinical judgment to attribute pathology to clients when appropriate environmental resources are not available to them (Howe 1983). Just as people with many supports can appear to have adequate coping skills, so those without supports may appear to lack coping skills. Social workers will need to adapt to the ecological perspective to help parents achieve their goals most successfully.

To judge a parent's ability to manage responsible care of self and children, the worker must be sure the parent has access to those services that facilitate coping. For this reason, the worker has the task of matching available resources with parent needs. A proper fit of services and innate coping skills can make the difference in a parent's ability to manage effectively. When appropriate services are not available, it is the environment rather than the family that should first be examined for lacks. Many families have had long histories of living in poverty and isolation, with little support from family and community. Their needs may be extreme, and poverty, isolation, lack of support, drift, stress, and depression may have become a way of life. People cannot be expected to make speedy or dramatic changes when their lives do not carry any thread of optimism.

Along with ecological theory, a growing body of literature advocates the use of social support networks as helping tools in the human services (Biegel and Naparstek 1982; Collins and Pancoast 1976; Froland et al. 1981; Swenson 1981; Whittaker and Garbarino 1983). According to Whittaker and Garbarino (1983), services to clients in diverse settings, including child welfare, may best be provided through integration of professional helping methods with informal helping approaches. Other writers underscore that natural support systems are actual or potential sources of strength in minority communities (Cochran and Brassard 1979; Delgado and Humm-Delgado 1982; Hill and King 1982; Walker 1981).

In addition, research has shown that the social networks of families can have a significant impact on child development (Whittaker and Garbarino 1983: 177–80). Along with potentially offering supports to the parents, social networks can influence the child by providing: (1) cognitive and social stimulation; (2) direct supports such as informal child care; (3) observational models for the child; and (4) opportunities for active participation in the network of his or her parents (Cochran and Brassard 1979: 604–05).

The collaboration between formal and informal helpers is just beginning to be examined as a service provision scheme, and the responsibility of the formal services to make such a network effective is being recognized (Froland 1980; Whittaker and Garbarino 1983). Whatever the mix of formal and informal services, however, the goals should be to bolster parents in their coping efforts, provide assistance that will prevent family deterioration, enable parents to test their capacity to keep their child, and give the opportunity for a more satisfying life style. Support services are used as adjuncts to the direct work carried out with parents and children (Chapters 10 and 11) and within the context of the assessment and treatment plan formulated in each case. Moreover, as noted in preceding chapters, support services are mandated by Public Law 96–272.

TYPES OF SUPPORT SERVICES

In addition to the individual or family counseling offered to family members, as described in Chapters 10 and 11, families often need other services to help them achieve a permanent plan for the child. These services, which will be discussed in this section, may include:

* *Financial supports:* Aid to Families with Dependent Children (AFDC); food stamps, food banks, local welfare, job training and placement.
* *Community resources:* churches, schools, recreation, community centers, adult education.
* *Support groups:* Parents Anonymous, Alcoholics Anonymous, hospital-supported day programs.
* *Parent education:* formal courses or workshops and informal parenting groups.
* *Family supports:* relatives, friends, neighbors.
* *Supports from foster parents and child care workers.*
* *Home-based services:* homemakers, visiting nurses, volunteer visitors, parent aides.

Financial supports

Often biological parents do not know about the financial support available to them. Parents who live in isolation, or who move frequently, may never get established to the point where they can take advantage of the resources designed to assist them. Social workers need to have a good working knowledge of available resources in their geographic areas. Case managers in particular should know about temporary shelters for people without housing, food banks for people without immediate cash, location of soup kitchens, or assistance for fuel payments. Those who dispense such temporary services are often helpful in directing clients to appropriate longer-term assistance.

Other resources are local welfare programs, which will offer temporary assistance while families await eligibility for state-supported programs like AFDC in the USA. Parents may need information on how to apply for public assistance, Food Stamps, or low income housing. These services can be significant in helping parents resume care of their children. Without the basic necessities, parents who want their children can be pessimistic about their ability to care for them. Case managers cannot leave this area of service to chance. They must be active, or see that someone else is active, in helping families to acquire appropriate assistance.

Community resources

Biological parents often do not avail themselves of resources existing in their community. Because they tend to be isolated, make frequent moves, and lack self esteem, they do not know of resources and do not comfortably reach out for them. The case manager or other members of the permanency planning team must help to fill in the gaps.

Churches are often a rich source of support. They may provide concrete help, such as used clothing or canned goods. They may have committees that reach out to those in need. Their youth programs provide good socialization for children. Church families may volunteer to take in children for a visit, thus giving parents some time off. For example, in one case, an adolescent boy was fighting and verbally abusing everyone in the home but not in school or at his job. When a hospital refused to admit the boy because they did not see him as sufficiently disturbed or 'out of control', it was a church family that offered to take the boy for the weekend. This provided a sense of relief for everyone, especially his parents, and allowed time for more constructive planning. Most churches are service oriented and welcome the challenge of being helpful to those in need. It may be only with the assistance and support of the worker that families will utilize this source of support. Direct contact with clergy can be an appropriate intervention on the part of the worker.

Schools are another source of support. Social workers should be active in assuring that children are receiving the appropriate services from the school. Parents may not be able to advocate for special education classes, resource room help, psychological testing, or school social work services. The social worker can accompany the parents to the school and model appropriate methods for obtaining services for their children. He or she may play a part in seeing that parents participate in school conferences and have an understanding of how their children are doing.

Schools often offer special programs for parents, such as lectures on child issues or other topics of interest, or adult education programs; workers should be aware of these so that they can encourage parents to participate. Contact with school social workers may help permanency planning workers become familiar with this resource. Because biological parents often tend to live in isolation, facilitating their involvement in community resources can be supportive and therapeutic for them.

In addition to churches and schools, there are community centers such as neighborhood clubs, YMCAs and YWCAs, recreation centers, and Jewish Community Centers. In a recent study of services desired by families reunited with their children, recreation services placed surprisingly high (Fein *et al.* 1983); recreational opportunities are needed by parents as well as children. Most centers offer varied programs at minimal cost. Opportunity for socialization, skill development, physical exercise, and emotional support are built into these programs.

Family Resources Centers (FRC) are emerging as a new approach, or actually a new application of the settlement house concept (Advisory Committee on Child Development 1976: 96–8). The Center's staff becomes a part of the parents' social network. Parent learning occurs in many ways, for example, modeling by other parents, formal sessions, and participation or observation in children's playrooms. The Centers also try to meet concrete needs of parents to encourage their participation. Some provide laundry services (washers and dryers), free coffee, supervised children's playrooms and organized recreational programs such as trips to community parks. The Centers thus offer parents opportunities to learn skills in child care, to obtain concrete services, to socialize with other parents and combat their typical sense of isolation, and to derive emotional support from interaction with staff members as well as other parents.

It is not unusual to find that parents are unaware of such community resources, or not accustomed to using them, or lack the required transportation. It can be appropriate to include the use of such services in a service agreement, recognizing that parents need a variety of supports for themselves if they are to be successful in providing emotional succor and adequate care for their children.

Support groups

Traditionally in child welfare social workers have relied almost exclusively on individual approaches in their work with parents. In recent years, however, there has been some use of groups in practice with parents of children in placement or at risk of placement. In particular, self-help group approaches are gaining attention, albeit slowly, as practitioners recognize the untapped resources and latent potentialities in clients themselves. The use of self-help groups is increasing especially in practice with parents involved in child abuse or neglect or whose children are placed in foster care (Cohn 1979; Carbino 1982).

Numerous support groups are available that can address the needs of biological parents. While some are sponsored by profit-making agencies, many are free or available at minimal, sliding scale cost. Some are run by professionals and some are self-help groups with professional assistance. There are many models for how they may function (Coplon and Strull 1983). The chief value of support groups is the benefit that comes from knowing that others are experiencing difficulties similar to one's own. Such sharing allows people to seek help without stigma; in the group process the person in need can be converted to a help-giver, further enhancing confidence and competence (Lemberg 1984). People in similar distress can offer an understanding to each other that observing professionals cannot always do. This help, based on experiential rather than professional knowledge, is a structured adjunct to the informal support networks people tend to develop on their own (Borkman 1984).

Self-help groups have proven effective with clients from varied socio-economic and ethnic backgrounds. For example, Leon *et al.* (1984) report on a self-help group for Hispanic mothers, which benefited participants in a number of ways: building personal relationships and mutual support systems with others sharing similar concerns and interests; feeling free to relate their problems and express their anxieties as parents; strengthening their self-esteem and increasing their self-confidence in parenting; and learning how to negotiate the various service delivery systems.

Since support groups will differ depending on locale, social workers need to be aware of the resources available in their communities. For example, parenting groups are frequently organized by local social agencies or community organizations such as the YWCA. These groups usually offer a combination of a didactic presentation and opportunity for discussion. They generally deal with norms for child development, guidelines for child management, and suggestions for appropriate discipline of children. Such groups offer basic education and an arena for discussing issues, to parents who lack skills in rearing children.

Another self-help group, Parents Anonymous, was originally designed for parents who had physically abused their children, but now is recognized as supportive for parents who feel frustrated in managing their children (Lieber and Baker 1977). A history, or even an incident, of abuse is not a prerequisite for participation in Parents Anonymous groups. Many parents who are afraid of 'losing control' with their children find strength and support in realizing that others feel the same way. Attendance at Parents Anonymous group meetings can help alleviate the guilt parents have for their angry feelings at their children. Relief of guilt can lead to reduction of the parents' anger, making it easier for them to handle children appropriately. The chance for contact with other adults, by itself, can be therapeutic for parents who are isolated with small children for long periods of time. The opportunity to discuss and learn about appropriate child management techniques is also available in Parents Anonymous groups.

Other support groups, though they do not directly relate to the area of child management, may be appropriate for parents. These may be groups that assist with particular problems such as recovery from mental illness or alcoholism (Alcoholics Anonymous, Recovery, Hospital Day Treatment Programs), groups organized around special interests or life situations (Parents Without Partners, Divorced Men's Association), or groups that deal with issues of personal growth and self-esteem. When parents participate in weight watching groups, personal insight groups, or physical fitness groups, they are enlarging their views of themselves in ways that may help them feel more secure, personally satisfied, and equipped to handle the day-to-day care of children.

Social workers cannot expect parents to know about existing support groups, or have the ability to mobilize themselves to attend such groups. Case managers in particular need to take pains to pave the way for parents to participate, and thereafter express interest in how the group is going. Without the worker's support, parents may not sustain attendance, even if the groups provide a measure of satisfaction.

Parent education

Parents of children who come to the attention of permanency planners often need help in the area of parenting; they need to learn or relearn skills in child care and to practice and enhance their skills as parents. Through such help, they are more likely to be able to care for their children on a permanent basis.

Relevant opportunities are provided by various community resources or support groups, such as schools, family service agencies, child welfare agencies, and self-help groups. Abidin (1980) and Turner (1980) delineate various kinds of resources for parent education, including formal courses or workshops and informal sessions or groups. Abidin (1980) also discusses work with specific groups of parents, such as Black parents, those with a disabled child, and so on. Other writers focus on curriculum objectives and content as well as training methods (Abidin 1976; Harman and Brim 1980; Schaefer 1978).

Workers in permanency planning generally find that most biological parents can make use of these resources, in conjunction with counseling services or other treatment programs. As with any social work intervention, it is important to assess with the parent what is needed. For instance, does the parent recognize any needs around his or her parenting? What are the areas in which he or she needs to build or improve skills in child care? What is the parent's competence in areas such as interactional skills, behavior management, and the stimulation of cognitive development?

There is a wide range of parent education curricula, including the more well-known such as Systematic Training for Effective Parenting or STEP (Dinkmeyer and McKay 1976) and Parent Effectiveness Training or PET (Gordon 1970), as well as those developed for specific populations (Abidin 1980).[1] To be useful to parents coming to the attention of workers in permanency planning, parent education classes or parenting groups should be chosen or designed in ways that are responsive to their particular needs, qualities, and cultural backgrounds, rather than merely being adapted from programs originally developed for middle-class parents. In short, as with any intervention on the part of the worker, the parent education activity should be congruent with what is happening in the parent's life or ecological context – within the family, the informal social network, and the formal service network.

Some examples of differential use of parenting education approaches follow:

* Parents with large families overwhelmed with the maintenance responsi-bilities of their children might be confused by another 'crowd' such as a group parenting class. They might profit from individual nurturance through a parent aide.
* Adolescent parents are usually more apt to be attracted to and participate in groups that meet their social needs as well as the needs they might have as parents. In addition, the program would have to have peer approval (e.g. it should be 'cool' or at least 'okay' to 'go there').

* With parents for whom the church is an important part of their family's formal social network, parenting programs organized under its auspices would be apt to be more successful.
* Parents who have had little positive feedback in their parenting roles might respond better to highly structured programs that involve teaching parents (by modeling) concrete skills for interacting with their children or teaching their children to use specific toys or books.

Family supports

In addition to support services available through formal or informal community agencies and institutions, permanency planning workers should explore the support that families may have available from relatives, as well as friends and neighbors. With highly functioning families, relatives readily get identified as temporary caretakers, relief parents, or sources of temporary financial assistance. With families that are functioning poorly, it often does not occur to workers that there may be potentially helpful relatives or friends to call upon.

Just as parents may not take advantage of community resources, they also may not appreciate the extent of family supports available to them. It is important for workers to explore these possibilities with parents, who may be able to think of how relatives can be of assistance. For some clients there may be informal relatives, long-time family friends who have the status of aunt or uncle. Sometimes workers can invite parents to bring such relatives or friends to therapy sessions, and this can be the beginning of a new source of support. A relative may offer to take a child for a weekend, supply temporary housing, provide babysitting services while a parent looks for a job, or just be available to listen.

When a parent cannot provide permanency for a child, a relative may be the best resource. Knowing that a child will be cared for by a relative sometimes enables a parent to make the decision to release the child for adoption. Keeping a child 'in the family' can make a big difference when releasing a child, and informal adoption by relatives can be a successful permanent plan for some children.

The informal kinship systems that are often available to Blacks, Puerto Ricans, and other ethnic groups are also an integral source of support (Delgado and Humm-Delgado 1982; Hill 1971; Hill and King 1982; Walker 1981). They provide tangible services to their members, such as meals, a place to sleep, and child care, as well as connectedness and a sense of moral support. It has been speculated that kinship systems may be credited in part with the positive outcomes shown by Black children on their return from foster care (Fein *et al.* 1983).

In many instances friends and neighbors can provide the support when families are not available. Often, clients need help in identifying such resources, using them without guilt, and learning how to reciprocate to cement the relationship.

Supports from foster parents and child care workers

As discussed by various authors, foster parents and child care workers can play a prominent role in providing supports to parents of children in their care. For instance, Finkelstein (1981) and Whittaker (1981) have discussed the active involvement of biological families in residential treatment programs and the use of the treatment center as a support system for parents; Watson (1982) has proposed a new model of foster family care in which the foster family is regarded as a temporary extension of the biological family; Lee and Park (1980) have prepared a manual for training foster parents to work cooperatively with biological parents; and others have described the participation of foster parents as resources and role models for biological parents (Davies and Bland 1978; Johnston and Gabor 1981; Ryan, McFadden, and Warren 1981; Seaberg 1981).

Foster parents and child care workers can be involved in a variety of ways:

* Supporting the biological parent in efforts to achieve goals necessary for resuming care of the child.
* Reaffirming the importance of permanence and sharing the belief that children need to know where they will grow up.
* Maintaining the involvement of biological parents by consulting them about decisions affecting their children.
* Modeling parenting skills for biological parents, through such means as:

    * discussing discipline techniques;
    * modelling appropriate conversations with the child in front of the parent;
    * suggesting possible topics of conversation to the parent for interacting with the child; and
    * modeling the ability to enjoy the child (relaxing with the child, finding the child in one's self, playing with the child).

* Blending an acknowledgment of the child's problems and progress. While biological parents want to hear that their children are doing well, they also feel supported and more competent when they know that the children currently present some of the same problems that were evident at home prior to placement.

Home-based services

These services include a range of options and are provided by staff members who are variously called homemaker, family care worker, parent aide, or similar names. Their use is increasing, as elements of the Adoption Assistance and Child Welfare Act of 1980 (Public Law 96–272) are being implemented (Cole 1984).

The provision of services in the home is essential for many biological families. For instance, for parents who are physically ill, visiting nurses can sometimes make the difference between home and hospital care, permitting a child to remain at home rather than being placed in foster care. Similarly, homemaker service can help a family remain intact. Assistance with day-to-day management of a household while parents rehabilitate may make it possible to keep families together. Such services, offered on a time-limited basis with the goal of having the parent resume full responsibility, can offer support and encouragement to families. The modeling of the homemaker can be the best way for parents to learn new skills.

Potential home-based services and innovative programs have been extensively described in a number of publications, particularly Maybanks and Bryce (1979) and Bryce and Lloyd (1981). In addition, a comprehensive model of family-centered services for child welfare agencies has been proposed by the National Resource Center on Family Based Services at the University of Iowa (Hutchinson *et al.* 1983). It is not possible to consider all pertinent programs here. However, in the next section we would like to describe in detail a model parent aide program, so as to present the provisions that make it particularly valuable in permanency planning, and to show the advantages of providing support services to biological families.

PARENT AIDES

Child welfare agencies are increasingly involving parent aides as integral members of the service team (Gifford, Kaplan, and Salus 1979). One such model program will be presented in this chapter. It was developed at a voluntary child welfare and mental health agency, with funds from the National Institute of Mental Health (Miller *et al.* 1984b; in press). The program employs parent aides who are para-professionals specially trained to work with parents in the home. The main requirements for the position are not formal education but rich life experiences that allow one to empathize with the plight of others. Most successful parent aides are people who have reared children of their own, are of ethnic and racial background similar to their clients, and have experienced some of the same hardships as the people with whom they work. They are familiar with community resources and skilled in manipulating systems to obtain legitimate services such as housing, welfare assistance, appropriate school programming, and other community services.

The primary role of the parent aide is to support the parent. Parent aides do not do housework for the parents, but may join in when a parent is trying to accomplish a certain project. The parent aide should nurture the parent, with the goal of freeing her energy to nurture the child. This nurturing can be accomplished in several ways. Parent aides can be good listeners. They can offer practical advice. They can accompany parents to the local donut shop for coffee, discuss recipes, or watch a favorite television program together. Parent aides may provide transportation to the housing authority, offer guidance in filling out forms for assistance, or accompany a parent to a neighborhood center. They can model appropriate interaction with children. Throughout this process, parent aides maintain a sense of professionalism, in that visits are planned and goals and tasks are clearly delineated.

Boundaries are less structured than in a traditional therapy hour, casual advice is acceptable, and sharing of personal experiences is considered appropriate. Parents often share information with aides that they would be reluctant to offer to the social worker. Although parents are aware that the aide and the social worker communicate with each other, trust in the aide often facilitates progress. The aide can sometimes help a parent build confidence in the social worker. For example, in one case a Black parent was transferred to a White worker when her Black worker left the agency. The new worker assigned a parent aide who was able to respond to the parent's questions about whether she would be able to trust the White worker. The aide sanctioned the trust, enabling the relationship to build without a long testing period.

Parent aide services can be delivered under a twelve-week contract, calling for two parent aide visits weekly, lasting about three hours each. As noted in Chapter 16, it is useful to write a parent aide service agreement involving parents, parent aides, and supervisor. The agreement sets forth appropriate goals for the twelve-week period, as well as plans to evaluate progress at the ninth week so that termination or contract renewal can be planned. The agreement should also contain a statement about the social worker and aide meeting weekly for at least a half hour to discuss progress, so that the parent will be aware of this communication.

Goals should be specific, concrete, clearly written, and as measurable as possible. They should deal with the outcome that is desired, not with a service that will be delivered, and should be pertinent to permanency planning goals. Examples are:

* The parent will take steps to find housing, such as reading advertisements in the newspaper, visiting the housing authority, and looking at available apartments. (*Not* The parent aide will help the family find housing.)
* The parent will be able to get up by 7 a.m. to assist the children in getting ready for school. (*Not* The parent aide will help get the children to school.)
* The parent will feel more able to prepare suitable meals for herself and the children (*Not* The parent aide will teach the parent how to prepare meals.)
* The parent will participate in community center parenting classes. (*Not* The parent aide will teach parenting skills.)
* The parent will discuss child management with the parent aide. (*Not* The parent aide will teach child management skills.)
* The parent will learn how to use time outs with children. (*Not* The parent aide will show better discipline methods.)
* The parent will pay more attention to personal care. (*Not* The parent aide will show parent better grooming.)

Goals like these make it possible to assess progress, and parents as well as professionals and paraprofessionals can monitor achievement. These goals describe what the parent will accomplish. In connection with each goal the aide has tasks that will assist the parent achieve success. For example:

* The parent aide will help the parent buy a newspaper and show her how to read the advertisements.

* The parent aide will teach the parent to lay out the children's school clothes the night before, and how to use an alarm clock.
* The parent aide will discuss nutrition and meal planning.
* The parent aide will accompany the parent to the community center to help her register for parenting classes.
* The parent aide will demonstrate and discuss child management skills where appropriate.
* The parent aide will discuss using time outs with children.
* The parent aide will use magazine and TV advertisements to reinforce cleanliness and hair care.

The central function of the parent aide is to be a source of nurturance for the parent. Parent aides must be accepting, offer genuine warmth, be empathic, and convey a sense of caring and concern. The uniqueness of the parent aide service is the ability of the aide to nurture the parent and to allow the parent to feel a deepening trust in another human being.

Parent aides need appropriate training if they are to be successful in their work. A training curriculum should contain units conveying:

* an appreciation of the characteristics of parents who abuse and neglect their children;
* a knowledge of child development;
* symptoms of severe pathology, particularly depression;
* a discussion of appropriate boundaries when working with parents;
* a discussion of confidentiality, particularly in the context of the team approach to permanency planning;
* child management skills; and
* a firm understanding of permanency planning principles and techniques.

Because their work may take them to undesirable locations and to people who are not glad to see them, parent aides themselves need support for their work. In addition to the opportunity to talk regularly with the case manager or supervisor, an ongoing educational/support group is useful for renewing their energy for difficult work. The opportunity to compare notes, frustrations, and accomplishments with other aides is a valuable deterrent to burnout.

Although volunteer parent aide programs do exist and can be successful (Ragan, Salus, and Schultze 1980), those with paid and trained paraprofessionals having strong agency support and supervision are more suitable for permanency planning work. Volunteers are usually less reliable and less able to give the time needed to participate in a total program. This in no way suggests that volunteer programs do not have value in situations where permanency is not the basic issue.

The use of trained parent aides as staff members and members of the permanency planning team is in its infancy. Agency administrative and financial concerns can make it difficult to develop such programs (Carroll and Reich 1978). The long-term cost benefits are still unmeasured, but workers who have been able to use parent aide services in permanency planning work find it a valuable addition to other available services (Baker et al. 1981; Miller et al. in press).

COORDINATION OF SERVICES

Coordination of services will be extensively considered in the discussion of collaboration for permanency in Chapter 14. It should be noted here that effective coordination begins with a high-quality referral that helps staff from the other agency to understand clearly the family's need and facilitates their use of the service.

As delineated by Ragan, Salus, and Schultze (1980: 42–4), effective referrals involve a series of tasks that may take considerable time and thought on the part of the worker:

* Determining which agency is able to provide the needed support to the family.
* Educating the family about the particular service.
* Helping the family understand how the service can be of benefit to them.
* Planning with family members the best way to initiate contact with the service.
* Accompanying the family to the agency providing the service, if necessary.
* Preparing the appropriate service provider to understand and assist the family.
* Establishing with the service provider a plan for regular contacts, including case conferences.

In referring parents for support services, often it is appropriate to pave the way. As in all sound social work practice, the goal is for clients to handle things on their own as much as possible. In that sense, we ideally would suggest to a parent that he or she inquire about services, such as parenting classes, in the community. Realistically, especially at the beginning, we will be more successful if we explain to a parent that a parenting class is available at a local school at a specific time; that there is no charge; that it starts on a particular date; and that the parent can sign up by telephoning a given number. Making it easy for a parent to negotiate the use of support services will facilitate progress.

It also makes sense to prepare the service provider for the contact. For example, the worker might say to the parent: 'I'll be glad to talk with Mrs Jones at the Housing Authority so that she will be expecting to hear from you.' We know that extra attention may be forthcoming to a client when the way has been paved by another professional. Some parents may find it easier to use support services if they feel that their 'story' is already known. Workers can help by getting their permission to share pertinent information in advance: 'If it's all right with you, I'll be glad to tell the parent aide about Johnny being in foster care and about your hospital stay before we all meet together.'

In essence, paving the way between a parent and a community resource can promote optimal use of support services. Beyond the initial referral, of course, there is the need for ongoing communication and collaboration, following the guidelines to be presented in Chapter 14. In particular, referrals to support services must be monitored to be certain that there was follow-through. The parents and all the professionals involved need to be aware that everyone is working together to achieve the goal of providing the child with permanency. Each of them should know that all the collaborators will be talking with one another so they can work effectively together, so decisions can be made in a timely way and with full cooperation and understanding of all participants.

It is important, for example, for the case manager to know if a parent is attending a parenting class, and it is legitimate for the case manager to discuss the parent's progress with the instructor. Case managers also must be aware of goals set in parent aide contracts and must discuss progress with the aide. If a parent is using day care services, case managers need to communicate with the day care staff, to learn if children are arriving and being picked up on time, and if they are adequately cared for. If Big Sisters or Big Brothers are involved, case managers should know if parents are cooperating with the program appropriately.

This communication between the case manager and all services used by parents should be clear to parents from the start and should be defined as important for several reasons. The first is to assure that appropriate planning is done and that there is no overlap of services or contradiction in messages. A second reason is to facilitate the team's or case manager's role as evaluator of progress. Parents must know from the start that workers have the dual task of assisting parents to make as much progress as possible, *and* evaluating progress so that a recommendation regarding a permanent plan for the child can be made. Workers must be clear and honest with parents about both of these tasks.

CASE ILLUSTRATIONS

The use of support services is illustrated in two contrasting cases: in one, support services helped a parent to be reunited with her child; in the other, it was found that it was not possible to rehabilitate the mother and parental rights had to be terminated, despite the extensive use of support services.

Case of Kent Mosher

Kent Mosher, age six, was placed in a foster family because of his mother's inability to provide appropriate supervision. Kent's problems included violent behavior at school (throwing things and biting), enuresis, hyperactive behavior and learning disabilities.

Ms Mosher was a Black, single mother who had grown up in an institution. Her background clearly did not prepare her for independent living and responsible care of her son. She was seen by agency staff as a woman who, despite average intellectual potential, had been denied opportunities to learn. She had friends and needed people to rely on, yet could not adequately assess who could offer the kind of emotional and educational support she needed. While she seemed at a loss to understand Kent's problems, she expressed a commitment to caring for him.

Over the course of nearly one year, support services made available to Ms Mosher, in addition to weekly counseling sessions, included: weekly therapy at a mental health clinic to work on issues separate from Kent; weekly attendance at Parents Anonymous meetings; regular attendance at adult education classes at her local high school, particularly a course on parenting; transportation to and from the agency to keep appointments with the worker and to visit Kent; close interaction with an older couple in her apartment building who were taking an interest in her and Kent; and telephone contacts with Kent's foster mother to discuss daily management of Kent.

In this case, Kent's mother readily availed herself of the services offered and responded positively to the efforts of others to assist and teach her. Kent was able to return home, an outcome which would probably not have been achieved without the extensive range of support services that have been outlined.

Case of Albert Porter

Albert Porter, a White, eight-year-old child, was placed in a residential treatment center because of impulsivity, self-destructiveness, and learning disabilities. Prior to placement, he had lived with his mother and, at various times, different relatives, including his father, stepmother, and both sets of grandparents. Reports of physical abuse had been made while he was living with his parents and grandparents.

Ms Porter, Albert's single mother, who expressed strong wishes for Albert to return home, was seen by agency staff as an immature 22-year-old woman whose own childhood had been characterized by physical and sexual abuse. Her strong desire to meet her own needs seemed an obstacle to her ability to see and understand her son's special needs. Assessment of the family indicated that extended family members were not available as supportive resources for Albert and his mother.

Support services made available to Ms Porter, in addition to weekly counseling sessions, included: participation in Alcoholics Anonymous, as mother acknowledged 'using liquor to calm my frazzled nerves and keep from going crazy'; weekly attendance at a Parents Anonymous group; introduction to programs available at a community recreation center; weekly sessions with a parent aide to assist in learning parenting skills particularly useful for hyperactive children; transportation to and from the agency for appointments; and regular contact with child care staff to discuss Albert's progress.

Ms Porter seemed unable to utilize support services. Despite the provision of transportation, she missed close to half of scheduled appointments. The parent aide service was used only minimally, with Ms Porter sometimes being surprised when the aide arrived. In addition, she was reluctant to visit the community center, even when the parent aide offered to accompany her. Her contact with child care staff did not facilitate new learning on her part, as she persisted in feeling that the onus should be on Albert to change. She did not participate in Alcoholics Anonymous or Parents Anonymous sessions.

In this case, the provision of supportive services was not successful in rehabilitating the mother. However, her response to the offer of services demonstrated her potential as a parent. In assessing Ms Porter's functioning the worker recognized that her narcissism was such that her own needs would always supersede those of her son; moreover, her inability to keep even late morning appointments because she needed her sleep, her failure to be present for appointments with the parent aide, her refusal to use public transportation though she was close to the bus, and her incompetence in delaying personal gratification in favor of the needs of her son all pointed to her lack of capacity to care for a child with special needs. As a result, the worker concluded that termination of parental rights and placement of the child in another permanent plan were the appropriate decisions.

SUMMARY

This chapter identified the range of support services essential to biological families and considered the rationale for support services in permanency planning. The involvement of parent aides as an innovative, home-based service for biological families was highlighted. The use of support services was illustrated in two contrasting cases, one in which support services helped a parent to be reunited with her child, and another in which parental rights had to be terminated despite extensive provision of supports.

It was stressed that the case manager plays an important role in assuring that appropriate services are provided and that progress is being made. The case manager also is responsible for the coordination of services and communication among service providers in order to achieve the goal of permanency.

NOTE

1. Brief reviews of an extensive sample of parent education programs and texts, including PET and STEP, may be found in Abidin (1980: 531–69).

SUGGESTIONS FOR FURTHER READING

Delgado, M. and Humm-Delgado, D. (1982) Natural Support Systems: Source of Strength in Hispanic Communities. *Social Casework* 27 (1): 83–9.

Hill, E. H. and King, G. C. (1982) Working with the Strengths of Black Families. *Child Welfare* 61 (8): 536–44.

Miller, K., Fein, E., Howe, G., Gaudio, C., and Bishop, G. (1984b) Time-limited Goal-focused Parent Aide Services. *Social Casework* 65 (8): 472–78.

Ragan, C. K., Salus, M. K., and Shultze, G. L. (1980) *Child Protection: Providing Ongoing Services*. Washington, DC: US Department of Health and Human Services Publication No. (OHDS) 80–30262.

Walker, F. (1981) Cultural and Ethnic Issues in Working with Black Families in the Child Welfare System. In A. N. Maluccio and P. A. Sinanoglu (eds) *The Challenge of Partnership: Working with Parents of Children in Foster Care*. New York: Child Welfare League of America, pp. 133–48.

Whittaker, J. K. and Garbarino, J. (eds) (1983) *Social Support Networks: Informal Helping in the Human Services*. New York: Aldine Publishing.

13 Maintaining the permanent plan

In addition to making a plan best suited to the child's needs and qualities, permanency planning involves deliberate attention to *maintaining* that plan in the aftercare period, that is, once the child is reunited with the biological family or placed with another family. Maintenance of the plan should be undertaken with the conviction that the decision is forever and that every effort, ordinary and creative, will be pursued to make the permanence work. The social worker's intervention with children and parents should not end abruptly once the plan is implemented; it should continue at least during the initial adjustment period, and often for longer periods afterward.

Following a brief review of research findings on aftercare services, this chapter offers guidelines for helping children and parents or other caretakers in their efforts to remain together in a way that is mutually satisfying and growth-producing. The focus is on the agency's responsibility and the worker's role in maintaining the permanent plan. Issues such as disruption of some permanent plans are also considered.

RESEARCH ON AFTERCARE SERVICES

Although there is general agreement that what happens to a child after leaving the child welfare system is a significant source of information for research, few studies have been published about the role of aftercare services. The latter can run the gamut from highly structured professional services (governmentally mandated or supported, provided by voluntary agencies, or supplied by private, market-based organizations) to more informal services (friends, relatives, and other natural helpers; self-help groups) (Froland 1980).

There have been numerous reports on these services. For example, Carbino (1982) discusses the value of group work with biological parents; Whittaker and Garbarino (1983) recognize the contribution of informal helpers; and Mitchell and Trickett (1980) are concerned with discriminating the variables that would define some dysfunctional influences of support networks.

There has been little research, however, on the role of these services in maintaining a permanent plan. A study by Taylor and Alpert (1973) was an early attempt to identify factors related to stability or permanency in the lives of children discharged from residential treatment. They found, not surprisingly, that children with family and other community supports were most likely to have successful aftercare experiences, regardless of the severity of the problems leading to their placement or the nature of the placement experience. In a more recent investigation of the outcomes of permanency planning, the authors concluded that many families, especially the biological ones, were in need of basic services in the aftercare period (Fein *et al.* 1983). In this study, many parents expressed their need for housing, employment, and financial assistance; in addition, recreation services emerged as a strongly perceived need. Workers also felt the families required counseling services.

In another study of the services needed and used by biological families after being reunited with a child returned from foster care, it was found that counseling services were most frequently needed and used, and that the continued involvement of the child welfare agency's social worker was often seen as desirable by the parents (Fein, Maluccio, and Goetzel 1983). Further, parents perceived a need for services not readily available to them – additional counseling, financial assistance, recreational programs, job training, and the like. Parents who lived alone with a child were found to need more services than those who had other adults in the house for support; the former parents used more services and would have preferred more attention from the social worker.

Aftercare services of a wide variety are beginning to be perceived as a necessary adjunct to good child welfare practice (Farber *et al.* 1984). Adults who were in foster care as children, in particular, have identified a range of services that would have been useful: employment and career planning, educational advice, financial counseling, housing, family planning, legal and insurance information, personal relations and marriage counseling, health, and nutrition advice (Festinger 1983).

THE AGENCY'S ROLE IN MAINTAINING PERMANENT PLANS

Management and administrative issues in implementing permanency planning are discussed in Chapter 17. As set forth in that chapter, the steps necessary to create an administrative context for initiating permanency planning can be extended to the aftercare services that maintain permanency: commitment to the concept, planning for its implementation, educating and training staff, allocating sufficient resources for implementation, and building in staff support. Aftercare services, however, may require conviction and dedication beyond this already formidable list. Some of the issues facing agencies in this task will be discussed in this section, along with implications for the agency's role in maintaining permanent plans.

Subsidizing aftercare

In most instances, aftercare services for youngsters who return home after placement outside the home are limited in scope. In voluntary agencies, for instance, only six weeks of aftercare, typically telephone contact, but sometimes interviews as well, are not unusual (Farber 1984). This is because payment by the public agency is based on days of placement rather than other services provided. Furthermore, the public agency itself is pressured by financial considerations to close cases as rapidly as possible.

Social workers from the public agency may keep in contact with children after they return to permanent placements and their cases are closed, but there is no evidence that much in the way of services is offered (Fein *et al.* 1983). Often, it becomes the responsibility of voluntary agencies to support aftercare and in effect subsidize it. This is a difficult fiscal position for agencies, but a reasonable one if endowment income is available. Voluntary agencies, however, are involved in only a limited number of cases. The public agency is the one legally responsible for services to children and should be the one charged with providing equal access to appropriate services for all its clients.

Cost effectiveness of aftercare

In urban areas in the USA, in 1983 it cost an average of $14,000 to maintain a child in an institution, $5,000 in a foster family, and $2,300 to provide special services at home with the family (Ward *et al.* 1984).

While there are no data on the costs of aftercare services, and indeed little information about the characteristics or the effectiveness of such care, it is apparent that there is a wide disparity of costs between community services and out-of-home care. If aftercare services can be perceived as preventing replacement, the cost advantage is obvious. For example, in Connecticut the average child in foster care is in placement forty-three months (Ward *et al.* 1984). At the rate of $5,000 per year, it would cost the state almost $18,000 for that child. That would purchase more than seven and a half years of aftercare services. Even if the same number of dollars were spent, the savings in emotional trauma and disrupted lives would be a clear benefit of aftercare.

It is conceivable that some families may require aftercare forever: their functioning without assistance cannot be counted on to provide a nurturing milieu for their children. Is it cost effective to deny those services and perpetuate the broken families, the abusive behavior, and the other sequelae of parental neglect? A society concerned about its children would act on such cost information. The benefits are beyond cost.

Advocating for aftercare

The cost benefits of aftercare services are so obvious that one would not expect that those in decision-making positions would need much convincing. The reality is, however, that resources for human services are in short supply, and crisis situations always have greater call on the public dollar. Money for prevention of crises usually gets allocated only as the result of strong advocacy efforts by individuals and organizations concerned about the need. Administrators must be forceful in leading their agencies in such advocacy. Working together with other agencies and citizen action groups, it is possible to have an impact on legislation, resource allocation, and regulations and practices.

Those voluntary agencies with advocacy programs or advocacy committees might well undertake a payment-for-aftercare-services project, working with their public agencies or legislatures. Public agencies can encourage the formation of advisory councils of lay persons, who might focus on support for aftercare. These groups can join with other voluntary or citizen groups concerned with the lives of children, such as associations of child caring agencies, child guidance clinics, or family service agencies, among others. Lobbying and building support for aftercare are reasonable activities for such advocacy groups. As they gain success, aftercare services will gain legitimacy, as dollars are allocated to them; to expect decent aftercare without fiscal support is unrealistic.

Continuum of care

Providing aftercare services and thereby maintaining the permanent plan may require putting into place an entire continuum of care system. Continuum of care refers to a model of delivering a *range* of services to promote healthy functioning and prevent dysfunctioning, strengthen and support children and families when dysfunctioning occurs, and place children in permanent homes following an out-of-home episode. The continuum of care model adopted by the public child welfare agency in the state of Connecticut, for example, assumes four levels of service, moving from least restrictive to most restrictive for children. The first level, *developmental and preventive* services, are those services in the community and school that enhance healthy development. They may include family life enrichment groups, recreational services, self-help groups, and so on. The second level of services, *support* services, are those services in the community, such as individual and family counseling, that are designed to strengthen families when difficulties occur. The third level, *supplementary* services, are also community-based, but offer some respite for families in order to prevent removal of the child from the home. These may include day treatment, respite day care, or extended day treatment. The more restrictive services, level four, are *substitute* services, that is, out-of-home placement such as foster family care, residential treatment, or emergency shelter care (Connecticut Department of Children and Youth Services 1982).

It is not reasonable to expect that any one agency can provide all levels of service. Many agencies are single purpose, for example residential care, while others offer only a small number of services on the continuum. Each agency, however, can provide easy movement between levels, and intake and transfer or referral systems that encourage workers to push families to their highest level of functioning. A youngster who is in foster care (Level IV) may have a parent participating in family life enrichment groups to increase parenting skills (Level I); when he returns home he may go into a day treatment program (Level III). The parent may use a parent aide for a time (Level II), and the entire family may be referred to various church and recreational programs (Level I).

While such a formulation of service provision is attractive in its logic and rationale, there are many barriers that may prevent its implementation. For example, agencies that provide foster care and are paid on the basis of days of care may be reluctant to return children home and arrange for a parent aide; a worker in a residential facility may not be accorded the time to search for, and prepare a parent to participate in, family education groups. Although extended day treatment may be a viable option, residential facilities may be unwilling to risk the fiscal consequences of empty beds in the middle of a year. Agencies must be encouraged, however, to develop an easy flow between the levels of services. They must permit workers the time, training, and support to learn about levels of service beyond the one they are working in primarily, and they should streamline the process by which such interchange can occur.

THE WORKER'S ROLE IN MAINTAINING A PERMANENT PLAN

Workers are in a difficult position when it comes to aftercare services. They must make peace with the agency's policies, the clients' needs, and their own feelings. These feelings are complex, and they are related to diverse aspects, including:

The agency
* Do the workers feel supported?
* Is there a good working atmosphere?
* Do agency policies and procedures enhance the workers' self-esteem?

The client
* Do workers feel successful with the clients?
* Is there optimism about the clients' future?
* Have counter-transference issues been handled adequately?

The worker
* Do the workers feel strongly enough about aftercare services to push hard for them in the face of obstacles?
* How can they maintain optimism about the future in working with families that have so many environmental and emotional barriers to overcome?
* Do they feel comfortable with the role of advocate forced on them by the paucity of aftercare services?

Although these feelings and reactions are real and often difficult to deal with, workers can play a useful role in aftercare, by considering certain principles in areas such as the following: relationship with family; use of case manager model; referral process; continued use of service agreements; threat of return to placement; and planning for aftercare.

Relationship with family

Whenever possible, maintenance of the established trusting relationship with the family is desirable, though this should be done with a view toward gradually decreasing dependence on this service. If group work can be designed, that modality has obvious cost advantages and probably therapeutic benefits as well (Carbino 1982). Except in the most utopian of situations, services will need to be provided with an understanding of the limits imposed by financial constraints.

Case manager model

Probably the optimum alternative for aftercare services is the continuance of the worker as case manager, a basic permanency planning role that was described in Chapter 5. Through leadership from the case manager, an appropriate amalgam of community services based on a continuum of care model can be added or discarded as the family's needs change, without unduly increasing the burden on the staff. Recreational services, crisis intervention, and ongoing outpatient services in a facility appropriate to the family's functioning can be designed. The search for services and their coordination is aided by the use of an aftercare checklist (see *Figure 6*). Such an instrument can remind the worker of services that might otherwise be overlooked, and serve as a monitoring tool to assure that timely decision-making is supported.

Figure 6   Aftercare checklist for the Jones family (Sally age 24, John 10, and Sue 2), September 1, 1984

service	recommended	time frame	for whom	re-evaluation time
Big Brother	X	1 year	John	9 weeks
Big Sister				
church				
counseling	X	open-ended	whole family	6 months
day care	X	in 3 months	Sue	
day treatment				
financial aid				
job training	X	in 3 months	Sally	6 months
parent aide	X	12 weeks	Sally	9 weeks
parenting group	X	open-ended	Sally	3 months
recreation center				
respite care				
school meeting	X	prior to return home	John and mother	3 months
scouting				
self help group				
service organization (YWCA etc.)				
summer camp				
transportation				
tutoring				
other				

Referral process

Implementing aftercare, whether as the sole worker or as the case manager, inevitably requires adequate referral procedures. These are dependent on:

Agency policies
* ★ How long can a case be carried after a child is discharged?
* ★ Who will be billed for services?
* ★ What agency budget will the worker's time be charged against?

Worker relationships
* ★ Can a personal relationship with a worker or supervisor in another agency help obtain services more easily or more quickly?
* ★ Can another worker be persuaded to accept the transfer of a difficult case?

Client needs
* ★ How is the way paved with the client to make the referral useful and desirable?
* ★ How is the new worker or service apprised of the client's needs without undue emphasis on deficits?

Referral guidelines generally omit consideration of the worker's response when a referral is not consummated. Typically it is the client who is 'blamed'. Often, however, it is the service that is inadequate: for instance, there are no evening appointments available; transportation to the facility is impossible; the worker breaks an appointment. The case manager must be intrusive enough to address with the agency those issues that must be faced on a systems level, but also must be sensitive to the importance of building competence and empowerment in clients, encouraging them to deal with such issues on their own.

Continued use of service agreements

Service agreements are as important in the aftercare period as they were previously. It is easy for expectations to outdistance reality when the concrete situation of the child being out of the home is no longer a constraint on – or incentive to – use of services. Typical questions to be considered include:

* ★ How long will the worker remain in touch with the family?
* ★ What should the family do if a crisis arises?
* ★ What are the consequences if referrals are not followed?

The obligations of the client and service provider, as well as the consequent effects, need to be articulated as carefully as in the original permanency planning work.

Threat of return to placement

Returning a child to placement is often used as a contingency in service agreements. It should be a choice based on rational considerations. Its importance in the aftercare period warrants special emphasis, since parents may be tempted to threaten a child with return to placement to force good behavior. The threat to place a child is not uncommon (Argles 1984); it has been estimated that up to 30 per cent of mothers use the threat as a form of punishment (Bowlby 1973).

Whether the threat occurs because of parental frustration with the child's behavior, marginal resources available for the family, ambivalence about parenthood, or stress on the parent or family, the impact is devastating on the child, the parent, and the siblings (Moss and Moss 1984). It is even more frightening when the reality of a placement has already occurred. Parents must be helped not to use such a threat, and its prohibition should be written into the service agreement. Consequences for breaking the prohibition might be recanting, discussion, and apology to the child; a call to the worker for support in this crisis; or re-entry into brief family treatment to help all family members with the trauma.

Planning for aftercare

Permanency planning places equal stress on 'permanency' and 'planning'. In that light, the planning for aftercare services becomes a prominent consideration. In the welter of plans that need to be made in the original work, the thinking about aftercare should be initiated as early as possible once a family comes to the worker's attention.

While the details will need to be designed in relation to the family's changing needs over time, the concept of aftercare should be introduced and underscored from the beginning. The client must understand that placement out of the home is not a discrete event, and that services will be provided to assist the family generally, not merely to reunite them. Similarly, the worker and the agency must make such a commitment. As with services for children, unless plans are made early, the provision of aftercare services will be haphazard, and the risk of drift will be magnified.

CASE EXAMPLE

To illustrate the use of aftercare services in maintaining permanency, a case example will be presented. It should be noted that in this case the social worker continued to provide services, served as a case manager, used referral procedures and service agreements, helped the parents to avoid threatening a return to placement, and was active in planning for permanency at every step.

Marie Porter is a ten-year-old who has been in residential placement for two years because of her parents' inability to handle her. Ever since the age of three, when she was first seen in an outpatient child guidance clinic, she has been hyperactive, with a short attention span and a low frustration tolerance. She was in and out of treatment with a social worker, two psychologists, and a social work intern. All were frustrated in their attempts to relate to and treat her. Eventually she was sent to a residential treatment center some distance away in the same state. Her parents and younger brother, now age eight, continued in outpatient treatment with the child guidance clinic.

After two years, the staff of the residential treatment center no longer felt that they were helping Marie, and they therefore recommended another facility or a return home. Because they had no permanency planning program, most of the aftercare planning was initiated by the outpatient worker who had been seeing the parents and the younger brother. The worker realized that unusual efforts would need to be expended to break the cycle of enmeshment and failure and achieve some stability in all their lives. The following specific plans were formulated:

1. A permanency planning treatment meeting was set up with the home school district, to begin planning before Marie's actual return.
2. Plans were made to have her return home in the spring, rather than at the end of the school year, so that educational testing and planning could begin and her school placement in the fall would be decided before the start of classes in September.
3. It was arranged with the agency's foster care unit to provide respite foster care one weekend a month, to give Marie and her family some break from each other.
4. Arrangements were made with the local Big Sister program for Marie's participation, to give her extra support, attention, and caring.
5. A teenage babysitter was engaged for every afternoon after school, even if the parents were home, to give Marie the undivided concentration of one person.
6. It was agreed to see the younger brother in therapy, to give him support in adjusting to the return of a disturbed child into the family.
7. It was recommended that enrollment in a summer day treatment program be explored.
8. A service agreement was drawn with the family to assist them in establishing a new equilibrium without slipping into the old pattern of parental splitting so common with a disturbed child. Mr and Mrs Porter were also to be helped not to use return to placement as a threat when Marie misbehaved; this threat had been used frequently in the past, especially when Marie had been home on weekend visits. In addition, the parents and worker together were to become alert to the recurrence of Marie's old behavior patterns, and how they served to trigger family crises. These characteristic patterns of Marie's reactions, her school behavior, and her relationship within the family were to be used as signals by the parents to call into play new reactions on their parts, coached by the worker, to cope with the confrontation.

On many fronts, therefore, a plan was formulated to maintain permanency. The worker not only provided counseling services after the return home, but also served as a case manager to orchestrate school planning and community services to help the family reunite. Marie and her parents may well require such specific and detailed services for many years. *What is the alternative?*

ISSUES IN AFTERCARE

The planning and implementation of aftercare services often do not proceed as smoothly as in the above case. Many issues emerge that need to be considered.

Program design

Many of the situations that typically present themselves in maintaining permanency planning are illustrated in Marie's case. The residential treatment facility would count her as a permanency planning success, since she was returned to her biological family. The aftercare concept, however, was not built into its programs; were it not for the intervention of the outpatient clinic's worker and the efforts of the parents, services might not have occurred or been as comprehensive.

Governmental support

The lack of planning for aftercare in Marie's case was not a consequence of evil intent on the part of the residential facility. As previously suggested, due to limited resources, planning for aftercare has a lower priority than coping with the needs or emergencies of the moment. Since placement facilities are paid for the duration of the child's care, aftercare appears to be a luxury that few can afford. States, or other governmental bodies, in turn are loathe to allocate funds to aftercare. It takes creative advocacy and extremely motivated parents, as Marie's were, to break this cycle. Perhaps legislative action, or the preventive services mandated by Public Law 96–272, will eventually create a different atmosphere.

Transfers in workers

When aftercare services are provided, they typically are for brief 'transition' periods before the case is finally closed. More extensive aftercare usually requires that the case be transferred to a worker who has more available time, to another program in the same agency (e.g. the outpatient service), or even to another agency (e.g. one located closer to the client; a child guidance clinic rather than a residential center; or a voluntary agency rather than the public agency).

Any transfer has the potential for creating tremendous barriers to successful work. Since families whose children have been removed from them are typically those that have problems with trust and with maintaining a relationship, it is easy to see how a transfer to a new worker can be perceived as a break in a relationship, with consequent feelings of rejection and loss on the part of a fragile client. This can defeat the gains previously made, heighten the regression normally expected when a child returns home, and undermine any newly found feelings of esteem and empowerment.

In many cases transfers are inevitable, and preferable to no service at all. In that event, change to the new worker or situation needs to be worked out with care. With sufficient lead time, so feelings of rejection can be anticipated and dealt with, the new worker can be introduced and made aware of the subtleties of the case, and other termination issues can be acknowledged and defused.

Gaps in aftercare services

Gaps in service delivery are especially evident in aftercare. Case managers often face such a paucity of services that coordination does not even become a possibility. Ideally, however, a variety of services should be available. For example, parent aide or homemaker services, used before a child is returned home to enhance parenting skills, may be needed in the aftercare period as well. Similarly, after school care or part of a day treatment program may be necessary once a child is returned to the home school district. Legal services, employment training, day care, housing, and other services useful in maintaining a family after a child comes home are all important.

Timing

Many residential treatment facilities claim to provide aftercare even if they are not reimbursed by the state or other authority. This usually turns out to be discharge planning, an interview or two, and a number of telephone contacts over a six-week period. In like manner, the public agency usually keeps a case 'open' for a few months after a family is reunified, though the intensity of service of necessity must diminish as the worker faces crises in other ongoing cases.

How long is long enough for aftercare? Are cases closed to minimize dependency or to balance the budget? It may be necessary to acknowledge that some children and families will need aftercare for long periods, perhaps for life. Balancing the clients' needs for more care with the desire to decrease dependency and minimize the financial burden for the agency may complicate the worker's decision-making on behalf of the client.

All aftercare services must face the issue of how much and how long is enough, as illustrated in the following case examples:

Case Example No. 1: Raymond, at age fourteen, returned to his biological mother after four years in foster care. He had not been doing well in the foster home despite concerned foster parents, weekly counseling, and a special education program. He was determined to return to his mother as had his older brother and sister, one after completing high school while living in a group home, and the other upon graduating from a residential treatment center.

The court approved his return home despite apprehension about his mother's ability to provide structure. Since it was recognized that many supports would be needed to help Raymond remain at home, the following services were arranged: counseling at a branch office of a social service agency located within walking distance of his mother's apartment; special arrangements for late enrollment in summer school in the new town, with the understanding that he would be eligible to attend the local technical high school if he passed English and Mathematics, two subjects he had failed; a part time summer yard job made available through the town's Youth Services Bureau; and bus tokens for transportation to and from summer school. In addition, Raymond's mother received a subsidy from the state public welfare department to provide for his care, and she changed her part time job hours so she could be home in the evenings to supervise him.

The services provided were used by the family in a marginal way. Raymond's handling of the summer job was less than responsible but he managed to earn some spending money. He did not attend summer school regularly and had to repeat ninth grade in the regular program. At sixteen, he dropped out of school. He missed counseling appointments so often that it was no longer suitable to make them available to him. At a later point, however, he returned to counseling on his own at the local child guidance clinic, a place of his own choosing. Raymond was able to remain at home until age seventeen, when he and his brother rented a small apartment together. When he moved out, he contacted a local job corps program for assistance in obtaining work.

Questions that arise from this case include:

* Would earlier return home have led to the same outcome, but with less separation trauma for the child?
* What role did the services play in Raymond's ability to remain at home?
* Would services have been used better if the child and mother had greater choice in the planning process?
* Was it the services themselves, or Raymond's awareness that assistance was available, that made the outcome successful?

Case example No. 2: Sam, age nine, was referred for outpatient counseling because of lying, stealing, poor school performance, and disobeying his adoptive parents. He had been with the adoptive family for two and a half years, a 'hard-to-place' child with emotional problems. There had been regular contacts with the adoption worker for the six months following the placement and then sporadic contact for the next six months. At the time the adoption worker closed the case, the parents were feeling encouraged about their progress with Sam. One and a half years later at the time of referral for outpatient counseling, the parents were at their wits' end, angry at Sam, critical of themselves for 'failing' as parents, and ambivalent about continuing with him.

Questions to be raised in this case include:

* Should the aftercare have been longer?
* Should there have been a plan for follow-up at least every three months?
* Was the family encouraged to view a need for services, particularly with a disturbed child, as their right and not as evidence of their failure?
* Would an ongoing support group for adoptive parents have been helpful?

Case Example No. 3: Stacy was referred to the outpatient clinic at age five by her adoptive parents. She had been in the home since age two, placed as a foster child after witnessing the murder of her parents. The foster parents adopted Stacy at the age of three. Aside from occasional contact with the public agency worker, no services were offered to Stacy or the adoptive parents following the placement. The parents were concerned that Stacy was not developing appropriately. An evaluation pointed out serious developmental delays, emotionally and intellectually. These delays were attributed to Stacy's difficulties around the death of her parents. The adoptive parents at this point were 'tired of a five year old who acts like a three year old', angry about her lack of growth, and discouraged about their own inability to help Stacy grow.

Questions to be raised include:

* Would an earlier developmental evaluation with baseline data about mental, psychological, and emotional levels have been appropriate?
* Could this child have been helped to deal with the death of her parents through play therapy at the time of placement in the adoptive home?
* Would a pre-school program with a developmental emphasis have been of value?
* Would the adoptive parents have benefited from a group for parents of children who had experienced similar traumas?
* Could counseling have assisted the adoptive parents to understand Stacy's needs and how to help her deal with the trauma?

Resistance of client

Parents who neglect or abuse are characteristically resistant to intervention in their lives. Treatment typically takes place when mandated by the public agency or the courts, though in some cases parents do enter into treatment voluntarily. Voluntary or not, parents are defensive about their handling of their children and resistant to efforts to change their child-rearing methods or their family interaction patterns. In Chapter 6 we already discussed a variety of treatment strategies that flow from a treatment philosophy based on the ecological perspective – strategies designed to empower parents, acknowledge their strengths, and convince them that we recognize them as the most important resource for their children. Even within this perspective, clients resist our best efforts to help them help themselves and their children. Frustrating as this is for workers, 'resistance' in many cases can be viewed as a strength – the resolution and purposefulness that may have prevented a surrender to crushing life circumstances.

As noted in Chapters 10 and 11, treatment techniques for working with the resistance of parents and children are basic to all therapeutic work (Anderson and Stewart 1983; Nelsen 1975). It should not be surprising, moreover, to encounter resistance after the treatment period is concluded and maintenance of permanency is the prime goal. Parents who have a child returned to them can easily feel that the trauma and pain of family treatment should be behind them, and that further intervention is an unnecessary intrusion.

Resistance can manifest itself in other ways as well: as dependence and reluctance to end treatment; in acting-out behavior (breaking appointments for aftercare interviews, not following through on referrals, 'forgetting' previously integrated parenting skills); and through passive-aggressive actions and attitudes that undermine the permanency of the plan. Anticipating, acknowledging, and working with this resistance are vital to permanence. The worker must have strong conviction about the absolute necessity for permanence, and must be decisive and creative in the face of the parent's – or the child's – resistance.

TYPICAL NEEDS IN VARIOUS PERMANENCY PLAN OPTIONS

Different issues emerge in aftercare services with parents and children in each of the major permanency planning options.

Biological families

Research has shown that biological families, more than adoptive, permanent foster care, or other types of families, have the greatest requirement for services when children are returned to them (Fein *et al.* 1983). Such services may be needed not only for the immediate functioning of the parents, but as an investment in their handling of other children they have, or may have in the future.

It is therefore essential that the worker make it clear, from the beginning of the permanency planning process, that aftercare support will be available for all family members, children and parents, regardless of the specific outcome of the case. When permanency plans require the removal of children from their biological families, it is imperative that aftercare services be available for the parents as well. However difficult parenting has been for them and however many opportunities they may have muffed to reunify with their children, the final termination of their rights is a tremendous loss. They need the support of the worker who knows the situation, for help in seeing the removal as a positive contribution on their part to the stability of the child's life. They must be assisted in rebuilding their fragile self-esteem despite the official judgment that they are unfit parents.

Case example: Wanda Peters was a twenty-year-old mother of two, Tommy, aged four and Judy, aged two. Both children came to the attention of the child protection agency because of neglect. It was clear that Mrs Peters' immaturity and personal needs made it difficult for her to care for the two children. With counseling, she was able to come to the decision to relinquish Judy for adoption because the care of the younger child was too demanding and her attachment too tenuous to hope for a different outcome. Tommy was to be placed in short-term foster care with the goal of returning home.

Over time, Mrs Peters was able to discuss her feelings about surrendering Judy. Sensitivities about separation and loss were often evident and came up particularly at holidays, birthdays, and the anniversary of the placement date. There was recurring concern for how Judy would understand what had happened. Mrs Peters was helped by the worker to write letters for Judy's adoption file about her feelings, and was able to express her hope to the worker that Judy would know she had been loved despite Mrs Peters's inability to give her what she needed. Mrs Peters was also able to admit her desire that Judy not grow up to hate and resent her. These themes were recurrent, but Mrs Peters was gradually able to feel more acceptance of herself as a responsible person. Eventually she wrote a letter that she wanted to become a part of Judy's Life Story Book, feeling that in this way she could bring closure for herself to a painful event.

This case illustrates how painful the issues of separation, loss, and guilt can be for biological parents. They may find it difficult to make use of continuing service and may be unwilling to go on with counseling after relinquishing a child. Workers need to enhance their skills in this area and be diligent in sincerely offering the opportunity to parents.

Adoption

Whether adoptive families make more use of mental health services than non-adoptive families is an open question (Taylor and Starr 1972). In general, after-care services tend to be readily available to the adopting family. Compared with biological families, workers tend to visit adoptive parents more often in the year before the adoption is finalized (Fein *et al.* 1983), and adoptive families tend to be proficient in obtaining and using services (Breetz, Starr, and Taylor, 1975). In addition, some agencies have begun offering supportive family therapy in the post-adoption period, to help adoptive families deal with issues such as a child's multiple loyalties; the impact on the family of telling the child about his or her adoption; and biological and emotional identity concerns (Bunin 1984). Other agencies are offering more extensive and longer-term service beyond the placement period (Hartman 1984).

There has been increasing concern, moreover, about the permanence of adoption (Fein, Davies, and Knight 1979). The disruption rate for adopted, hard-to-place children has been difficult to determine. Research studies have been flawed by insufficient follow-up periods and other methodological difficulties, although the Child Welfare League of America is presently engaged in a more rigorous study of adoption outcomes (Nelson, in press). Some authors estimate as few as 15 per cent of hard-to-place adoptions disrupt (Churchill 1984). One factor involved in disruptions is the vulnerability of adoptees to identity conflicts (Depp 1982); this is especially true in instances of transracial adoption (Silverman and Feigelman 1984).

A recent response to this quest for identity has been the increasing acceptance of the adoptive 'search', the process by which adoptees seek specific information, or even reunion, with their biological parent(s). Although the adoption search is usually undertaken by older adolescents or young adults, the possibility of the search presents anxieties for adoptee and parent alike (DiGiulio 1979). Parents need the assistance of the social worker in accepting the legitimacy of the identity quest and coping with the anxiety of the implied rejection. Similarly, the adoptee needs support for whichever dimensions of the search he or she is interested in and for ultimate re-acceptance by the adoptive parents.

Maintenance of adoption as a permanent plan can be enhanced by considering the following service issues:

1. There should be forthright recognition of the need for ongoing supportive services. The need is legitimate and not a sign of failure.
2. Workers should help parents understand that the need for support will vary. As children reach new stages of development, different issues about their pasts come up. Adolescents have identity concerns; eight-year-olds may need new explanations for the adoption they seemed to understand at age four; planned or unplanned encounters with the past may be troublesome; or anniversaries such as birthdays, placement dates, or death dates may raise anxieties.
3. There should be consideration of open as well as closed adoptions for older children who know their biological parents. The closed adoption has the advantage of the new parents not feeling in direct competition with the biological parents. It has the disadvantage, however, of allowing for fantasies of reunion and the denial of past problems. Continued, though limited, contact may help maintain a sense of reality about the problems that caused the separation.
4. Efforts should be made to promote the use of groups for parents and children throughout the post-adoptive period. Currently there are probably more such groups for parents than for children. Since many of the concerns are similar, support groups for both can be helpful.
5. Parents must be helped to accept from the start that older, hard-to-place children will make life difficult for them. They may not relate to them as parents, may not allow themselves to feel close, and may not trust them. This is intensely painful for the adults who look forward to a loving relationship, and they need preparation and support for this outcome.
6. Potential adoptive families should be assessed for their sensitivity to realistic expectations for a child. This includes the ability to allow a child to move at his or her own pace of relating, and not to feel rejected by avoidance or other examples of the child's discomfort with intimacy.

Permanent foster care

Maintaining permanency for youngsters placed in long-term foster care has been a problem because of the danger of multiple placements, the inadequacies of foster homes in providing a sense of permanence, and the loosening of ties with the biological family (Fanshel and Shinn 1978; Knitzer and Allen 1978). Children growing up in foster care see themselves as different from others; they are keenly aware of their status as foster children, and their self-perception is damaged by their awareness of their parental rejection.

As found in a study by Rest and Watson (1984), therapeutic intervention was not as successful as had been hoped in dealing with the pain experienced by children in out-of-home placement. While in care, the functioning of the children was not as positive as those whose permanent plan had been return to biological family or adoption. Despite this concern, long-term foster care did not seem to present overwhelming obstacles to adequate functioning. A number of recent studies, moreover, have reported good results for adults who grew up in foster care (Festinger 1983; Rest and Watson 1984; Triseliotis 1973). The major finding has been that children who grow up in a stable, long-term foster home generally do well in their functioning in basic life areas.

Social worker services should be geared to easing the dilemmas presented by a child's damaged self-image. Casework or other therapeutic services alone are not sufficient. Foster children should be helped to gain experiences that will enable them to feel competent. Education, training, socialization opportunities, and supportive connections to families and community should be encouraged by the social worker seeking to maintain permanency.

DISRUPTION OF PERMANENT PLANS

With all our emphasis on permanency and stability, little consideration has been given thus far to the possibility that 'permanent' plans may disrupt. In fact, as reviewed in Chapter 2, various studies raise questions about the stability of permanent plans (Claburn, Magura, and Chizeck 1977; Fein, Davies, and Knight 1979; Fein et al. 1983; Block and Libowitz 1983). Although major methodological problems are encountered in efforts to define and measure recidivism or disruption, it is known that a substantial proportion of children placed in 'permanent plans' re-enter the foster care system and are likely to remain in care indefinitely; others enter the mental health or juvenile justice systems. There is extensive evidence that many of the children come from families with limited social supports, insufficient income, and multiple needs and problems in such areas as health, day care, education, housing, employment, and family relationships (Fanshel and Shinn 1978; Fein et al. 1983; Festinger 1983; Fein, Maluccio, and Goetzel 1983; Giovannoni and Billingsley 1970; Jenkins, Schroeder, and Burgdorf 1981; Shyne and Schroeder 1978).

Case example: Sally, age eleven, is a precocious pre-adolescent who has lived with her adoptive parents for four years. Despite the diligent efforts of the adoptive parents to win her over, she remains distant, aloof, secretive, and moody. In addition, she resists attachment, offers no affection, and is lax in meeting family expectations. The adoptive parents are discouraged, feel as though they have failed, and are questioning their ability to continue with Sally in their home.

The adoptive parents and Sally were actively involved in outpatient treatment for two years, with minimal progress. Sally has had a recurring fantasy of seeing and returning to her biological parents, who had given her up when she was six, acknowledging their rejection of her.

When it became clear the adoptive parents could not continue with Sally, it was apparent that her chance of succeeding in another home was minimal, since there had been no acceptance of the loss of her biological parents. The worker decided to seek out the biological parents to determine their willingness to meet with Sally and go over, once again, the reasons for their inability to keep her.

The biological parents were found to be cooperative. They had not forgotten Sally, and thought about her often. They talked openly about their problems and also shared their present ongoing struggle with the three children still at home. They described financial and marital difficulties, along with the special educational needs of their youngest child. They were clear about continuing to feel unable to care for Sally and agreed to tell her so.

While a bond between the biological parents and Sally clearly did exist, it was not possible to pursue a reunion. Since it was apparent that a bond did not exist between Sally and her adoptive parents a group home placement, where renewed contact with the adoptive parents could be promoted, was agreed upon as the best plan.

The above case illustrates the willingness of the worker and the adoptive parents to recognize that the permanent plan was not working. While this is extraordinarily difficult and there is the tendency to persist rather than admit failure, the best interests of the child must be given priority. The worker must be challenged to think of creative ways to deal with the inevitable disruption and minimize the trauma of a painful situation.

Despite a worker's strongest efforts, families and children may find themselves unable to maintain the elements of the plan that promised stability. On these occasions, it is the worker's responsibility to be sensitive to the family's and child's needs, and not keep a child in an untenable situation just to pay lip service to permanency.

SUMMARY

This chapter has presented some of the issues and principles involved in maintaining a permanent plan. The importance of aftercare services was stressed, and the agency's and worker's roles in providing such services were delineated. Such issues as program design, role of support by the public agency, delicacies of transferring cases, kinds of services, timing of services, and client resistance were discussed, and an aftercare service checklist was presented. Disruptions of permanency, and special considerations that various placement options present, were also noted, and a plea for advocacy, based on the cost effectiveness of aftercare services, was made.

SUGGESTIONS FOR FURTHER READING

Fein, E., Maluccio, A. N., Hamilton, V. J., and Ward, D. (1983) After Foster Care: Outcomes of Permanency Planning for Children. *Child Welfare* 62 (16): 485–560.

Hartman, A. (1984) *Working with Adoptive Families Beyond Placement*. New York: Child Welfare League of America.

Taylor, D. and Alpert, S. (1973) *Continuity and Support Following Residential Treatment*. New York: Child Welfare League of America.

PART III

COLLABORATIVE AND ADMINISTRATIVE ASPECTS

14 Promoting collaboration

Collaboration among different organizations, disciplines, and persons is highly regarded in the human services field, since it is a means of utilizing community resources efficiently and meeting client needs effectively. In permanency planning, collaboration is essential – a *sine qua non* of practice; in most case situations, formulation and implementation of a permanent plan for a child involve the efforts of a range of agencies, professionals, and other service providers. It may be said, without exaggeration, that the quality and quantity of collaboration in a particular case can make or break a permanent plan. For these reasons, in Chapter 1 we identified collaboration as a prominent component of the framework for permanency planning.

In this chapter we discuss the rationale for collaboration in permanency planning, the variety of potential collaborators, guidelines for promoting effective collaboration, the role of the case manager in the collaborative process, and the issue of maintaining confidentiality. A case example illustrating the range of roles and tasks that facilitate collaboration is also presented. For our purposes, we define collaboration as the process of all concerned parties actively sharing in examining a child's and family's needs and qualities, reaching a decision regarding the most appropriate permanent plan for the child, working together to implement that plan, taking joint responsibility for what occurs, and evaluating the outcome.

RATIONALE FOR COLLABORATION

In their guide to coordination and planning among human service agencies, Rossi, Gilmartin, and Dayton (1982: 11–13) point to the following benefits of interagency coordination:

* improved staff effectiveness;
* improved public image;
* improved accessibility for clients;
* reduced fragmentation of services;
* greater efficiency.

These general benefits also apply in permanency planning practice. In addition to coordination, however, there must be *collaboration*, to accomplish the goal of permanency planning. As implied in the definition of collaboration given in the introduction to this chapter, we regard it as a proactive rather than a reactive process – a process in which all collaborators play continuing roles related to the goal of achieving permanence for children and youth. It involves more than simply coordinating services. It is an ongoing, dynamic interaction that requires concerted activity and determined efforts to succeed. It is a process that presents social workers and others with innumerable challenges and dangers, as reflected in the following typical experiences drawn from actual permanency planning cases:

* Currently working with Mr and Mrs Brown and their three children in foster care are representatives of a public child welfare agency, a residential treatment center, a training school for delinquent youth, a child guidance clinic, and a public assistance program – in addition to the mother's psychiatrist, the father's probation officer, and personnel from several schools. How can these extensive resources be mobilized on behalf of this family, whose children seem destined to a life of foster care in one setting or another?

* An inter-agency conference is scheduled to discuss a controversial question that has been dividing staff members of a residential treatment center and a public agency: Should Bobby, age ten, return to his biological home, as the public agency worker believes, or should he go into adoption, as the residential care staff argues?

* At a case review, a young mother expresses her confusion about plans for her two children; she had understood from her social worker at the family service agency that her children would be returned to her care as soon as she stopped drinking, but now the worker from the child welfare agency is saying that she is not ready. What must she do to get her children back?

* A foster mother calls the agency, very upset and angry, to ask why her foster child's father was allowed to visit in the foster home with his 'girlfriend' and to bring all kinds of gifts to Tommy, his eight-year-old son. How can she help Tommy if the agency doesn't make things clear to everyone?

* Following extensive therapy, the worker in a child guidance clinic concludes that six-year-old Judy is ready for adoptive placement. The foster parents, however, disagree, feeling that the child is not yet able to give enough emotionally to succeed in adoptive placement.

As these examples only begin to suggest, in permanency planning work many problems and dangers can result from poor or insufficient collaboration. Among the more typical ones are these:

* Children and families may be confused, overwhelmed, and uncertain. How can they relate to so many different people from diverse agencies or

systems? How quickly is their energy depleted? How can they make sense out of multiple messages from different sources?

* Agency services and other community resources may be duplicated, wasted, poorly coordinated, or underutilized.
* Social workers, foster parents, child care workers, and other service providers may be working at cross purposes, canceling each other's contributions, having discrepant or unrealistic expectations of each other or of family members, or not providing the service needed by the family.

These common problems and dangers may be avoided, or at least minimized, through planned, purposive, and systematic collaboration. This is the best rationale for collaboration in permanency planning. Or, to put it more positively, collaboration is required for many purposes, particularly to help in:

* achieving consensus regarding a permanent plan;
* ensuring that everyone is working on *one* focused plan;
* identifying and engaging necessary services and matching them with client needs;
* making judicious and effective use of community services;
* monitoring the delivery of services to a particular family and evaluating its effectiveness;
* highlighting gaps, duplication, or other issues in the service delivery system.

In addition, the formal or informal team of collaborators can serve as a mutual support group, particularly in cases that are unusually difficult, demanding, frustrating or slow-moving. For example, when the social worker and parent aide discuss a parent's continued lack of consistency with a child, both will feel strengthened as they come up with strategies that complement each other's efforts. The worker's discussions about appropriate child management skills with the parent will be illustrated and modeled by the parent aide during visits in the home, and each of them will be contributing to the outcome of the intervention.

CASE ILLUSTRATION

The following case illustrates selected principles in collaboration and the kinds of roles and tasks that need to be carried out to facilitate collaboration within a permanency planning context. We shall return to this case at various points throughout this chapter.

Case summary

Henry Hogan, age twelve, is seen in an outpatient child guidance clinic. He has recently been discharged to his parents from a residential school specializing in learning disabilities and behavior problems. The psychiatrist at the school had recommended inpatient care in a psychiatric hospital because, despite educational gains, Henry had made no significant therapeutic progress while in the treatment center. While he could behave satisfactorily with adequate supervision, there was no evidence of an ability to internalize norms for behavior. Henry's parents decided to take him home after a two-year placement and seek outpatient services. The situation is clearly one of high risk for replacement of the child out of the home.

The outpatient clinic offered weekly individual sessions to Henry and weekly individual or joint sessions for the parents. Collaborators were Henry's parents; the clinic outpatient worker who served as case manager; the former residential school staff; personnel at Henry's current school; the clinic psychiatrist; the public child welfare agency; the special tutor assigned to Henry; and the staff of a summer day camp for children with behavior problems.

Henry was discharged from the residential school in April, 1984. Prior to the discharge, Mr and Mrs Hogan contacted an outpatient clinic worker, requesting ongoing help in keeping Henry at home.

Plan for initial collaboration

Following discussion with the parents, the clinic staff, and the worker from the residential school, the outpatient clinic worker, as case manager, set up the following plan for initial collaboration:

1. The residential school was asked to forward records to the outpatient clinic and to Henry's home school.
2. A school conference was set up for Henry's parents, the school personnel from the residential school, and the outpatient clinic worker.
3. A session was set up for Henry and his parents and the clinic psychiatrist so that Henry's medication, which had been started at the school, could be continued, monitored, and evaluated.
4. The parents agreed to contact the local school to get appropriate application forms for a special tutor.
5. An appointment was arranged with a summer day camp for children with behavior problems, to assess its appropriateness for Henry.
6. The public child welfare agency was contacted to initiate the process of obtaining financial assistance for the summer day camp experience.

Plans for ongoing collaboration

Following continued discussion and a meeting of the potential collaborators that also included the parents, the following plan for ongoing collaboration was agreed upon:

1. The outpatient clinic worker will attend the school planning meeting when it is time for recommendations for Henry's schooling in September.
2. The parents will attend a weekly meeting of the summer day camp staff to discuss Henry's adjustment and progress during the summer program.
3. The outpatient worker will contact the worker from the public child welfare

agency at the end of the seven-week summer day camp to discuss the benefits of the program for Henry.

4. The parents will discuss appropriate guidelines for the special tutor's work with Henry.
5. The special tutor will confer with Henry's classroom teacher to coordinate their teaching activities.
6. The outpatient clinic worker will communicate informally with the clinic psychiatrist about day-to-day progress and will set up bi-monthly or monthly checks for medication supervision.
7. In the weekly sessions with Henry and his parents, the outpatient clinic worker will share pertinent information from collaborators.
8. A review of all collaborators will be held in three months.

POTENTIAL COLLABORATORS

As the above example suggests, in any case of permanency planning there is a vast range of potential collaborators, that is, persons, disciplines, organizations or systems that directly or indirectly may be called upon to play a role throughout the duration of the case or at some specific point.

Service systems

Many different service systems may be involved in a permanency planning case. The most typical ones may be categorized as follows:

* *Child welfare service delivery system:* Public and private child welfare or child caring agencies, such as protective service departments, foster care agencies, children's institutions or residential treatment centers.
* *Legal/judicial system:* Courts, probation department; and legal counsel or legal aid firms.
* *Public assistance:* Income maintenance programs.
* *Educational system:* Schools.
* *Health care:* Hospitals; clinics; private practice.
* *Mental health system:* Counseling agencies; psychiatric hospitals and clinics; private practice.

In addition, as discussed in Chapter 12, potential services include family service agencies, other counseling programs, religious organizations, self-help groups, and recreational programs, among others.

These service systems often have different auspices, missions, orientations, organizational structures, and staffing patterns. As a result, achieving collaboration among them is no easy task.

Disciplines

Various professions or disciplines are involved in the service system outlined above. The most common ones include social work; psychiatry; psychology; law;

education; medicine; nursing; child care; and recreation; others, such as the clergy, may also be involved.

Although there may be overlapping among them, these professions or disciplines emphasize different theories and ideologies, address different human or social needs, and stress different approaches to understanding and working with human beings.

Service providers

In these service systems and professions are found diverse types of 'service providers' who are potential collaborators in permanency planning cases. They are located within the agency with major responsibility for the case as well as other agencies and organizations in the community. These collaborators may include:

* Social workers; psychologists; and other professional helpers.
* Judges; attorneys; court monitors; probation officers; and others affiliated with the legal or judicial system.
* Teachers; principals; guidance counselors; and others in the school system.
* Child caring personnel such as foster parents; child care workers; houseparents; and others.
* Parent aides; homemakers; home service specialists; and other paraprofessionals.
* Physicians; nurses; health aides; and other members of the medical system.
* Members of the clergy or other religious institutions.
* Recreation specialists.
* Volunteers.
* Informal helpers such as neighbors; friends; relatives; and members of self-help groups like Parents Anonymous and Alcoholics Anonymous.

In light of their frequently diverse orientations, training, qualifications, functions and frames of reference, it can be expected that there will be differences and disagreements in the ways these potential collaborators regard and approach a particular permanency planning case. For instance, some may identify primarily with the child and wish to protect him or her from the biological parents through placement in an adoptive home. Others may identify more with the parents and be inclined to return the child to them prematurely. Similarly, some social workers may consider adoption as the optimal type of permanent plan for young children, whereas others may prefer reunification of placed children with their biological families.

In addition to differences in their orientations, biases, or preferences, service providers bring different qualities, strengths, or resources to the permanency planning enterprise. Thus, some may be more proficient in working with the child than with the parents; some have already formed a strong and trusting relationship with the parents; and others may have better access to community resources.

Since there exists such a great variety of protagonists in the drama of permanency planning, collaboration is needed to maximize their contributions to the cause of securing a permanent plan for each child coming to their attention. In light of such an urgent purpose, it is not an exaggeration to say that collaboration in permanency planning is as crucial as in any other type of case. For instance, it is not enough to know that different agencies are providing particular services. There must be clarity of goals, honest sharing of progress and concerns, adequate attention to accountability, and a serious, shared commitment to a child's right to permanency. All of this must occur despite the agencies' concerns about territoriality and the workers' anxieties about sharing power and exploring personal inadequacies. We therefore need to consider ways of promoting such collaboration.

GUIDELINES FOR PROMOTING COLLABORATION

If we keep the purposes of collaboration in mind, we find that the typical challenges and potential dangers noted earlier in this chapter can be translated into opportunities to use human and community resources on behalf of children and families. To accomplish this goal, service providers should be guided by principles of collaboration and teamwork that have been found valuable in the human services in general. Here we delineate those principles or guidelines most crucial in permanency planning.

Adopting a team approach

Collaboration is enhanced as service providers adopt a team approach, that is, as they consider themselves a team pooling their resources and expertise to help a particular child or family. Although team participation initially increases the cost of service provision, the ultimate cost-effectiveness makes this approach worthwhile.

Writing on working together in the human services, Brill (1976: 22) offers the following concise definition of a team: 'A team is a group of people each of whom possesses particular expertise; each of whom is responsible for making individual decisions; who together hold a common purpose; who meet together to communicate, collaborate, and consolidate knowledge, from which plans are made, actions determined and future decisions influenced.'

There are different types of teams – from those that are loosely organized and informal to more formal ones with clearly designated leaders and structures. According to Brill (1976: 16), 'there is no one model of teamwork that can be considered the ultimate model. Many different models are being used and tested.' There is, therefore, no one type that is best for all permanency planning situations. Each group should develop and use the model that is most conducive to their collaboration in a particular case.

Whatever model may evolve or be chosen, 'flexibility, open-mindedness, and adaptability are particularly important in both workers and systems' (Brill

1976: 16). Furthermore, effective teamwork requires on the part of members qualities such as mutual respect, trust, and appreciation of each person's contribution. Collaborators must work hard to build a sense of common purpose, while avoiding typical obstacles to inter-agency coordination, such as inflexibility, turfsmanship, bureaucracy, and politics (Rossi, Gilmartin, and Dayton 1982: 38–42).

In permanency planning practice, service providers can learn in particular from the experiences of child protection teams, as analyzed by Schmitt (1978). Such teams, based either in hospitals or community settings, have been used increasingly in recent years to deal with problems of child abuse and neglect. Their 'overriding goals are effectively to diagnose and treat child abuse, and to coordinate the efforts of the many agencies involved' (Schmitt 1978: 7). Each team is multi-disciplinary and generally composed of:

* *nuclear members:* social worker, physician, and coordinator;
* *consultative members:* psychiatrist or psychologist; attorney; developmental specialist; law enforcement representative; and public health nurse;
* *ad hoc members:* other professionals who are not the primary workers with a given family and who are not permanent members of the team but join it for a particular case. Some examples are social workers, physicians, and educators (Schmitt 1978: 9–12).

In permanency planning, team members would also include, as appropriate child care workers or foster parents.

Clarifying goals and tasks

In his discussion of team purpose and structure, Schmitt (1978: 8) notes that, 'once team purposes are agreed on, role definition, task assignment, case reevaluation techniques, and team policies easily follow.' There may be some utopian thinking involved in considering that this is such an easy process; but there is no doubt that collaboration is facilitated through clarification of – as well as agreement upon – the central goals to be achieved in each case and the specific functions and tasks of each team member.

All of this is especially true in permanency planning, in which complex and crucial decisions often must be made in a timely fashion and in the midst of doubt, confusion, inexact knowledge, incomplete information, and conflicting values. Given such a context, it is understandable that the views of service providers are influenced by their particular biases and perspectives and subjective interpretations. The process of sharing and assessing available evidence and knowledge, reaching decisions, and clarifying goals and tasks in a collaborative fashion serves to minimize such risks.

Using a service agreement

The service agreement or contract can be used as a dynamic tool for facilitating collaboration among service providers, just as it is used in work with parents and children, as discussed in Chapter 9. Without the collaborative framework created through the contract, 'problems can arise to hinder goal attainment' (Stein 1981: 232). With clients as with service providers, the process of negotiating and renegotiating the contract can help to 'establish mutual concerns, clarify the purposes and conditions of giving and receiving service, delineate roles and tasks, order priorities, allocate time constructively for attaining goals, and assess progress on an ongoing basis' (Maluccio and Marlow 1974: 30).

The application of the service agreement to child welfare practice is extensively considered by Stein and his associates (Gambrill and Stein 1978; Stein 1981; Stein and Rzepnicki 1983; Stein, Gambrill and Wiltse 1974). These authors offer various suggestions and guidelines for formulating and using agreements. In addition, much of the discussion of service agreements in practice with parents and children (Chapter 9) is applicable to the use of contracts among service providers. In essence, collaboration works best where there is a system which assures selection of a case manager; clarity of roles; specificity of goals, tasks, and time frames; emphasis on the prime purpose, namely, decision-making toward a permanent plan; and provision for periodic review of progress.

Overall service agreements or contracts can be developed to encompass collaborative efforts among all team members or service providers involved in a given case. Specific contracts can also be formulated to focus on key members of the team. In particular, it is essential to clarify the objectives and tasks of service providers who will be working directly with the child and his or her family, as illustrated by the sample contract below, which comes from the Hogan case summarized earlier in this chapter.

Also, in cases of foster children, it is useful to develop a written agreement or contract between the agency and the foster parents. It is not unusual for foster parents to 'complain that they are not informed about their role or helped to understand their rights and responsibilities. Many are confused about their role and unsure of exactly what is expected of them' (Horejsi 1979: 22). Although some foster parents may be uncomfortable with a written agreement, some type of contract 'patterned after . . . but not duplicating, the one developed between the parents and the worker could help to remedy these complaints' (Blumenthal 1983: 320). Moreover, through full participation in developing a contract, foster parents can be helped to feel – and be – integral members of the service team, that is, as members who contribute prominently to accomplishment of the permanent plan on behalf of their foster child.

A contract with foster parents should cover:

* commitment to support the achievement of permanency for the child, including, as appropriate, efforts to reunite child with biological parents;
* a parent–child visiting schedule, as worked out by social worker, foster parents, and biological parents;
* arrangements to transport a child for scheduled agency appointments;
* agreement to meet with biological parents on a regular basis to discuss child management;

SAMPLE CONTRACT – HOGAN CASE

To facilitate collaborative efforts regarding Henry, the following contract is agreed to by Alan Snow, outpatient clinic worker; Russell Adams, outpatient clinic psychiatrist; Janet James, child welfare worker; and Mr and Mrs Hogan, Henry's parents.

1. *Alan Snow, outpatient clinic worker:* agrees to meet with Mr and Mrs Hogan for weekly counseling; meet with Henry weekly for ongoing therapy; initiate appropriate referral procedures for Henry's admission to a summer day camp for children with behavior problems; arrange for the clinic psychiatrist to supervise Henry's medication; and set up progress review meetings involving all collaborators every three months.
2. *Russell Adams, outpatient clinic psychiatrist:* agrees to meet with Henry and his parents to review medical history; prescribe appropriate medication for Henry; and see Henry as needed to supervise and evaluate his medication needs.
3. *Janet James, child welfare worker:* agrees to meet with Mr and Mrs Hogan to assess their need for financial assistance for the summer day camp and to make such determination by June 15, the deadline for holding a space for Henry in the program.
4. *Mr and Mrs Hogan, Henry's parents:* agree to contact the public school to set up a conference to plan for Henry's return and apply for a special tutor for Henry; and attend sessions with clinic psychiatrist, child welfare worker, summer camp staff, and school personnel.

All parties agree to attend review meetings every three months.

---

* agreement to work with child in appropriate areas, such as the supervision of homework, regular school attendance, or peer relationships.

Evaluating progress and outcome

As service providers collaborate in a permanency planning case, they follow a problem-solving approach patterned after the traditional phases of the scientific method of study: 'recognition and systematic formulation of a problem: collection of data surrounding the problem through observation and experimentation; development and testing of tentative hypotheses or explanation of the problem; and the emergence of a valid theory or law on which practice principles can be built' (Brill 1976: 126–27).

A central component of the scientific approach to problem-solving is ongoing review and evaluation of the activities of service providers and the outcome in relation to the family's goals and needs. Consequently, 'there must be provision not only for dissemination of information about what is going on but also built-in requirements and opportunities for feedback/feedforward and commitment to responsible, critical examination of the work being done' (Brill 1976: 127). Through periodic reports or conferences, team members share information and scrutinize their activities and results on an ongoing basis, leading to necessary revisions in goals, priorities, or tasks. Case conferences can thus serve to identify actual or potential sources of dysfunctioning in the client's service network and maximize the contribution of service providers (Compher 1984). In addition, team meetings can provide mutual support to collaborators in their difficult decision-making process.

In sum, periodic team meetings of service providers from all of the agencies or systems involved serve a number of important purposes, as delineated by Ragan, Salus, and Schultze (1980: 50):

' ★ to promote working relationships among the service providers
  ★ to share progress made by the family in each service area
  ★ to present *specific* questions that need to be answered and/or *specify* family problems that remain unsolved
  ★ to determine whether services are being duplicated, are not being used effectively by the family, or are no longer necessary
  ★ to develop future intervention strategies
  ★ to assign specific tasks that are to be completed jointly or individually by the service providers prior to the next meeting.'

Dealing with conflict

Conflict between collaborators often is an inevitable feature of permanency planning practice. Because of the difficult decisions that need to be made with insufficient time, information, or resources, disagreements typically arise in areas such as formulation of goals and tasks, assignment of responsibilities, and, in particular, selection of the best permanent plan. Often these disagreements are resolved through consultation or discussion at team meetings. But there are occasions when the issues are not resolved to everyone's satisfaction. Particularly troublesome are disputes involving the public agency with statutory responsibility for the child on one side, and one or more other collaborators on the other side.

Some disputes may center on a child's capacity to adapt to a particular environment. For example, the staff of a residential treatment center may judge a child ready for a home environment because of the excellent adjustment while in residence. The consulting psychiatrist may feel that the adjustment is only a reflection of the neutrality of the setting where there is little demand for intimacy.

Often, because of a lack of understanding about the importance of permanency to a child, a recommendation is made by one of the workers involved to move a child from one time-limited placement to another. The example of Henry, presented above, illustrates such a conflict. The psychiatrist's recommendation for inpatient care in a psychiatric hospital was based on a sound assessment of the child's personality. The social worker's view, based on the perspective that multiple placements are detrimental, was equally sound. The parents, with the assistance of the outpatient clinic worker, based their decision on their ability to secure enough community support to maintain Henry at home.

LEADERSHIP ROLE OF CASE MANAGER

Effective collaboration in permanency planning, as in the human services in general, does not happen easily or automatically, even when service providers are clear about their roles and proceed with the best intentions; service providers are human beings confronted with complex personal and professional pressures and demands. For instance, ostensibly minor frustrations mount when phone calls are not returned; requests for information not honored; appointments not kept; or reports not submitted. These dissatisfactions can escalate and contribute to the breakdown of a working relationship.

Making collaboration work consequently requires not only painstaking and persistent efforts, but also continuous leadership from a team member. This task generally falls to the social worker who plays the role of case manager. As noted in Chapter 5, the case manager role involves particular functions such as keeping services coordinated between multiple providers and bringing clients into constructive contact with various community and social resources. The explicit assignment of a leadership role to the case manager is a further means of promoting collaboration.

In keeping with his or her overall responsibility to orchestrate services on behalf of the family, the case manager must be ready to assume such a leadership role; establish himself or herself as the focal point for continuing exchange of information issues, or problems in the delivery of services to the family; and hold himself or herself accountable to all parties involved (Ragan, Salus, and Schultze 1980: 50).

Tasks of case manager

Specific tasks of the case manager in the area of collaboration, in conjunction with those delineated in Chapter 5, may include:

* *ensuring that a decision is made* regarding a permanent plan for the child, and that the family is involved as much as possible in the decision-making process;
* *negotiating respective roles and tasks* with the various providers involved in a case, if this has not been accomplished through formal or informal team meetings;
* *monitoring the implementation of roles and tasks* assigned to service providers;
* *identifying breakdowns or gaps in service delivery*, bringing them to the attention of the appropriate parties, and seeking solutions;
* *referring clients* to appropriate community resources in areas such as health care, transportation, housing, or education;

* *mediating* between the clients and service providers;
* actively *advocating* for clients in cases where other agencies are unwilling to provide service;
* *helping clients develop social resources*, including reestablishment of ties with family and friends and becoming involved with local community groups;
* *planning and managing parent–child visitation* in those cases in which children have been removed from the home; and
* *obtaining legal consultation*, to be certain of rights, liabilities, and responsibilities of parents, workers, and agencies.

This is an obviously complex set of demanding tasks. In some cases or agencies, it may be found that it is more desirable or feasible to allocate these tasks among several workers. It should be underscored, however, that effective collaboration only happens when there is a prime collaborator, usually the case manager, who makes certain that the process flows smoothly and that everyone is following through as agreed.

Relationships with informal providers

In carrying out such a pivotal role, the case manager must maintain not only good intra-agency and inter-agency relationships but also good relationships with informal providers of service. As discussed in Chapter 10, in permanency planning work there is frequent involvement of informal helpers, such as neighbors, relatives, or friends. To use these resources effectively, the case manager needs to follow guidelines such as these:

'   * Delineate with the client what steps the client can undertake to make use of the resource in a way that will make it easier for the client to do so on his or her own.
* Request permission from the client to release the kinds of information that service providers may need.
* Interpret, as necessary, the family's needs to the service provider and explain how the service provider can be helpful.
* Call to explain any missed appointments or other "breakdowns".
* Share feelings of appreciation for the service provider's interest in and help for the family.
* Provide the service provider with a contact, in case problems arise.
* Keep communication channels open among worker, client, and service provider through follow-up calls or personal contacts.'

(Ragan, Salus, and Schultze 1980: 48)

Participation of the family

In the midst of the many pressures and responsibilities that confront them in permanency planning practice, it is easy for workers to plan *for* – rather than *with*

– the family and to neglect or overlook its participation in collaboration. At times, collaboration proceeds as if it were – or should be – a secret endeavor. Another prominent function of the case manager, therefore, is to ensure that the family in each case is appropriately involved in the process of formulating and implementing collaboration. This may include, as appropriate, participation in team meetings; information as to who the collaborators and their roles and tasks are; and clarification about each participant's contribution to decision-making.

Such participation should be encouraged for many reasons. Most important of all, family members have a right to be involved in the process of making decisions affecting their lives. In addition, parents and other family members have much that they can contribute to this process, especially if we define them as resources in their own behalf, as suggested in Chapter 6. Moreover, their participation can have therapeutic value as well, as it helps to enhance their sense of competence and control over their destiny.

In the earlier case of Henry, the parents' participation in collaboration was crucial, especially since they maintained custody of Henry and were therefore in a position to make decisions. An example of reluctance to involve fully Henry's parents follows:

> A representative from the residential school attended a conference in Henry's local school to plan for his return. Also in attendance, besides local school personnel, were Henry's parents and the outpatient clinic worker. The residential school representative had various reports from the residential center. A question was raised about a psychiatric evaluation and recommendation. It became clear that the center's representative was hesitant to share the content of the psychiatric evaluation in the presence of Henry's parents, seemingly wanting to protect them from hearing the psychiatrist's recommendation that Henry be referred for inpatient care in a psychiatric hospital.

> This tendency to want to protect parents does not facilitate good collaborative work in permanency planning. In Henry's case, the parents had been informed of the psychiatrist's recommendation; they were nevertheless frustrated, because the psychiatrist's recommendation was shared with them by the social worker and they had had no direct conversation with the psychiatrist. A review meeting with both parents and psychiatrist present would have allowed for more satisfying communication and collaboration.

CONFIDENTIALITY AND COLLABORATION

Collaboration among service providers in a permanency planning case raises serious problems and issues regarding confidentiality, since sufficient information about the family needs to be shared by the collaborators with each other, to enable them to carry out their responsibilities. The need to share information while also protecting the rights of clients presents service providers with ethical dilemmas:

'Decisions involving the child's welfare can infringe on the parents' right to privacy, and professionals such as lawyers and mental health practitioners may be reluctant to reveal information given them in confidence. There is then a delicate balance to be maintained between the rights of the individuals about whom records are kept and the ability of professionals to treat individuals effectively.'

(Ragan, Salus, and Schultze, 1980: 44)

Agency regulations and state statutes in the area of confidentiality vary. In some states, the statute mandating reports of suspected child abuse to the child protection agency is in apparent contradiction to the statute defining privileged communication between psychiatrists/psychologists and patients. Also, there can be disagreements or tensions between service providers as to what constitutes confidential information or whether the child's needs or the parents' rights should be safeguarded.

A further related concern is the potential danger posed by clients who threaten violence to themselves or others. What obligation does the social worker have to report the threat and warn the intended victim? How is that obligation reconciled with the confidentiality inherent in the social worker–client relationship? The issues raised here were those decided in two *Tarasoff* decisions in the 1970s (Tarasoff I – 1974; Tarasoff II – 1976). The litigation concerned the case of a client who told his therapist that he intended to hurt his girlfriend. Despite the therapist's attempts at dissuasion and his consultation with others, including temporary detention by the institution's security force, ultimately the client killed the young woman. The woman's parents sued the therapists, the police, and the institution, and the courts found there was a basis for a negligence suit for 'failure to warn'. A re-hearing found there was cause for action against the therapist but not the police, and the court established a duty to 'use reasonable care to protect'.

While the *Tarasoff* decision does not impose a clear duty to warn intended victims, it does require social workers to make decisions weighing the client's right to confidentiality against a potential danger to a third party. Case law that has developed since *Tarasoff* has tested some of the issues, and Southard and Gross (1982) have proposed some guidelines for decision-making. Confidentiality should be breached if there is:

* a clear threat, as opposed to a vague one;
* serious danger, as opposed to marginal danger;
* a specific victim, rather than one not identifiable;
* imminent danger.

In all cases supervisors should be consulted or notified and documentation of reasons and actions taken should be specified. Actions may include family therapy, if appropriate; warning the victim; calling the police; and involuntary commitment of the client.

How can social workers and other service providers deal with issues of confidentiality? As suggested by Ragan, Salus, and Schultze (1980: 47), some guidelines for agencies and workers are:

* using release forms and obtaining informed consent;
* explaining to family that release of information is essential and done *only* when essential;
* sharing with the family what is released;
* being absolutely clear regarding professional responsibility to keep information confidential; and
* taking reasonable and appropriate steps to protect intended victims from danger.

Honesty with families is especially essential. Avoidance of a discussion of confidentiality is not helpful. Even when families willingly sign a group of release forms giving their permission for information to be shared, the issue must be carefully discussed. By way of explanation, families need to know that responsible decision-making regarding a child's permanency cannot be made when there is no responsible sharing of information. Collaborators cannot be expected to do a competent job, progress cannot be thoroughly evaluated, nor can courts make responsible decisions without accurate and complete information.

In addition, families need to appreciate that all collaborators are part of the decision-making team and can only contribute responsibly with full understanding of the problems and goals. Chances are that families will appreciate the honesty about the need for information to be shared. This has more credence than typical statements such as: 'Everything you say to me is strictly confidential.'

Most helpful is the presence of families when information is being shared. If we assume that parents are important members of the collaborative team, we should not keep secrets from them. As they participate in the sharing of important information, there is less risk of suspicion or worry over what was said.

Confidentiality of course must be maintained regarding parties not involved in the permanency planning process. Families need to know that information will not be discussed with people outside of the collaborative team without their specific consent.

SUMMARY

In permanency planning, collaboration among different organizations, disciplines, and persons involved in formulating and implementing a permanent plan for a child is an integral feature of practice. In this chapter we defined collaboration as the process of actively sharing in examining a child's and family's needs and qualities, reaching a decision regarding the most appropriate permanent plan, working together to implement that plan, taking joint responsibility for what occurs, and evaluating the outcome.

We also explained that collaboration is required for a number of reasons, such as avoiding the innumerable problems and dangers that can arise in complex case situations involving diverse service providers; achieving consensus regarding a permanent plan; clarifying expectations, roles and tasks of family members as well as service providers; ensuring that everyone is working on *one* focused plan; and effectively using and continuously monitoring services provided for the family.

We noted that in any given case there is a vast range of potential collaborators; their effective collaboration can be promoted through such means as adopting a team approach; clarifying goals and tasks; using a service agreement; evaluating progress and outcome periodically; dealing with conflict; and assigning a leadership role to a case manager. The responsibilities of the case manager in collaboration were described, particularly in respect to his or her leadership role, relationships with formal and informal service providers, and participation of the family. Issues in maintaining confidentiality in the process of collaboration were considered. Finally, a case example was presented to illustrate selected principles and the roles and tasks that need to be delineated to facilitate collaboration within a permanency planning framework.

SUGGESTIONS FOR FURTHER READING

Brill, N. (1976) *Teamwork: Working Together in the Human Services*. Philadelphia, PA: J. B. Lippincott.

Ragan, C. K., Salus, M. K., and Schultze, G. L. (1980) *Child Protection: Providing Ongoing Services*. Washington, DC: US Department of Health and Human Services. Publication No. (OHDS) 80–30262, especially Chapter 4.

Rossi, R. J., Gilmartin, K. J., and Dayton, C. W. (1982) *Agencies Working Together – A Guide to Coordination and Planning*. Beverly Hills, CA: Sage Publications.

Schmitt, B. D. (ed.) (1978) *The Protection Team Handbook*. New York and London: Garland STPM Press.

must be aware of legal doctrines —

15 Working with the legal system

This chapter will discuss the interplay of the legal system with permanency planning efforts. It will give a brief history of legal doctrines, define some confusing terms, and discuss conflicting roles and rights. A review of Public Law 96–272 and its implications for permanency planning will be presented, as well as guidelines for court appearance and testimony by social workers. A case example of termination of parental rights will conclude the chapter.

BACKGROUND

Permanency planning workers must be aware of the framework of conflicting legal doctrines, varying definitions of the legal status of children, new legal criteria resulting from Public Law 96–272, and new procedures mandated by the same law.

Conflicting legal doctrines

Laws dealing with child protection and child custody have a long evolutionary history in the USA. The earliest laws, deriving from English common law on property, were based on the concept of the father's 'natural right' to his children. In disputes, the father was legally entitled to the custody of his offspring. In the nineteenth century, the 'parens patriae' power of the state, protecting property rights, was extended to the jurisdiction over incompetent adults and children even when no property was involved. This led to an awareness of the psychological and developmental needs of the young child, the 'tender years' doctrine, which guided the courts in considering the 'benefit of the child' and awarding custody to the mother in parental disputes. The entry of the state as a disinterested third party in protecting a child in the absence of property did not emerge till the middle of the nineteenth century. Only then did adoption statutes appear; the first ones required consent of any living parent for legal adoption. Changing a child's custody without parental consent proceeded initially under the 'parental right' test – the parent was entitled to custody unless he or she was shown to be 'unfit' (Hegar 1983).

In recent years, 'the best interests of the child' concept relegated the fitness of the parent to only one of a number of considerations in awarding custody, others being the physical surroundings, the emotional ties between parent and child, the child's wishes, and the physical, psychological, and social characteristics of child and parents. Most recently, the concept of the 'psychological parent' has been promulgated (Goldstein, Freud, and Solnit 1973) to settle disputes solely on the basis of the emotional ties the child has formed with one parent or with surrogate parents.

The power of the state over children, especially as expressed in termination of parental rights, it can be seen, is a relatively modern legal concept in a constant state of change and redefinition. While the state's interests have been extended, constitutional guarantees found in the 14th amendment of the US Constitution protecting individuals from loss of life, liberty, or property without due process have been broadened to include family privacy and even family integrity, thus limiting the power of the courts to intervene in family life. At the same time, the burden of proof that cases be decided on the 'preponderance of evidence' has been shifted, by a 1982 Supreme Court decision, *Santosky* v. *Kramer* (1982), to the more rigorous standard of 'clear and convincing' evidence (Hegar 1983). Only conviction 'beyond a reasonable doubt' is more difficult to prove.[1]

In applying these concepts and legal doctrines, state courts must deal with a variety of conflicting concerns: the 'best interests of the child', the 'psychological parent', the due process guarantee to the family, and the child's right to permanency and stable relationships. This is especially true once the child has been removed from the home: the child's 'right to care' by biological parents (Houlgate 1980) comes into conflict with the right to 'treatment' (in this case nurturing stable relationships), the emotional attachments formed as a result of foster placements, and the disengagement from biological parents that a lengthy period away from home may entail. Major areas of tension may exist when considering:

* parents' rights *v.* children's rights;
* biological parents *v.* psychological parents;
* the right to privacy inherent in family integrity *v.* children's rights to safety and protection;
* the best interests of the child *v.* the least detrimental alternative (Mnookin 1973; Wald 1975, 1976); and
* foster parents' rights *v.* the right of the state to control the child when it has guardianship.

The worker must deal with the complexities presented by these alternatives and come to accept that such conflicts are inherent in the decisions that must be made for permanency planning.

Legal status of children

In addition to the difficulties posed by these legal doctrines, the worker must understand some of the intricacies of the child's legal status. For example, when a child's situation is so serious that the state must intervene to remove the youngster permanently from the biological parents who should have been the natural care-givers, the child welfare agency petitions the court to legally *terminate parental rights*. Before this serious step is undertaken, however, various temporary options may be explored when minor children need to have their care and supervision attended to by others. If parents are unable to provide such care, courts have the power to award 'custody', 'guardianship', or 'wardship' to public agencies or to responsible adults. The custodian or guardian then has certain rights and respon-sibilities in dealing with the child. If the custodian is the state's child welfare agency, the child is often said to be *committed* to the commissioner or other authority. The state then becomes the child's parent, and is, in effect, empowered to make decisions and give permissions for a variety of events vital to the child's well-being. When Juvenile Courts dealing with situations of abuse or neglect award *custody*, this includes the right to make important decisions for the child (where to live, authorization for emergency medical care, and so on) as well as the duty to provide for and protect him or her.

In some Juvenile Courts the category of *guardianship* may also be awarded, granting additional decision-making rights such as authorizing enlistment in the armed forces, major medical treatment, and marriage. In other jurisdictions, guardianship may be awarded only by the Probate Court, the state court involved with estates, conservators, and guardianship of property as well as persons. The rights and responsibilities are similar to those in Juvenile Court proceedings except that, generally speaking, they permit custody without ongoing involve-ment of the state's child welfare agency.

Social workers in each state must familiarize themselves with the laws and judicial procedures in their locality since, for the most part, matters of family relations in the USA are left to states, and they all differ in smaller or greater detail. The federal government influences many aspects of children's lives through the policies and funding patterns of the Social Security Act, the Uniform Child Custody Jurisdiction Act, the Juvenile Court Act, the Adoption Assistance and Child Welfare Act, and other laws. The Federal role is also based on the provisions of the Constitution and other laws and case decisions promulgating legal doctrines and practices. The states, for their part, must, by codes and regu-lations, put into effect the laws decreed by the federal government in order to obtain the funding promised. This must be done in congruence with the practices reserved to the states and developed over the years concerning issues of family life. The dichotomy between the roles and functions of the federal government and those of the states creates a dynamic tension that accounts for the evolutionary nature of so much of the law in this area.

The remainder of this chapter will discuss, within the context of Public Law 96–272 in the USA, some of the legal considerations in permanency planning, especially those issues that need attention in seeking termination of parental rights, the most frustrating legal situation apt to be encountered by permanency planning advocates.

Legal criteria and Public Law 96–272

Permanency planning work is complicated by the conflicting legal doctrines discussed above, as well as the inconstancy presented by the legal system itself. Although Public Law 96–272 is the major component of the legal context within which permanency planning is carried out, each state has its own laws, regulations, and procedures as does the federal government, and this variability, combined with frequent legislative changes, makes it difficult for non-lawyers to learn. It is important, however, to be aware of the legal conditions that prevail, and Public Law 96–272 is a good starting point. As noted in Chapter 2, this Act, passed by the US Congress in 1980, provides for federal financial incentives to states to discourage family breakup and, by implementing specific procedural reforms, to encourage permanency for children. To qualify for increased funding under Title IV B of the law, states are required to develop alternative services to those foster care or adoption subsidy services already in place, and to create preventive and reunification service programs. Other requirements are case plans for each child, case reviews, a statewide management information system, a one-time inventory of children in care, and a specific reunification program. These services are to prevent placement, assist children in placement, and reunify families.

The Title IV E programs, on the other hand, provide subsidies for foster care or adoption, but only if efforts have been made to prevent placement or to reunify the family. Case plans and case reviews are required. In order to motivate states to find alternatives to out-of-home care, those states that have implemented the law's requirements may transfer unused Title IV E funds (foster care payments) to Title IV B programs (preventive and reunification programs). In addition, under Title IV E, there is federal matching money for adoption subsidy, and those children automatically become eligible for the Medicaid program.

New procedures mandated by Public Law 96–272

The current legal framework for permanency planning in the USA is extensively described in a guide by Dodson (1983a), which includes, in addition to a review of Public Law 96–272 and narrative discussion of legal issues, a variety of checklists for evaluating state laws; annotated references to exemplary state laws and regulations and model legislation; and references to the legal literature on topics such as preventive services, foster care reviews, parent–child visitation, termination of parental rights, and adoption.

Social welfare agencies, represented by their social workers, now need to become familiar with the new federal requirements and their own state's compliance with Public Law 96–272. In part, these are:

★ *Reasonable efforts*. 'Reasonable efforts' must be made to prevent out-of-home placement of a child or to make it possible for the child to return to the biological home when placement cannot be avoided.[2] Furthermore, removal of the child from the home requires a judicial determination that such reasonable efforts were made. While the law is emphatic in this regard, it does not clearly define what constitutes 'reasonable efforts'; yet this is the heart of the law, designed to shift the emphasis away from the use of foster care to the application of prevention services for families at risk. Agencies, courts, and practitioners are currently struggling with the issue of what constitutes 'reasonable efforts'.

* *Case plans*. Case plans are required for each child. A case plan is a written document maintained on each child in out-of-home care, which must include:

    * reasons for removal from the home;
    * information ensuring that placement is in the least restrictive setting, in the child's best interests, and close to the parent's home;
    * a description of the placement setting and its appropriateness;
    * a plan for the child's receipt of proper care and the provision of appropriate and necessary services to facilitate reunification or adoption; and
    * the agency's and parents' expected conduct to assure permanency.

* *Case reviews*. A double review system is mandated. Every six months, throughout care, there must be a court or administrative review of case plans. Where the review is carried out by other bodies than the court, there must be at least one individual attending not party to the delivery of services in the case. The review monitors the need and appropriateness of the placement, progress being made in the case plan, and a likely date for return home or other permanence. Parents should be welcome to participate in the review.

   The other part of the review system is a dispositional hearing by a court (or its sanctioned agent) within eighteen months of placement, to determine the child's future and the services needed to provide a permanent family. These reviews are clearly delimited to provide for checks and balances in the state's care of children. The state must apply procedural safeguards to assure that each child has a dispositional hearing and on behalf of the parents to assure their rights with respect to removal, visitation, and changes in placement.[3]

* *Procedural protections*. Safeguards must be afforded parents and children whenever a child is removed from the home, a placement is changed, or a child is placed voluntarily. These safeguards are not specifically provided in the law, but pertain to speedy hearings, the child's proximity to parents so visiting can occur, fair hearings for parents, and assurance of non-coercion for voluntary placements, including a court hearing within 180 days.

* *Preventive and reunification services*. Although specific programs are not set forth, Congress intended that a range of services be provided, tailored to the needs of individual children. Social workers must become familiar with homemaker, day care, crisis intervention, shelter, and other services that can play a preventive or reuniting role in the achievement of permanency

(Chapter 12). The law provides for a fair hearing for families contesting the adequacy of service provision.

* *Management information system.* The importance of timely, accurate record-keeping is underscored by Public Law 96–272. An information system that monitors the status, characteristics, goals, and location of each child provides for accountability, permits for timely scheduling of case reviews, and can help determine the appropriateness of case plans. The need to provide such reports to the federal government for reimbursement is the motivation for developing a strong information system.

Compliance with the mandates set forth in Public Law 96–272 is complicated to monitor, since compliance at the policy level may be different from what occurs at the practice level. A number of organizations, such as the Children's Defense Fund in Washington, DC, may be helpful to advocates who are seeking to monitor their own state's compliance, by providing materials relevant to such oversight. Monitoring is further complicated by the absence of regulations that define 'reasonable efforts', 'preventive services', 'least restrictive setting available', and other such non-specific requirements. Varying interpretations of the legislation are inevitable, and state legislatures may have to revise state laws to be in compliance. Legal challenge may be the ultimate resource that will provide the impetus for compliance, by forcing change either in the laws or the regulations that implement the laws.

It may be that with Public Law 96–272 the legal system in the USA will become the prime mover in a new revolution in child welfare. Just as institutional care gave way to foster care, and the limbo of foster care is giving way to permanency planning, the efforts to implement permanency planning may lead to a new network of home-based preventive and reunification services as the prime emphasis of child welfare. This revolution may be created by legal challenges to out-of-home care. The law seems to point in that direction, with its emphasis on family integrity, due process for parents throughout a case, the right to treatment and preventive services, and the concepts of least restrictive alternative and reasonable efforts to prevent placements.

An attorney representing children or parents, in attempting to prevent removal of the child from the home, has a variety of strategies available which, in their totality, create a movement away from out-of-home placement. These include:

* negotiating with the child caring agency to refer the family for home-based services;
* opposing removal from the home unless there is 'imminent danger' of physical harm or serious emotional trauma;
* assuring the rights to parental hearing by the court before removal;
* petitioning for a hearing by the child caring agency when services required by law or case plan are not forthcoming;
* using an expert witness to argue against removal, citing the services needed to ensure safety and accomplish family rehabilitation;

* aggressively pursuing the child caring agency to determine what home-based service alternatives have been pursued or offered, and why they were rejected;
* countering claims of insufficient resources to provide home-based services with the costs of foster care;
* pursuing court orders for home-based services if the child caring agency is not willing to provide them voluntarily (Dodson 1983b).

Attorneys for the child and for the parents may use many of these techniques permitted by the provisions of Public Law 96–272 to create a climate of change, in which home-based, family supporting services, rather than removal from the home, become the norm of service provision for the child caring agency. Case-by-case litigation, however, is only one element in the creation of change. Legislative mandates are needed at the state level to support and fund preventive services. In addition, the assumption of responsibility by the child caring agency for broad education, specific training, and concrete technical assistance is necessary for effective home-based programs to succeed.

ROLES OF COURTS, LAWYERS, AND SOCIAL WORKERS

In each state there is often a number of courts dealing with child welfare. Juvenile Courts, Domestic Relations Courts, and Probate Courts present a tangled web to those who must deal with the judicial system. More than one court may have responsibility for the decisions about termination of parental rights, custody, or other issues around out-of-home children. Often the system is fragmented, one court having jurisdiction over custody, another over case review, and still another over determination of 'reasonable efforts' to provide reunification services. Each court has its characteristic administrative procedures, staff competencies, and financial inadequacies (Dodson 1983a). The social worker must learn the particulars of the court system in his or her own state, and try to find access to legal assistance to assure that all permissible steps are being taken to create permanency for children in care.

The attorney has many roles to play in permanency planning. He or she must investigate the facts in a case; review case plans to assure their appropriateness whether the client is the child, a parent, or an agency; represent the client with vigor and advocacy; prepare witnesses for court testimony; and become comfortable working with children and mental health professionals and agencies. The attorney must be prepared to present the case creatively in the complexity of a court situation (juvenile, domestic relations, or probation), where elements of both civil and criminal procedings may each be appropriate. In addition, litigation may involve divorce law, tort law, constitutional law, or other reliefs; the proceedings usually occur more quickly when children are involved than in adult matters; and the relative informality of procedures in family relations may be disconcerting (Hewitt 1983). A good family law attorney is a rare find; the financial rewards are meager, whether the attorney is employed by the state representing the agency, by the parents who most often are poor, or by the court that appoints a guardian *ad litem* to represent the child.

A social worker's close interaction with the law depends a good deal on his or her employment situation. In some jurisdictions a social worker may qualify as an expert witness, one whose special knowledge can help the court in coming to a decision. Such a worker is usually in private practice or employed by a voluntary agency, and may be called to testify by the attorney for any of the parties involved. Most often, however, the social worker has been involved with the child or family as an employee of the state agency, or a voluntary agency providing services, and has come to an advocacy position on behalf of the child against the parents in a petition for termination of parental rights. It should be noted that each agency has its own guidelines for social workers seeking or using legal consultation. Some may have staff attorneys readily available, some state agencies may have attorneys assigned from the Attorney General's or State Attorney's Office, and some may need to contract for legal consultation on a case-by-case basis.

Differing perspectives of social workers and attorneys

Permanency planning work, in order to be effective, requires a close knowledge of, and collaboration with the legal system. This is often difficult for social workers to accept for a variety of reasons. First, the essence of social work is listening and helping; in law the essence is advocacy, and these two philosophic stances may appear to be in opposition. Social workers are trained to facilitate and mediate, while lawyers must ethically use those skills only on behalf of their clients, even to the detriment of other family members.

Second, the terms used by the legal and judicial systems are similar to those used by laymen, but meanings may vary and therefore give rise to confusion. 'Disposition', 'expert witness', 'proof', and 'evidence' are some examples of the disparity between lay and legal language usage. 'Disposition' often refers to the judicial hearing at which a placement decision is made; this may be separate from the adjudication hearing at which a finding of abuse may be entered. In lay terms, 'disposition' is the outcome of any hearing, clearly not as specific a meaning as the legal term. 'Expert witness' is a professional who may be qualified by law or by the judge to testify because he or she possesses knowledge and can offer opinions beyond that of the layman that can help the court in coming to a decision; in lay terms an expert witness is any professional, with no recognition of the legal requirements that an expert be specially qualified by the court in order to offer evidence and opinions beyond those matters observed directly.

Similarly 'proof' is subject to a wide variety of standards and interpretations. There is a 'preponderance' of evidence, 'clear and convincing' evidence, and evidence 'beyond a reasonable doubt'. Each has its own legal and judicial implications, all more rigid than the layman's understanding. This is also true with 'evidence', around which there are definitions and legal constraints perplexing and intimidating to the layman. The burden of proof for custody in the state of Connecticut, for example, may be schematically displayed as follows:

Figure 7 Burden of proof

Standard of proof	Description	Typical applicability
Beyond a reasonable doubt	No question exists about the proof	Not used in Connecticut, but applied in some states in termination of parental rights
Clear and convincing evidence	Though some doubts may exist, it is insufficient to challenge the decision; the evidence is highly probably true	Termination of parental rights
Preponderance of evidence	More than 50 per cent true	Custody hearings
Ex parte	Reason to believe the evidence	Judicial decision, based on a lawyer's petition, for a brief, time-limited period of custody

In addition to the confusion of legal terms, social workers find the legal system difficult to work with because it is so cumbersome. While the social worker may be passionately committed to the protection of the child who is being abused, and have less conviction about the integrity of the family, the legal system is charged with everyone's protection. The child's safety and right to permanency must be balanced with the rights of the parents. The complex rules and procedures that have evolved to provide balance when conflicting issues are at stake often appear counter-productive. The US Supreme Court, for example, has recently ruled that a state must prove parental unfitness by 'clear and convincing evidence' before terminating parental rights (*Santosky* v. *Kramer* 1982). In many states the standard had been a 'preponderance of the evidence', a less stringent requirement favoring parental rights. The conflicting doctrines and legal constraints that characterize the adversarial system in the USA give no evidence of being any worse than various non-adversarial systems in Europe and elsewhere in coming to timely, 'fair' decisions. The complexity of human interaction mitigates against quick, easy decision-making, but the frustration with complexity is not easily dissipated.

The social worker as witness

The social worker may be called into court to testify under two circumstances:

1. As a courtroom witness, one who can be subpoenaed to appear by any attorney in a case and give information about the professional relationship with the clients.

2. As an expert witness, one whose professional expertise qualifies him or her to give an opinion that will assist the court in coming to a decision. An expert witness does not have to testify only to those things directly observed, as does a courtroom witness, but may also deliver opinions about hypothetical situations that will help the court understand the issues and the case under consideration.

COURTROOM WITNESS

Most commonly, the social worker is called as a courtroom witness. As the confidant and helper of one of the parties to the litigation, the worker may be called by the child's attorney, the parents' attorney, or the attorney for the state.Logically, it would be the attorney who felt the social worker's testimony would be helpful to his or her client who would ask for the subpoena. In that instance, the social worker and attorney can become a working team, since presumably they have an identity of interest in the outcome of the case. The social worker, however, must obtain releases from the client to share information with attorneys before the trial; although testimony in court can be ordered, the confidential relationship cannot be breached under other circumstances without client consent.

Many of the points to be discussed in the next section on 'Preparation for court activity' are important as the social worker prepares for his or her own court appearance. Case documentation, assertive negotiation with the attorney, an outline of the case history, and updated assessments and other information are all necessary elements. As advised for the client, it is essential for the social worker to know the case material well; here the chronology of events and list of important points are a good memory aid.

In addition, the social worker should prepare a strong resumé, detailing education, professional employment, and other professional experiences such as memberships, honors, and publications, which lend credibility to the testimony. Helpful to the attorney might be a list of questions and a list of collaterals whose testimony could be useful. If the attorney has the inclination and the time to enlist the social worker as a team member, other participation could include discussing the trial, contacting and preparing witnesses,and listing and describing exhibits or other demonstrative evidence such as pictures of bruises or anatomically correct dolls to illustrate a child's testimony.

So far as actual appearance on the stand is concerned, physical and mental preparedness minimizes difficulty. Physical preparation consists of dressing conservatively, wearing comfortable clothes so as to appear at ease, and perhaps having tissues or a handkerchief available. Mental preparation is a little more complicated. The social worker should be able to take a position, but only after presenting the facts fairly and without hostility to parent or attorney. Fair presentation of facts includes mentioning positive as well as negative aspects; since the positive points in all probability will emerge during cross-examination, prior acknowledgement of them lends credibility.

EXPERT WITNESS

When the social worker is called as an expert witness, there is great likelihood that opposing attorneys will attempt to impeach the qualifications, discredit the accomplishments, and personally attack the social worker.

All the guidelines that pertain to the courtroom witness are relevant to the expert witness, but with the additional concerns that responding to hypothetical questions engender. The expert witness must be prepared to present a resumé in a form that will qualify him or her for legal status as expert, and must be ready to give an opinion about a case 'like this one' without necessarily testifying to the facts in the case. Most often, however, that opinion as well as one's entire professional stance and value system will need to be defended strongly in the face of attack by opposing counsel.

Reconciling divergent views in the literature or explaining opposite professional opinions are also required of the expert witness. In general, a strong defense against intimidation is essential. The expert witness must speak authoritatively and with inner conviction. He or she can admit to not knowing an answer, ask for explanations of a question, ask the judge to allow for more than a 'yes' or 'no' response, or even respond 'half yes, half no' to maintain respectful integrity in the heat of hostile cross-examination.

It is as important for the expert witness as for the courtroom witness or the client to prepare for, rehearse, and role play the court appearance. In general, the courts are considering due process for parents with the gravity previously accorded the best interests of the child. This is in keeping with the intent of Public Law 96–272. Testimony must take into account this judicial leaning, and clinical judgments that go against this tendency must be buttressed by specific reasons and concrete documentation.

GUIDELINES FOR TESTIMONY

A checklist for testimony as either a courtroom or expert witness follows:

* Accept your mounting anxiety. Despite your pounding heart and sweating palms you can testify calmly. Take a deep breath before responding, and speak louder and slower than you think is normal.
* Do not take any question – or even your being summoned to appear – personally. Especially on cross-examination, whose purpose is to discredit your testimony, the probing hostile attorney is focused on you as a witness against his or her client rather than you as a person.
* Listen to the questions carefully, answer only the question asked and let the attorney develop the line of questioning.
* Be sure you are telling the truth; state facts, not opinions or what others have reported to you. You may bring the case chronology or other data sheets to help your memory, and you may consult your notes.

* Do not attempt to answer questions when you do not know the answer. 'I don't know' is honest and acceptable. If you do not understand the question, it is reasonable to ask for clarification.
* Use the judge to help you. For example, you can ask the judge to allow you to give more than a 'yes' or 'no' answer if the simple response needs explanation, or you can ask the judge to curb an overly aggressive attorney or a client or spectator making threatening gestures.
* Speak as neutrally as possible, not as a biased advocate, but speak with conviction and use vivid language to make your point. A child can have 'bruises on his body', or he can have 'five or six welts and lacerations on each arm or leg, some black blue and some bleeding'. Vivid language, however, does not include professional jargon, 'psychobabble', hostile jibes at parent or attorney, or sarcastic references.
* Be prepared to state your recommendation in the case, to defend it, and to discuss the pros and cons of alternative recommendations.

PREPARATION OF SOCIAL WORKERS FOR COURT ACTIVITY

In addition to being ready to provide court testimony, social workers should prepare for court activity through careful record-keeping, negotiating with attorneys, maintaining an outline of the case record, forming a list of potential witnesses, and preparing clients for court appearance.

Careful record-keeping

The most important preparation for court activity is the documentation that should occur during the course of a case. Careful record-keeping or organization of records is an absolute requirement for successful legal action. A good social history, a service agreement with the parents, and specific case notes monitoring compliance with the agreement as well as other relevant facts in the case as they occur are essential. Such a case record assists the attorneys in constructing their legal action, is necessary to jog the social worker's memory about feelings and events, and is more convincing to the court than unverified impressions and recollections. A case record that is factual, specific, free of hearsay reports and professional jargon, and nonjudgmental has the greatest documentary value.

Good documentation begins at the first client contact. If parents are being seen, complete honesty must be the basis of the therapeutic relationship, as noted in Chapter 8. Although it is a tricky position, the social worker must forthrightly convey the ability to function as a helper to the clients and as a monitor of their progress at the same time. Clients must know that their service agreements will be documented, and the monitoring must occur periodically, preferably in writing, so there will be proof of the seriousness of the process. The client must also understand the possible results if monitoring shows no progress.

Progress notes about events outside the service agreements should also become part of the case record, as discussed in Chapter 16. These should deal not only with occurrences with the client but also contacts between the child caring agency and other service providers working with the child and family.

The case notes, as much as possible, should be factual, objective, and free of jargon. If a client frequently misses appointments or is late for visits, those observations are best stated as facts rather than summarized with a judgmental 'resistant to treatment'. Similarly, it is more effective to note that a parent stays all day in a dark, cold apartment, staring at the wall, than that she is 'suffering from depression'.

Negotiating with attorneys

The social worker should not only be a conciliator and mediator concerned with the best interest of the child, but also an assertive advocate for the child/client. Telephone calls to attorneys to indicate concern for the status of the case in the justice system, to negotiate or bargain for a better position for the child, to suggest witnesses, or to arrange for an interview with the child or other important parties are all reasonable activities for the social worker.

The worker can quickly get a sense for whether these interventions are considered helpful by the attorney; very often they make the difference between an inadequately presented case and one that is well-prepared. Social workers should not be in awe of the mysteries of the legal world. Their attitude should be 'nothing ventured, nothing gained'.

Maintaining an outline of the record

An outline of the case record – a chronology of important dates and important events in the case – is essential. In addition, a list of points important to the case is a valuable aid, and even a list of questions may be appreciated. The chronology, the list, and the questions can be shared with the state's attorney or with the child's attorney, each of whom can probably use such assistance to formulate the specific inquiries they will make of witnesses during direct and cross-examination.

Formulating list of witnesses

The worker should prepare a list of potential witnesses – those professionals or other reliable observers who have had contact with the child or family and can testify as to the facts in the case. All of these are good resources for the attorney.

The social worker can prepare a list of such people along with a brief statement of what they can testify to. Since courts tend to decide on the 'preponderance of the evidence' rather than 'clear and convincing evidence' or 'beyond a reasonable doubt', collateral witnesses may easily strengthen a case.

Preparing clients

The social worker can be of invaluable assistance to a child or parent client appearing in court. The preparation can range from simple explanations that will remove some of the mystery from the judicial process, to the most complicated role-playing and testimony rehearsal. These are some of the ways the social worker can help:

* Inform the client about the court procedures, who the various courtroom actors are, and what purposes they serve. Clients should be prepared for long tedious waits in court, for continuances for a variety of reasons, and for legal maneuvers that cause delays. The client should know that it is the state, not an individual social worker, prosecuting; if a youngster is testifying to abuse, the child similarly should be aware that he or she is not the accuser but that the state's interest is being represented. The purposes of cross-examination, its hostile tones, and how to cope with it (as detailed in the preceding section on testimony) should all be rehearsed.

* Be in contact with attorneys to arrange for meetings with the client. An assessment of the client's ability to testify and hold up under cross-examination is important for the attorney in formulating successful questions or in negotiating agreements with opposing attorneys. Ideally, a pre-trial conference between the social worker and attorney will clarify the functions and expectations of each. The social worker can prepare a case summary which will be useful to the attorney in anticipating problems in evidence and law. The attorney can role-play with the worker so there will be no surprises in the questioning, can entertain suggestions about witnesses, and can summarize the main points of the case that will be emphasized to make the strongest impression.

* Accompany the client to all pre-trial meetings and conferences. Be an advocate and support for the client.

* Inform the client if there is a possibility that you, the social worker, will be called as a witness. Inform the client in general terms about the content of your testimony, without being specific about the details if your statements will be neutral or negative in tone. Be careful not to emphasize positives, if they are inappropriate, out of guilt for testifying in the presence of the client.

* Prepare an outline from the case record, documenting all events and points the client will need in testifying. Remind the client of past occurrences that are in the record but that may be forgotten. Use drawings, audio tapes, or video tapes to rehearse your time together, so that details become fixed in the client's mind. Drawings of a houseplan, for example, can help a youngster remember and explain where physical abuse occurred; listening to or viewing tapes can be a vivid memory aid and desensitizer when painful details must be recounted.

* Rehearse the chronology and important events. Enable the client to use specific details about embarrassing or painful events. Direct graphic language, rather than euphemisms, will permit the client to become more comfortable with difficult material. For example, helping a child describe how her breasts were touched is more convincing than allowing her to say: 'He did something wrong.' Rehearse, rehearse, rehearse.

* Role-play the complete testimony, beginning with the swearing-in and personal identification. Cross-examination is especially important to anticipate.

Playing the devil's advocate role with the client will enable him or her to deal with the confrontive questions and hostile tone of the opposing attorney.

★ Coach the client in how to testify – to listen to the attorney's questions carefully, remain calm, answer clearly, and seek relief from the judge if difficulties arise, such as threatening gestures or tone from the opposing attorney or being forced to answer 'yes' or 'no' when a more complete response is necessary. The client should also be advised about appropriate dress for court, how to address the judge, and other details of comportment that might affect the judge.

★ Visit the courthouse with the client before the trial. Try to gain access to an empty courtroom so the physical surroundings will become familiar to the client, and some of the awe and mystery will be neutralized.

★ Be an assertive – even aggressive – advocate. Call attorneys for information, to check times for meetings, and to confirm court dates in advance. Make arrangements to use the victim assistance room if one is available. Even with the most careful planning, much time is spent in the court-house waiting around; if the client can do this away from chance encounters with those on the opposing side, there is less likelihood of emotional upset and distraction.

★ Be responsible about talking with the client after a court appearance. If the client is a child, it is important to review the experience, in order to explain misperceptions, minimize guilt, rebuild self-esteem after a damaging cross-examination, and clarify decisions and their consequences. With a parent the same effort is necessary, especially if the court proceeding was for termination of parental rights and rights were terminated. In that case the parent needs to hear again that the termination was in the best interests of the child, that the parent is not a bad person for having become involved in this tangled web, and that the social worker is available for continued help if needed. Being non-judgmental is difficult when the lives of children are in question, but in order to help the parent, the social worker must accept this professional stance.

★ Be as clear as possible about your own feelings. This perhaps should be the first point about preparation instead of the last. It is natural to feel conflicted about children in the child welfare system and to express those feelings by assigning blame, becoming a zealous advocate of one side or the other, or becoming indecisive about an appropriate course of action. We were all once children and many of us are parents; our hurts and defenses around separation, loss, discipline, and nurturing are easily aroused and it is natural to find them unconsciously translated into ambivalences about the case. Team review and peer support are excellent aids in this area.

TERMINATION OF PARENTAL RIGHTS

Adoption was not statutorily recognized in the USA until 1851, when Massachusetts passed the first comprehensive adoption statute. The intent of that law, and others following, was to serve the interests of the adults rather than protect the children. This was necessary because children without parents lived in foster care and often informally entered into adoption without clear legal procedures.

Beginning in the 1950s, the rights of biological parents came to be more legally recognized and protected, and the informal adoption process gave way to more circumscribed procedures. Now each state has its own requirements. Most states specify that the petition to terminate parental rights must provide 'clear and convincing evidence' of parental fault or acts of omission or commission such as abandonment, non-support, repeated or severe abuse, substance abuse, imprisonment, improper care due to mental illness or retardation, or failure of the parent to improve (Hewett 1983). Some states require a waiting adoptive home. In all proceedings, the legal matters, the best interests of the child, and the leanings of the presiding judge determine the ultimate outcome for permanency.

This chapter will conclude with an abstract of a case history prepared for a Termination of Parental Rights hearing. The level of specifity of events, the documentation of facts, and the efforts to involve the parents are fundamental elements.

Witness: Marilyn Ogden, social worker-therapist and case manager for both Robert Little and his mother, Mrs Ethel Little. After working with the family for one year she has recommended that the agency pursue Termination of Parental Rights to free Robert for adoption.

State's attorney: Susan Rikes. She is representing the petitioner, the public child welfare agency.

Parent's attorney: Eugene Diaz. He is representing Mrs Ethel Little.

Robert Little: Age four. Committed to the public child welfare agency since age two. Presently living in the Grant foster home. Prior to this year, he had two foster placements and two hospitalizations. Robert presents as an anxious, insecure child who damages furniture and fights with others, is easily distracted, and constantly runs around displaying a high level of activity. He hits other children without provocation, becomes disturbed when he cannot complete a task or game perfectly, and reverts to more baby-like behavior when his routine is disturbed.

Mrs Little: Age 22, is a single parent. She has not been employed since quitting high school at age sixteen. She did not marry Robert's father; she was married briefly and divorced prior to living with Mr Pauley for two years. She relinquished an infant child for adoption five years ago. She has denied all allegations in the present hearing and is contesting the termination. She fully participated in the hearing.

Mr Pauley: Age thirty-three. Robert Little's father. His whereabouts have been unknown since Robert was nine months old and he moved out of the home. He has never financially supported Robert or his mother. His name is on Robert's birth certificate. Efforts to locate Mr Pauley by Mrs. Little and the child welfare agency proved futile. His family's whereabouts are also unknown. He was given notice of the upcoming hearing by publication in the newspaper serving his last known place of residence. He did not appear to participate in the hearing. As provided by state law, the petition for termination of parental rights is sought on the ground of abandonment by the natural father, and on the ground of acts or omissions of the mother denying Robert the care, guidance, or control necessary for his well-being.

Date of petition: March 16, 1983
Name: Robert Little
Date of birth: 2/15/79 (4½)
Placed: 4/10/82 (Grant)
Committed to public child welfare agency: August 1980

Record of living arrangements

Birth – November 13, 1979: Lived with Mrs Little and Mr Pauley.

11/79	Mr Pauley abandoned family (no contact since); Robert was nine months old.
12/79–3/80	Lived with Mrs Little, January 1980 – Child protection agency received complaint from neighbor, who reported child cut with glass by Mrs Little as a punishment for breaking a dish. Agency investigated.
3/80	Child broke arm, according to hospital report; 'fell down stairs', according to Mrs Little. Child removed from home.
4/80–10/80	Placed in foster home (Brown) August, 1980 – commitment to public child welfare agency.
10/80–12/80	Home with Mrs Little. Emergency Room of local hospital twice: 10/1 with cigarette burns; 11/2 with Valium overdose (Mrs Little's pills).
12/80	Placed in foster home (James).
7/81	Discharged to mother. Mrs Little appears stabilized; new boyfriend, Mr Jensen. Mrs Little told worker that Mr Jensen didn't like kids, they made him nervous. Mr Jensen tied him to bed at night because he kept getting up. Locked him outside when he was 'bad', 'He was uncontrollable.'
11/81	Admitted to Children's Hospital – 'Extremely oppositional, highly active, negativistic three-year-old . . . underweight . . . anemic . . . obsessive personality style.' Inpatient until 4/82.
4/82	Placed in specialized foster care home (Grant).

Specialized foster care events since 4/82

6/10/82	While child visiting at home, agency's parent aide observed iron plugged in within child's reach, butcher knife left out on counter.
7/5/82	Social worker saw child playing in road (unsupervised).
7/5/82	Robert – hospital resuscitation – water accident.
8/12/82	Robert admitted to hospital – broken leg; 'fell down stairs'
11/10/82	Parent aide reports mother not at home. Child left in care of nine-year-old neighbor.

12/26/82	Mrs Little called social worker to end Christmas visit (premature – to spend a week) – 'Robert soiling his pants, spit in my face, temper tantrums everyday. He doesn't listen to me, I can't stand him anymore.'
1/14/83	Mrs Little picked up Robert a day late for home visit. *Excuse:* Mrs Little, 'I had a date.' *Comment:* 'He acts like a brat . . . just like his father.' Returned to foster home four hours early.
1/22/83	Neighbor reported to child protection agency that Robert was locked out of home for misbehavior.
1/30/83	Phone call from mother to social worker: 'I don't want any more visits, I can't stand him . . . he's so immature.'
2/83	Mrs Little refused Robert for home visit.
3/83	Mrs Little agrees to voluntary termination but wants legal guarantee of yearly visits in order to sign. When told this not possible she said she will 'fight for him'.

Additional facts to note

* Mrs Little kept most of her weekly therapy appointments with Mrs Ogden.
* Mrs Little did not attend 'Parents Anonymous' as advised by Mrs Ogden.
* Mrs Little refused to enroll in a free Parent Behavior Training course.
* Mrs Little broke 10 out of 32 appointments, and was 'no-show' five times with parent aide June 1982–January 1983.
* Mrs Little repeatedly was one–three hours late picking Robert up from Grant foster home and repeatedly brought him back early from home visits. She excused herself from weekend visits due to being sick five times and 'working' four times on weekends between May 1982 and January 1983.

Discussion

The parent's attorney, in his arguments and examination of witnesses, made an attempt to dwell on Mrs Little's positive qualities; he admitted the difficulties she had but tried to minimize them. He brought out the problems inherent in dealing with any child, and related the worker's testimony to situations anyone might face in child-rearing. He emphasized that Mrs Little was doing as well as anyone could expect with a troubled child, and tried to refute the worker's statements with contradictory testimony by friends and relatives. In his summary to the judge, the attorney stressed Mrs Little's interest in Robert, her positive attempts to parent in the past, and the need to continue to give a loving mother an additional chance.

Despite the spirited argument, the presentation by the attorney for the state, buttressed by the strong factual evidence of the worker's efforts to involve the mother, well-documented and clearly set forth, provided 'clear and convincing' proof to the judge that parental rights should be terminated. The Grants eventually adopted Robert, giving him promise of a permanency he had sorely lacked before.

SUMMARY

This chapter outlined legal doctrines of importance to permanency planning work, including the father's 'natural rights', the 'tender years', 'the best interests of the child', and 'the right to care'. It was pointed out that the complexity of relating to the legal system is compounded by misunderstandings about terms such as termination of parental rights, commitment, custody, and guardianship. Complicating this legal thicket is the variability of state laws and regulations. This is especially apparent when state laws seek to implement federal mandates as, for example, in Public Law 92–272. The requirements of this Act were reviewed: 'reasonable efforts' to prevent placement, written case plans, case reviews, procedural protections, preventive and reunification services, and a management information system.

The different roles of the courts, attorneys, and social workers were discussed, and guidelines for the social worker's appearance in court were set forth. Other elements in preparation for court activity include careful record-keeping, negotiating with attorneys, preparing an outline of the case record, suggesting witnesses, and preparing clients. The chapter concluded with a case example of a Termination of Parental Rights petition, illustrating the specificity required, the importance of documentation, and the involvement of parents.

NOTES

1. The diverse standards and interpretation of 'proof' are discussed later in this chapter, in the section on 'Differing Perspectives of Social Workers and Attorneys'.
2. The 'reasonable efforts' clause may be found in Section 471 (a) (15) of Public Law 96–272.
3. See Allen, Golubock, and Olson (1983) for extensive discussion of the requirements of Public Law 96–272 regarding periodic case review.

SUGGESTIONS FOR FURTHER READING

Dodson, D. (1983a) *The Legal Framework for Ending Foster Care Drift: A Guide to Evaluating and Improving State Laws, Regulations, and Court Rules*. Washington, DC: Foster Care Project, National Legal Resource Center for Child Advocacy and Protection, American Bar Association, Young Lawyers Division.

Goldstein, J., Freud, A., and Solnit, A. J. (1973) *Beyond the Best Interests of the Child*. New York: Free Press.

Hardin, M. (ed.) (1983) *Foster Children in the Courts*. Boston, MA: Butterworth Legal Publishers.

Mnookin, R. H. (1973) Foster Care – In Whose Best Interest? *Harvard Educational Review* 43 (4): 599–638.

16 Keeping records

Social work records, like medical records, have always been the bane of clinicians. Records are necessary because we live in an age of accountability (Briar 1973), and they should be used to facilitate supervision and teaching, permit administrative oversight, and allow research to occur. We allow ourselves to accept these goals, however, with little hope of attaining them adequately. Records often have vital information missing (Willer and Santoro 1975), are disorganized, fragmentary, and 'subject to the caprice of the clinician' (Gilandas 1972: 336), and are rarely used for clinical decisions, administrative monitoring, or research (Hayes-Roth, Longabaugh, and Ryback 1975). Other weaknesses are an absence of procedures to systematically measure therapeutic changes, a lack of effort to address treatment effectiveness (Miller and Willer 1977), and the ease with which the subjectivity of records gets identified as case facts (Holbrook 1983). In addition, records are sometimes written 'to deny the failure of interventions' or 'to justify the refusal to serve "bad clients"' (Bush 1984: 1).

Despite these difficulties, adequate and relevant record-keeping is essential in permanency planning, not only because it helps ensure program accountability and case monitoring but also because it can help to structure service delivery, guide worker activity, and facilitate the participation of clients. How can we minimize the negative aspects of record-keeping and maximize its use? What goals should be served by record keeping for permanency planning? What is the essential content of permanency planning records? How can we use records to further our work with families? This chapter will discuss these questions, proposing a format for permanency planning records to facilitate the assessment of progress and appropriate decision-making about where children will grow up. In addition, goal-oriented recording will be introduced and illustrated as a new technique for achieving clarity in the planning for permanency, enforcing decision-making, and monitoring the attainment of desired goals and plans.

GOALS FOR RECORD-KEEPING

For permanency planning, record-keeping serves the following goals:

* case planning and management, with timely decision-making;

* structuring service delivery so that there is clarity in what is occurring;
* helping clients participate in what is happening to their families and in achieving a permanent plan;
* ensuring program accountability;
* documenting case progress for possible court appearance.

Any plans for record-keeping, however, must take into account the realities of service delivery. Administrators and researchers can design seemingly logical forms, but practitioners must find them usable. The criterion of usability often creates difficulties for the social worker, whose professional comfort may be more with 'doing' than 'writing'; whose priorities when time is short are crises and important client issues rather than record-keeping; whose orientation is more to people than to paper. If the requirement to keep records is further undermined by the demonstration that the records are not used, the social worker's motivation for careful documentation is greatly weakened. For these reasons, basic conditions for a good record-keeping system should include the following:

* The format should be as streamlined and simple as possible. Social workers do not like to write voluminously.
* Time should be allocated to demonstrate that records are used. Supervisors and administrators need to read records, and make plans or ask questions based on the information contained. Otherwise social workers perceive no result from the efforts they expended in writing records.
* Training in record writing and record review should be included in every social worker's job orientation, especially if the recording requirement is different in any way from the free-flowing narrative recording in which most students are trained. Examples of acceptable and unacceptable records should be used to demonstrate what is expected.
* The responsibility for case and program accountability must be assumed by administrators. If actionable information is included in records and no action results, there is not much positive reward for writing useful records. For example, if a number of case records document the unwillingness of the child protection agency to take appropriate legal action, and caseworkers have been unable to negotiate satisfactorily, there must be administrative response to the problem. Otherwise the records are useless, the workers perceive their efforts as fruitless, and record-keeping becomes another example added to the alienation phenomenon commonly labelled 'burn-out'.

CONTENT OF RECORDS

To be useful in the processes of assessment, intervention, and evaluation, the record kept in each case should document the following areas:

* initial and subsequent goals and objectives
* each family member's strengths and needs

* tasks assigned to the worker, the family, and any other service providers
* services selected to meet the family's needs
* strategies used to implement the services
* barriers (client, worker, service provider, and community) that interfered with completion of assigned tasks and effective service provision
* services needed by the family which are unavailable or inaccessible'.

(Ragan, Salus, and Schultze 1980: 57)

Social workers in child welfare are accustomed to voluminous case records, and equally accustomed to 'combing' them when a particular piece of information is needed. Extraneous materials wend their way into already crowded folders, resulting in documents that are cumbersome and difficult to use.

It is important that permanency planning records be structured and professional in appearance, particularly since they may be used in court; therefore, an orderly format is necessary. The content of the record should comprise:

* identifying information about the child and family
* initial assessment
* referral materials
* service agreement
* case activity log
* correspondence
* psychiatric, psychological, educational, or other evaluations
* progress review

For convenience, a sectioned record is suggested. For children who are in placement, there is the additional need for a medical section and a document section for such items as commitment papers, birth certificates, and baptism papers.

Identifying information

Each record should begin with a face sheet of information that a worker will want to refer to frequently. Included should be:

* child's name and birthdate
* child's legal status
* child's current placement (if any) and address
* date of present placement
* names and current addresses of biological parents
* names, addresses, and phone numbers of important collaborators such as the child protection agency worker, school social worker, and lawyer

Optional, but recommended, additions might be the date for decision-making regarding permanency planning and a date targeted for implementation of a permanent plan.

Initial assessment

The initial assessment is a well-organized narrative that presents factual and reported information in as objective a fashion as possible; this is followed by a clinical formulation of the social, emotional, and psychological characteristics of the family, which should highlight the child's need for permanency within a reasonable length of time and stress the decisions that need to be made in order to address the child's need.

Care must be taken to assess each family member's strengths and needs, and to evaluate the barriers to effective use of service faced by the family in the present or the past. As discussed in Chapter 8 on work with parents and children, the important ingredients in the assessment include:

* identifying information
* presenting problem
* history of presenting problem
* developmental history of the child
* health history
* pertinent past history
* clinical formulation
* treatment plan

Referral materials

Since children who need permanency planning often are known to more than one agency, it is common for records to include referral materials. These may include reports from the child protection agency, reports from schools, psychiatric or psychological evaluations from other resources, information from other placement agencies, etc.

A summary of the pertinent information from referral materials should be included by the worker in the initial statement of the assessment. The details of referral materials are often helpful to the worker in identifying patterns and in noting changes in functioning, and therefore belong in the record, but an abstract is more useful for getting relevant information to administrators, supervisors, and reviewers in one document.

For legal purposes, it is important that information from referral sources be so labelled, particularly when the information is being summarized in the assessment; for example, 'The report submitted by the protective service worker states that mother has a drinking problem.'

Service agreement

The service agreement should also be included because, as discussed in Chapter 9, it contains:

* the most succinct statement of a child's right to permanency;
* the desired permanent plan;

* the time frame for a permanent plan;
* the goals which must be attained for the permanent plan to be achieved;
* the roles of all parties in working toward goal achievement; and
* the dates for review of progress.

The service agreement is an essential part of the record and should be used periodically as progress is evaluated. A copy of the service agreement in the record should be made available to parents and all collaborators in the permanency planning process. Despite some evidence in outpatient counseling that written and verbal service agreements are equally effective (Klier, Fein, and Genero 1984), in permanency planning there should not be a choice between verbal and written agreements. As emphasized in Chapter 9, they must be in writing, in clear and simple language, and should state specific times for making decisions about permanency.

The chapter on service agreements (Chapter 9) goes into further detail on their use and content, and offers guidelines for writing them. While they are not considered legal documents, their use in court proceedings can offer clarity about goals and progress.

Case activity log

Permanency planning requires careful documentation of all activity directed toward decisions about where children will grow up. This means that notations need to be made about kept and missed appointments; phone contacts with parents and collaborators; meetings held for progress review or other purposes; and correspondence. A simple form (see *Figure 8*) facilitates this kind of documentation, which then permits easy assessment of the level of case activity. It provides information to support the efforts of both worker and family. It can also point out weaknesses, perhaps alerting a worker to the need to be more active or providing data for the worker to share with families in a way that enables them to become more responsible.

Figure 8   Case activity log

Date	Nature of activity	Comments
1/18/83	Appointment with mother	Appointment not kept
1/19/83	Phone call to mother	She 'forgot' appointment Rescheduled for 1/26/83
1/25/83	Progress review meeting	See report in record

Correspondence

Copies of all correspondence are necessary to document communication among workers, families, and collaterals. For example, letters are used to convey important information such as visiting schedules and appointment dates. Correspondence may be especially important in cases where there is reason to believe that parents are not able to participate in a way that will enable them to resume care of their children. For families whose addresses change frequently or parents who state they have not received mail, the use of registered letters is advocated. Receipt of such correspondence can then be documented.

Correspondence from families and collaterals should also be kept in the record. As we have noted repeatedly, in permanency planning decision-making is the major goal. Since decision-making requires sound clinical judgment based on accurate information, the ability to support clinical judgment with well-documented evidence is essential. This in turn reinforces the confidence that the courts have in the social worker's judgment, and facilitates the judicial decision-making process.

Progress review

At agreed-upon intervals, case progress must be reviewed for decision times to be taken seriously. At a progress review meeting, ideally attended by worker, family, and collaborators, the terms of the service agreement and the content of the goal-oriented record should be reviewed, and progress and lack of progress noted. Implications for decision-making should be discussed. The outcome of the meeting should be recorded as objectively as possible. An important feature of permanency planning records is that they be written in a way that makes them available to families and collaborators. For this reason it is important that they be objective and descriptive, and that they use simple language. Each item in the record and on the service agreement should be reviewed. For example:

* 'Mother agreed to keep weekly appointments with worker. All appointments were kept.'
* 'Mother agreed to learn and try new child management techniques. While she agrees with the idea of a reward chart, she has not actually implemented its use.'
* 'Mother agreed to pick up her son for visits each Saturday. She picked him up four times but missed four times. On one of those occasions she called to say that she was ill.'

The progress review should include a statement that relates to decision-making, such as: 'Progress is such at this point that the plan for child to return home seems an appropriate goal'; or 'Progress at this point is limited and it may be necessary to consider other options as a permanent plan for child.'

The report of the progress review should also include any changes in the goals or tasks stated in the record or the service agreement. For example, if a goal to find new housing was achieved, there might then be a new goal of investigating supportive community resources in the new neighborhood.

As discussed in Chapter 14, copies of the report of the progress review meeting should be available to worker, family, and collaborators in order to assure clarity of progress and future planning.

GOAL-ORIENTED RECORD-KEEPING

In permanency planning, traditional narrative recording or periodic case summaries will not reinforce the case management, decision-making, and assertive casework needed by children and families. A technique tailored to these objectives is the goal-oriented record, which will be presented and illustrated in this section.

Background

This new development in record-keeping is a variation of the problem-oriented system, which has been described as the most exciting change in record-keeping in hundreds of years (Grant and Maletzky 1972). Problem-oriented records began as a modification of medical records. Medical records, because medicine deals with particular, specifiable complaints and elements of patient care, were likely, regardless of format, to contain the important information about a patient's care, but in a disorganized and non-integrated form. The problem-oriented record, originally developed by Weed, is organized according to a problem list with a matching treatment plan, in contrast to the traditional narrative medical record, in which each entry is filed by source of writer (i.e. all nursing notes are together, all X-ray reports are together, etc.).

Despite the increasing popularity of the problem-oriented record, its extension to related fields has been slow. The hospital setting has encouraged some applicability to psychiatry and to hospital-based social work, but general acceptance in the field of social work has been sluggish (Windle 1972). In social work there is still little uniformity about what goes into the records, much less how it is organized (Chea 1972; Kagle 1984).

This stems not only from the general opposition to innovation that any change, and the Weed system in particular, faces (Goldfinger 1973), but also to a special problem in mental health and child welfare, namely, the lack of problem and goal orientation. Social workers, psychologists, and psychiatrists have traditionally worked with clients on whatever issues seem important for however long it takes to explore them. Efforts to change this orientation have included the development of task-centered casework, time-limited therapy, and goal-attainment scaling (Garwick and Lampman 1972; Mann 1973; Reid and Epstein 1972). The new task and goal orientation, reflected in the latter approaches, however, needs to be matched by a similar change in record-keeping. This is beginning to occur as the original promise of the problem-oriented record is being applied to social work settings (Kane 1974), and modifications are constantly being sought by administrators and researchers alike (Beinecke 1984; Hartman and Wickey, 1978). The search is for a system that will give a clear picture of problems, their treatment, and follow-up; encourage planning of treatment and assessment of progress; facilitate the integration of many diverse facets of the client's case; foster training of students and staff; permit auditing of treatment; and ultimately sharpen the decision-making ability and competencies of social workers.

Goal-oriented records as a technique for permanency planning

One response to the search for applicable record-keeping has been the creation of the *goal*-oriented record, developed from a modification of medical problem-oriented records, using that record-keeping system's emphasis on focus, structure, and conceptualization.[1] The goal-oriented-record, however, is not based on a medical model of service delivery; it is not focused only on problems to be solved but also on the strengths of clients and the resources and planning efforts in each case situation. This shift in emphasis should help define case plans in actionable terms rather than psychological formulation. It also mirrors how families are being treated by social workers using the ecological approach that was discussed in Chapter 6.

The goal-oriented record is a technique for recording assessments, plans, progress, and accomplishments in a case. It is designed to help social workers think in a goal-oriented way, to keep track of important elements in a case, and to communicate efficiently the major issues. Record forms are designed to document three key stages in permanency planning:

* identification and assessment of a range of permanency planning options;
* formulation and review of a specific permanent plan; and
* goals and plans for treatment of specific problem areas, based on resource-building interventions.

In addition, the forms are designed to encourage systematic planning and periodic review. They cannot readily be used to document daily activity on a case, as the previously mentioned case activity log or narrative recording can. They are intended to force social workers to think about cases in a permanency planning framework, with a goal orientation based on tight time considerations and active planning. The records encourage constant review for evaluation and recommendation of alternatives, thus permitting a worker to take a broad view of what is occurring over time in order to make new decisions and take corrective action when necessary.

Sections of the goal-oriented record

The goal-oriented record contains three sections:

* *Section A: Permanent Placement Decision Form*
  This form (see *Figure 9*) sets the stage for the record, giving limited information about the child and forcing a conscious choice for the social worker and others about permanency planning. The reasons for circling *No* or *Yes* about a permanency planning decision should be the subject for case review by the supervisor or service team.
* *Section B: Permanent Plan Form*
  This form (see *Figure 10*) sets forth the option for a permanent plan that has been selected by the social worker and others involved in the case. It requires a target date by which that option will be filled, other placement

options that may be considered if the first one fails, and goals that must be met by child and adults for the option to be viable.

In addition, to emphasize the importance of time in a child's life, dates are required for achievement of each goal, overall goal achievement, and physical placement of the child. These dates should be the subject of ongoing periodic review by the social worker and the supervisor, as well as the team when appropriate, to assure that work is proceeding suitably and that the option for permanency will be exercised.

★ *Section C: Treatment and Resource Development Form*
This form (see *Figure 11*) is the heart of the goal-oriented system. It documents what the case is about, what has happened in the progress of the case, and what planning has occurred to achieve specified goals. It requires that the social worker consider each of a list of potential problem areas, and then write a problem definition, statement of resources and strengths, goals for the client, and worker plans to address these areas of difficulty. It further requires that a modality of service for each plan be identified, and that achievement of goals and plans be reviewed and rated.

The review and ratings can be done as frequently as program supervisors decide that they are useful; the minimum would be at least at case closing. Assessments at closing time are important for evaluation of case progress and for learning through careful consideration of past successes and failures. Supervisors need to monitor the use of the forms for these purposes and demonstrate their value for teaching purposes. (See *Figure 12* for Rating Guide.)

The 'Treatment and Resource Development Form' requires thinking and writing in four major areas:

1. Definition of the problem: *What's the problem?*
   The definition of a problem should be as *explicit* as possible so that a clear image emerges. The statement of the problem should be *relevant* to how it affects the individual's or family's functioning and ability to cope. The language should be *direct* and informal; technical jargon will probably produce inadequate problem definitions.

   Examples:
   ★ 'Poor mother–child relationship' – Better stated as: 'Mother and child fight frequently and rarely show affection.'
   ★ 'Child has low self-esteem' – Better stated as: 'Child feels he is too dumb to do well in school or to make friends.'

2. Consideration of the client's strengths and resources: *What can I build on?*
   The client's strengths or resources are abilities, ways of functioning, social connections, or any positive aspects of his or her life that presently exist, or can be found or mobilized on behalf of the client. They may be personal characteristics, social connections, or environmental conditions that will be

applicable to the problem area. They should be relevant and explicitly stated.

> Examples:
> * *Problem:* Mother and child fight frequently.
>   *Client strengths:* Many fights occur because mother fears child will get hurt if she doesn't watch him; she is concerned for her child's welfare. Mother and child do *not* fight over schoolwork.
> * *Problem:* Child feels he is too dumb to do well in school or to make friends.
>   *Client strengths:* Child does average work in school; he is not failing. Child's small number of friends keeps him close to one or two and keeps him from associating with trouble-making groups.

3. Creating a goal for the problem. *How will we know when we're successful?* The goal states how the *client* or his or her situation will be different, not what the social worker will do to make that happen. The goal should be stated in such a way, however, that the social worker can *assess* whether it is accomplished. In addition, the goal should be able to be accomplished in a clearly stated *time period*, so that a feeling of success can emerge from the client's interactions with the social worker. Explicit, observable, assessable goals must be balanced with *clinical relevance*. This is the most difficult part of goal-oriented record-keeping. It requires serious thought on the part of the social worker and anticipation of how things can be different for the client; it needs a mind-set unlike the usual one of letting events unfold.

> Examples:
> * *Problem:* Mother and child fight frequently about meal time.
>   *Goals:* Mother will serve smaller portions.
>   Mother will ask child's participation in meal planning.
>   Child will agree to try new foods.
>   *Not explicit enough:* Mother and child will cooperate at meal time.
> * *Problem:* Child feels he is too dumb to do well in school or to make friends.
>   *Goals:* Child will feel confident in ability to read.
>   Child will feel more accepted by peers.
>   *Too explicit:* Child will talk to two new friends each day.
>   *Not appropriate clinically:* Child will volunteer for extra work after school.

4. Making a treatment plan. *What do I do to get there?* Plans are a statement of what the social worker will do to help the client achieve his or her goals. Each plan should be *explicit*, able to be carried out in a relatively *brief time* period, and *assessable* as to its accomplishment. Plans should be reasonable and specific enough so that the social worker can be held accountable.

Examples:
* *Problem:* Mother and child fight frequently about meal time.
  Plans: Discuss with mother her child's need to assert himself and ways mother can allow this, particularly at meal time.
  Not explicit: Help mother and child with communication.
* *Problem:* Child feels he is too dumb to do well in school or to make friends.
  Plans: Refer child to social skills group to help overcome fear of peers.
  Provide tutoring to enhance child's reading skills.
  Not assessable: Build self-esteem in weekly therapy sessions with child.

Sample of goal-oriented record

To illustrate the use of the goal-oriented record in permanency planning practice, we are including in this section a sample of a completed record (*Figure 13*). As the reader reviews this record the following story will emerge.

From Section A we learn that Mary Peters, previously in a foster home of a public child welfare agency and most recently in an emergency placement in a residential facility, came to this agency's attention on May 1. Her situation required a decision for a permanent placement. Section B tells us that by September 1 it was decided that Mary would return to live with her biological mother if certain goals were met within four months. Her mother needed to find an apartment and maintain it for three months; regularly attend alcoholism counseling sessions for three months; show evidence of being able to set appropriate limits on Mary's behavior; and make plans for dealing with Mary's father should he appear and start acting violently. In addition, there needed to be evidence that Mary would no longer be afraid of daily interaction with her mother. If these goals were not met by January, alternative permanent placement options in order of priority would be long-term foster care with Mary's maternal grandmother, adoption by the grandmother following termination of parental rights, and adoption by a non-family member.

What were the family issues that were contributory to the decisions outlined above? Section C, the *Treatment and Resource Development Form* tells us that three major problems were identified August 1:

1. Mary needed a stable permanent home while permanent placement options were being worked on;
2. Mary was fearful of being alone because of intense difficulties around separation and rejection; and
3. Mary, at age seven, had little school experience and her math and reading skills were deficient.

It can be seen that each problem has a concomitant resource or strength identified, along with goals for the client and plans for the social worker. For the first problem, the foster family care program of the agency was a resource, and the goal for Mary was placement. The plans the social worker needed to make so Mary could achieve that goal consisted of specific actions with collaterals and foster parents – presenting the case, selecting a family, arranging for placement, and meeting with the foster parents.

For the second problem, Mary's fear of being alone, the strengths were Mary's good response to firmness and affection and her attachment to significant role models. The goals were for Mary to be able to be alone for short periods without fear and to learn to trust the foster parents. (These goals, in another record-keeping format, could easily have been stated in more intra-psychic terms. As emphasized earlier, the statements here aim for explicitness, specificity, and ease in assessment.) The social worker's plans to help Mary achieve these goals consist of individual child therapy focusing on separation conflicts and reinforcement of feelings of self-worth, as well as work with her foster parents to help them deal with Mary's fears of rejection.

For Mary's academic problem (problem 3), the resources were Mary's eagerness to learn and her responsiveness to structure. The goal was for her to be in a public school program; to accomplish that, the social worker collaborated with the foster parents to help them enroll Mary in school and consulted with the teacher on Mary's individual needs.

By September, three additional problems were identified, at which time the permanent plan and goals for its achievement were set down on Section B, the *Permanent Plan Form*.

In January, when goal achievement was rated on Section C, *The Treatment and Resource Development Form*, Mary had been placed in a foster home but there was little to no progress in regard to her fears. The work on those goals was continued. Her school goals were being met and her mother had found a place to live. Her mother, however, had not been able to reduce her drinking and that goal was abandoned. Because of this inability to meet her goal, the first option for permanency planning, Mary's return to her mother, was not viable, and the second option, placement in long-term foster care with the maternal grandmother was selected. A new *Permanent Plan Form* was then filled out, with new goals that needed to be met by June 1. (See *Figure 13*, Section B, Permanent Plan Revision.)

At the same time, on the *Treatment and Resource Development Form*, Mary's goal to be unafraid while interacting with her mother was rated as partially achieved and modified to a new goal, feeling comfortable when alone with her mother. A new problem arising from Mary's move to her grandmother's house was identified – the grandmother's lack of understanding Mary's need for structure. The resource to work on that problem was the grandmother's commitment to keeping Mary with her, and the goal was for the grandmother to understand Mary's need for structure. The social worker's plans were for individual interviews with the grandmother and family interviews with the grandmother and Mary together, to work on these issues.

This record-keeping example has no case history or narrative recording, yet the broader elements of case progress are apparent. Decisions were made about the child's placement, goals were set, and contingency plans were enforced when they were not met on time. Continuing work with the family was noted, and areas of success and failure were clearly set forth. The amount of writing, considering the breadth of information conveyed, was minimal. What was required was the capacity to think differently about case flow and case notation – to demonstrate a strong focus on goals and planning, a commitment to time frames, and a determination to follow through on what the review of information in the record conveyed.

USE OF GOAL-ORIENTED RECORD IN PARENT AIDE PROGRAM

The same departure from the traditional thinking about case progress presented in the preceding section can be demonstrated in a record-keeping system developed for a paraprofessional parent aide program. In this program parent aides work with families whose children are at risk for child abuse or neglect. The aide works with the mother to help her develop parenting skills so the child can remain safely and permanently at home. The feature that distinguishes this program from others similar to it is its goal-oriented, time-limited structure; administrative and record-keeping procedures were developed to reinforce and monitor that structure.

Typically, a referral for a parent aide would come from a social worker working with the family. She would send the supervisor, who served as program coordinator, a form describing the client, case issues, parenting concerns, and possible roles for the aide. The supervisor would assign the aide and meet with the social worker, aide, and client to draw up a service agreement, outlining the general goals that would be addressed in a twelve-week period (see sample agreement in *Figure 14*).

Three weeks after the service begins, the social worker, aide, and program coordinator meet to become more specific about case problems and goals. For each problem a separate record sheet is filled out, stating the goal it is hoped the parent will achieve, and specifying the activities the aide will engage in to help the parent achieve that goal. As in the permanency planning records discussed earlier, the goals should be stated in terms of what the *client* will *achieve*, not what the social worker or aide will do, and should be as concrete as clinical relevance will permit; they should be achievable within the twelve-week period; and they should be assessable. Similarly, the aide's interventions should be specific, clinically appropriate, and goal-related.

After nine weeks, the social worker, aide, and program coordinator meet again to assess the progress made. A rating of goal achievement for each problem is made on a 20 point scale ranging from -10 (much worse) through 0 (no change) to $+10$ (goal completely achieved). If the aide service is to be terminated at twelve weeks, the goal review at nine weeks allows three weeks to work on termination. If the goal review indicates that further service is needed, new goals may be set or plans made for improvement or maintenance of the work in the first period (see *Figure 15*).

In a parent aide program such record-keeping has many advantages (Miller *et al.* in press). It clarifies the role of the aide and helps the social worker understand what is going on in the home. The concrete plans assist the aide in her work and give a sense of professional contribution to the progress of the case. The ratings of goal achievement give information about attainment, permitting modification of plans when there is little success or giving a feeling of satisfaction when success is observable. These assessments are important in building worker or parent aide pride and preventing burnout; ordinarily the cases are so difficult that it is easy to overlook the small but significant gains that do occur. A further advantage of the record-keeping is that it keeps all professionals involved keenly aware of time. Contracts are set for specified periods, reviews occur regularly, and service is terminated or extended according to plan.

Such record-keeping requires serious commitment on the part of the program administrator. It is not cumbersome to implement, but it is time-consuming and requires investment in training of staff. Although it meets with resistance because practitioners who are used to other systems must learn to think differently about their work and how they document it, for those who try the new system the reward is usually an exciting feeling of accomplishment in their new orientation. This system has been used by the parent aide program at Child and Family Services since 1980, with satisfaction and success. The aides, in particular, find it a valuable focusing and evaluative tool (Miller *et al.* 1984b and in press).

SUMMARY

This chapter discussed the values and uses of record-keeping, especially as they facilitate clarity and decision-making in permanency planning. A goal-oriented record-keeping format was suggested to include sections on identifying information, assessment, referral materials, service agreements, a case activity log, correspondence, and progress review. The goal-oriented record was presented as an effective technique for achieving clarity in permanency planning, enforcing decision-making, and monitoring progress. In addition, its use was illustrated through discussion of sample records involving a social worker and a family in one case, and an in-home parent aide program in another.

NOTE

1. Many modifications of problem-oriented records have been developed at Child and Family Services, a voluntary child welfare and mental health agency in Hartford, CT, for use in alcoholism programs, child sexual abuse projects, homemaker services, and walk-in mental health facilities. The goal-oriented record was created for use in a Social Work Training Project funded for three years by the National Institute of Mental Health. It was used to train, monitor, and evaluate students in techniques and practices of permanency planning (Miller and Fein 1984).

SUGGESTIONS FOR FURTHER READING

Kane, R. A. (1974) Look to the Record. *Social Work* 19 (4): 412–19.

Klier, J., Fein, E., and Genero, C. (1984) Are Written or Verbal Contracts More Effective in Family Therapy? *Social Work* 29 (3): 298–99.

Miller, K., Fein, E., Howe, G., Gaudio, C., and Bishop, G. (in press) A Parent Aide Program: Record-Keeping, Outcomes, and Costs. *Child Welfare*.

Wilson, S. J. (1980) *Recording – Guidelines for Social Workers*. New York: Free Press.

Figure 9   Goal-oriented record

SECTION A: PERMANENCY PLACEMENT DECISION FORM

Identified Client: Mary Peters

Case Number: 00430

Social Worker: J. Doh

Date Assigned: 5/1/81

Child's place of residence at date of case assignment: Children's Institution – emergency placement; had been in foster home of public child welfare agency.

Does this case involve a permanency planning decision? (circle one)

NO (If No, also complete Section C of goal-oriented record.)

YES (If Yes, also complete Sections B and C of goal-oriented record.)

Figure 10 Goal-oriented record
SECTION B: PERMANENT PLAN FORM

Identified Client: Mary Peters

Worker: J. Doh

PERMANENT PLAN: Return to biological mother, contingent on various goals being met within the the next four months. These are listed in detail below.

DATE: 9/1/81

OTHER PLACEMENT OPTIONS (IN ORDER OF PRIORITY)

Second: Placement in long-term foster care with maternal grandmother.

Maintain supervised contact with mother.

Third: Adoption by maternal grandmother, following termination of parental rights.

Fourth: Adoption by non-family mother, following termination of parental rights.

GOALS WHICH MUST BE MET FOR FIRST OPTION TO BE ACCEPTABLE	Date Formulated	Date Met
1 Mother must find a suitable residence and have maintained it for 3 months.	9/8/81	
2 Mother must have been attending alcohol counseling sessions for 3 months, on a regular basis.	9/8/81	
3 Mary must be unafraid of contacts with her mother.	9/8/81	
4 Mother must show evidence of being able to set appropriate limits on Mary's behavior.	9/8/81	
5 Mother must show evidence of plans for dealing with Mary's father, should he appear and begin acting violently as in the past.	9/8/81	

PROJECTED DATE BY WHICH THESE GOALS MUST BE ACHIEVED: _____1/1/82_____

PROJECTED DATE FOR PHYSICAL PLACEMENT (if applicable): _____3/1/82_____

(USE GOAL SHEETS IN SECTION C TO RECORD ACTIVITIES UNDERTAKEN TO HELP CLIENTS MEET THESE GOALS.)

Figure 11 Goal-oriented record

SECTION C: TREATMENT AND RESOURCE DEVELOPMENT FORM

| Identified Client: Mary Peters |
| Worker: J. Doh |

Consider each of the following areas in defining problems, goals and plans:

Child's behavior	Relations between child and parents
Child's feelings towards self	Relations between child and foster parents
Potential developmental lags	Relations between child and peers
Child's emotional state	Other family relationships
Child's school functioning	Sexual relationships
Parent's behavior	Home management
Parent's feelings toward self	Community support systems
Parent's emotional state	

Health (each family member)
Alcohol or substance abuse
Educational needs
Employment needs
Finances
Housing and transportation
Criminal justice system

Use as many extra pages as necessary to identify all problem areas to be worked on. Add new problems to the list as they emerge.

PROBLEM: 1. Mary is currently at a children's institution; needs a stable, consistent temporary home

while permanent options are pursued.

Date Identified: 8/1/81

Resources & Client Strengths: Specialized Foster Care Program — Child & Family Services Agency.

RATING

Goals: 1 Placement in a foster home with foster parents who can provide
          necessary structure for Mary.

Plans: 1 Present case to Team in Specialized Foster Care Program.

       2 Select appropriate foster family.

       3 Arrange for placement.

       4 Meetings with foster parents to discuss Mary's specific needs for
          structure, and to provide consultation for them as needed.

PROBLEM: 2

Date Identified:

Resources & Client Strengths:

RATING

Goals:

Plans:

Figure 12 Rating guide for review of goal-oriented record

GOALS

I. <u>Focus</u>

Over the past few months, has this goal been:

1 A MAJOR FOCUS of your work

2 A MINOR FOCUS of your work

3 NOT WORKED ON during this time

II. <u>Goal State</u>

At this time, is this goal:

A ACHIEVED

B CONTINUED

C ABANDONED

D Not yet achieved, but MODIFIED (to _____)

II. <u>Success in Goal</u>

What level of success has been reached with this goal at this time?

Become Much Worse	Become Somewhat Worse	Shown No Change	Partially Achieved Goal	Completely Achieved Goal

```
-10  -9  -8  -7  -6  -5  -4  -3  -2  -1  0  1  2  3  4  5  6  7  8  9  10
 +---+---+---+---+---+---+---+---+---+---+---+---+---+---+---+---+---+---+---+---+
```

PLANS

This particular plan has been:

A Carried out as planned; and to be continued

B Carried out as planned; not to be continued

C Not yet carried out, but still planned

D Abandoned

Figure 13   Goal-oriented record

SECTION A: PERMANENCY PLACEMENT DECISION FORM

Identified Client: <u>Mary Peters</u>

Case Number: <u>00430</u>

Social Worker: <u>J. Doh</u>

Date Assigned: <u>5/1/81</u>

Child's place of residence at date of case assignment: <u>Children's</u>
<u>Institution – emergency placement; had been in foster home of</u>
<u>public child welfare agency.</u>

Does this case involve a permanency planning decision? (circle one)

NO   (If <u>No</u>, also complete Section C of goal–oriented record.)

YES (If <u>Yes</u>, also complete Sections B and C of goal–oriented record.)

Figure 13 (cont.) Goal-oriented record
SECTION B: PERMANENT PLAN FORM

Identified Client: Mary Peters

Worker: J. Doh

PERMANENT PLAN: REVISION: Mary placed in long-term foster care with maternal grandmother.

Mother's visitation to be on a regular basis.

DATE: 1/15/82   REVISED:

OTHER PLACEMENT OPTIONS (IN ORDER OF PRIORITY)

Second: Adoption by grandmother followed Termination of Parental Rights; maintain only

supervised contact with mother.

Third: Adoption by non-family mother, following Termination of Parental Rights.

Fourth:

GOALS WHICH MUST BE MET FOR FIRST OPTION TO BE ACCEPTABLE	Date Formulated	Date Met
1 Grandmother and mother to develop visitation arrangement agreeable to both	1/15/82	
2 Grandmother to understand Mary's special needs for structure.	1/15/82	
3 Grandmother to show evidence of being able to set appropriate limits for Mary.	1/15/82	

PROJECTED DATE BY WHICH THESE GOALS MUST BE ACHIEVED: 6/1/82

PROJECTED DATE FOR PHYSICAL PLACEMENT (if applicable): 7/1/82

(USE GOAL SHEETS IN SECTION C TO RECORD ACTIVITIES UNDERTAKEN TO HELP CLIENTS MEET THESE GOALS.)

Figure 13 (cont.) Goal-oriented record

SECTION B: PERMANENT PLAN FORM (PERMANENT PLAN REVISION)

Identified Client: Mary Peters

Worker: J. Doh

PERMANENT PLAN: Return to biological mother, contingent on various goals being met within the next four months. These are listed in detail below.

DATE: 9/1/81   REVISED: 1/15/82

OTHER PLACEMENT OPTIONS (IN ORDER OF PRIORITY)

Second: Placement in long-term foster care with maternal grandmother.

    Maintain supervised contact with mother.

Third: Adoption by maternal grandmother, following termination of parental rights.

Fourth: Adoption by non-family mother, following termination of parental rights.

GOALS WHICH MUST BE MET FOR FIRST OPTION TO BE ACCEPTABLE	Date Formulated	Date Met
1 Mother must find a suitable residence and have maintained it for 3 months.	9/8/81	1/1/82
2 Mother must have been attending alcohol counseling sessions for 3 months, on a regular basis.	9/8/81	1/1/82
3 Mary must be unafraid of contacts with her mother.	9/8/81	
4 Mother must show evidence of being able to set appropriate limits on Mary's behavior.	9/8/81	
5 Mother must show evidence of plans for dealing with Mary's father, should he appear and begin acting violently as in the past.	9/8/81	

PROJECTED DATE BY WHICH THESE GOALS MUST BE ACHIEVED: __1/1/82__

PROJECTED DATE FOR PHYSICAL PLACEMENT (if applicable): __3/1/82__

(USE GOAL SHEETS IN SECTION C TO RECORD ACTIVITIES UNDERTAKEN TO HELP CLIENTS MEET THESE GOALS.)

Figure 13 (cont.) Goal-oriented record

SECTION C: TREATMENT AND RESOURCE DEVELOPMENT FORM

Identified Client: Mary Peters

Worker: J. Doh

Consider each of the following areas in defining problems, goals and plans:

Child's behavior   Relations between child and parents   Health (each family member)
Child's feelings towards self   Relations between child and foster parents Alcohol or substance abuse
Potential developmental lags   Relations between child and peers   Educational needs
Child's emotional state   Other family relationships   Employment needs
Child's school functioning   Sexual relationships   Finances
Parent's behavior   Home management   Housing and transportation
Parent's feelings toward self   Community support systems   Criminal justice system
Parent's emotional state

Use as many extra pages as necessary to identify all problem areas to be worked on. Add new problems to the list as
they emerge.

PROBLEM: 1 Mary is currently at a children's institution; needs a stable, consistent temporary home

while permanent options are pursued.

Date Identified: 8/1/81

Resources & Client Strengths: Specialized Foster Care Program - Child & Family Services Agency.

	1/15/82		RATING

Goals: 1 Placement in a foster home with foster parents who can provide
      necessary structure for Mary.   **1   A   10**

Plans: 1 Present case to Team in Specialized Foster Care Program. **A**

     2 Select appropriate foster family. **B**

     3 Arrange for placement. **B**

     4 Meetings with foster parents to discuss Mary's specific needs for **A**
       structure, and to provide consultation for them as needed.

Figure 13 (cont.) Goal-oriented record
SECTION C: TREATMENT AND RESOURCE DEVELOPMENT FORM

Identified Client: Mary Peters
Worker: J. Doh

PROBLEM: 2 Mary has intense conflicts around separation and rejection. As a result, she is very fearful of being alone.

Date Identified: 8/1/81

Resources & Client Strengths: 1 Mary attaches well to significant role models.
2 Mary responds well to firmness and affection.

1/15/82 RATING

Goals: 1 Mary's conflicts about separation to be reduced to a point where she can trust her foster parents. — 1. B 3

2 Mary to be able to be alone for short periods without fear. — 2. B 0

Plans: 1 Weekly therapy with Mary to focus on conflicts around separation. — A

2 Weekly therapy with Mary to focus on increase in her feelings of self-worth. — A

3 Weekly meetings with foster parents to discuss how they can help Mary deal with her fears of rejection during daily interaction. — C

PROBLEM: 3 Mary, aged 7, has little school experience, and her math and reading skills are below

expected level.

Date Identified: 8/1/81

Resources & Client Strengths: 1 Mary's teacher reported she seemed eager to learn, and was receptive

to structure.

1/15/82 RATING

	1	B	8				

Goals: 1 Mary to be in public school program with appropriate services to help

her make up any deficits.

Plans: 1 Help foster parents to enroll Mary in school.   B

2 Weekly meetings with foster parents to discuss how they can help Mary   C

deal with her fears of rejection during daily interaction.

Figure 13 (cont.) Goal-oriented record

SECTION C: TREATMENT AND RESOURCE DEVELOPMENT FORM

Identified Client: Mary Peters

Worker: J. Doh

PROBLEM: 4. Mother has no permanent residence, and a history of transiency.

Date Identified: 9/8/81

Resources & Client Strengths: 1 Mother's church has provided help in such areas before.

2 Child & Family Services Parent Aide Program might have available

services.

	1/15/82 RATING		
Goals: 1 Mother to find and maintain suitable residence.	3	A	10
Plans: 1 Discuss problem with Reverend Johnson.	D		
2 Refer to Parent Aide Program.	D		
3 Discuss lifestyle changes with mother in individual therapy.	D		

PROBLEM: 5   Mother's excessive drinking interferes with her parenting time and skills.

Date Identified: 9/1/81

Resources & Client Strengths: 1   Child & Family Services Agency's Adult Counseling Services.

		1/15/82	RATING			
		2	C	0		

Goals: 1   Mother to reduce her drinking to a point where it will not interfere
with parenting.

Plans: 1   Refer to Adult Counseling Services – Child & Family Services Agency.   B

Figure 13 (cont.) Goal-oriented record

SECTION C: TREATMENT AND RESOURCE DEVELOPMENT FORM

Identified Client: Mary Peters

Worker: J. Doh

PROBLEM: 6 Mary is fearful of being around Mother.

Date Identified: 9/1/81

Resources & Client Strengths: 1 Mary has responded well to individual therapy situation.

2 Mary wants to be with her mother sometimes.

	1/15/82 RATING		
Goals: 1 Mary to work through the basis of her fear.	1	B	4
2 Mary to be unafraid while interacting with mother.	1	D	5
Plans: 1 Individual therapy to focus on basis of fears.	A		
2 Meetings between Mary and Mother to begin to desensitize Mary.	A		

PROBLEM: 7 Grandmother does not understand Mary's special needs for structure.

Date Identified: 1/15/81

Resources & Client Strengths: 1 Grandmother committed to keeping Mary with her.

RATING

Goals: 1 Grandmother to understand Mary's need for structure.

Plans: 1 Discuss issues with grandmother.

2 Meet with grandmother and Mary together, to develop roles for home life.

Figure 14 Parent aide program

AGREEMENT BETWEEN PARENT AND PARENT AIDE

CASE: JOAN EVANS

As Parent Aide, I agree to help this parent:

1) Better cope with problems in daily life.
2) Increase understanding about children's needs and child care.
3) Organize and manage daily activities.
4) Locate and use services in the community.
5) Work on the goals agreed upon with the parent and supervisor.

I also agree to keep anything said during our meetings confidential, sharing such information with no one outside of the Child & Family Services team, without direct permission from the parent. I will discuss my work with the case supervisor.

As parent working with a Parent Aide:

I understand my own responsibility in working with the Parent Aide to reach any goals on which we agree.

I understand that the Parent Aide is part of a team of helpers, and must be free to share any experiences with the other members of that team, when necessary.

I realize that Parent Aide services are limited, and that the Parent Aide cannot:

1) Babysit when I leave the home.
2) Lend money, or hold money for me.
3) Provide transportation (unless approved by supervisor).
4) Provide food, or do housework for me.

The Parent Aide will begin to visit with the parent on ___June 1, 1983___.

I agree to meet with the Parent Aide on the dates we agree upon. IF FOR SOME REASON, IT IS NECESSARY FOR ME TO CANCEL MY MEETING WITH THE PARENT AIDE, I WILL CALL THE PARENT AIDE OR THE CASE SUPERVISOR.

Together we agree:
To meet on a regular basis, __2__ days per week, for 12 weeks. The days we agree upon are __Monday/Wednesday__, time __9:30 A.M.__. To work toward the following specific goals:

1) To learn to set limits and be consistent with children.
2) To learn to budget and comparison shop for nutritious food.
3) To become involved in specific community activities.

_____
(Parent Aide)

_____
(Parent)

_____
(Date)

As supervisor of the Parent Aide, I agree to meet with parent and Parent Aide if either feels this agreement needs to be altered in any major way.

_____
(Supervisor)

Figure 15 Parent aide
PROBLEM/GOAL LIST

PROBLEM NUMBER: 1

CLIENT: Joan Evans

AIDE: Estelle Brentwood

PROBLEM: Mrs Evans doesn't know how to care for her infant. DATE IDENTIFIED: 6/10/83

INITIAL GOALS AND PLANS (At third week conference)   Date: 6/24

Goal PA will address: 1 Mrs Evans to be able to parent infant.

Parent Aide Plans: 1 Mrs Brentwood will role model appropriate parenting skills.
                      2 Mrs Brentwood will discuss infant care with Mrs Evans.

FIRST CASE REVIEW (At ninth week)   Date: 8/5

Plans which were accomplished:1 Talked about infant care, Mrs Brentwood's mothering
                                 experience.
                               2 Parent Aide modeled loving, caring for, playing with
                                 baby.

Progress Mrs Evans very receptive, no longer calls baby 'it', has clearer understanding
          of developmental stages, is more confident and comfortable with baby.

Status of goal: [ ] Goal Achieved   [ ] Goal Abandoned

LOF = 7   [X] Goal Continued   [ ] Goal Changed to:

(Level of Functioning)
New Plans: Continue same plans, work for more progress

SECOND CASE REVIEW   Date: 10/28

Plans which were accomplished: Same as above.

Progress Mrs Evans more capable mother.

Status of goal: [X] Goal Achieved   [ ] Goal Abandoned

LOF = 9   [ ] Goal Continued   [ ] Goal Changed to:

New Plans: Terminate case 11/15.

17 Creating the administrative context

Up to now we have been dealing with permanency planning as a helping process, without attention to how such a program becomes viable. In this chapter we shall discuss broader agency management and administrative implementation: the impact that adoption of a permanency planning philosophy can be expected to have on an agency, the barriers it must face, the importance of administrative commitment, and the extra resources required. These administrative issues will be discussed in general; in addition, issues of burnout and training will be discussed in greater detail, and a suggested curriculum will highlight the scope of training necessary to support the administrative initiative.

INITIATING PERMANENCY PLANNING

As outlined in earlier chapters, adoption of a permanency planning philosophy requires the incorporation into practice of the following key components:

* Early consideration of long-term plans for each child, beginning immediately upon referral.
* Identification of different options for averting out-of-home placement or moving the child out of temporary care, with establishment of priorities.
* Creation of a time-limited service plan to achieve an appropriate permanent placement.
* Record-keeping that structures documentation and organization of evidence for legal action, if necessary (e.g. for termination of parental rights).
* Use of periodic case reviews to monitor progress in plan achievement.
* Collaboration with other community agencies to obtain the optimum assistance and support for the family.
* Provision of comprehensive services to the biological family to support and maintain permanency.

These components may be perceived as threats to the traditional ways of delivering services in an agency. We shall examine some of the resulting barriers and issues as they pertain to the worker, the administrator who represents the service delivery system, and society in general as it defines and influences what is being accomplished. Additionally, we shall offer suggestions useful to administrators in dealing with these issues, particularly in instituting a permanency planning process and creating a supportive administrative context. Other suggestions may be found in Dreyer (1978), Villone (1982), and Ward *et al.* (1982).

Barriers related to the worker

As early as 1976, the Oregon Project recognized the crucial role of the worker's beliefs in implementing permanency planning: 'Decisions about planning possibilities for the foster child are a function of the workers' information and optimism, their attitudes and opinions, their decisiveness and experience, and their perception of the constraints under which they operate' (Regional Research Institute 1976). It was discovered, for example, that caseworkers become less optimistic about permanency planning as the child gets older. There is also evidence that adoption of the older, handicapped, and minority child is dependent on workers' attitudes (Temporary State Commission on Child Welfare 1977); the difficulty of placing severely handicapped children in adoptive homes leads workers to believe that permanency planning is not effective.

Workers' experiences on the job, moreover, strongly influence the type of placement they feel will be permanent and that they therefore encourage. For instance, less experienced workers may favor adoption as the outcome of foster care with the greatest potential for stability. Those with experience in residential treatment may prefer remedial work with children over work with families. Some workers with strong beliefs about the importance of bonding may not be in a hurry to move a child from foster care, despite an intellectual belief in permanency planning. Program directors and supervisors must be sensitive to such proclivities on the part of workers, in order to create the strongest context for permanency planning.

In addition to the experiences workers have had, certain biases – against the paperwork that documentation requires, the confrontation that a service agreement may necessitate, or the action against biological parents that non-compliance with the agreement may call for – may affect the implementation of a permanency planning program. In the same vein, discomfort with case reviews may exist: can the worker be assured that the review is of case planning and not of the worker, that it is a technique of case monitoring and not of witch-hunting? Similarly, a worker with a strong clinical orientation may lack belief or comfort in mobilizing available community resources to maintain the permanent plan. Again, it is the program director or supervisor who must assess such resistances and design strategies to deal with them.

Other significant challenges to the worker are the complexities of the roles they must assume and the variety of systems in which they must do their work; the anticipation of burnout, a phenomenon that seems to accompany work particularly with abusing, multi-problem families; and the never-ending task of finding, developing, and maintaining homes that will provide permanence.

Clearly, the values, skills, experiences, and attitudes of the worker are crucial in dealing with the threats that the introduction of a permanency planning orientation poses. It is too simplistic, however, to expect changes in workers without the guidance and support of the unit or agency in which they work. The difficulties the workers perceive may be countered most effectively when responsibility for change is assumed up and down the entire administrative hierarchy.

Policy issues

In order to demonstrate commitment to permanency planning, many difficult administrative decisions about policy and programming need to be faced. One concern, for example, is the population to be served. Logically all children and families are entitled to permanency services; in the real world of scarce resources, however, logic may not prevail. Since more than half of all foster children are twelve and over (Knitzer and Allen 1978), there must be increased attention to the needs of older children. Yet this must be balanced by the urgency of moving younger children as quickly as possible. Which group should be the target population if such a choice needs to be made in an agency or community?

Another example of a difficult administrative decision is caseload size. It has been stressed that fifteen cases is a worker's maximum efficient load (Emlen *et al.* 1977). The complexities of the roles the worker must assume, as discussed in Chapter 5, necessitate commitment to a small caseload. In most agencies, most caseworkers have caseloads larger than this (Knitzer and Allen 1978). Although there is no conclusive evidence that caseload size is correlated with successful outcome, work with client populations where interactions among complex and overlapping systems is required, as in permanency planning, typically limits the cases that can be handled. In one program in which sexual abuse cases were treated, it was found that on an average only eight cases a week of the caseload of twenty could receive worker attention (Bander, Fein, and Bishop 1982). The administrator must reconcile the large number of cases and relatively low number of workers with the demands for time that permanency planning requires. The administrator must be convinced that over time planful activity in non-crisis situations will avert crisis calls, that the total time on a case will not necessarily increase with permanency planning work, and that time and energies will be used more efficiently once clear objectives and explicit strategies are formulated. Evaluating time use and case outcomes is an essential administrative function to maintain the oversight necessary in allocating personnel.

Administrators are also faced with the need to create policy guidelines that will help workers deal with controversial questions. These may include such dilemmas as:

* What criteria determine whether a child who has been in 'temporary' foster care for several years should remain and avoid the trauma of another move, or be placed elsewhere with the expectation of legal permanency?
* Should a young child currently placed with elderly relatives be considered

for a permanent placement elsewhere? Is that a present problem or one that should be postponed?

★ What are the determinants in the conflict between continuity of relationships with inadequate caretakers and moving a child to give the child a permanent legal home?

Specific procedures for making such decisions need to be in place before the thorny issues arise. A permanency planning team, peer support groups, or consultation with permanency planning experts are some of the ways decision-making can be effected. For instance, staff planning groups have been found to be particularly effective in expediting permanency planning within large agencies (Villone 1982).

Related to decision-making are administrative techniques for dealing with inter-agency conflicts. When a public agency places a child with another agency, at least two workers become involved in the case. Who 'owns' the child? Who is responsible for planning? Who implements what pieces of the plan? In the best interests of the child and family, as discussed in Chapter 14, these jurisdictional questions should become part of a service agreement that is subject to review and monitoring.

Similarly, conflicts in orientation may arise, as when a child is being cared for by one agency and a parent is in treatment with another agency. The adult's worker, convinced of the significance of permanency planning, may be creating expectations that the parent conveys to the child's worker who may not have as much conviction about permanency. Or the situation may be reversed, and the child's worker may be pushing for permanency while the parent's worker prefers more traditional, psychiatrically oriented clinical treatment. The workers in both of these examples obviously need to meet to negotiate the differences between them. But on a recurring basis, if negotiations fail and agreements are not adhered to, there needs to be an administrative response. Too often the conflicts are left to smolder between workers who have no power to resolve differences. It then becomes the responsibility of the administrator to facilitate inter-agency conflict resolution. Such an administrative response is not only helpful in postponing or eliminating the burnout phenomenon, but it displays creative leadership in implementing policy, and models the assertiveness and decisiveness that workers in permanency planning need to see demonstrated.

Finances

One of the biggest problems the administrator faces in permanency planning work is the financial one. Aside from the usual problems of resources too scarce adequately to cover service needs, permanency planning presents economic concerns of great sensitivity. It costs more to do good permanency planning than to merely maintain a roof over a child's head. While the costs in the long-term, considering board and other payments for years of foster care, may be less for the public agency, in the short-term they are higher in servicing each case. It takes more time to develop special services such as parent aides, find adoptive homes, work carefully with parents on visiting and other therapeutic action plans, and move families through the complex legal and other systems with which they are involved. From where is the money to come? Supportive legislation, such as Public Law 96–272, in the USA, is part of the answer. Moving money from one program to another is another possibility, though robbing Peter to pay Paul requires keen sensitivity to political realities. Strong program planning – long-term planning with periodic review and update – is probably the safest way to insure continued financial support.

Funding problems are idiosyncratic to particular agencies, and few generalizations can be made for their resolution. Perhaps the most meaningful statement is that the competent administrator must display a commitment to the implementation of policy sufficient to obtain the wherewithal to accomplish it. The allocation of expensive resources for long-term benefit requires an exquisite obligation on the part of administrators, and each must find his or her own way of meeting the challenge.

BURNOUT

Administrators also must deal with the loss of energy, purpose, and enthusiasm that can be experienced by social workers over a period of time as a result of a variety of causes: client overload, insufficient training, too many things to do in too little time, low pay, unchanging clients, and bureaucratic constraints (Edelwich and Brodsky 1980). This 'burnout' phenomenon has been recognized as a special vulnerability of permanency planning work. Suggestions for dealing with it range from responses that individuals can make (e.g. leaving the job) to those more relevant to organizational action. Kahn (1978) proposes, for example, that organizations develop social supports as well as reduce the amount of time spent working directly with clients, while Maslack (1978) advocates peer support groups on the job, and Edelwich and Brodsky (1980) recommend an application of reality therapy principles to staff burnout issues (that is recognizing the problem, interpreting successes and failure, supporting constructive changes).

Given the demands of complex permanency planning work, the need for support to staff to prevent burnout cannot be overestimated (Ward *et al.* 1982). Support includes training, adequate time for job performance, manageable case-loads, peer support groups, and opportunity to deal with personal feelings.

Support for case managers

As discussed in Chapter 14, the role of case manager is crucial in permanency planning work, especially to promote coordination and collaboration among service providers. Case managers need to be recognized for the complex work they do. They also need opportunities to share work with others who are interested and willing to offer insight and suggestions. A case manager cannot function well alone, particularly when important decisions are to be made. In addition, because the work is concerned so much with issues of separation and loss, the emotional strain on workers is great. They need the opportunity to discuss the painful feelings that arise in working with families experiencing the trauma of loss. A formal administrative structure to provide peer support is essential to maintain the vitality of permanency planning work.

Administrative supports for permanency planning include consistent sensitivity and attention to morale-building as well as allocation of sufficient time and physical resources to accomplish the tasks. The reality is that some desirable supports will not be available (e.g. manageable case loads, grateful clients, adequate pay scales), but others (e.g. training, support groups, established criteria for measuring competence) can be established. A preventive approach to burnout can have the advantage of keeping trained workers interested in doing permanency planning and thus minimizing the expense and morale problems of staff turnover.

Support for foster parents and child care workers

Caring for someone else's child is both satisfying and frustrating. The satisfaction comes from the growth and development of the youngster, the pleasures of providing nurturance, and the self-esteem derived from altruistic behavior. On the other hand, the frustrations are many. Children may resent the care, regardless of its quality, because of the confusion about loyalty. They may have an idealized view of their parents that must be dealt with sensitively. The children may manifest inappropriate behavior, attitudes, and emotional states, and must be handled with compassion. Everyone hopes the foster parents can miraculously erase the emotional scars.

Additionally, biological parents may resent the foster parents for taking the child from them, dividing the child's loyalty, and being able to do the job they cannot do. Biological parents will seek opportunities to find flaws in the ability of foster parents to care for the child, and criticisms will be free-flowing.

With all of this, foster parents need appropriate support services to sustain their strength for the important work they do. These may include:

* *Training* of foster parents about child development, emotional problems of children, issues of separation and loss, working with biological parents, child management skills, and use of community services.
* *Support groups* for foster parents to provide the opportunity to share experiences with each other.
* *Recognition* of foster parents as significant team members, by providing adequate financial reward for their work; appropriate training; opportunities for group meetings; and annual dinner, picnics, and other informal rewards.
* *Regular contact* with the case manager for the opportunity to discuss painful feelings related to permanency planning work, as other team members do.

* Assistance in developing an *informal support network* (Froland 1980). A buddy system in which foster parents can call other foster parents to discuss general issues, a child's particular behavior, disciplinary actions, or an incident that occured during a parent's visit can sometimes get things into a manageable perspective and help avoid crises.
* *Expansion of communication* networks by sharing articles to read, newsletters about foster parent activities, and special recognition for the difficult work being done.

Support for parent aides or homemakers

Paraprofessionals who work with biological families in their homes to offer support to parents also need assistance to avoid burnout. These parent aides or homemakers are engaged in difficult, front-line, often thankless work. They need:

* *Recognition* for the difficulty and importance of their work by the professionals with whom they have contact. The courtesy and respect of the other permanency planning team members, who will treat parent aides as those with a particular expertise whose time is as valuable as that of workers with higher educational qualifications, are vital supports.
* *Training* in specific techniques for working effectively with parents who may be dependent, isolated, hostile, depressed, and uninterested.
* A *support group* to discuss their work with other parent aides where insight and assistance are available.
* A record-keeping system that helps paraprofessionals develop and monitor *criteria for reviewing* their accomplishments. Thankless jobs become more manageable when successes can be recognized periodically and failures used as a basis for learning.
* *Tangible supports*, such as adequate pay, career movement opportunities, perquisites to which staff have access (use of an agency automobile, travel to conferences, inclusion in planning meetings, and so on).

Support for volunteers

Permanency planning often involves the use of volunteers, who may be used as home visitors for biological parents, tutors for children, drivers for parents or children, or case monitors and reviewers. Volunteers will not remain long on the job without recognition and support from those who recruit them. Agency support may be less significant in those situations where the work with families and children itself becomes the reward. In permanency planning, the return from work with the families may be slow in coming, and volunteers will need to feel a sense of accomplishment from some other source. They need support services of their own, such as training events, social get-togethers, appreciation luncheons, and certificates.

SOCIETAL ISSUES

Permanency planning raises many issues about how service is delivered, not only for workers and administrators, but for the child welfare establishment and indeed for society in general. Changes will need to be made to put our philosophical beliefs into practice. For example, as more foster children are freed for the permanency of adoption, the recruitment of adoptive homes will need to be increased as well. This in turn will have an impact on the screening process for potential adoptive parents, the agency programming required to help parents accept the hard-to-place child, and the flexibility an agency will need to develop to deal with poor or unusual adoptive parents and adoptive practices.

Legal processes, too, will need to change as permanency planning becomes viable. As considered in Chapter 15, social workers, through mandated reviews, termination of parental rights proceedings, and child protection testimony are coming into contact with attorneys and the judiciary with increasing frequency. Social workers' approach to human services is through mediating, encouraging self-esteem and self-respect, and pursuing the best interest of all parties involved. Attorneys, on the other hand, are advocates, dedicated to the protection of the rights of the individuals they are representing (Knierim 1983). The stereotypes of the social worker who deals with feelings, not facts, in a soft-hearted manner, and the attorney who is single-mindedly concerned only with the client's interest are being challenged as contact between social workers and legal practitioners increases. Attorneys are beginning to admit that improvements in the rights of individuals are often the result of problem identification and public advocacy by social workers; in turn social workers, as they become more familiar with the law, can respect its concern with facts and the protection of the individual, and can appreciate the negotiating skills attending any advocacy position.

The judicial system is also part of this systemic interaction. Both lawyers and judges are being asked to make permanency planning decisions without a feeling of confidence in their expertise in this area. In addition, increasing attempts to obtain termination of parental rights, or increasing pressures for frequent judicial reviews of committed children, stretch the court backlog even further than do the usual delays in setting hearing dates, continuances, and postponements. The judicial system, designed for a different era, is being challenged by the neds of permanency planning. More effective relationships among social agencies, judges, and attorneys are being fashioned in a number of ways:

* Use of volunteers as case monitors to relieve the burden on court personnel.
* Inter-professional cooperation on 'children and the courts' committees designed to improve communication.
* Concerned legislative lobbying on such issues as foster care review, guardians *ad litem*, and termination of parental rights.
* Inter-professional education about child welfare and the courts.

A further challenge to the child welfare system stems from a concern over services for biological families (Maluccio and Sinanoglu 1981). Since over half of all foster children have been in temporary care for two or more years (Knitzer and Allen 1978), returning children to their biological families, which is often the preferred treatment plan, will require difficult adjustments for all family members. What support can society promise? What value is placed on the integrity of the family? For example, funding for board and care payments for foster care continues to be more readily available than financial support for preventive services, or supportive services for biological families. This creates a systematic bias encouraging agencies to place children in foster care as an expedient solution to a family's problem. Incentives that keep a child out of the family are a revelation of the values of society (Wolock and Horowitz 1984).

Over a decade ago legislation was introduced in the US Senate requiring a family impact statement of all federal programs which might be expected to have significance for families before being funded, something akin to the environmental impact statements that are now mandatory. The defeat of that legislation made a statement about the value of families in our national consciousness. If we are to broaden our concern for family life, there needs to be a more general awareness of the importance to families of adequate housing, income, and education. Thus the quest for permanence may be said to pose some questions about our entire economic system and how responsive it can be to the basic needs of our families. A society displaying instability in many of its aspects (hunger, housing, education, nuclear safety) may be hard-pressed to provide permanence and stability for its most vulnerable children. In a wide sense, efforts to increase permanency for all children are necessary as a base for permanency planning for youngsters at risk.

TRAINING

The administrative conflicts and decision-points discussed above may be applied to the particular consideration of training for permanency planning. The issues in introducing and implementing a training program will be discussed in response to a series of questions that will be asked of permanency planning in general, and of training in particular (Ward *et al.* 1982).

What is the target group?

All workers in the program can be trained, a special unit doing permanency planning can be created and trained, or certain workers within the program can be selected and trained (e.g. only supervisors, only those with a special commitment). Decisions about the target group need to be made on the basis of political realities as well as program effectiveness and efficiency. A big issue may arise about workers who, for a variety of reasons, may be uneducable in permanency planning. What should be done with them – invest in further training, reassign them, limp along as well as possible?

Who will do the training?

There are a variety of options for delivering training:

* outside experts to train a whole staff;
* outside experts to train a small part of the staff (e.g. supervisors) who will then train line staff;
* staff workers who have received training elsewhere who then train others; and
* training unit combining in-house and outside expertise.

In order to make an appropriate decision, the administrator needs to consider what the training is attempting to accomplish. For instance, trainers within the agency can provide ongoing support, essential in permanency planning work, as well as impart information; but certain information is best obtained from outside sources, as with legal guidance in documentation and testimony for court or procedures in working with local school districts.

What will be accomplished?

In most training, information and skill acquisition are prime objectives. In permanency planning especially, skill building should be based on participants' strengths rather than deficits. What needs to be conveyed, beyond the basic information that will be discussed later, is a certain style in dealing with people and institutions. It incorporates an appropriate assertiveness and comfort in confrontation, depends on careful attention to monitoring deadlines, and reinforces the importance of decisiveness. Because decision-making must take place in ambiguous situations, and because the families are usually so difficult to work with, ongoing support for workers to develop such a style is essential. The training must emphasize this, and the administrator must make time available for it to occur.

What does training consist of?

The following curriculum is proposed as a model for a six- to ten-week course in permanency planning. The purposes are to:

* increase knowledge of permanency planning components, processes, and techniques;
* build conviction about the importance of permanent families for children;
* strengthen attitudes of decisiveness and assertiveness that are conducive to a permanency planning approach;
* develop skills in assessment and intervention;
* create an appreciation of the diverse and interlocking roles of the social worker and other intervenors in achieving permanency; and
* heighten sensitivity to issues of ethnicity, minority groups, and socio-cultural aspects.

Each of the major sections is a content area that should contain didactic elements. The conveyed information should be combined with readings, case examples, and experiential exercises. The particular methods used singly and in combination should be consonant with the objectives of each content area. For example, lectures and readings are efficient in giving factual information; case examples are helpful in involving participants; experiential exercises foster the growth of new skills and attitudes; and general discussion and sharing provide support as people work from strengths to remedy deficits. In particular, as discussed in Chapter 15, role-playing may be useful in preparation for serving as a court witness, as may visits to the court to become familiar with the physical surroundings.

SAMPLE CURRICULUM

A comprehensive curriculum on permanency planning should incorporate the content areas covered in this book. Following is an outline of these areas.

I. Introduction to Permanency Planning
   A. Background
      1. Problem of foster care drift
      2. Evaluation of foster care system
      3. Emergence of permanency planning movement
      4. Adoption Assistance and Child Welfare Act 1980 (Public Law 96–272)
   B. Permanency planning
      1. Definition and rationale
      2. Different options and strategies
      3. Major components
      4. Multiple roles of worker
      5. Importance of team approach
      6. Influence of worker's feelings and attitudes
II. Working with Families
   A. The ecological/competence perspective on practice
      1. Interactional view of child abuse and neglect
      2. Role of environment
      3. Cultural awareness, racial and ethnic diversity, socio-cultural variations
      4. Implications for permanency planning
   B. Needs, feelings, and reactions of parents
      1. Impact of loss and separation on parents
      2. Awareness of worker's own feelings and reactions
      3. Importance of parental involvement in the helping process.
      4. Role of parent–child visiting
III. Working with the Child
   A. Psychological assessment within an ecological perspective

    B. Needs, feelings, and reactions of the child
       1. Variations, according to age, developmental phase, reason for placement, socio-cultural factors
       2. Impact of loss and separation
       3. Awareness of worker's own feelings and involvement
IV. Case Planning
    A. Formulating a comprehensive assessment
       1. The family as the unit of attention
       2. Variables of environment, ethnicity, family strengths, personalities
    B. Goal formulation
       1. Involving parents
       2. Mobilizing family strengths
       3. Criteria for selection among permanency planning options
       4. Specificity and attainability
       5. Use of service agreement
    C. Writing a service agreement
       1. Appropriate content
       2. Timing
       3. Participation of family
       4. Review and monitoring
    D. Treatment planning
       1. Role of worker as therapist and monitor
       2. Correlation of monitoring with decision-making
       3. Involvement of parents and child – establishing and using the therapeutic relationship
       4. Varieties of treatment strategies
       5. Use of resources – parent aides, homemakers, day care
       6. Outreach and advocacy – child protection agency, adoption
       7. Clarification of roles of all professionals involved
       8. Use of goal-oriented records to plan, document, and monitor
    E. Working with outside systems
       1. The child protection agency – treatment planning, service agreements, administrative issues
       2. Legal system – documentation, testimony
V. Maintaining Permanent Plans
    A. Providing support to families regardless of permanency options selected
    B. Providing aftercare services

An adequate training program will begin with a curriculum such as the one outlined above, but ongoing training is also vital. It should have three distinct aspects:

1. *Didactic* – Seminars, literature reviews, and presentations by experienced practitioners and researchers are necessary to maintain a level of proficiency and to become acquainted with new developments.

2. *Supervision* – Case review and monitoring are important to assure that all permanency planning standards are being met. The reviews should not be seen as administrative oversight of workers; they should be conducted in the spirit of discovering aspects of cases that need further discussion, support, and learning for the benefit of all. The more experienced workers need to be given responsibility for this aspect of program implementation.

3. *Support* – Peer training, support group, or team review are various names attached to the cooperative efforts required for a viable agency program. As part of the training package, support from other staff engaged in the same work is invaluable because permanency planning work is so taxing. It requires decisiveness in ambiguous situations; assertiveness and appropriate confrontation; work with families with many problems; adequate response to a high incidence of child abuse; acceptance of frequent disappointment in the outcomes of cases; and dealing with administrative policies and decisions that are frustrating and correlated with worker burnout. Without support from peers, the turnover in workers will exacerbate the difficulties and costs, and doom the permanency planning effort to a weak shadow of what it should be.

Further details regarding content of in-service training programs may be obtained from various curricula and training materials that have been developed to communicate the essence of permanency planning. Selected exemplary materials are concisely described below (Maluccio, in press, b).

1. Creative Associates. *Child Welfare In-Service Training Curriculum*. Washington, DC: Creative Associates Inc., 1982.
   The most comprehensive, up-to-date curriculum available for in-service training in the field of child welfare. Its overall purpose is to enhance the knowledge and skills of workers in supporting families and reducing incidence and duration of substitute care. Each of the following thirteen modules, which comprise a 168-hour curriculum, can be used as designed or adapted to individual agency requirements:

   * Family assessment
   * Developing a service plan
   * Assessing progress
   * Serving families
   * Children in need of special services
   * Adolescents in need of special services
   * Planning for permanency planning
   * Preparing for substitute care
   * Facilitating placement
   * Providing services to children in care
   * Reuniting families
   * Constitutional and statutory framework of child welfare services
   * Working with the court

Also included is a guide on 'Training Resources with Cultural Perspectives'.

2. Drews, K., Salus, M. K., and Dodge, D. *Child Protective Services: In-Service Training for Supervisors*. Washington, DC: Creative Associates, 1981.

A training package designed for use by supervisors in training of protective service workers in public agencies. Training is provided through dialogue on audio cassettes and through self-instructional modules in each of these areas:

* Role and tasks involved in supervision in children's protective services
* Intake
* Investigation
* Ongoing services
* Court system
* Cultural responsiveness

3. *Permanency Planning: The Black Experience – A Training Curriculum*. Knoxville, TN: Office of Continuing Education, University of Tennessee, School of Social Work, 1982.

A set of trainer's and resource manuals on permanency planning with Black children and families, designed for in-service training for caseworkers and supervisors with basic knowledge and skills in permanency planning. The focus of training is in areas such as:

* Afro-American history and culture
* Communication between Black and White human service workers
* Agency policies and practices as related to permanency planning work with black families and children.

In view of the disproportionate number of children and families from minority groups coming to the attention of permanency planners, training curricula and programs should reflect sufficient recognition of the importance of cultural awareness, and therefore of content relating to ethnicity, socio-cultural aspects, and minority groups.

SUMMARY

Permanency planning is a term applied not only to a method of case planning and management, but also to an agency program. This chapter emphasized that, in order to succeed as a new way of delivering services, permanency planning must have the strong commitment of administrators, who must be responsive to the obstacles such an initiative presents. Challenges are faced by the worker who needs to deal with the discomforts of becoming familiar with a new orientation; the administrator who represents the service delivery system and must provide consistent support; and even the larger society which must choose the values it wishes to promote. One of the greatest challenges is the increased cost that permanency planning entails in the short term. The phenomenon of burnout and the issue of training were used as illustrations of particular administrative concerns. In addition, a specific curriculum was detailed, as well as some of the extra resources required.

SUGGESTIONS FOR FURTHER READING

Dreyer, L. (1978) *Permanent Planning in Foster Care: A Guide for Program Planners*. Portland, OR: Regional Research Institute for Human Services, Portland State University.

Maluccio, A. N. (in press, b) Education and Training for Child Welfare. In J. Laird and A. Hartman (eds) *A Handbook of Child Welfare*. New York: Free Press.

Villone, P. (1982) Staff Planning Groups: Internal Advocates of Permanency Planning for Children in Foster Care. *Social Work with Groups* 5 (4): 81–93.

Ward, D. E., Maluccio, A. N., Hamilton, J., and Fein, E. (1982) Planning for Permanency Planning in Foster Care. *Children and Youth Services Review* 4 (3): 223–37.

18 Epilogue

The theme of this book has been how to help children grow up in a family – the essence of permanency planning. We have seen that permanency planning emerged as a response to the problem of children languishing in substitute care originally designed to be temporary. Gradually, it also evolved as a movement to prevent placement of children in out-of-home care and to reunify children with their families when placement could not be avoided.

We have also seen that permanency planning is not a panacea, that services to children and families are insufficient, and that our ability to prevent family breakdown is limited. Still, we are promoting the concept and practice of permanency planning to emphasize a key issue: the urgency of each child having a nurturing family in which to grow up and to which he or she belongs.

Permanency planning is a sound framework for all child welfare practice. As we stressed throughout the book, it is based on social workers' conviction about each child's right to be reared in a family setting; timely and emphatic decision-making; and assertive case management. Its finest practice demands early identification of vulnerable children, provision of prevention services for at-risk families, and adequate aftercare services to avert recidivism to out-of-home placement. It is hoped that the philosophic orientation to permanency planning will be heartily accepted by social workers, and that its practice will be applied with sensitivity in each case on an individual basis, with appropriate consideration for the unique qualities and needs of each child and family.

GAPS AND ISSUES

The positive and progressive aspects of the permanency planning movement hold great promise for the future of our children, although there are gaps in our knowledge in many areas, uncertainties about some practices, and issues ripe for further study. For example, the long-term success of permanent plans has not yet been assessed because of the recency of the movement. Not enough time has elapsed to study the adult adjustment of youngsters who were the beneficiaries of permanency planning. In particular we lack knowledge about the extent and implications of the unusual practices around adoption that have emerged – open adoptions, hard-to-place adoptions, searches for biological parents, more responsible roles for children in the process, and increased support services for adoptive parents of adolescents.

We cannot yet understand the impact of changing legal and judicial practices around the needs of children and the rights of parents. The changes in law are so frequent, the effect on judicial climate so varying, and the outcomes of advocacy efforts so unpredictable that uncertainties about the impact on children and their families abound.

Further, the effectiveness of training for permanency planning has not been studied. How expensive is an adequate training program? What cost in effectiveness can be expected with short-cuts in training? What are the best ways to inculcate decisive and assertive case management, and how can we monitor it so that it does not become an intolerant and insensitive force?

Other areas of uncertainty about permanency planning exist because we have not provided for them in a strong enough effort to understand their impact. These include services for aftercare, prevention, and family support. What mix of such services can be designed for maximum benefit for families? What is the cost-benefit outcome? We accept the value of these services on faith, face validity, and some research evidence. Will advocacy lead to services in sufficient quantity to enable us to measure their impact?

Many gaps in our knowledge exist because we live in a world of interlocking systems whose workings are too complex to predict completely. We cannot be sure about what the reactions will be to the stresses imposed by the implementation of permanency planning. We have already seen that the legal system has responded with increased emphasis on the rights of biological parents – but we have not as yet committed sufficient resources to maintain or rehabilitate families. In the area of adoption, can we expect effects on the number, quality, and nature of adoptive family recruitment? Will the homes become more caring or more business-like? In residential treatment, will that large system meet the challenges of permanency planning by decreasing the number of institutions but increasing in specialization? Will economic realities enforce obsolescence, or will some other unpredicted outcome result? In regard to foster family care, should it become an acceptable permanency planning option for some youngsters?

REALITIES OF IMPLEMENTATION

Other areas of controversy and criticism about permanency planning center around the harsh realities of its implementation. One is the clash with vested interests, alluded to previously in the questions about residential treatment. Although permanency planning need not be perceived as a threat to residential facilities, in some cases that has been the first reaction. Others have responded with creative programs for families as well as children, with incorporation of permanency planning procedures into their services, and with movement into broader outpatient and community programming.

Other vested interests that may perceive a threat from permanency planning are the bureaucracies that by nature move slowly in response to any new challenge. For example, the judicial and child protection systems need to find ways to work together in an effective review mechanism; this involves territoriality, cost, and power issues. Collaboration, and an appreciation for the evolutionary nature of complex compromises, may be the best that can be expected in such a situation. Similarly it may be realistic to anticipate difficulties with the mental health and child guidance interests as permanency planning and the ecological perspective are implemented. The clash in ideologies is real, and much effort will need to go into defining the appropriate domains and functions of the professionals involved.

Implementation of permanency planning faces difficulties with its own constituency. While social workers may subscribe to the purpose of the movement and agree with its goals, resistance may arise over the new way of thinking about case management; procedures that may be conceived of as an uncongenial style of assertiveness; or the requirements of unfamiliar paperwork or new patterns of collaboration. In addition, professionals may need to reconsider their diagnostic and treatment orientations so that families' strengths rather than their pathologies are reinforced. Can we involve biological parents more effectively as partners in permanency planning for their children? Can we truly accept that a client's functioning in many cases is a reaction to environmental stresses, and can we make concrete treatment plans to alleviate those stresses? Can a mother be helped to find an apartment in a better school district, can she be provided transportation to visit her family, and can she be connected with the social group in her church or neighborhood, rather than being treated for depression? Can we transfer a child to a school that will provide him with an after-hours program to keep him constructively occupied, rather than have an outpatient clinic simply see him weekly to offer therapy? Should these services be an integral part of the helping process? Are our treatment services too defined and bound by our middle-class sensibilities and training?

An additional concern is the support professionals need as they go about their difficult decision-making. Timely permanent plans may be unfair to parents, taking children from them before they have had a chance to improve their parenting, while delays may be damaging to children, keeping them in temporary care situations for long periods. Can agencies and institutions assist workers in the task of creating stability and permanency in lives and situations that are at best impermanent and changing?

The harshest reality about permanency planning is the lack of resources to implement it properly. Insufficient financial recompense for those working in permanency planning, not enough money for prevention, support, and aftercare services, and wavering commitment to services for children and families in general are the most common complaints. It is easy to lose sight of the key idea of helping children grow in a family when we face vacillating hopes and commitment evidenced by lack of economic support.

NEED FOR SOCIETAL COMMITMENT

The areas of uncertainty outlined above should not be permitted to diminish the importance of the permanency planning movement. Instead we should concern ourselves with what must occur to bolster, maximize, and implement the best in permanency planning. To begin, we must attend to the acute problems faced by our minority children and families. Despite our sensitivity to the issues, this book, like most written by White middle-class authors, has not given enough space or attention to this national disgrace. Minority children are over-represented in our child welfare system, as they are in all systems dealing with the negative effects of their underclass status. Their families by and large receive second-class services, with little recognition or respect for their cultural and ethnic differences from the mainstream. We wish this were not so. We wish there were some way all of the prescriptions and procedures advocated here could be intensified for minority families in order to make up for their longer and deeper sufferings. Perhaps an awareness on the part of social workers of the depth of this issue is a first step.

A related area of concern is the commitment our society should make to child welfare. What are the social and fiscal costs if we do not promote permanency planning? There is some evidence of the interconnectedness of the numbers of children in the child welfare, mental health, and juvenile justice systems. For instance, extrapolation from data of the Minnesota Department of Public Welfare leads to the suspicion that those children not adequately served by the child welfare system end up in the juvenile justice system (Krisberg and Schwartz 1983). In particular, the private sector, through third party payments, has been assuming a large role in paying for residential care and substance abuse treatment for growing numbers of youth. In addition to the lack of control and monitoring such a 'hidden' system presents, the stress on health care costs is considerable (Krisberg and Schwartz 1983).

A more basic concern is how we as a society think about the welfare of our children, and how we define child maltreatment. Although there is strong evidence that child neglect is more prevalent and more serious in its consequences than child abuse, we have chosen to focus on the more visible and newsworthy problem of abuse (Wolock and Horowitz 1984). This focus on child abuse may stem from its identification by and with the medical profession since it was first publicized by Kempe *et al.* (1962), and with the ease with which parental disturbance and blame could be attached to it. The etiology of neglect, on the other hand, is more closely related to basic social and economic structures of our society (Gil 1975). Consequently, it has been suggested that coping with poverty and its sequelae is the most feasible way to deal with problems of neglect – a solution clearly unpopular politically:

'It is our belief that we must attend now to the full dimensions of the agenda of societal changes required to give children their rights . . . We must be ready to develop new mechanisms for resource allocation and new models of service programs for children that would avoid the categorical and deficit-focused child intervention schemes that have not met our goals up to now.'

(Wolock and Horowitz 1984: 541)

What is society's role in alleviating the situation of the multi-problem under-class? What must the community do to make education an avenue of social mobility? Is the most meaningful response money and employment? Perhaps we must address the ultimate question of all: can a society moving towards greater instability in all its aspects provide permanence and stability for its children?

CONCLUSION

Such issues have been with us for a long time. They should not be minimized. Yet an effort to address them must begin somewhere, and we feel the permanency planning movement holds the greatest optimism for some success. It is an affirm-ative and progressive family-centered approach requiring dramatic changes in social policy as well as social work practice. It calls for highly skilled workers, sufficient support from society, a great deal of hard work, and full collaboration among diverse community agencies, professionals, and formal as well as informal helping systems. Although the criticisms discussed here may appear overwhelm-ing, there are many encouraging signs: there is indication of substantial pro-fessional commitment to families; there is evidence of a range of innovative approaches; and there is a great deal of knowledge about how to help children and parents.

The movement can succeed in its goal of achieving permanent families for all children. Although this may appear unrealistic in light of the limits to many of the world's physical resources, human resources have been long undervalued and underused, especially the resources of biological parents. Perhaps we are now ready to shift from our historical focus on *saving children from their families* to a more vital focus on *saving families*. Perhaps we are ready to shape public policy to implement the broadest implications of permanency planning. This requires a willingness to change – societally, institutionally, and professionally – an awesome task, but the least we should expect for the millions of children touched by the child welfare system.

References

Abidin, R. R. (1976) *Parenting Skills*. New York: Human Sciences Press.
—— (ed.) (1980) *Parent Education and Intervention Handbook*. Springfield, IL: C. C. Thomas.
Advisory Committee on Child Development (National Research Council) (1976) *Toward a National Policy for Children and Families*. Washington, DC: National Academy of Sciences.
Aldgate, J. (1980) Identification of Factors Influencing Children's Length of Stay in Care. In J. Triseliois (ed.) *New Developments in Foster Care and Adoption*. London and Boston, MA: Routledge & Kegan Paul, pp. 22–40.
Allen, M. L. and Knitzer, J. (1983) Child Welfare: Examining the Policy Framework. In B. McGowan and W. Meezan (eds) *Child Welfare: Current Dilemmas–Future Directions*. Itasca, IL: F. E. Peacock, pp. 93–141.
Allen, M. L., Golubock, C., and Olson, L. (1983) A Guide to the Adoption Assistance and Child Welfare Act of 1980. In M. Hardin (ed.) *Foster Children in the Courts*. Boston, MA: Butterworth Legal Publishers, pp. 575–609.
Anderson, C. and Stewart, S. (1983) *Mastering Resistance – A Treatment Guide to Family Therapy*. New York, Guilford Press.
Argles, P. (1984) The Threat of Separation in Family Conflict. *Social Casework* 65 (10): 610–14.
Aust, P. (1981) Using the Life Story Book in Treatment of Children in Placement. *Child Welfare* 60 (8): 535–36, 553–60.
Backhaus, K. (1984) Life Books: Tool for Working with Children in Placement. *Social Work* 29 (6): 551–54.
Baker, B., Grant, J., Squires, J., Johnson, P., and Offerman, L. (1981) Parent Aides as Preventive Intervention Stategy. *Children and Youth Services Review* 3: 115–25.
Bander, K., Fein, E., and Bishop, G. (1982) Evaluation of Child Sexual Abuse Programs. In S. M. Sgroi (ed.) *Handbook of Clinical Intervention in Child Sexual Abuse*. Lexington, MA: Lexington Books, D. C. Heath, pp. 345–76.
Beinecke, R. H. (1984) PORK SOAP, STRAP, AND SAP. *Social Casework* 65 (9): 554–58.
Bentovim, A. and Tranter, M. (1984) A Family Therapy Approach to Decision Making. *Adoption & Fostering* 8 (1): 25–32.
Bernstein, B. E. (1975) The Social Worker as a Courtroom Witness. *Social Casework* 56 (9): 521–25.
—— (1977) The Social Worker as an Expert Witness. *Social Casework* 58 (7): 412–17.
Beste, H. M. and Richardson, R. G. (1981) Developing a Life Story Book Program for Foster Children. *Child Welfare* 60 (8): 529–34.

Biegel, D. E. and Naparstek, A. J. (1982) *Community Support Systems and Mental Health*. New York: Springer Publishing Co.

Black, J. (1982) Assessment in Child Custody. Unpublished paper presented at Child and Family Services, Hartford, CT.

Block, N. M. and Libowitz, A. S. (1983) *Recidivism in Foster Care*. New York: Child Welfare League of America.

Blumenthal, K. (1983) Making Foster Family Care Responsive. In B. G. McGowan and W. Meezan (eds) *Child Welfare: Current Dilemmas – Future Directions*. Itasca, IL: F. E. Peacock Publishers.

Blumenthal, K. and Weinberg, A. (eds) (1984) *Establishing Parent Involvement in Foster Care Agencies*. New York: Child Welfare League of America, pp. 295–342.

Bolton, F. G. Jr. (1983) *When Bonding Fails: Clinical Assessment of High Risk Families*. Beverly Hills, CA: Sage Publications.

Borkman, T. (1984) Mutual Self-Help Groups: Strengthening the Selectively Unsupportive Personal and Community Networks of Their Members. In A. Gartner and F. Riessman (eds) *The Self-Help Revolution*. New York: Human Sciences Press, pp. 205–15.

Bowlby, J. (1973) *Attachment and Loss – Vol. III: Separation*. New York: Basic Books.

Brady, J. (1982) Advantages and Problems of Using Written Contracts. *Social Work* 27 (3): 275–77.

Breetz, S., Starr, P., and Taylor, D. (1975) *Helping Services Used by Adoptive and Natural Parents*. Hartford, CT: Child and Family Services. Mimeographed.

Briar, S. (1973) The Age of Accountability. *Social Work* 18 (1): 2 and 114.

Brill, N. (1976) *Teamwork: Working Together in the Human Services*. Philadelphia, PA: J. B. Lippincott.

Bronfenbrenner, U. (1979) *The Ecology of Human Development*. Cambridge, MA: Harvard University Press.

Brown, J. H., Finch, W. A., Northen, H., Taylor, S. H., and Weil, M. (1982) *Child, Family, Neighborhood – A Master Plan for Social Service Delivery*. New York: Child Welfare League of America.

Bryant, B. (1980) *Special Foster Care: A History and Rationale*. Verona, VA: People Places.

Bryce, M. E. and Ehlert, R. C. (1971) 144 Foster Children. *Child Welfare* 50 (9): 499–503.

Bryce, M. E. and Lloyd, J. C. (eds) (1981) *Treating Families in the Home*. Springfield, IL: C. C. Thomas.

Bunin, S. (1984) The Role of Family Therapy in Supporting Adoptions. *Permanency Report* (Child Welfare League of America) 2 (3): 5.

Burns, R. C. (1982) *Self-Growth in Families – Kinetic Family Drawings – Research and Application*. New York: Brunner/Mazel.

Buros, O. K. (ed.) (1972) *The Seventh Mental Measurements Yearbook*. Highland Park, NJ: Gryphon Press.

Bush, M. (1984) The Public and Private Purposes of Case Records. *Children and Youth Services Review* 6 (1): 1–18.

Bush, M. and Gordon, A. C. (1982) The Case for Involving Children in Child Welfare Decisions. *Social Work* 27 (4): 310–11.

Carbino, R. (1982) Group Work with Natural Parents in Permanency Planning. *Social Work With Groups* 5 (4): 7–30.

Carroll, N. A. and Reich, J. W. (1978) Issues in the Implementation of the Parent Aide Concept. *Social Casework* 59 (3): 152–60.

Chea, M. W. (1972) Research on Recording. *Social Casework* 53 (3): 177–80.

Chestang, L. W. (1978) The Delivery of Child Welfare Services to Minority Group Children and Their Families. In *Child Welfare Strategy in the Coming Years*. Washington,

DC: US Department of Health, Education and Welfare. DHEW Publication No. (OHDS) 78–30158, pp. 169–94.

Churchill, S. R. (1984) Disruption: A Risk in Adoption. In P. Sachdev (ed.) *Adoption: Current Issues and Trends*. Toronto: Butterworths, pp. 115–27.

Churchill, S. R., Carlson, B., and Nybell, L. (eds) (1979) *No Child Is Unadoptable*. Beverly Hills, CA: Sage Publications.

Claburn, W. E., Magura, S., and Chizeck, S. P. (1977) Case Reopening: An Emerging Issue in Child Welfare Services. *Child Welfare* 56 (10): 655–63.

Claburn, W. E., Magura, S., and Resnick, W. (1976) Periodic Review of Foster Care: A Brief National Assessment. *Child Welfare* 55 (6): 395–405.

Cochran, M. M. and Brassard, J. A. (1979) Child Development and Personal Social Networks. *Child Development* 50 (3): 601–16.

Cochran, M. M. and Woolever, F. (1980) Programming Beyond the Deficit Model: The Empowerment of Parents with Information and Informal Support. Ithaca, NY: Cornell University. Mimeographed.

Cohn, A. H. (1979) Effective Treatment of Child Abuse and Neglect. *Social Work* 24 (6): 513–20.

Cole, E. S. (1984). In Support of Families. *Permanency Report* (Child Welfare League of America) 2 (1): 1–2.

Collins, A. H. and Pancoast, D. L. (1976) *Natural Helping Networks*. Washington, DC: National Association of Social Workers.

Colon, F. (1978) Family Ties and Child Placement. *Family Process* 17 (3): 289–312.

Compher, J. V. (1984) The Case Conference Revisited: A Systems View. *Child Welfare* 63 (5): 411–18.

Connecticut Department of Children and Youth Services (1982) *Five Year Master Rolling Plan –1982–1987*. Hartford, CT: Connecticut Department of Children and Youth Services. Mimeographed.

Cooper, S. and Wanerman, L. (1977) *Children in Treatment*. New York: Brunner/Mazel.

Coplon, J. and Strull, J. (1983) Roles of the Professional in Mutual Aid Groups. *Social Casework* 64 (5): 259–66.

Cowan, B., Currie, M., Krol, R., and Richardson, J. (1969) Holding Unwilling Clients in Treatment. *Social Casework* 50 (3): 146–51.

Creative Associates (1982) *Child Welfare In-service Training Curriculum*. Washington, DC: Creative Associates.

Crompton, M. (1980) *Respecting Children: Social Work with Young People*. London: Edward Arnold.

Cutler, J. P. and Bateman, W. (1980) Foster Care Case Review: Can It Make a Difference? *Public Welfare* 38 (4): 45–51.

Davies, L. and Bland, D. (1978) The Use of Foster Parents as Role Models for Parents. *Child Welfare* 57 (6): 380–86.

Delgado, M. and Humm-Delgado, D. (1982) Natural Support Systems: Source of Strength in Hispanic Communities. *Social Casework* 27 (1): 83–9.

Depp, C. H. (1982) After Reunion: Perceptions of Adult Adoptees, Adoptive Parents, and Birth Parents. *Child Welfare* 61 (2): 115–19.

Derdeyn, A. P. (1977) A Case for Permanent Foster Placement of Dependent, Neglected, and Abused Children. *American Journal of Orthopsychiatry* 47 (4): 604–14.

DiGiulio, J. F. (1979) The 'Search': Providing Continued Services for Adoptive Parents. *Child Welfare* 58 (7): 460–65.

Dinkmeyer, D. and McKay, G. D. (1976) *Systematic Training for Effective Parenting:*

Leader's Manual. Circle Pines, MN: American Guidance Service.

Dodson, D. (1983a) *The Legal Framework for Ending Foster Care Drift: A Guide to Evaluating and Improving State Laws, Regulations, and Court Rules*. Washington, DC: Foster Care Project, National Legal Resource Center for Child Advocacy and Protection, American Bar Association, Young Lawyers Division.

—— (1983b) Advocating at Periodic Review Proceedings. In M. Hardin (ed.) *Foster Children in the Courts*. Boston, MA: Butterworth Legal Publishers, pp. 86–127.

Dohrenwend, B. S. and Dohrenwend, B. P. (eds) (1977) *Stressful Life Events: Their Nature and Effects*. New York, John Wiley.

Downs, S. W., Bayless, L., Dreyer, L., Emlen, A. C., Hardin, M., Heim, L., Lahti, J., Liedtke, K., Schimke, K., and Troychak, M. (1981) *Foster Care Reform in the 70's: Final Report of the Permanency Planning Dissemination Project*. Portland, OR: Regional Research Institute for Human Services, Portland State University.

Drews, K., Salus, M. K., and Dodge, D. (1981) *Child Protective Services: In-Service Training for Supervisors*. Washington, DC: Creative Associates.

Dreyer, L. (1978) *Permanent Planning in Foster Care: A Guide for Program Planners*. Portland, OR: Regional Research Institute for Human Services, Portland State University.

Ebeling, N. B. and Hill, D. A. (1983) *Child Abuse and Neglect – A Guide With Case Studies for Treating the Child and Family*. Boston, MA: John Wright PSG Inc.

Edelwich, J. and Brodsky, A. (1980) *Burnout*. New York, Human Sciences Press.

Emlen, A. C. (1981) Development of the Permanency Planning Concept. In S. W. Downs, L. Bayless, L. Dreyer, A. C. Emlen, M. Hardin, L. Heim, J. Lahti, K. Liedtke, K. Schimke, and M. Troychak. *Foster Care Reform in the 70's – Final Report of the Permanency Planning Dissemination Project*. Portland, OR: Regional Research Institute for Human Services, Portland State University, pp. 1.1–1.15.

Emlen, A., Lahti, J., Downs, G., McKay, A., and Downs, S. (1977) *Overcoming Barriers to Planning for Children in Foster Care*. Portland: OR: Regional Research Institute for Human Services, Portland State University.

Epstein, L. and Heymann, I. (1967) Some Decisive Processes in Adoption Planning for Older Children. *Child Welfare* 46 (1): 5–9, 46.

Faller, K. C. (1981) *Social Work with Abused and Neglected Children*. New York: Free Press.

Fanshel, D. (1971) The Exit of Children from Foster Care: An Interim Research Report. *Child Welfare* 50 (2): 65–81.

—— (1975) Parental Visiting of Children in Foster Care: Key to Discharge? *Social Service Review* 49 (4): 493–514.

—— (1981) Foreword. In A. N. Maluccio and P. A. Sinanoglu (eds) *The Challenge of Partnership: Working with Parents of Children in Foster Care*. New York: Child Welfare League of America, pp. ix–xi.

—— (1982) *On The Road to Permanency*. New York: Child Welfare League of America.

Fanshel, D. and Shinn, E. B. (1978) *Children in Foster Care – A Longitudinal Investigation*. New York: Columbia University Press.

Farber, S., Bishop, G., Armstrong, B., and Fein, E. (1984) Aftercare Services – Report to the Department of Children and Youth Services and the Connecticut Council of Child Caring Agencies. Hartford, CT: Child and Family Services. Mimeographed.

Fassler, J. (1978) *Helping Children Cope*. New York: Free Press.

Fatis, M. and Konewko, P. (1983) Written Contracts as Adjuncts in Family Therapy. *Social Work* 28 (2): 161–63.

Fein, E. (1984) Dangerous Clients. *Social Casework* 65 (9): 531.

Fein, E., Davies, L., and Knight, G. (1979) Placement Stability in Foster Care. *Social Work* 24 (2): 156–57.

Fein, E., Maluccio, A. N., and Goetzel, R. (1983) Reunification of Families: Issues for Practitioners. Hartford, CT: Child and Family Services. Mimeographed.

Fein, E., Maluccio, A. N., Hamilton, V. J., and Ward, D. (1983) After Foster Care: Outcomes of Permanency Planning for Children. *Child Welfare* 62 (16): 485–560.

Fein, E., Miller, K., Olmstead, K., and Howe, G. (1984) The Roles of the Social Worker in Permanency Planning. *Child Welfare* 63 (4): 351–60.

Festinger, T. (1983) *Nobody Ever Asked Us . . . A Postscript to Foster Care*. New York: Columbia University Press.

Finkelstein, N. E. (1980) Family-Centered Group Care. *Child Welfare* 59 (1): 33–41.

Finkelstein, N. E. (1981) Family-Centered Group Care – The Children's Institution, from a Living Center to a Center for Change. In A. N. Maluccio and P. A. Sinanoglu (eds) *The Challenge of Partnership: Working with Parents of Children in Foster Care*. New York: Child Welfare League of America, pp. 89–105.

Fischer, J. (1978) *Effective Casework Practice – An Eclectic Approach*. New York: McGraw-Hill.

Fitzgerald, J., Murcer, B., and Murcer, B. (1982) Building New Families Through Adoption and Fostering. Oxford, England: Basil Blackwell.

Fox, L. (1982) Two Value Positions in Recent Child Care Law and Practice. *British Journal of Social Work* 12 (3): 265–90.

Frank, G. (1980) Treatment Needs of Children in Foster Care. *American Journal of Orthopsychiatry* 50 (2): 256–63.

Froland, C. (1980) Formal and Informal Care: Discontinuities in a Continuum. *Social Service Review* 54 (4): 572–87.

Froland, C., Pancoast, D. L., Chapman, N. J., and Kimboko, P. J. (1981) *Helping Networks and Human Services*. Beverly Hills, CA: Sage Publications.

Gambrill, E. (1977) *Behavior Modification – Handbook of Assessment, Intervention, and Evaluation*. San Francisco, CA: Jossey-Bass.

—— (1983) *Casework: A Competency-Based Approach*. Englewood Cliffs, NJ: Prentice-Hall.

Gambrill, E. D. and Stein, T. J. (1978) *Supervision in Child Welfare: A Training Manual*. Berkeley, CA: University of California Extension Press.

Gambrill, E. D. and Stein, T. J. (1981) Decision Making and Case Management: Achieving Continuity of Care for Children in Out-of-Home Placement. In A. N. Maluccio and P. A. Sinanoglu (eds) *The Challenge of Partnership: Working with Parents of Children in Foster Care*. New York: Child Welfare League of America, pp. 109–34.

Gambrill, E. D. and Stein, T. J. (1983) *Supervision: A Decision Making Approach*. Beverly Hills, CA: Sage Publications.

Garbarino, J. (1982) *Children and Families in the Social Environment*. New York: Aldine Publishing.

Garbarino, J. and Gilliam, G. (1980) *Understanding Abusive Families*. Lexington, MA: Lexington Books, D. C. Heath.

Garwick, G. and Lampman, S. (1972) Typical Problems Bring Patients to a Mental Health Center. *Community Mental Health Journal* 8 (4): 271–80.

Germain, C. B. (1979) Ecology and Social Work. In C. B. Germain (ed.) *Social Work Practice: People and Environments*. New York: Columbia University Press, pp. 1–22.

Germain, C. B. and Gitterman, A. (1980) *The Life Model of Social Work Practice*. New York: Columbia University Press.

Gifford, D., Kaplan, F. B., and Salus, M. K. (1979) *Parent Aides in Child Abuse and Neglect Programs*. Washington, DC: US Department of Health, Education, and Welfare. DHEW Publication No. (OHDS) 79–30200.

Gil, D. (1964) Developing Routine Follow-up Procedures for Child Welfare Services. *Child Welfare* 43 (5): 229–40.

—— (1975) Unraveling Child Abuse. *American Journal of Orthopsychiatry* 45 (3): 346–56.

Gilandas, A. J. (1972) The Problem-Oriented Record in a Psychiatric Hospital. *Hospital and Community Psychiatry* 23 (11): 336–39.

Giovannoni, J. M. and Billingsley, A. (1970) Child Neglect Among the Poor: A Study of Parental Adequacy in Families of Three Ethnic Groups. *Child Welfare* 49 (4): 196–204.

Goldfinger, S. (1973) The Problem-Oriented Record: A Critique from a Believer. *New England Journal of Medicine* 288: 606–08.

Goldstein, J., Freud, A., and Solnit, A. J. (1973) *Beyond the Best Interests of the Child*. New York: Free Press.

Goldstein, J., Freud, A., and Solnit, A. J. (1979) *Before the Best Interests of the Child*. New York: Free Press.

Gordon, H. L. (1941) Discharge: An Integral Aspect of the Placement Process. *The Family* 22 (2): 35–42.

Gordon, T. (1970) *P.E.T – Parent Effectiveness Training*. New York: Peter H. Wyden.

Grant, R. L. and Maletzky, B. M. (1972) Application of the Weed System to Psychiatric Records. *Psychiatry in Medicine* 3: 119–29.

Greenspan, S. I. (1981) *The Clinical Interview of the Child*. New York: McGraw-Hill.

Gruber, A. R. (1978) *Children in Foster Care*. New York: Human Sciences Press.

Halper, G. and Jones, M. A. (1981) *Serving Families at Risk of Dissolution: Public Preventive Services in New York City*. New York: City of New York, Human Resources Administration.

Harari, T. (1980) *Teenagers Exiting from Foster Family Care: A Retrospective Look*. Unpublished Doctoral Dissertation, University of California at Berkeley, Berkeley, CA.

Hardin, M. (ed.) (1983) *Foster Children in the Courts*. Boston, MA: Butterworth Legal.

Harman, D. and Brim, O. G. (1980) *Learning to Be Parents: Principles, Programs, and Methods*. Beverly Hills, CA: Sage Publications.

Harris, J. C. and Bernstein, B. E. (1980) Lawyer and Social Worker as a Team: Preparing for Trial in Neglect Cases. *Child Welfare* 59 (8): 469–80.

Hartman, A. (1984) *Working with Adoptive Families Beyond Placement*. New York: Child Welfare League of America.

Hartman, A. and Laird, J. (1983) *Family-Centered Social Work Practice*. New York: Free Press.

Hartman, B. and Wickey, J. M. (1978) The Person-Oriented Record in Treatment. *Social Work* 23 (4): 296–99.

Hayes-Roth, F., Longabaugh, R., and Ryback, R. S. (1975) Should the Psychiatric Hospital be Hospitalized? *International Journal of Social Psychiatry* 21: 147–56.

Hegar, R. L. (1983) Foster Children's and Parents' Rights to a Family. *Social Service Review* 57 (3): 429–47.

Helfer, R. E. and Kempe, C. (1974) *The Battered Child*. 2nd edition. Chicago, IL: University of Chicago Press.

Hess, P. (1982) Parent–Child Attainment Concept: Crucial for Permanency Planning. *Social Casework* 63 (1): 46–53.

Hewett, C. (1983) Defending a Termination of Parental Rights Case. In M. Hardin (ed.) *Foster Children in the Courts*. Boston, MA: Butterworth Legal, pp. 229–63.

Hill, E. H. and King, G. C. (1982) Working with the Strengths of Black Families. *Child Welfare* 61 (8): 536–44.

Hill, R. B. (1971) *The Strengths of Black Families*. New York: Emerson Hall.

Holbrook, T. (1983) Case Records: Fact or Fiction? *Social Service Review* 57 (4): 645–57.

Hollis, F. and Wood, M. (1981) *Casework: A Psychosocial Therapy*. 3rd edition. New York: Random Press.

Holman, A. M. (1983) *Family Assessment – Tools for Understanding and Intervention*. Beverly Hills, CA: Sage Publications.

Holmes, T. H. and Rahe, R. H. (1967) The Social Readjustment Rating Scale. *Journal of Psychosomatic Research* 11: 213–17.

Horejsi, C. R. (1979) *Foster Family Care*. Springfield, IL: C. C. Thomas.

Horejsi, C. R., Bertsche, A. V., and Clark, F. W. (1981) *Social Work Practice with Parents of Children in Foster Care – A Handbook*. Springfield, IL: C. C. Thomas.

Houlgate, L. (1980) *The Child and the State: A Normative Theory of Juvenile Rights*. Baltimore, MD: Johns Hopkins University Press.

Howe, G. (1983) The Ecological Approach to Permanency Planning: An Interactionist Perspective. *Child Welfare* 62 (4): 291–301.

Hubbell, R. (1981) *Foster Care and Families*. Philadelphia, PA: Temple University Press.

Hutchinson, J. R., Lloyd, J. C., Landsman, M. J., Nelson, K., and Bryce, M. (1983) *Family Centered Social Services: A Model for Child Welfare Agencies*. Oakdale, IA: National Resource Center on Family Based Services, University of Iowa School of Social Work.

Iowa Department of Social Services, Foster Care Research Project (1977) *Increasing the Effectiveness of Foster Care Through the Use of the Service Contract with Children, Natural Parents, Foster Parents and Workers*. Des Moines, IA: Iowa Department of Social Services, Division of Community Services. Mimeographed.

Jackson, A. D. and Dunne, M. J. (1981) Permanency Planning in Foster Care with the Ambivalent Parent. In A. N. Maluccio and P. A. Sinanoglu (eds) *The Challenge of Partnership: Working with Parents of Children in Foster Care*. New York: Child Welfare League of America, pp. 151–64.

Jameson, B. and Sugg, M. (1979) *The Monitoring and Evaluation System to Assure Permanent Plans for Children in Foster Care: An Assessment*. Midlothian, VA: Social Research Associates. Mimeographed.

Janchill, M. P. (1981) *Guidelines to Decision Making in Child Welfare*. New York: Human Services Workshops.

Jenkins, S. (1981) The Tie That Binds. In A. N. Maluccio and P. A. Sinanoglu (eds) *The Challenge of Partnership: Working with Parents of Children in Foster Care*. New York: Child Welfare League of America, pp. 39–51.

Jenkins, S. and Diamond, B. (1985) Ethnicity and Foster Care: Census Data as Predictors of Placement Variables. *American Journal of Orthopsychiatry* 55 (2): 267–76.

Jenkins, S. and Norman E. (1972) *Filial Deprivation and Foster Care*. New York: Columbia University Press.

Jenkins, S. and Norman, E. (1975) *Beyond Placement: Mothers View Foster Care*. New York: Columbia University Press.

Jenkins, S. and Sauber, M. (1966) *Paths to Child Placement – Family Situations Prior to Foster Care*. New York: Community Council of Greater New York.

Jenkins, S., Schroeder, A. G., and Burgdorf, K. (1981) *Beyond Intake: The First Ninety Days*. Washington, DC: US Department of Health and Human Services, DHHS Publication No. (OHDS) 81–30313.

Jewett, C. (1978) *Adopting the Older Child*. Harvard, MA: Harvard Common Press.

Jewett, C. L. (1982) *Helping Children Cope with Separation and Loss*. Harvard, MA: Harvard Common Press.

Johnston, E. and Gabor, P. (1981) Parent Counselors: A Foster Care Program with New Roles for Major Participants. In A. N. Maluccio and P. A. Sinanoglu (eds) *The Challenge of Partnership: Working with Parents of Children in Foster Care*. New York: Child Welfare League of America, 200–08.

Jones, M. A., Neuman, R., and Shyne, A. (1976) *A Second Chance for Families*. New York: Child Welfare League of America.

Jones, M. L. (1978) Stopping Foster Care Drift: A Review of Legislation and Special Programs. *Child Welfare* 57 (9): 571–80.

—— (1980) Developing Training Resources for Permanency Planning. *Children Today* 9 (2): 25–6.

Kadushin, A. (1980) *Child Welfare Services*. 3rd Edition. New York: Macmillan.

Kagle, J. D. (1984) Restoring the Clinical Record. *Social Work* 29 (1): 46–50.

Kahn, R. (1978) Job Burnout: Prevention and Remedies. *Public Welfare* 36 (2): 61–3.

Kane, R. A. (1974) Look to the Record. *Social Work* 19 (4): 412–19.

Keith-Lucas, A. and Sanford, C. W. (1977) *Group Child Care as a Family Service*. Chapel Hill, NC: University of North Carolina Press.

Kempe, C. H., Silverman, F. N., Steele, B. F., Droegemueller, W., and Silver, H. K. (1962) The Battered Child Syndrome. *Journal of the American Medical Association* 181: 17–24.

Klier, J., Fein, E., and Genero, C. (1984) Are Written or Verbal Contracts More Effective in Family Therapy? *Social Work* 29 (3): 298–99.

Knierim, G. (1983) Social Work and the Law. *Interchange*. New England Resource Center for Children and Families.

Knitzer, J. and Allen, M. L. (1978) *Children without Homes*. Washington, DC: Children's Defense Fund.

Krisberg, B. and Schwartz, I. (1983) Rethinking Juvenile Justice. *Crime and Delinquency* 29 (3): 333–64.

Krymow, V. L. (1979) Obstacles Encountered in Permanent Planning for Foster Children. *Child Welfare* 58 (2): 97–104.

Kufeldt, K. (1984) Listening to Children – Who Cares? *British Journal of Social Work* 14 (3): 257–64.

Lahti, J. (1982) A Follow-up Study of Foster Children in Permanent Placements. *Social Service Review* 56 (4): 556–71.

Lahti, J. and Dvorak, J. (1981) Coming Home from Foster Care. In A. N. Maluccio and P. A. Sinanoglu (eds) *The Challenge of Partnership: Working with Parents of Children in Foster Care*. New York: Child Welfare League of America, pp. 52–66.

Lahti, J., Green, K., Emlen, A., Zendry, J., Clarkson, Q. D., Kuehnel, M., and Casciato, J. (1978) *A Follow-up of the Oregon Project*. Portland, OR: Regional Research Institute for Human Services, Portland State University.

Laird, J. (1979) An Ecological Approach to Child Welfare: Issues of Family Identity and Continuity. In C. B. Germain (ed.) *Social Work Practice: and Environments*. New York: Columbia University Press, pp. 174–209.

Lee, J. A. B. and Park, D. N. (1980) *Walk a Mile in My Shoes – A Manual on Biological*

Parents for Foster Parents. West Hartford, CT: University of Connecticut School of Social Work. Mimeographed.

Lemberg, R. (1984) Ten Ways for a Self-Help Group to Fail. *American Journal of Orthopsychiatry* 54 (4): 648–50.

Leon, A. M., Mazur, R., Montalvo, E., and Rodrieguez, M. (1984) Self Help Support Groups for Hispanic Mothers. *Child Welfare* 63 (3): 261–68.

Levitt, K. L. (1981) A Canadian Approach to Permanent Planning. *Child Welfare* 60 (2): 109–12.

Lieber, L. and Baker, J. (1977) Parents Anonymous and Self-Help Treatment for Child Abusing Parents: A Review and an Evaluation. *Child Abuse and Neglect* 1 (2): 133–48.

Lieberman, F. (1979) *Social Work with Children*. New York: Human Sciences Press.

Littner, N. (1956) *Some Traumatic Effects of Separation and Placement*. New York: Child Welfare League of America.

Maas, H. S. (1971) Children's Environments and Child Welfare. *Child Welfare* 50 (3): 132–42.

Maas, H. S. and Engler, R. E. (1959) *Children in Need of Parents*. New York: Columbia University Press.

McAdams, P. T. (1972) The Parent in the Shadows. *Child Welfare* 51 (1): 51–55.

McDonnell, P. and Aldgate, J. (1984) An Alternative Approach to Reviews. *Adoption and Fostering* 8 (4): 47–51.

Macintyre, J. M. (1970) Adolescence, Identity, and Foster Family Care. *Children* 17 (6): 213–17.

Magura, S. and Claburn, W. E. (1978) Foster Care Review: A Critique of Concept and Method. *Journal of Social Welfare* 5 (2): 25–34.

Maluccio, A. N. (1979a) Promoting Competence Through Life Experiences. In C. B. Germain (ed.) *Social Work Practice: People and Environments*. New York: Columbia University Press, pp. 282–302.

—— (1979b) *Learning From Clients – Interpersonal Helping as Viewed by Clients and Social Workers*. New York: Free Press.

—— (1981a) An Ecological Perspective on Practice with Parents of Children in Foster Care. In A. N. Maluccio and P. A. Sinanoglu (eds) *The Challenge of Partnership: Working with Parents of Children in Foster Care*. New York: Child Welfare League of America, pp. 22–35.

—— (1981b) Competence-oriented Social Work Practice: An Ecological Approach. In A. N. Maluccio (ed.) *Promoting Competence in Clients: A New/Old Approach to Social Work Practice*. New York: Free Press, pp. 1–24.

—— (1981c) A Task-Based Approach to Family Treatment. In C. Getty and W. Humphreys (eds) *Understanding the Family*. New York: Appleton-Century-Crofts, pp. 435–57.

—— (1984) Permanency Planning: Implications for Practice with Natural Parents. *Adoption and Fostering* 8 (4): 15–20.

—— (in press, a) Biological Families and Foster Care: Initiatives and Obstacles. In M. Cox and R. Cox (eds) *Foster Care: Current Issues, Policies, and Practices*. Norwood, NJ: Ablex Press.

—— (in press, b) Education and Training for Child Welfare. In J. Laird, and A. Hartman (eds) *A Handbook of Child Welfare*. New York: Free Press.

Maluccio, A. N. and Fein, E. (1983) Permanency Planning: A Redefinition. *Child Welfare* 62 (3): 195–201.

Maluccio, A. N. and Fein, E. (in press) Permanency Planning Revisited. In M. Cox and R. Cox (eds) *Foster Care: Current Issues, Policies, and Practices*. Norwood, NJ: Ablex Press.

Maluccio, A. N. and Libassi, M. F. (1984) Competence Clarification in Social Work Practice. *Social Thought* 10 (2): 51–58.

Maluccio, A. N. and Marlow, W. D. (1974) The Case for the Contract. *Social Work* 19 (1): 23–36.

Maluccio, A. N. and Sinanoglu, P. A. (eds) (1981) *The Challenge of Partnership: Working with Parents of Children in Foster Care*. New York: Child Welfare League of America.

Maluccio, A. N., Fein, E., Hamilton, V. J., Klier, J., and Ward, D. (1980) Beyond Permanency Planning. *Child Welfare* 59 (9): 515–30.

Mann, J. (1973) *Time Limited Psychotherapy*. Cambridge, MA: Harvard University Press.

Maslack, C. (1978) Job Burnout: How People Cope. *Public Welfare* 36 (2): 56–58.

Maybanks, S. and Bryce, M. (eds) (1979) *Home-Based Services for Children and Families*. Springfield, IL: C. C. Thomas.

Mayer, J. E. and Timms, N. (1970) *The Client Speaks – Working-Class Impressions of Casework*. Boston, MA: Routledge & Kegan Paul.

Mech, E. V. (1983) Out-of-Home Placement Rates. *Social Service Review* 57 (4): 659–67.

Meddin, B. J. (1984) Criteria for Placement Decisions in Protective Services. *Child Welfare* 63 (4): 367–73.

Meezan, W. (1983) Toward an Expanded Role for Adoption Services. In B. McGowan and W. Meezan (eds) *Child Welfare – Current Dilemmas – Future Directions*. Itasca, IL: F. E. Peacock, pp. 425–477.

Meier, E. (1965) Current Circumstances of Former Foster Children. *Child Welfare* 44 (4): 192–206.

Meyer, C. H. (1984) Can Foster Care Be Saved? *Social Work* 29 (6): 499.

Miller, K. and Fein, E. (1984) *Evaluation of Training in Permanency Planning*. Hartford, CT: Child and Family Services. Mimeographed.

Miller, G. H. and Willer, B. (1977) An Information System for Clinical Recording, Administrative Decision Making, Evaluation, and Research. *Community Mental Health Journal* 13 (2): 194–204.

Miller, K., Fein, E., Bishop, G., Stilwell, N., and Murray, C. (1984a) Overcoming Barriers to Permanency Planning. *Child Welfare* 63 (1): 45–55.

Miller, K., Fein, E., Howe, G., Gaudio, C., Bishop, G. (1984b) Time-Limited Goal-Focused Parent Aide Services. *Social Casework* 65 (8): 472–77.

Miller, K., Fein, E., Howe, G., Gaudio, C., Bishop, G. (in press) A Parent Aide Program: Record-Keeping, Outcomes, and Costs. *Child Welfare*.

Minuchin, S. (1970) The Plight of the Poverty-Stricken Family in the United States. *Child Welfare* 49 (3): 124–30.

Mishne, J. M. (1983) *Clinical Work with Children*. New York: Free Press.

Mitchell, R. E. and Trickett, E. J. (1980) Task Force Report: Social Networks as Mediators of Social Support. *Community Mental Health Journal* 16 (1): 27–44.

Mnookin, R. H. (1973) Foster Care –In Whose Best Interest? *Harvard Educational Review* 43 (4): 599–638.

Moore-Kirkland, J. (1981) Mobilizing Motivation: From Theory to Practice. In A. N. Maluccio (ed.) *Promoting Competence in Clients – A New/Old Approach to Social*

Work Practice. New York: Free Press, pp. 27–54.

Morris, C. (1982) *The Permanency Planning Principle in Child Care Social Work.* Social Work Monograph 21, University of East Anglia, Norwich.

Moss, S. (1966) How Children Feel About Being Placed away From Home. *Children* 13 (4): 153–57.

Moss, S. and Moss, M. (1984) Threat to Place a Child. *American Journal of Orthopsychiatry* 54 (1): 168–73.

Murphy, H. B. M. (1974) Long-Term Foster Care and Its Influence on Adjustment to Adult Life. In E. J. Anthony and E. Koupernik (eds) *The Child in His Family.* New York: John Wiley, pp. 425–46.

Nayman, L. and Witkin, L. (1978) Parent/Child Foster Placement: An Alternate Approach in Child Abuse and Neglect. *Child Welfare* 57 (4): 249–58.

Nelsen, J. (1975) Dealing with Resistance in Social Work Practice. *Social Casework* 56 (10): 587–92.

Nelson, K. (in press) *Parents View Special Needs Adoption.* New York: Child Welfare League of America.

Neubauer, P. (1976) (ed.) *The Process of Child Development.* New York: Jason Aronson.

Newberger, E. H., Newberger, C. M., and Hampton, R. L. (1983) Child Abuse: The Current Theory Base and Future Research Needs. *Journal of the American Academy of Child Psychiatry* 22 (3): 262–68.

Northen, H. (1982) *Clinical Social Work.* New York: Columbia University Press.

Olmstead, K. A. (1983) The Influence of Minority Social Work Students on an Agency's Service Methods. *Social Work* 28 (4): 308–12.

Olmstead, K. A., Hamilton, J., and Fein, E. (1985) Permanency Planning for Children in Outpatient Psychiatric Services. In C. B. Germain (ed.) *Advances in Clinical Social Work.* Silver Spring, MD: National Association of Social Workers.

Olsen, L. (1982) Services for Minority Children in Out-of-Home Care. *Social Service Review* 56 (4): 572–85.

Oxley, G. B. (1981) Promoting Competence in Involuntary Clients. In A. N. Maluccio (ed.) *Promoting Competence in Clients – A New/Old Approach to Social Work Practice.* New York: Free Press, pp. 290–316.

Pare, A. and Torczyner, J. (1977) The Interests of Children and the Interests of the State: Rethinking the Conflict Between Child Welfare Policy and Foster Care Practice. *Journal of Sociology and Social Welfare* 4 (8): 1224–245.

Permanency Planning: The Black Experience – A Training Curriculum (1984) Knoxville, TN: Office of Continuing Education, University of Tennessee, School of Social Work.

Pike, V. (1976) Permanent Planning for Foster Children: The Oregon Project. *Children Today* 5 (6): 22–25.

Pike, V., Downs, S., Emlen, A., Downs, G., and Case, D. (1977) *Permanent Planning for Children in Foster Care: A Handbook for Social Workers.* Washington, DC: US Department of Health, Education, and Welfare. Publication No. (OHDS) 78–30124.

Plenk, A. M. and Hinchey, F. S. (1985) Clinical Assessment of Maladjusted Preschool Children. *Child Welfare* 64 (2): 127–34.

Poertner, J. and Rapp, C. A. (1980) Information System Design in Foster Care. *Social Work* 25 (2): 114–19.

Ragan, C. K., Salus, M. K., and Schultze, G. L. (1980) *Child Protection: Providing Ongoing Services.* Washington, DC: US Department of Health and Human Services.

Publication No. (OHDS) 80–30262.

Regional Research Institute for Human Services (1976) *Barriers to Planning for Children in Foster Care*. Portland, OR: Regional Research Institute for Human Services, Portland State University.

Reid, W. and Epstein, L. (1972) *Task-Oriented Casework*. New York: Columbia University Press.

Reid, W. J. and Shyne, A. W. (1969) *Brief and Extended Casework*. New York: Columbia University Press.

Rest, E. R. and Watson, K. W. (1984) Growing Up in Foster Care. *Child Welfare* 63 (4): 291–308.

Rossi, R. J., Gilmartin, K. J., and Dayton, C. W. (1982) *Agencies Working Together – A Guide to Coordination and Planning*. Beverly Hills, CA: Sage Publications.

Rowe, J. and Lambert, L. (1973) *Children Who Wait*. London: Association of British Adoption Agencies.

Rowe, J., Cain, H., Hundleby, M., and Keane, A. (1984) *Long-Term Foster Care*. London: Batsford Academic and Educational, in association with British Agencies for Adoption and Fostering.

Rutter, M. (1972) *Maternal Deprivation Reassessed*. Harmondsworth, Middlesex (England): Penguin Books.

Ryan, P., McFadden, E. J., and Warren, B. L. (1981) Foster Families: A Resource for Helping Parents. In A. N. Maluccio and P. A. Sinanoglu (eds) *The Challenge of Partnership: Working with Parents of Children in Foster Care*. New York: Child Welfare League of America, pp. 189–99.

Sachdev, P. (ed.) (1984) *Adoption: Current Issues and Trends*. Toronto, Canada: Butterworths.

St Ignatius (1964) *The Spiritual Exercises of St Ignatius*. Translated by Anthony Mottola. Garden City, New York: Image Books. (1548.)

Santosky v. Kramer (1982) 102 S. CT 1388. As cited in M. Hardin (ed.) *Foster Children in the Courts*. Boston, MA: Butterworth Legal, p. 252.

Schaefer, C. E. (1977) The Need for 'Psychological Parents' by Children in Residential Treatment. *Child Care Quarterly* 6 (4): 289–99.

Schaefer, C. E. (1978) *How to Influence Children: A Handbook of Practical Parenting Skills*. New York: Van Nostrand Reinhold.

Schmitt, B. D. (ed.) (1978) *The Child Protection Team Handbook*. New York and London: Garland STPM Press.

Seaberg, J. R. (1981) Foster Parents as Aides to Parents. In A. N. Maluccio, and P. A. Sinanoglu (eds) *The Challenge of Partnership: Working with Parents of Children in Foster Care*. New York: Child Welfare League of America, pp. 209–20.

Seabury, B. A. (1979) Negotiating Sound Contracts with Clients. *Public Welfare* 37 (2): 33–8.

Sgroi, S. M. (ed.) (1982) *A Handbook of Clinical Intervention in Child Sexual Abuse*. Lexington, MA: Lexington Books.

Shaffer, G. L. (1981) Subsidized Adoption in Illinois. *Children and Youth Services Review* 3 (1 and 2): 55–68.

Shaw, M. and Hipgrave, T. (1983) *Specialist Fostering*. London: Batsford Academic and Educational, in association with British Agencies for Adoption and Fostering.

Sherman, E. A., Neuman, R., and Shyne, A. (1973) *Children Adrift in Foster Care*. New York: Child Welfare League of America.

Shireman, J. F. (1983) Achieving Permanence After Placement. In B. G. McGowan and W. Meezan (eds) *Child Welfare: Current Dilemmas – Future Directions*. Itasca, IL: F. E. Peacock, pp. 377–423.

Shulman, L. (1984) *The Skills of Helping Individuals and Groups*. 2nd Edition. Itasca, IL: F. E. Peacock.

Shyne, A. W. (1980) Who Are the Children? A National Overview of Services. *Social Work Research and Abstracts* 15 (1): 26–33.

Shyne, A. W. and Neuman, R. (1974) *A Commitment to People*. New York: Child Welfare League of America.

Shyne, A. W. and Schroeder, A. G. (1978) *National Study of Social Services to Children and Their Families*. Washington, DC: US Department of Health, Education, and Welfare. Publication No. OHDS 78–30150.

Sifneos, P. E. (1972) *Short-Term Psychotherapy and Emotional Crisis*. Cambridge, MA: Harvard University Press.

Sigel, I., Flaugher, J., and Johnson, J. (1977) *Parent–child Interactions Observational Manual*. Princeton, NJ: Educational Testing Service.

Silverman, A. R. and Feigelman, W. (1984) The Adjustment of Black Children Adopted by White Families. In P. Sachdev (ed.) *Adoption: Current Issues and Trends*. Toronto: Butterworths, pp. 181–94.

Simmons, G., Gumpert, J., and Rothman, B. (1973) Natural Parents as Partners in Child Care Placement. *Social Casework* 54 (4): 224–32.

Sinanoglu, P. A. (1984) From Drift to Permanency: The US 1980 Legislation. *Adoption and Fostering* 8 (4): 10–14.

Sinanoglu, P. A. and Maluccio, A. N. (eds) (1981) *Parents of Children in Placement: Perspectives and Programs*. New York: Child Welfare League of America.

Sisto, G. W. (1980) An Agency Design for Permanency Planning in Foster Care. *Child Welfare* 59 (2): 103–11.

Sluckin, W., Herbert, M., and Sluckin, A. (1983) *Maternal Bonding*. Oxford, England: Basic Blackwell.

Snyder, E. and Ramo, K. (1983) *Deciding to Place or Not to Place*. Revised edition. Cheney, WA: School of Social Work and Human Services, Eastern Washington University.

Solomon, B. (1976) *Black Empowerment – Social Work in Oppressed Communities*. New York: Columbia University Press.

Southard, M. J. and Gross, B. H. (1982) Making Clinical Decisions After Tarasoff. In B. Gross and I. Weinberger (eds) *New Dimensions for Mental Health Services. The Mental Health Professional and the Legal System*. San Francisco, CA: Jossey-Bass, pp. 93–101.

Spinelli, L. A. and Barton, K. S. (1980) Home Management Services for Families with Disturbed Children. *Child Welfare* 59 (1): 43–52.

Stark, F. (1959) Barriers to Client–Worker Communication at Intake. *Social Casework* 40 (4): 177–83.

Stehno, S. M. (1982) Differential Treatment of Minority Children in Service Systems. *Social Work* 27 (1): 39–46.

Stein, T. J. (1981) *Social Work Practice in Child Welfare*. Englewood Cliffs, NJ: Prentice-Hall.

Stein, T. J. and Rzepnicki, T. (1983) *Decision Making at Child Welfare Intake*. New York Child Welfare League of America.

Stein, T. J., Gambrill, E. D., and Wiltse, K. T. (1974) Foster Care: The Use of Contracts *Public Welfare* 32 (4): 20–5.

Stein, T. J., Gambrill, E. D., and Wiltse, K. T. (1978) *Children in Foster Homes –
Achieving Continuity of Care*. New York: Praeger.

Sundel, M. and Homan, C. C. (1979) Prevention in Child Welfare: A Framework for
Management and Practice. *Child Welfare* 58 (8): 510–21.

Sundel, S. S. and Sundel, M. (1983) *Be Assertive: A Practical Guide for Human Services
Workers*. Beverly Hills, CA: Sage Publications.

Swenson, C. R. (1981) Using Natural Helping Networks to Promote Competence. In A. N.
Maluccio (ed.) *Promoting Competence in Clients – A New/Old Approach to Social
Work Practice*. New York: Free Press, pp. 125–51.

(Tarasoff I – 1974) *Tarasoff vs. Regents of the University of California*, 13 Cal. 3rd. 117,
529 P. 2d. 553, 118 Cal. Rptr. 129.

(Tarasoff II – 1976) *Tarasoff vs. Regents of the University of California*, 17 Cal. 3rd. 425,
551 P. 2d. 334, 131 Cal. Rptr. 14.

Taylor, D. A. and Alpert, S. (1973) *Continuity and Support Following Residential Treatment*. New York: Child Welfare League of America.

Taylor, D. A. and Starr, P. (1972) The Use of Clinical Services by Adoptive Parents: A
Review of Some Practice Assumptions. *Journal of the American Academy of Child
Psychiatry* 11: 384–99.

Temporary State Commission on Child Welfare (1977) *The Children of the State –
Incentives to Adoptive Placements*. Report submitted to New York State Governor and
Legislature by Honorable Joseph Pisani, Chairman.

Tomlinson, R. and Peters, P. (1981) An Alternative to Placing Children: Intensive and
Extensive Therapy with 'Disengaged' Families. *Child Welfare* 60 (2): 95–104.

Triseliotis, J. (1973) *In Search of Origins: The Experiences of Adopted People*. London:
Routledge & Kegan Paul.

——(1980) Growing up in Foster Care and After. In J. Triseliotis (ed.) *New Developments
in Foster Care and Adoption*. London and Boston, MA: Routledge & Kegan Paul,
pp. 131–61.

Triseliotis, J. (ed.) (1980) *New Developments in Foster Care and Adoption*. London and
Boston, MA: Routledge & Kegan Paul.

Turner, C. (1980) Resources for Help in Parenting. *Child Welfare* 59 (3): 179–87.

Turner, J. (1984) Reuniting Children in Foster Care with Their Biological Parents. *Social
Work* 29 (6): 501–05.

US Department of Health and Human Services (1984) *Report to Congress on Public Law
96–272 – The Adoption Assistance and Child Welfare Act of 1980*. Washington, DC:
US Department of Health and Human Services, Office of Human Development
Services, Administration for Children, Youth, and Families. Mimeographed.

Villone, P. (1982) Staff Planning Groups: Internal Advocates of Permanency Planning for
Children in Foster Care. *Social Work with Groups* 5 (4): 81–93.

Wald, M. S. (1975) State Intervention on Behalf of 'Neglected' Children: A Search for
Realistic Standards. *Stanford Law Review* 27 (4): 985–1040.

Wald, M. S. (1976) State Intervention on Behalf of 'Neglected Children': Standards for·
Removal of Children from Their Homes, Monitoring the Status of Children in Foster
Care, and Termination of Parental Rights. *Stanford Law Review* 28 (4): 623–706.

Walker, F. (1981) Cultural and Ethnic Issues in Working with Black Families in the Child
Welfare System. In A. N. Maluccio and P. A. Sinanoglu (eds) *The Challenge of
Partnership: Working with Parents of Children in Foster Care*. New York: Child
Welfare League of America, pp. 133–48.

Ward, D., Maluccio, A. N., Hamilton, J., and Fein, E. (1982) Planning for Permanency
Planning in Foster Care. *Children and Youth Services Review* 4 (3): 223–37.

Ward, H., Fletcher, C., Fuzesi, N., and Sayer, A. (1984) *Growing up at Risk in Connecticut*. Hartford, CT: Connecticut Association for Human Services and Junior League of Hartford. Mimeographed.

Ward, M. (1984) Sibling Ties in Foster Care. *Child Welfare* 63 (4): 321–32.

Watson, K. W. (1982) A Bold, New Model for Foster Family Care. *Public Welfare* 40 (2): 14–21.

Weed, L. L. (1968) Medical Records That Guide and Teach. *New England Journal of Medicine* 278: 593–600.

Weinstein, E. (1960) *The Self-Image of the Foster Child*. New York: Russell Sage Foundation.

Weissman, H. H. (1978) *Integrating Services for Troubled Families*. San Francisco, CA: Jossey-Bass.

Weitzel, W. J. (1984) From Residential Treatment to Adoption: A Permanency Planning Service. *Child Welfare* 63 (4): 361–65.

Wert, S., Fein, E., and Haller, W. (in press) *Children in Placement: A Model for Citizen-Judicial Review. Child Welfare*.

Wheeler, C. (1978) *Where Am I Going? Making A Life Story Book*. Juneau, AK: Winking Owl Press.

White, M. S. (1981) Promoting Parent–child Visiting in Foster Care: Continuing Involvement Within a Permanency Planning Framework. In P. A. Sinanoglu and A. N. Maluccio (eds) *Parents of Children in Placement: Perspectives and Programs*. New York: Child Welfare League of America, pp. 461–75.

Whittaker, J. K. (1979) *Caring for Troubled Children: Residential Treatment in a Community Context*. San Francisco, CA: Jossey-Bass.

Whittaker, J. K. (1981) Family Involvement in Residential Treatment: A Support System for Parents. In A. N. Maluccio and P. A. Sinanoglu (eds) *The Challenge of Partnership: Working with Parents of Children in Foster Care*. New York: Child Welfare League of America, pp. 67–88.

Whittaker, J. K. and Garbarino, J. (eds) (1983) *Social Support Networks: Informal Helping in the Human Services*. New York: Aldine Publishing.

Willer, B. and Santoro, E. (1975) The Reporting Habits of Staff in a Psychiatric Hospital. *Hospital and Community Psychiatry* 26 (6): 362–65.

Wilson, S. J. (1980) *Recording – Guidelines for Social Workers*. New York: Free Press.

Wiltse, K. T. (1981) Decision Making Needs in Foster Care. In G. Sorozan (ed.) *A Trainer's Guide for Permanency Planning*. Boston, MA: Massachusetts Department of Social Services. Mimeographed.

Wiltse, K. T. and Gambrill, E. D. (1974) Foster Care, 1973: A Reappraisal. *Public Welfare* 32 (1): 7–14.

Windle, C. (1972) NIMH Perspectives and Frustrations. Paper presented at the Annual Meeting, American Psychological Association, Honolulu. Mimeographed.

Wolock, J. and Horowitz, B. (1984) Child Maltreatment as a Social Problem: The Neglect of Neglect. *American Journal of Orthopsychiatry* 54 (4): 530–43.

Wood, P. E. (1981) Residential Treatment for Families of Maltreated Children. *Child Welfare* 60 (2): 105–08.

Name index

Subject index